Apart from Modernism

Apart from Modernism
Edith Wharton, Politics, and Fiction before World War I

Robin Peel

Madison • Teaneck
Fairleigh Dickinson University Press

© 2005 by Rosemont Publishing & Printing Corp.
All rights reserved. Authorization to photocopy items for internal or personal use, or the internal or personal use of specific clients, is granted by the copyright owner, provided that a base fee of $10.00, plus eight cents per page, per copy is paid directly to the Copyright Clearance Center, 222 Rosewood Drive, Danvers, Massachusetts 01923. [0-8386-4079-6/05 $10.00 + 8¢ pp, pc.]

Associated University Presses
2010 Eastpark Boulevard
Cranbury, NJ 08512

The paper used in this publication meets the requirements of the American National Standard for Permanence of Paper for Printed Library Materials Z39.48-1984.

Library of Congress Cataloging-in-Publication Data

Peel, Robin.
 Apart from modernism : Edith Wharton, politics, and fiction before World War I / Robin Peel.
   p. cm.
 Includes bibliographical references and index.
 ISBN 0-8386-4079-6 (alk. paper)
 1. Wharton, Edith, 1862–1937—Criticism and interpretation. 2. Politics and literature—United States—History—20th century. 3. Wharton, Edith, 1862–1937—Political and social views. 4. Modernism (Literature)—United States. I. Title.
   PS3545.H16Z758   2005
   813'.52—dc22
                                                           2005004432

PRINTED IN THE UNITED STATES OF AMERICA

Contents

Acknowledgments	7
1. "Schooling an Intelligence": An Ideological Apprenticeship	11
2. Skirting Modernism: Novels, Novellas, and Short Stories (1900–1909)	43
3. Apart from Modernism? Mr. Proust, Mr. Bennett, and Mrs. Wharton (1910)	80
4. *Ethan Frome,* Modernism, and a Political Argument (1911)	123
5. Vulgarity, Bohemia, and *The Reef* (1912)	155
6. John Jay Chapman, "Social Order and Restraints": *The Custom of the Country* (1913)	197
7. Money, Politics, and Art: Questions of Commerce, Imperialism, and Gender	225
8. Politics and Paradoxes: Toryism, Modernism, and War	263
Appendixes	280
Notes	297
Works Cited	331
Index	341

Acknowledgments

I WOULD LIKE TO THANK JUDITH BAXTER FOR ENCOURAGING ME TO start work on Edith Wharton and to the staff at the Beinecke and Houghton Libraries for their unfailing help with manuscript research. Thanks are also due to Amy Gorelick for her enthusiasm for the project and to a variety of anonymous but dedicated readers for their helpful comments. I am also grateful to Nick Smart for helping me to think about Edith Wharton as an American Tory and to Sarah Churchwell, Hermione Lee and Frederick Wegener for their valuable observations. Finally, and most importantly, there is the understanding, support and encouragement of Mary Peel, to whom I owe most of all.

For permission to quote from the manuscripts held at the Houghton Library, Harvard University I would like to thank the Houghton Library, and for permission to quote from the works of Edith Wharton I would like to thank the Estate of Edith Wharton and the Watkins/Loomis Agency. I would also like to thank Lawrence Buell and the Department of English and American Literature and Language at Harvard University for their support during the time I spent there as a visiting scholar.

Parts of chapter 5 appeared in *American Literary Realism* 37 Spring 2005.

Apart from Modernism

1
"Schooling an Intelligence": An Ideological Apprenticeship

> Do you not see how necessary a World of Pains and troubles is to school an Intelligence and make it a Soul?
> —Passage marked by Edith Wharton in her own copy of Keats's *Letters*

IN THIS STUDY I WILL BE SEEKING TO ANSWER TWO PAIRS OF QUESTIONS. The first concerns the relationship between Wharton's fiction and turn of the century beliefs about state and society. What kind of politics and ideology informs Wharton's pre–World War I fiction, and how does this relate to the politics and ideology she and her peer group publicly espoused? The second pair concerns the relationship between this politics and the aesthetics of early modernism. Is it the case that before World War I there is significant evidence in Wharton's fiction of the influence of ideas about the need for a different kind of new writing, one that reflects a sympathy and commitment to the theories of naturalism, symbolism, or impressionism, and is this influence so striking that we could justifiably call Wharton an early modernist? My argument will be that the answer to this final question is a firm no, and that this conclusion must be reached despite the siren calls of novels such as *Ethan Frome* and *The Reef*, whose formal qualities might lure us into believing otherwise. My central argument will be that this rejection of the label "modernist" is inevitable if we give due weight to the rhetoric of the fiction, which despite its political polyphony ultimately confirms the enduring influence of the ideological and class discourses that shaped Wharton as a young woman. These conservative discourses, which surrounded her from childhood and were questioned by her but never rejected, led her to esteem duty and the power of society above the individual, and made anathema to her Old New York principles the anarchy implicit in her reading of the aesthetic and cultural implications of modernism. Despite this temperamental antipathy to the culture of the new, however, her fiction provided a space in which she could explore the meaning of change in complex and subtle ways, and I will not be arguing that her fiction is a manifesto for her beliefs in the way that *The Ragged Trousered Philanthropists* (1915) is a manifesto for Robert Tressell's socialism. Wharton's fiction does not overturn her ideological inheritance, but it certainly interrogates it.

After her return from Europe as a ten-year-old child in 1872, Edith Newbold Jones spent the next two decades, arguably the most formative years of her life, back in cosmopolitan New York, more precisely the aristocratic New York that was to be the subject of the successful fiction published under her married name of Edith Wharton. By 1900, when her fiction publishing career began, she had absorbed and identified with an ideology that loathed a new-money vulgarity that seemed to enjoy privilege without responsibility. Shaped by her own class and genealogy, her public statements and letters were to consistently contain a rhetoric that distanced itself from the swirling money-driven urban politics of the metropolis that posed such a challenge to the values of noblesse oblige that formed the necessary cornerstone of the just society.

This condensed description of Wharton's political leanings forms the backdrop to the case I wish to advance here. In essence I will be arguing that in contrast to the narrow strictness of the conservatism with which she was happy to be identified publicly, something more complex is evident in her fiction, where she explores and interrogates a range of political beliefs, some progressive and radical, which are presented in a far more liberal and subtle way than her public posture of what I will later label an American Toryism would lead us to expect. These contrasting responses to ideologies (unequivocal in life, more reflective in fiction) help explain her complex attitude to the movement known as modernism. On the one hand her interrogation of early modernism is informed by an antipathy to change, but on the other it is informed by a developed aesthetic recognition that all art, including literature, has evolved and must evolve, if it is to be vital and serious. I will be arguing that rather than the forms, it is the politics of modernism, where it privileges the individual over society and history, that causes Wharton most unease. The new writing is seen as undiscriminating and irresponsible, charges that have their roots in Wharton's ideological apprenticeship.

"A World of Pains and Troubles"

In her autobiography *A Backward Glance*, completed and published after World War I, Edith Wharton looks back from Europe to the

America in which she grew up in the second half of the nineteenth century. In the chapter in which she reminisces about Henry James, she comments: "The truth is that he belonged irrevocably to the old America out of which I also came, and of which—almost—it might paradoxically be said that to follow up its last traces one had to come to Europe."[1]

The title of her autobiography, with its allusion to Whitman's essay "A Backward Glance O'er Travel'd Roads," and the emphasis of the passage marked in her copy of Keats's *Letters*,[2] suggest an identification with hardship, suffering, and loss[3] that would seem to make her sympathetic to the social and democratic needs of the populace, a sympathy seemingly at odds with Wharton's social origins. The "old America" out of which she came is not the America of the frontier, or even of Concord and the transcendentalists (even though as a child Wharton had met the daughter of Emerson's cousin), but refers to a social elite that was "Old New York." It was a highly privileged, materially comfortable, politically conservative world that Edith Wharton inhabited before 1900, a world whose shallowness and follies she had remorselessly exposed in her fiction, but whose retreat after World War I now filled her with regret. The raison d'être of the world that had guarded its leisure, conventions, and tastes jealously, and provided her with the privileges of inherited wealth, was reassessed increasingly favorably by the political worldview espoused by Wharton in late middle age. Yet she was all too aware that it may partly have contributed to its own demise. Wharton blames the failure of that world to realize the good society on the weakness of unspecified institutions, not least of which, as Wharton's own experience had revealed, was the prison-house of Victorian marriage, with the loss to society of those imprisoned. The comment in her autobiography is less specific, deflecting criticism to the general waste of talent: "In every society there is the room, and the need for, a cultivated leisure class; but from the first the spirit of our institutions has caused us to waste this class instead of using it."[4]

Wharton's autobiography glides over the collapse of her own marriage and her subsequent divorce. *A Backward Glance* is not a confessional work. Wharton passes over her breakdown in the 1890s, and conceals the brief joy and subsequent pain brought about by her affair with Morton Fullerton. She says little about the work with war refugees for which she was awarded the Cross of the Légion d'Honneur in 1915. Wharton is silent about many things in her autobiography, but the title she has chosen hints at the matters about which she feels she cannot speak openly. It is a clue to the way we should approach the many paradoxes in her work, looking for the hint rather than the open statement, accepting unresolved ambiguities as evidence of unresolved political debates. Wharton provides us with the shadow of Whitman, and leaves it at that.

How should we assess the Edith Wharton of the beginning of the twentieth century from the perspective of the beginning of the twenty-first? By "Wharton" I mean her writing, principally her fiction writing, and the politics of its rhetoric, because the complex human being is another matter. Yet I will be referring to Wharton's own reading of politics where it can be glimpsed in published letters and nonfiction writing so that this can be mapped alongside the political positions inscribed, often more implicitly than explicitly, in her fiction. She never published a developed political exposition of her beliefs, but much can be observed from an examination of the implicit politics of her imaginative work.

Edith Wharton has been the subject of a number of important biographies over the past thirty years, from the long anticipated study by Hermione Lee to the earlier substantial biographies by R. W. B. Lewis, Cynthia Griffin Wolff, and Shari Benstock.[5] Enough has been said about Wharton, both in these studies and in the memoirs of Wharton's contemporaries, to justify and then challenge a portrait of an aloof, cold, rather snobbish, self-centered individual enjoying and comfortable with all the privileges of class and relative wealth.[6] She mixed with a patrician group of men who frequented gentlemen's clubs and seemed to enjoy considerable leisure time. She insisted on protocol. She could refuse an invitation to dinner from her neighbor at St. Bernard because she had sent a spoken rather than a written invitation.[7] She disapproved of her neighbor Marie Laure de Noailles's avant-garde friends, and expressed this disapproval as a sustained frostiness. But such an incident as the dinner refusal, even if it tells us something about Wharton's adherence to formal procedure and her dislike for the unconventional, ignores the picture of Wharton as a joking, sociable, and generous host, the woman of tremendous energy and enthusiasm who was capable of a monumental achievement in dedicating so much of her life to charity work for World War I refugees. On the one hand she seems staid and proper, on the other we learn that Henry James's sister-in-law thought her an immoral woman.

Her achievements are impressive. In an era before the emancipation of women she showed striking independence, in supporting herself through her writing, through managing and promoting her own work, through refusing to take the easy option of becoming the wife of a wealthy man following her divorce, and through the extent of her scholarship and erudition, despite having been denied a formal education. In her energy, love of dress, intelligence, fondness for male company, resourcefulness, and public rejection of feminism, she had some qualities in common with Margaret Thatcher, Britain's first woman prime minister, though such a comparison immediately foregrounds differences in class between the two women, and the changes in the political status and education of women that occurred only after World War I.

A more contemporary comparison, which emphasizes as many differences as it does similarities, is with the highly successful British-born writer, Frances Hodgson Burnett.[8] Born in 1849, Burnett traveled along many of the same roads as Wharton, but often in the opposite direction. She was born in England but spent much of her life in America, crossing the Atlantic almost as many times as Wharton. Frances Hodgson Burnett's father was an ironmonger in Manchester, and he died when she was very young. As she became successful as a writer, she left the Tennessee world behind her and knocked as an outsider on the doors of fashionable New York society. The differences between the two women are therefore considerable. Like Wharton she experienced an unsuccessful marriage, but Hodgson Burnett had children and went on to marry a second time. She was thirteen years Wharton's senior, but supported the women's suffrage campaign, which Wharton opposed. She met Henry James, but did not become part of his circle. She was converted to the New Thought, a mystical philosophy that interested William James and owed much to Swedenborg, Emerson, and Phineas Parkhurst Quimby. Wharton had no time for what she regarded as its completely muddled thinking.

What links these two writers, however, is their successful use of the market for fiction, which allowed them to achieve financial independence at a time when they both desperately needed to do so. For Frances Hodgson Burnett this was at a very early age. Soon after she arrived in Tennessee at the age of fifteen she was helping the family fortunes by earning an income from her magazine stories. She became an enormously successful commercial writer of stories for adults, such as *The Lass of Lowrie* (1877) and earned much from the successful dramatization of her work. She is now most remembered for her enormously popular children's stories such as *Little Lord Fauntleroy* (1886) and *The Secret Garden* (1911).

Wharton published her most experimental work in 1911. The Edwardianism, not to say Victorianism, of *The Secret Garden*, with its debt to *Jane Eyre*, contrasts with the deliberate enigmas of *Ethan Frome*, a novel that stands on the verge of modernism. Though Wharton's achievement as a commercially successful woman writer was not unique, as the precedent of Frances Hodgson Burnett shows, their class difference meant that Wharton had greater social obstacles to overcome. Despite the indifference, not to say disapproval, of her parents' class, Edith Wharton became a writer, a very fine and popular writer of prose fiction at a time when the art of fiction which had brought her commercial success, was being challenged by an apparent revolution. Having fought and won her place in the market, thus satisfactorily becoming independent enough to ignore the censor of the philistines from Old New York society, she now found that the model of fiction that had brought her success was under fire from another quarter, the avant-garde. The second strand of discussion, therefore, will assess the complexity and diversity (as is now increasingly claimed) of the politics of Wharton's writing in the context of early modernism.

As Bradbury and McFarlane observe, the movement toward sophistication and mannerism, toward introversion, technical display, and internal self-skepticism has often been taken as a common base for a *definition* of modernism.[9] Ortega y Gasset suggests another defining feature, noting that the aesthetics of modernism involve the dehumanizaton of art, the consequence of "the progressive elimination of the human, all too human elements in romantic and naturalist production."[10] David Lodge argues that symbolist bias of modernist fiction is traceable in the use of metaphor in modernism,[11] while for those who associated modernism with the antibourgeois stance of bohemia, the new writing arose simply from a desire to shock. Put like this, it is not difficult to represent a version of modernism with which Wharton clearly has little in common. Although I shall argue that Wharton and modernism have parted company by 1915, I shall try to avoid loading the dice in this way.

Nevertheless, Edith Wharton's writing does seem quite divorced from the first wave of modernism that appeared soon after she achieved popular success. Her novels are not characterized by the apparently radical experiment with form that we associate with Virginia Woolf and James Joyce. If *Ethan Frome*'s naturalism is only part of the story, then the earlier Conradian impressionism with its uncertain narrator, rather than the contemporary Steinian modernism of *Tender Buttons*, is the relevant comparison and descriptive category. While Wharton's 1912 novel, *The Reef,* may have been a nod toward the psychological novel favored by Henry James, it was not a nod toward the emerging post–1910 modernism, and she was not to continue the experiment.

This is not surprising. Wharton was born in 1862, in the middle of the American Civil War. Woolf and Joyce were born twenty years later and were a generation younger. Pound and Lawrence were born in

1885, and so were younger still, while Eliot had been born in 1888, and was twenty-six years younger. In Europe her contemporaries were H. G. Wells and W. B. Yeats, four and three years older respectively. The generation of "new" writers who were publishing as she grew up included some distinctively late Victorian authors such as George Moore, who had been born in 1852, Wilde who had been born in 1854, and Hardy, who was born in 1840. Her reading as a child and as a young woman, as revealed in *A Backward Glance,* was of a distinctly Victorian flavor. Her favorite English novels were by George Meredith.

Later, as a young adult with regular contact with French culture, she became aware of influential writers such as Zola, who was twenty-two years older than Edith Jones. This is a large gap in years and it is always salutary to remember that Henry James, with whom the now married Wharton became very friendly after 1900, was born in 1843 and was also nearly twenty years older than Wharton. Yet writers such as Henry James and Joseph Conrad[12] cross the watershed into early twentieth-century modernism, and both writers had published their most experimental work before Wharton's first successful novel, *The House of Mirth,* appeared in 1905. Age, therefore, cannot be the sole explanation for her aesthetic and narrative sympathies. Wharton, however, confessed to liking James the individual more than his later books, and her career and reputation were established before the appearance of the first wave of modernist experimental writing in the years before World War I. Wharton's depiction of the story of Lily Bart places her closer in method to Theodore Dreiser than to James or Dorothy Richardson, and Virginia Woolf would no doubt have placed Wharton in the naturalist/realist camp of "Mr. Bennett" rather than that of the Georgians, later known as modernists, such as herself. In her examination of the influence of family and the importance of property, her writing was seen by an early reviewer such as H. L. Mencken as having something in common with John Galsworthy, whose first *Forsyte Saga* novel, *The Man of Property,* appeared in 1906.[13] And if there is one writer cast in the role of Edwardian author whose work was made to look dated by the arrival of modernism, it is John Galsworthy.

❖

Throughout this discussion of Wharton's work the word "politics" is taken to mean the way human beings have gone about formulating and implementing the policy that will bring about the organization of the state or city (the word derives from the Greek word for citizens) in the way they consider desirable. In this process agency, class, and gender are important factors, and for Wharton, agency and class are as important as gender. Inasmuch as it can be considered to embrace a coherent set of beliefs, modernism is an expression of a particular political view that argues that societies should be shaped by a recognition that artistic perception is in the vanguard of the development of civilization. It is not just a case of "make it new" but "see it new."

There is a particular meaning of modernism, however, that predates the twentieth-century one. It is a meaning given by the Webster Collegiate Dictionary in 1916: [C]ertain methods and tendencies which, in Biblical questions, apologetics and the history of dogma, in the endeavor to reconcile the doctrines of the Roman Catholic Church with the conclusions of modern science, replace the authority of the church by purely subjective criteria; so called officially by Pope Pius X.[14]

The artistic response to modernity also became known as modernism. Well under way by 1916, it shares with spiritual modernism this emphasis on the subjective, and the emphasis on the individual is a political position rooted in romanticism. It is a position and an issue, I will argue, that set Wharton's fiction apart from what Halliwell calls the "modernist rejection of moralism."[15] In so doing, her politics on this issue can be situated alongside other later critics of modernism who have decried its "flaccid melancholia."[16] The matter, however, is complicated by the fact that writers we now describe as modernist criticize one another. Virginia Woolf found fault with Joyce. Katherine Mansfield had reservations about Dorothy Richardson's work.[17]

If we take politics to mean only a political awareness or activism, then it is often assumed that it was World War I that forced a political awareness on Wharton. Speaking of Wharton's close circle of male friends, for example, Susan Goodman says that "[t]he war . . . politicized the group."[18] Yet the broader implications of the word politics have not been completely ignored, as a title such as *Edith Wharton's Brave New Politics* (1994) suggests.[19] In his early study of Wharton's fiction Blake Nevius is at pains to locate her in a political environment, and to address the charge of snobbery that had so damaged her post–World War I reputation.[20] Carol J. Singley makes this passing apologetic reference, as if eager to move on to the more positive aspects of her work: "Always politically engaged, Wharton seems from today's perspective to have had a limited perspective on some issues: most troubling are her views on eugenics and race."[21]

The understandable emphasis in many other critical works is the politics of gender, and if gender politics are not the solitary focus, then they are brought into relationship with psychoanalytic theory, as in *Edith Wharton's Prisoners of Shame* (1991)[22] and *Gender and the Gothic in the Fiction of Edith Wharton* (1995),[23] studies that are informed by affective theory and Jung's theory of individuation respectively. Materialist readings of the class-based discourses that surrounded Wharton, and the political assumptions that underpin the interrogation in her fiction of new-money economics, have been limited largely to individual essays, with the notable exception of Jennie Kassanoff, whose new historicist and cultural materialist readings of Wharton have been full of brilliant insights.[24] The wider matter of discussions of international politics and its relationship to Wharton's pre–World War I writing, the third strand of my analysis here, has not been considered a very fertile topic, except in one important respect. Both Janet Beer[25] and Judith L. Sensibar[26] have applied the discourse of colonization to a reading of Wharton's fiction, drawing on Wharton's encounters with North Africa. Sensibar's work, however, emphasizes the appearance of this discourse in Wharton's wartime propaganda and fiction, and in her postwar novel *A Son at the Front* (1923). Her prewar work is largely discussed in terms of sexual politics.

Two recent studies of Wharton's work, Stephanie Lewis Thompson's *Influencing American Tastes* (2002) and Jennie A. Kassanoff's *Edith Wharton and the Politics of Race* (2004), show in the one case the continuing emphasis on gender and in the other a willingness to locate the work in a wider political perspective. In her study of three writers Thompson argues that recent attempts to place Wharton, Willa Cather, and Fannie Hurst in the canon of American modernism are misplaced. Instead Thompson argues for a new model, one that resists the well rehearsed three part American literary parading of realism, naturalism and modernism on the one hand, and its corollary, the popular-author-writing-for-middle-brow America on the other. Instead, Thompson sees Wharton as questioning modernism from a gendered perspective, so that the modernist aesthetic, as seen in the Vance Weston novels, is interrogated quietly but devastatingly by the cultured and cultivated feminine authority of Halo Spear. Thompson is concerned primarily with the later work, and rather too content with the American identification of 1925 as the year of modernism and a reading which sees World War I as "the war many see as ushering in the modern era."[27]

Much more searching is Kassanoff's study that confronts the issue of Wharton's conservatism and her anxieties about the consequences of American pluralism, drawing on cultural concerns about racial extinction (in the discussion of *The House of Mirth*), corporate America, the body and the machine (in relation to *The Fruit of the Tree*) and the sinking of the Titanic (in the discussion of *The Reef*). Kassanoff is the most astute interdisciplinary reader of Wharton writing today, and she rightly points to Wharton's often self-contradictory statements on modernism, whose main fault is that it replaces the order of structured language with the demotic babble of the populace. It is the willingness to see Wharton as part of an often disturbingly dominant eugenicist, racial and antidemocratic political discourse that is the most refreshingly challenging aspect of Kassanoff's work, however.

Wharton, like many writers who adopt a life of voluntary exile, reassessed American culture from her vantage point in Europe.[28] This reassessment is not politically overt, nor traceable in anything so obvious as membership of a political party. More subtly, it is that process of reviewing America from Europe, that realignment and reestimate so previously dominated in fiction by Henry James, Wharton's close companion, that is significant for Wharton's reading of politics in her fiction. Her first published novel, *The Valley of Decision*, is an extended exploration of politics, ideology, and power in Italy, set at a time when there was an ideological confrontation between the old and the new orders. Wharton was very conscious of coming from what, in American terms, was considered the old order, a group whose values were under threat from the forces of the new.

In 1862 Wharton was born into a privileged, wealthy family, and as a child and young woman she possessed intelligence, she was physically attractive, and she never knew poverty. Despite such advantages, she arrived at a philosophical position that concurred with Keats's view that intelligence was schooled by a "World of Pains and troubles"[29] In her poem "Life" Wharton shows that the reed must be cut if it is to become a pipe that produces music. Keats's romanticism was of a melancholy kind, his personal melancholy deriving from frustrations caused by class, illness, and thwarted love. Privilege had not insulated Wharton from some painful experiences, including illness and the pain of being an intellectual woman in a deeply conservative nonintellectual family. She knew she had learned much from these experiences, and came through the melancholia.

By 1910 she had experienced a breakdown, her marriage had collapsed, the affair with the journalist Morton Fullerton was over, and she was dependent on her writing as a source of income now that her husband had squandered much of the family wealth. She had experienced pain and trouble, cushioned to a certain extent by her social status, but also exacerbated by that status and the values that accompanied and governed it. Her acute intelligence allowed her to see beyond the political conventions that accompanied privilege.

In her writing Wharton repeatedly traces out a cold world in which the longing for passionate experience is crushed by disappointment, restraint, rules, conventions, and the callousness of others. Idealism is often compromised, love ends in disappointment, and independent women are crushed. The conclusions seem almost Marxist in their recognition that economic interests rather than moral values ultimately drive history. Yet in 1908 she wrote of her excitement at the discovery of Nietzsche, whose "power of breaking through conventions . . . is most exhilarating."[30] There was a yearning to escape, fleetingly seized in a few excursions with Fullerton. Earlier it had been the subject of a last flowering of her late-Victorian version of romanticism, later to be subjected to a different political gloss.

Wharton's 1899 short story, "Souls Belated," has a Nietzschean rebel, not in the man, but in the woman. It is she who wishes to defy conventions. The story announces many of the themes that appear in the writing from 1910–14, the prewar period with which this study is particularly concerned. These themes, some of which may not sound political at all, include the person who has been trapped in a loveless marriage who longs for love, the failure of the cautious man who lacks the courage and recklessness to love fully, and the hypocrisy of society's rules. Lydia and Ralph are on a train in Italy, runaway lovers for whom there is already the sense of strain. She wants more than he can give, she wants the freedom of love and sexual expression. He talks of marriage. The conventions are turned on their head because the man does not understand that remarrying in these circumstances would be worse than the scandal of an affair. The directness of being "cut" by society is preferable to the readmission into a society in which she would be encouraged to cut others who find themselves in her present circumstance. Trouble and pain are rooted, therefore, in marriage, convention, and the failure of love, failures in the very traditions to which she publicly subscribed. In drawing attention to ideological and social issues, there will be no attempt to lessen the importance of the powerful, but often suppressed, emotional issues that the texts convey. But these feelings, often expressed as a loss, can be metonymies indicating primal feelings not only about individuals, but about ways of life. They are rooted in politics.

The sense of loss is conveyed by *A Backward Glance*'s dedication, with its suggestion that Wharton is haunted by the ghosts of those who have passed out of her life: "To the friends who every year on All Souls Night come and sit with me by the fire."[31] Ghosts, real or imagined, had always interested Wharton, and ten years after "Souls Belated" Wharton wrote the series of stories published as *Tales of Men and Ghosts*. Only two or three are ghost stories and the ghost story may seem a strange one for her to choose. But Wharton admired the form. Her last short story "All Souls" is a ghost story, and she concluded the preface to *Ghosts,* the collection in which it appeared soon after her death in 1937, with a sentence that suggests that fear was as great a familiar, and perhaps more of a revelation, than love had ever been: "The only suggestion I can make is that the teller of supernatural tales should be well frightened in the telling; for if he is, he may perhaps communicate to his readers the sense of that strange something undreamt of in the philosophy of Horatio."[32]

Modernism and ghost stories may seem far apart as cultural phenomena, but they share a desire to go beyond the familiar and material world. Wharton enjoyed the genre of the ghost story, and like Henry James in *The Turn of the Screw* she uses it to explore the repressed and the unfamiliar. Freud published his essay "The Uncanny" in 1919, and one translation of Freud's term *unheimliche* is not just "uncanny" or "unfamiliar" but the more literal "unhomelike." Exile and defamiliarization are features of modernism that have something in common with Wharton's own displacement, as well as with her sense of the fearful experience of the unknown. Such a fear was explored much earlier by Burke in his 1757 discussion of the sublime,[33] and the uncanny is seen by some[34] as an extension of Burke's aesthetic theory of the sublime and the beautiful, where the overawing experience of the sublime is more powerful than the experience of beauty because it creates a feeling of obliteration and the infinite. The feeling of astonishment and awe that characterizes the Burkean sublime is largely omitted from Wharton's novels but, like the return of the repressed, appears in her stories of the uncanny. This, however, is a feature of romanticism rather than modernism. Wharton is still concerned with the individual and his or her social relations, however much the focus may be on the individual's troubled psychology. These stories are concerned with modern, psychological conditions, but they are not to be reduced to thinly disguised explorations of that modernist subject par excellence, artistic alienation.

What links ghost stories and social narrative is the sense of a powerful external force beyond the individual's control, and this helps us understand why Wharton always retained an interest in the social and the anthropological, as opposed to the emphasis on individual consciousness that we associate with modernism. After 1910 it is the cold cruelty of unfeeling human spirits that appears to have increasingly appealed to her, for in the novels of 1911 to 1913, *Ethan Frome, The Reef,* and *The Custom of the Country,* individuals who would be passionate are paralyzed by the chilling influence of those close to them. As for the shorter ghost stories, the genre provided an alternative to the world of scientific realism and sociological naturalism to which her novel writing paid artistic allegiance. It is easy to make the assumption that ghost stories offered an alternative that seemed to look backward, compared with modernism's response to realism, with the rallying cry of "make it new." The matter is more complicated than that.

In considering the politics of Wharton's fiction it will be necessary to discuss the assumptions, beliefs, and discourses with which she interacted during what is a long period of young and mature adulthood. From the late-Victorian vantage point of 1880, when she was eighteen, to 1915, when *The Book of the Homeless* was edited and the world was at war, is a period of thirty-five years. At the beginning the values and politics of her parents and immediate social circle provided a key influence, but throughout her youth and adulthood her reading of literature, science, and philosophy helped shape her views, as did her contact with her close circle of friends. A sense of noblesse oblige remains constant. It will be necessary to consider the readings of history, human behavior, evolution, the role of women, art, aesthetics, bohemianism, economics, and masculinity that she encountered over a period ranging from the Gilded Age to the Progressive, or in English terms, from the late-Victorian to the Edwardian. The twentieth century, which is regarded as a beginning historically, may not have been considered a beginning for many married woman who were forty years of age, but it was certainly a beginning in Edith Wharton's career as a successful writer.

Dale M. Bauer has stressed the important need to locate Wharton in the context of contemporary political discourses: "Wharton critics have neglected her politics, in part because her views are often conflicting and in part because her work has not been read in the light of the relevant intellectual debates of her day." To redress this neglect, Bauer argues for a recognition of "Wharton's connection to the political world around her, a connection her critics have often fervently denied or misrepresented."[35] Bauer concentrates on the period from 1917 onward. In concentrating on the years *before* 1914 I wish to argue that Wharton's involvement in war work in France is a logical and consistent development from the rhetoric of her imaginative writing and the political questions it addresses. What appears to be an abrupt and unexpected commitment to social work should not really come as a surprise. Wharton's 1900 to 1914 novels and short stories are important barometers of the diversity of political ideas to which she was sensitive, and we should not be misled by her statements in her letters, by her apparently comfortable prewar lifestyle, or by her autobiographical defense of Old New York into thinking that she never interrogated the politics of her class or the American preoccupation with individual achievement. Implicit in much of her early fiction, this interrogation emerged explicitly in the middle of the war, during a discussion of the New Frenchwoman. In 1917 she wrote: "If the collective life which results from our individual money-making is not richer, more interesting, more stimulating than that of countries where the individual effort is less intense, then it looks as if there is something wrong about our method."[36] In the light of this gentle querying of individualism and capitalism, and by implication the construction of the new individual per se, Wharton's apparent disregard for the experiments of modernism can be explained by her rejection of its perceived solipsism and lack of social commitment as much as by her disposition to avoid unnecessary innovation. Wharton's fiction explores how society shapes and constrains the individual. The sensibility of the artist, when it is represented, is represented as the sensibility of the collector, painter, or writer preoccupied with self. Such individuals are less innovative and culture forming than they would like to think, Wharton often shows us. The artist or art collector with bohemian tendencies, whether poor or rich, is not a figure who emerges with any credit in her novels. The political idealist, on the other hand, even when he or she fails, is presented as a weary, but attractive, individual. But what the dispossessed of the world most need is practical action, not to build new worlds but to repair old damage.

The world of pain and troubles is a cold one, and the soul searches for warmth and reasons for this coldness. In a religiously intense exploration of the imprisonment of human souls, Wharton interrogates the political assumptions of a culture that entraps women and the poor in particular, producing fiction whose rhetoric is sometimes at odds with the political position that the writer takes up when she defends the status quo in her letters and published autobiography. It is this political paradox, where the conservative public pronouncements are challenged by the argument of the novels, that this study will explore. In so doing it will be necessary to consider key questions, such as the effect on her work of viewing America from Europe, the interrogation of the American dream from the center of Paris, her reading of class and society, and most revealingly, her relationship to early modernism, in an attempt to historicize and reexamine the paradoxical nature of her work. Most important of all, there will be a need to show how Wharton's own assumptions about individual freedom, aesthetics, and culture were shaped both by the political discourses in which she was immersed and her fatalistic belief in the implacable Furies, the classical equivalent of Puritanism's belief in the inevitability of the Last Judgment. Her wide reading included fiction, history, science, sociology, psychology, anthropology, poetry, and philosophy, a process explored by Jennie Kassanoff in her study of Wharton and the politics of race.[37] The reading of articles written by Morton Fullerton and John Jay Chapman, both of whom entered her life at the same time, contributed to her perspective on national and international politics, and the representation of events in such papers as the *Times*, the *Times Literary Supplement, Punch,* and the illustrated papers, which we know she read,[38] provides evidence of the way some of the debates were couched. As Althusser shows in "Ideology and Ideological State Apparatuses,"[39] such discourses were mediated by institutions to persuade individuals that they enjoyed more autonomy than they in reality had. Thus, argues Althusser, so many individuals come to submit to the dominant ideology of society because they believe that it is in their best interest to do so. Is this true of Wharton, or is the assumption itself flawed? It may be that the paradoxes in Wharton's political representation and fictional rhetoric demonstrate the shortcoming in Althusser's view of the operation of ideology, for as Eagleton says,[40] the one thing that many human subjects exhibit is a willingness to struggle, a political struggle that is acted out not in Wharton's public life but in her fiction. It is these paradoxes that provide evidence of Wharton's formation by and questioning of significant political and historical ideologies.

Privileging the Political in Wharton's Life and Fiction

The instinctive political assumptions that underpinned Edith Whartons's worldview during the period of her emergence as a successful writer are not easy to pinpoint because they break through to the surface only occasionally. In an undated letter, probably written in 1910 in the middle of the wave of strikes that swept Britain at the end of the Edwardian period, Wharton writes to Sara Norton: "I have a very cut off feeling as I reflect that this beastly strike may be closing in on us in 24 hours."[41] That this comment was not the product of a specific moment's irritation but part of a set of political attitudes shared by those in her immediate circle is suggested by a letter to Wharton from Henry James written in 1912, in the middle of that period of social unrest in England, which saw protests from suffragists, miners, and even schoolchildren. "There is nothing here of any actuality save the great looming coal strike which really quite blackens all the sky & is in fact the most appalling of prospects, so appalling, however, that I can't believe the general national energy won't avail somehow to avert it. On the other hand we may be on the edge of evil days."[42]

James follows this up in a letter written a month later, expanding on his general apprehension over the anarchy of the moment, but expressing hope that the insurrections will be put down: "The impossible wears on us, but we wear a little here, I think, even on the coal-strike & the mass of attendant misery, though they produce an effect & create an atmosphere dismal and depressing, to which the window-smashing women add a darker shade. I am blackly bored when the latter are at large & at work; but somehow I am still more blackly bored when they are shut in Holloway,[43] & we are deprived of them."[44] James finally puts his political cards on the table: "We continue here up to our ears in crisis, though a light does seem to be at last dimly to break. I am with the Government, wholly,—& should go even further."[45]

In citing these comments from James, I am not assuming that he and Wharton shared identical political views, although it is likely that there would be signals in his letter if he thought that a reader, who by 1912 he knew so very well, were likely to be in disagreement. Neither am I claiming that there is anything here that should surprise us. The view expressed by Wharton and echoed by James was the dominant view of the class with which they most identified, and not the most reactionary view of that class by any means. The government, for example, was Liberal, but it was still opposed to the strikers and to votes for women. The English magazine *Punch*, read by both Liberals and Conservatives, featured a full-page cartoon on 6 March 1912, which, above the caption "The Victim," showed a frightened Britannia bound by ropes and cowering beneath a dark-skinned figure with "Coal War" on his turban, thus conflating fears of the so-called "white slave trade" and the power of the striking miners.[46] Such attitudes were the norm in England at the time. All that Wharton and James's comments provide is a reference point for a discussion of Wharton's own politics.

Central to this is an understanding of her view of art. Art, she believed, could only be produced by a leisure class, and only the very best art would do. Susan Goodman, citing Wharton's friend Bernard Berenson, comments on the political implications of this view, which was shared by those in her inner circle and cherished most religiously by James, the "master" of the group: "In societies where art flourished, they were largely willing to overlook the miseries caused by a rigid class system, whether intellectual or economic, for 'then a few of the highest class devote themselves to culture without harm, and perhaps to the greater advantage of the community.'"[47]

It is generally accepted now that too much has been made of James's influence on Wharton the artist, but the important, if not defining influence of his political aesthetic should not be similarly watered down. James wrote what were delightfully performed, and gracefully constructed, letters to his friends. The tone of this correspondence (until the outbreak of war in August 1914) was often wickedly self-mocking and playful, but when it came to the subject of the failure of other writers to commit themselves to their art with the same serious dedication that he himself gave to it, the voice invariably changed to one of steely dismissal and ruthless judgment. In a letter to Gosse, commenting on the Meredith who has been revealed through the publication of his letters, James crushingly concludes: "[H]e clearly lived even less than one had the sense of his doing in the world of art."[48]

In the disagreement with H. G. Wells, the writer he had previously championed and who, in James's view, had returned the kindness with what James felt to be a caricature of him in Wells's novel *Boon*, it was on the conception of art that the two writers most profoundly disagreed. Wells had written that he would as well be considered a journalist as an artist, and that to him literature was like architecture, a means, whereas to James literature, like painting, was an end. To this James wrote back bluntly, that he disagreed totally with Wells's distinction, because it was "art that makes life."[49]

Evidence that this view of the sacredness of art was shared by Wharton is to be found in many places, as, for example, in a letter to Bliss Perry, the editor of *Atlantic Monthly*. Perry commissioned the studies of France that eventually became *A Motor-Flight Through France*. Between 1909 and 1912 Wharton's work appeared in this periodical at least once a year, with the poems "Ogrin the Hermit" in 1909,[50] and "The Comrade" in 1910,[51] and the short story "The Long Run" in 1913.[52] Prior to this, in a letter to Perry dated August 8, 1905, Wharton lauded the editorship of this former professor of English: "I can't tell you how much praise I think you deserve for maintaining the tradition of what a good magazine should be in the face of our howling mob of critics & readers; & I hope the Atlantic will long continue to nurse the little flame of sweetness and light in the chaotic darkness of American 'literary' conditions. . . . If you are ever in this part of the world, do come and see me, & let us despair together of the Republic of letters.[53]

Elsewhere in this letter Wharton praises articles by Sedgwick and

Thayer that *Atlantic Monthly* had recently published. Both the items she cites are revealing. Thayer's article on "The Outlook of History,"[54] which sought to reinstate the individual of influence in the story of history, is discussed later in this study. It impressed Wharton enough to write to him personally on November 11, 1905, expressing her admiration for his essay on historical method. She also seizes the opportunity to acknowledge the extent to which she made use of *The Dawn of Italian Independence* in writing her "Italian novel," *The Valley of Decision*.[55] Henry Dwight Sedgwick's article "The Mob Spirit in Literature"[56] offers a broad patrician attack on "the mob" from the time of Mark Antony to the Gordon Riots. Its premise is that "[a]rt is a matter based on the experiences, not of all men, as in science, but of the few." As the article progresses, Sedgwick warms to his theme: "Here then we have art, the experience of the few, and authority, the judgment of the few, both antithetical to that mob spirit, which knows neither law nor authority, and follows the gusty impulses of instinct."[57] Good critics are sorely missed in the United States, Sedgwick argues, adding the wish that Henry James paid more attention to America. As the schools cannot provide the critical tools that are needed, art and critical authority must.

In her discussion of the acceptance in Edith Wharton's inner circle of the need for inequality as long as art is preserved, Susan Goodman makes a distinction between Wharton and the art critic Bernard Berenson: "Unlike Wharton, Berenson has an enormous faith in what he liked to call humanity, and she called the rabble."[58] Such a statement is at odds with Wharton's actions at the beginning of World War I, when she worked tirelessly for the Belgian refugees that both she and James identified as anything but "rabble." Such terms as "mob" and "rabble," if they were used by Wharton, may have been reserved for those from the world of literature who did not share her assumptions about taste, narrative crafting, and seriousness of artistic purpose.

Edmund Wilson argued that Edith Wharton was New York/Massachusetts Puritan to the core in her belief that we must always face the unpleasant and the ugly,[59] and that however much society may influence the individual, the individual can usually resist. On some subjects she seemed to subscribe to a version of the nineteenth-century Liberalism favored by Henry James. Yet she was enthusiastic about Roosevelt, enjoyed the company of titled Europeans, and was certainly no progressive when it came to matters of class and race. In his reading of her first full-length novel, *The Valley of Decision,* Blake Nevius concludes that not only was Wharton conservative in manners, but that manners themselves mattered to her more than the organization of government: "Nothing is clearer than that for Edith Wharton, with her conservative, anti-Rousseauistic bias, and her preference for gradual, orderly reform within the existing social structure, the French Revolution was a disaster comparable to the American Civil War and . . . the First World War, both of which brought about a revolution in manners as deplorable, in her mind, as a revolution in government."[60]

As a broad description of her politics of manners, this comment has not been seriously challenged, but it is something that is often seen as less important when compared to her achievements, which have led to increasingly vigorous celebration of her belated recognition as a major writer. In her recent introduction to *A Historical Guide to Edith Wharton,* Carol J. Singley writes: "Wharton's critical reputation has never been higher . . [she] is by critical and popular acclaim one of the United States' finest novelists and short story writers."[61] In some of the more enthusiastic attempts to represent Wharton as a progressive and subversive writer, many arising from the continuing reappraisal of her post–World War I fiction, several of the assumptions that supply the general framework for this writing, and of its prewar predecessors, are overlooked, with the consequent dehistoricization of her work. It is fruitful to look more closely at the evolution of her beliefs that commenced after the death of her mother in 1901, an evolution that was interrupted and paralyzed by the outbreak of war. Although this pre–war phase became in some ways a more difficult period in her life, because of the responsibilities and pressures that came to bear on her, the ability to take control, rather than be controlled, brought with it a sense of increasing freedom and liberation. The combination of an American home and a European perspective was crucial in facilitating this sense of autonomy between 1900 and 1915, and prepared her psychologically for the stressful demands of her war work. But there was never anything like a rupture with her past. Instead there was a reassessment.

For the young Edith Wharton, the extensive experience of Europe before World War I, and the timing of her permanent transfer, threw into relief the Old New York values with which she had grown up, many of which she never abandoned. The attraction of Europe for Wharton, and the timing of her decision to make it her permanent home, are circumstances rich with the irony of historical specificity. Malcolm Bradbury has alluded to this in his study of the expatriate tradition in American literature: "Europe was . . . becoming a place where American artists and writers could pursue an aesthetic and a social dissent from contemporary American culture."[62] This part of Bradbury's comment is applicable to Wharton, who despaired of the crassness and materialism of the American new-money class, and although wintering in Paris suited Teddy as much as it did Wharton, for her it was a chance to immerse herself in an environment in which the values and manners to which she subscribed did not seem to be disappearing as they were in America.[63] But Bradbury points to a danger in embracing Europe in this way: "One risk—mocked by Mark Twain in *Innocents Abroad* (1869) and more elaborately analyzed by James in his portrait of Gilbert Osmond—was that of 'museumizing' European culture, turning it into commodity, an object of study."[64]

Bradbury cites the cases of Logan Pearsall Smith in England, Leo Stein in France, and Bernard Berenson and George Santayana in Italy "whose quest was essentially aesthetic." These men sought Europe not for its manners but for its art, and a culture that was not predominantly Anglo-Saxon, which was their experience in America. Berenson and Santayana were originally from Lithuania and Spain respectively. Though Wharton confessed to being Celtic at heart, the more Celtic parts of Europe did not seem to detain her long, and like Berenson and Santayana she loved the architecture and history of Mediterranean Europe. But sympathetic to the warning of *A Portrait of a Lady*, she clearly did not see herself as "museumizing" Europe, a charge that was also to be brought by John Jay Chapman, the contemporary and acquaintance who attacked certain types of acquisitive American exiles then living in Paris. In the short story "The Daunt Diana" (1909), Wharton offers one of her own several portraits of the precious, mannered art collector, who is indeed a sad museumizer.

There is thus a subtle difference between what brought to Europe an American like Berenson, with his Jewish and Lithuanian heritage, and what took Wharton there. It is true, however, that they occupied the same cultural world once they began their permanent exile, and in Bradbury's comment, American upper-class Jews and East Coast patricians are bracketed together in their longing for what Europe had to offer: "Certainly they were expressions of a new era of American culture hunger—of the new immigration of educated, intellectual, upper class Jews into America; of the unsettlement growing within the East Coast patriciates, of the attempts by many richer Americans to recover the aesthetic senses through Europe."[65] But as Bradbury goes on to point out, there was a tremendous irony in the timing of this move for someone like Wharton: "Their 'aesthetic' preoccupation thus represented an important transition; turning, often to Europe as the repository of a past culture of the arts, they found it the active environment of a present one, and played their part in the discovery, authentification and promotion of Modernism."[66]

Bradbury has in mind, no doubt, Pound and Yeats. Settling in Europe at almost exactly the same time, Wharton, for reasons of class, background, and generation, found that she could not identify with the new movements that were challenging the conventions of art in a way that paralleled the challenges to manners posed by the arrival of the new moneyed barbarians invading New York.

The importance of the political and historical moment for Wharton's prewar writing has for a long time been neglected by full-length text studies, partly because other, more personal events in Wharton's life have seemed to offer a more obvious way into her work, and partly because her several years' active involvement in World War I refugee work has been seen as the more decisive moment of reorientation. Individual and important studies there have been, as we shall see, looking at subjects as diverse as sawmill technology in New England, the legacy of Darwinism and Emersonian transcendentalism, turn of the century architecture and the sense of space, and Wharton's reading of Morocco and colonialism. Yet, with the notable exception of Kassanoff, these more political and ideological readings have tended to remain the subject of individual essays, such as Nancy Bentley's influential study of the "science of manners,"[67] rather than complete books.

A significant reason behind this continuing neglect has been the success of recent critical discussion in drawing attention to the important debates about aesthetics, writing, and gender that are inscribed in Wharton's pre–1914 fiction. One example is the illuminating discussion of the place in the fiction of metaphors drawn from mythology and the spirit world. Candace Waid's study *Edith Wharton's Letters from the Underworld*,[68] for example, argues persuasively that Wharton's preoccupation with the myth of Persephone, who spends part of each year in the Underworld with Pluto because she has eaten the pomegranate seed, can be traced in fiction ranging from "The Muses's Tragedy" and *The Touchstone* to *The House of Mirth* and *The Custom of the Country*. Persephone becomes a symbol of the woman writer who moves between two worlds and lives a kind of ghostly existence. In the ramifications of her argument, the Persephone trope can be seen in many different ways. In one sense the mother, Demeter, that Persephone has to abandon each year is America, and Europe, the Underworld. Equally, the Underworld, and the pomegranate seed in particular, which Persephone has tasted there, can stand for the erotic, and as I shall argue in a discussion of *The Reef*, the bohemian. But as a woman who also identified with scientific rationalism and logic, Wharton was also keen to expose the hollowness of the sentimental, which allocates to women the role of muse or art object. All of these issues have a central place in any discussion of Wharton's work, and I would not wish to challenge the value of the debates about aestheticism, marriage, writing, and gender, which have been identified as central to her fiction.

There is, however, a strong argument for privileging the political in those prewar years to see how it affects our reading of Wharton. Whatever one's reaction to the debate about whether the personal is also the political, there is also a less individualistic, more collective reading of culture that sees self-development as the agent of collective development, and not the other way around. Such a reading is in sympathy with that of the "Hegelian historicist for whom the art that matters is one flushed with the dynamic forces of its age."[69] Such a view is frequently traceable in Wharton's work, and the belief that we need to recognize the way we are constructed[70] is one that has been articulated through the twentieth century.[71]

I use "politics" here and throughout in the narrower sense in which it was used before more recent cultural theory broadened its meaning. Politics in this discussion will be used to signify the organization and administration of local, state, or international affairs by governmental organizations. Politics, in other words, involves the functioning of the state and its agencies, or what is defined by Hague, Harrop, and Breslin, and glossed by Axford "as the process by which groups make collective decisions."[72] This is not to accept the binary categories of individual/state, questioned by gender theory, which sees sexual politics in *all* relationships, and by cultural theory, which sees agency as a principle informing thought and behavior so pervasively that the category "individual" is itself questionable. It will be precisely my argument that Wharton came to reassess the forces impinging on her as a writer in ways that represent her own politicization. In her autobiography she discussed herself primarily in relation to imaginative writing, art, and immediate personal relationships. Her relationship to the state was secondary. She was well aware of cultural pressures particularly on women, and began to recognize these as functions of society and capitalism. Such a claim is at odds with the argument, put forward by some critics, that Wharton misunderstood the politics of capitalism. Wharton's prewar fiction may not offer an explicit critique of the operation of the rampant capitalism of the Gilded Age, but it fully recognizes the meaning of marital prostitution, conspicuous consumption, the infantilization of women, and the connectedness between the behavior of the individual and the material world she inhabits. If anything, Wharton is rather too willing to attribute all present-day social ills to centuries of history.

Wharton's observations on architecture and art frequently raise historical questions, and these give rise to religious, philosophical, and political questions. There is a revealing moment in *A Motor-Flight Through France* (1908) in which she is discussing French cathedrals: "The world will doubtless always divide itself into two orders of mind: that which sees in past expression of faith, political, religious or intellectual, only the bonds cast off by the spirit of man in the long invincible struggle for 'more light'; and that which, while moved by the spectacle of the struggle, cherishes also every sign of these past limitations that were, after all, each in its turn symbols of the same effort toward a clearer vision."[73] The rhetorical position is announced by the affectionate word "cherishes." While sympathetic to the need for change, Wharton cannot overlook the history of change and the important record of that development that these cathedrals provide. Her instinct is to conserve rather than change, something I explore in the discussion of *The Reef* in chapter 5.

Wharton had a serious interest in history, but it was a particular Victorian liberal humanist version of history that she seemed to favor, or one that recognized the achievements of the great and the good, as in Carlyle's version of history, which was seen as increasingly Victorian and dated by the new historians, inspired by German scientific methods of historical analysis. Wharton had applauded[74] an article by William Roscoe Thayer[75] that challenged this development in historical studies, and in his relegation of politics to the world of effects rather than causes, we can see something of Wharton's own view:

> But what is History? Freeman, in an epigram which has helped to desiccate many of his disciples, declared that it is only "past politics" and that present politics will be future history. His dogmatic tone jars on us. Unless politics be defined so broadly as to lose all meaning it does not cover the field: for we see that political action is usually not a cause, but an effect, and we have grown hungry to know causes. . . . The publication of Tom Paine's *Common Sense*, or Mrs. Stowe's *Uncle Tom's Cabin*, would not fall within Freeman's definition of "political" and yet the historian who should ignore such symptoms as these books must himself be ignored.[76]

It may be true that books by Paine and Stowe fall outside the late nineteenth-century versions of history, but Thayer (and thus Wharton) wish to restore them not as political agencies, but as examples of individual influence and achievement. Today economic history would indeed see these works as part of the technology of politics, but not in a way that would have won Wharton's approval.

Edith Wharton grew to adulthood during a resurgence of capitalism and period of great expansion, change, and growth in America. Her childhood in New York took place against the background of Reconstruction, but Old New York was a long way from the impoverished South, and as a girl Edith Jones was more familiar with the other side of the Atlantic than with the South or West of the United States, having lived in Europe permanently between the ages of four and ten, mainly in Spain, Italy, and France. The psychological and political effect of this period of her life has generally been understood as one that strengthened feelings of conservatism. In discussing the reading regime imposed by her mother in France, Shari Benstock observes that an education in European practices meant that Wharton was drawn to a "cultural conservatism that valued preservation over innovation."[77]

There is an important element of truth in these comments, but it is a mistake to regard Europe as a single entity. Furthermore, the history of France and Italy, the countries she was most familiar with, can hardly be regarded as having been stable and settled over the previous hundred years. France had experienced a revolution and Italy had been born. The aftershocks of these events were still evident.

The Jones family returned to New York in 1872 in the belief that their period of relative money-saving in Europe meant that it was safe to resume their former lifestyle. Unfortunately the post–Civil War boom was about to end and on September 19, 1873, the so-called "Black Friday," there was a major financial panic on Wall Street leading to numerous bankruptcies and the failure of several banks. The Jones family remained in America, however, and continued to keep up both their Newport and New York houses, to socialize, and to entertain. Gradually economic conditions became more favorable and the national changes that led to the so-called "Age of Gold" tended to reinforce the dominance and strength of the North and improved the fortunes of those who traded in the stock market or invested in industrial development. But the Joneses were not an industrial family, and with much of their money tied up in property, the depression in real estate values caused financial losses that were a great worry to Edith's father, George Frederic Jones, particularly in 1879, the year in which Edith Jones made her formal entry into Newport and New York society. She was then seventeen years old.

Although we tend to associate the adult Edith Wharton with the twentieth century, because that is when her reputation as a writer was established, her birth year of 1862 shows us how close she was to a much earlier world that was quickly being transformed by the shift from rural to urban, brought about by the enormous economic success of the industrial revolution in the United States. The America of the yeoman farmer was one of recent memory, but it was a world that was vanishing.[78]

During the Gilded Age the population of the United States rose enormously, as the flow of immigrants continued to arrive at Ellis Island. Both rural and urban populations rose steeply, but the urban population grew most startlingly, and in 1914 equaled the rural population for the first time. By 1914 and the outbreak of war in Europe Wharton had completed an adjustment to her nineteenth-century political education and produced the bulk of the fiction on which her reputation rests. By then she had also substituted for the company of Old New York society with its inability to question or reflect, the company of a circle of cerebral male friends. Apart from Bernard Berenson, the Wharton circle included Walter Berry, Howard Sturgis, Paul Bourget, Gaillard Lapsley, Percy Lubbock, Henry James, Morton Fullerton, Egerton Winthrop, Bay Lodge, Robert Norton, John Hugh Smith, and Ogden Codman. These ranged from successful writers like James and Bourget, working architects and journalists such as Codman and Fullerton, to the more leisured and privileged professionals and art lovers such as Berry and Lubbock. Some, like John Hugh Smith and Robert Norton, were English, but the majority were American. Most tended to have a Harvard or Oxbridge education and a "distinguished" family background.

By nature democratic and liberal, in nineteenth-century terms, their beliefs were not inconsistent with a patrician outlook. Henry James, for example, was a close correspondent of Sir George Trevelyan, who had been a Liberal MP in the Gladstone government before retiring as an MP in 1897. Trevelyan had been at the very center of British politics, particularly during the introduction of Gladstone's Home Rule Bill, and had written a distinguished biography of his uncle Lord Macaulay and a six-volume study of the American War of Independence. Yet when James and Wharton knew him, he was enjoying his country house, Wallington Hall, in Northumberland, where he spent some of his time shooting pheasant and woodcock. That kind of privilege does not always lead to orthodoxy and conservatism in politics, but to resist the social conditioning of the establishment class, it is usually necessary to leave it, and this is something that this intimate inner circle of friends and their close acquaintances did not do.

The Politics of Privilege

The journey from Old New York to partician Europe was not so vast as the miles might suggest, and it was a slow and gradual one. In 1879, as a seventeen-year-old debutante, Edith Wharton had become old enough to review some of the assumptions of the society into which she had been born and in which she had grown up. The values of that society, the Old New York aristocracy of family, inherited wealth, and property, are indicated in the opening chapters of her autobiography, *A Backward Glance,* where she describes her ancestry at considerable length. Descended from merchant ship owners traceable to colonial New York, she comments that her own ancestry was "purely middle-class."[79] It may not have had a genealogy traceable to the aristocracy of the ancestral country but it had family members who mixed freely with those who did make such claims. As merchants, bankers, and lawyers, the members of both her mother's and father's families gained acceptance in a society that rigorously excluded "all dealers in retail business."[80] When, in the 1920s, Wharton came to reflect on the value of this self-styled "polite society," she draws on notions of refinement and honor to justify its privileged and exclusive status: "I believe their value lay in upholding two standards of importance in any community, that of education and good manners, and of scrupulous probity in business and private affairs."[81] It is unlikely that this political defense of a privileged society would have been articulated in Wharton's childhood home in quite these terms, but such beliefs were the implicit assumption behind all judgments and behavior. From hearing family comments on those who fell short of this set of standards, a group that included most of the new-money people, most members of the shopkeeping and retail class, and most members of the working class, Edith Jones would have been inducted into the values of what *was* acceptable and desirable in Old New York society's eyes. In 1934, at the age of seventy-two, Edith Wharton looked back on that society with nostalgia and affection: "At any rate I should say that the qualities justifying the existence of our old society were social amenity and financial incorruptibility; and we have travelled far enough from both to begin to estimate their value."[82]

Yet even reviewing that society from the rose-tinted distance of sixty or so years, Wharton did not offer it unqualified approval. She concedes that it was conformist, complacent, and "blind to innovation."[83] It was a class without curiosity ("No one in our set had any intellectual interests"),[84] and authorship was regarded as a practice that fell somewhere between manual labor and the black arts. It had a morbid fear of sexual scandal, and it had a Puritanical view of woman as temptress in every such heterosexual case. She was never able to forget the scornful "some" of her mother's murmured "Some woman" as the explanation for the excommunication of cousin George from the family circle. But in her old age, having seen the World War and the upheavals that preceded it sweep aside Old New York, Wharton seemed able to forgive it these things. Writing in the 1930s she reverts to a view of it that would have surrounded her in Old New York when she was seventeen. This contrasts with the more critical argument embedded in most of her prewar fiction, and she acknowledges the revisionism contained in her later *Backward Glance* assessment:

> Now I see that one of its uses lay in preserving a few drops of an old vintage too rare to be savoured by a youthful palate; and I should like to atone for my unappreciativeness by trying to revive that faint fragrance.[85]

It is not unusual for people in their older years to become unashamed apologists for the habits and standards of the past that at the time irked them. Such a reaction is partly a reflection of a genuine concern that something important is being lost and denied to fresh generations, but it is also a response that reflects unease about the bewildering and disorientating effects of change. Elsewhere in her autobiography Wharton draws attention to the change she has lived through, born as she was into an age "in which telephones, motor cars, electric light, central heating, X rays, cinemas, radium, aeroplanes" and the wireless were unknown and largely unimagined.[86] She not only coped with these changes, but as is clear from her infatuation with the automobile, for example, she sometimes positively embraced them. Several of her pre-1915 nonfiction books, such as *The Decoration of Houses, Italian Villas and Their Gardens, A Motor-Flight Through France,* and *Fighting France,* happily include photographs to illustrate her argument. Unlike E. M. Forster, who regretted the arrival of cars and planes from their first appearance, she was not by nature a conservative in technological matters. In an undated letter that was almost certainly written in 1909, she writes with tremendous enthusiasm of seeing her first plane:

> And what do you think happened to me last Monday? I was getting out of the motor at the door of the H.de Crillon, when I saw two or three people looking into the air. I looked also, & there was an aeroplane high up against the sky, just above the "Chevaux de Marly" & emerging on the Place de la Concorde. It sailed obliquely across the Place, incredibly high above the obelisk, against a golden sunset, with a new moon between flitting clouds, & crossing the Seine in the direction of the Pantheon, lost

itself in a flight of birds that was just crossing the sky, reappeared far off, a speck against the clouds & disappeared at last into the twilight. And it was the Comte de Lambert in a Wright biplane, who had first flown across from (Invisy?)—& it was the <u>first time</u> that an aeroplane had every crossed a great city!! I think "what soul was mine"—and what a setting in which to see one's first aeroplane flight![87]

There is much to note here, including the move from car to plane, the satisfaction that the plane is being flown by an aristocrat, and the irony in Wharton's failure to see that both car and plane would lead to the further encroachment of the "new barbarians." For now Wharton saw them as agencies that would allow welcome segregation from the larger populace, and more privacy for the traveler. The political conservatism of her later autobiography should be read in its own political context. As a younger woman she had been religiously accepting of her class and its formal rigidity and, as this letter shows, she was not resistant to the process of material change where it did not seem to threaten the established order.

Although at the age of seventeen Edith Jones was imaginative and enterprising enough to have completed her first novella, no critical reflections on the character of her early ideological apprenticeship appear in any of her published letters from this period or its sequel. Benstock offers this explanation for the general absence of discursive and essayistic paragraphs on political issues in her correspondence: "Her letters were not a stage for intellectual debate, nor did she often fully explore a topic in 'letter talk,' as Sand and Flaubert did, for example. Rather, she suggested topics for future discussion—the talk itself to take place in person."[88]

Carol J. Singley[89] also remarks on Wharton's relative "silence" on theoretical issues in both letters and essays. Wharton's first biographer, Percy Lubbock, claimed that this derived from an inability to discuss theoretically. More likely is the explanation that Wharton avoided this form because of the cultural expectations of women, which regarded the intellectual woman as "unwomanly." As the narrator says in *The Touchstone* (1900): "Genius is of small use to a woman who does not know how to do her hair."[90] Even in France, which became her preferred cultural home, the intellectual woman had to dissemble, so as not to be mistaken for the New Woman.[91]

It is possible that this French feminist ploy of covert tactics appealed to Wharton, allowing as it did for subversion in beautiful clothes. It also required a strategic reticence on abstract matters and in her study of the New Woman in fin de siècle France Mary Louise Roberts[92] considers how such a compromise could be the dupe of patriarchy and the product of internalized sexist belief. It is equally possible, however, that Wharton genuinely thought abstraction a waste of time in a world where there were so many practical things that eventually needed to be done, from organizing finances, to running a house, dealing with publishers, and nursing an ailing husband and an ailing friend. Such organizational demands came after her marriage, however. Pressure of responsibilities would not explain this absence of discursive writing in her early youth, and the cultural disapproval in Edith Wharton's class of the "bluestocking" is the more likely explanation.

❖

What then of the political climate in the America in which she lived as a girl and young woman? In many ways the last quarter of the nineteenth century was to be a relatively stable and uneventful period in the United States for the privileged class into which Wharton had been born. American politics of the following decades were dominated by Republicans and the presidents (Hayes in 1876, Garfield in 1880, Arthur, his vice president who succeeded him after his assassination, Cleveland in 1884, and Harrison in 1888) have collectively earned the rather unfortunate sobriquet "unmemorable presidents." Reconstruction fervency had passed and trusts, big business, and large corporations held sway over the economy and the lives of ordinary people. This inevitably provoked a measure of resistance: the emergence and initial success of Populism was one sign of a grumbling agrarian revolt, and in 1892 the Democratic candidate Cleveland was returned. In 1896 the Republicans were reelected with McKinley, who returned again in 1900, only to have his period of office cut short by his assassination in 1901. Two presidential assassinations in twenty years compounded the startling, shocking nature of each, but they were not the symptom of a country in a state of anarchy.

For Edith Jones the loss of her father in 1882 and her marriage to Edward Wharton in 1885 were more memorable and troubling events, and she had never fully recovered from the psychological aftereffects of contracting typhoid fever in 1870 when she was eight,[93] though whether these three events contributed to what amounted to a depressive illness and breakdown in the 1890s, as once generally assumed, is now open to question.[94] On the broad political front the arrival in the presidency in 1901 of a leader who favored the carrying of a big stick and who had ridden with the Rough Riders reassured many in the nation that the country was again in safe hands. The supremacy of Republicanism would have been reassuring to Old New York, and particularly gratifying to Edith Wharton, who had close links with Roosevelt.

Because contemporary issues are matters to which Wharton refers only rarely in her letters, it might be thought that the young Edith Wharton was isolated from politics. That is not the case, because it was impossible for members of the wealthy East Coast class to be isolated from politics, as they *were* the governing class. Even if their families did not mix with politicians, they would know the governors and senators of the region and they would have a clear view of how the country ought to be governed. In fact, Edith Wharton had close links with members of the Harrison administration. Her brother-in-law William Wharton, who earlier had been a member of the Massachusetts House of Representatives, became an assistant secretary of the state in Benjamin Harrison's government, while Levi Parson Morton, whose wife was a close friend of Wharton's mother Lucretia, became vice president to Harrison following his election in 1888.

Edith Wharton's *A Backward Glance*[95] reveals a version of her politics before the World War I, influenced by the consolidation of the conservatism that she seemed to espouse after it. It should not come as a surprise, however, that there is no explicit endorsement of any particular ideology or party in the book. Like many conservatives, in her public, nonfiction writing she appeared to hold the view that politics is something not practiced by the better members of her class, unless they achieved the office of president, and then it was only the policy of sound common sense. Theodore Roosevelt, a member of a privileged Dutch New York family, was a friend of Edith Wharton. They were linked by family: his second wife was her distant cousin. In *A Backward Glance* she recalls arranging a party for him in Paris and visiting him at Sagamore, his country house.[96] Wharton does not have to mention that he is a Republican any more than she has to mention that she does not spend much time with suffragettes, bohemians, anarchists, or socialists. There is a silent understanding of accepted values between those who share the same Old New York roots. It does not have to be articulated.

The same assumptions held sway in London and Paris. In England the values and assumptions of the landed, property-owning class, called Tories ever since the English civil war, were under attack from both the new business class and socialist ideology. The London magazine *Punch,* for example, which Wharton read from time to time, knew exactly what it could assume in its readers. In a cartoon in 1908 socialism is shown as a menacing little mongrel dog lunging to bite a recoiling "gentleman" in top hat and fur-collared topcoat. The dog's master reassures the man that he has the dog under control, and then in an aside to the dog says "Wait till you've grown a bit, my beauty, and you'll get a bigger mouthful."[97] The class sympathies of the magazine could not be clearer.

In her autobiography Wharton expressed opposition to those who challenged some of the assumptions of this silent understanding. Her willingness to be ranked with those sharing antipathy to women's suffrage is clear from her remarks about the damaging effect of education on young women's domestic skills and knowledge.[98] This is the elderly Wharton writing: in the period 1890–1914, Wharton's fiction had given voice to a diversity of views, many quite different from the instinctive conservatism generally shared by the privileged class to which she belonged. It was a conservatism tempered by a reformist streak that characterized the dominant political mood in the Progressive Era, 1890–1916, the period of her young adulthood and early middle age. In Roosevelt's case the reformist mission was driven by a genuine desire to bring about change, and his antitrust campaign was carried out with evident enthusiasm following his assumption of the presidency in 1901. But it was compromised by the panic of 1907, when Roosevelt had to rely on the help of the banker and trust owner, J. P. Morgan, to bail out the country, a man he had earlier fought against. Forced to give way to Taft, Roosevelt eventually renewed his reformist crusade by forming the Progressive Party in 1912, but did not win electoral success. At least some of these reformist issues and debates are traceable in Wharton's early fiction, whose political argument is not only more liberal than that of the Old New York of her parents (not surprisingly) but is also more grounded than the somewhat detached aesthetics of the circle of male friends who provided sustenance for her artistic and intellectual needs.

Wharton's 1907 novel *The Fruit of the Tree*, for example, reflects this reformist mood, though halfheartedly. *The House of Mirth* had earlier offered an indictment of some of the values of the Gilded Age, while the verse and ghost stories of 1908–9 reflect a concern with desire and a fascination with the concealed and the irrational that seemingly takes us away from an interest in the power of institutions and corporations. *Ethan Frome* (1911), despite its rural Massachusetts setting, is the novel that lends itself to the most political reading, as spotted by an early reviewer: a society that allows its people to be reduced to this level of despair is a society in need of reform. Such a rhetoric is discernible in the text, but that is not its whole, or even central, argument. *Ethan Frome*, the most modernist of her texts, also offers a parallel analysis of the entrapment of marriage and the impossibility of a successful life outside it, but this time in a setting of rural poverty. It is the most self-consciously artistic of her texts, suggesting a move toward the practices of modernism, on a bare, white, wintry canvas. It is a world seemingly very different from that occupied by Lily Bart in Wharton's 1905 novel, but *The House of Mirth* examines a completely different kind of poverty, the poverty of ethical values in a materialist society. *The Custom of the Country*, which Wharton worked at over a number of years, is the novel whose title announces the most sociopolitical theme, and it is indeed the book that shows how both male and female behavior is warped and damaged by a culture's norms and expectations. The book offering the most explicit and extensive political discussion is the early and uncharacteristic one disguised as an exploration of the genre of historical romance, *The Valley of Decision* (1902). This novel, along with *The House of Mirth* (1905), *The Fruit of the Tree* (1907), and the pre-1910 novellas provide strong evidence of the range of political positions examined by Wharton as she confronted challenges, both social and artistic, to her own fundamental belief in the need for stability, tradition, and custom.

2

Skirting Modernism: Novels, Novellas, and Short Stories (1900–1909)

> [T]he usual closet-theorists that are too busy planning Utopias to think of planting turnips.
> —Edith Wharton, *The Valley of Decision*

As Edith Wharton moved into the opening phase of her successful writing career, Henry James moved into the final phase of his, a career that never brought him the material success he longed for. Wharton began cautiously, starting with magazine short stories before moving on to novels. James concluded his career adventurously, beginning the twentieth century with his three most ambitious studies of human sensibility, perception, and the development of refined consciousness. Even though *The Wings of the Dove* (1902), *The Ambassadors* (1903), and *The Golden Bowl* (1904) stand as a stylistic bridge between the psychological practices of the French nineteenth-century novel and the modernism of the early twentieth, this was a bridge that Wharton was not eager to cross. She was not inclined to be James's imitator, and in her writing she skirts a stylistic practice she privately found obscure and uncongenial. Yet the closeness of their friendship was evidence that there was much else that they did have in common, and significant among their shared perceptions was their mutual disappointment with America. Their differing response is very revealing, however. James's despair at what he saw as the shortcomings of American culture reinforced his desire to examine the intricate workings of cultured minds, in ways that leave behind the vulgar details of the material world. Wharton's interest was in the forces and influences that shaped that society, and produced that vulgarity.

In the early years of the new century Edith Wharton expressed a recurring disenchantment with her native country. In a letter to Sara Norton she describes the overwhelming feeling of depression that accompanied her return to The Mount in June 1903:

> My first few weeks in America are always miserable, because the tastes I am cursed with are all of a kind that cannot be gratified here, & I am not enough in sympathy with our "gross public" to make up for the lack on the aesthetic side. One's friends are delightful; but *we* are none of us American, we don't think or feel as the Americans do, we are the wretched exotics produced in a European glass-house, the most déplacé & useless class on earth! All of which outburst is due to my first sight of American streets, my first hearing of American voices, & the wild, dishevelled backwoods look of everything when one first comes home! You see in my heart of hearts, a heart never unbosomed, I feel in America as you say you do in England—out of sympathy with everything. And in England I like it *all*—institutions, traditions, mannerisms, conservatisms, everything but the women's clothes, & the having to go to church every Sunday.[1]

While Wharton is describing something she acknowledges to be a temporary reaction ("My first few weeks in America . . .") her identification with the customs, conventions, and conservatism of England reveals a taste for the security and isolation of privilege that is possible in Europe, and a dislike for the popular democratic pressures and tastes of her own country. It is a prejudice that is given public voice five years later, in *A Motor-Flight Through France*,[2] where Wharton applauds a society in which each "man" is comfortable in his class, recognizes the value of manners, and fits into the pattern of things. As Blake Nevius notes in discussing Wharton's comments on the Seine country, "Not even in the final chapter of *The Valley of Decision* is the conservative position more complacently expressed."[3] In France, for Wharton, there exists a true "intelligence of life."

The conflict between the aristocratic model of the small state and the revolutionary aims of the large one is a subject she had explored in the novel to which Nevius refers. *The Valley of Decision* was published a year before her 1903 complaint about America, and notwithstanding her claim that the changes in eighteenth-century Italy that the novel explores are intellectual rather than political,[4] it is clear that this is the most explicitly political of her long fiction. But by making the central characters neither oppressors nor oppressed, but idealists who inherit power, and by setting the novel in an earlier century, she was also being very politic, not to say Machiavellian, in her publishing career strategy.

The Valley of Decision and Reactionary Politics (1902)

Wharton's first published novel, a historical romance set in Italy in the eighteenth century, is dedicated "to my friends Paul and Minnie

Bourget in remembrance of Italian days together."[5] It represents the first of three books from what is sometimes lightly characterized as Wharton's Italian period, *The Valley of Decision* (1902) being followed by two nonfiction works: *Italian Villas and Their Gardens* (1904) and *Italian Backgrounds* (1905). There is a fourth Italian work, actually written in that language, and Gian Franca Balestra speculates that Wharton's unpublished short tale, written as an exercise in Italian, is later and dates from 1908.[6] Unlike Wharton's earlier Italian novel this unpublished "exercise" has a contemporary setting and is an example of a not unfamiliar Wharton device, the short story told from the maid's point of view. Wharton did not revisit it.

In both America and Europe at the turn of the century there was a palpable sense that the pace of change was gathering speed. Reactions ranged from excitement to anxiety. The excitement was manifest in the Paris Exposition of 1900 where a huge dynamo was displayed. Unease is to be found in Henry Adams's response and his determination to rescue history from a theory in which acceleration leads to entropy.[7] Anxiety is to be found in the worries about the degeneration of the human species and its ultimate extinction, about decadence, and from those who enjoyed political power the threat posed by the emergence of socialism. For campaigners for social reform this was an exciting time, however, and the social reform movements posed questions as challenging to the hegemonic classes as the Reformation had to the Roman Catholic Church. If Henry Adams represents the response of the historian to these changes, Paul Bourget's series of novels exploring ethical and moral issues (1892, 1893, and 1902) provided a more immediate narrative discourse absorbed by Wharton as she prepared her own first novel.

The Valley of Decision explores the nature of revolution, and its argument seems to be an authoritarian one, namely that people are not yet ready for the freedom they are demanding.[8] Although the setting is Lombardy, the question of the perfectibility of humankind is also a revolutionary one advanced in both England and America. In his *Enquiry Concerning Political Justice*, published originally in 1793 and revised for the final edition of 1798, William Godwin had argued that "man is perfectible," though he made it clear that the phrase did not mean that "man" could be made perfect, but was used to indicate "the faculty of being continually made better and receiving perpetual improvement."[9] In contrast, however, the early Puritan settlers in America had wrestled with the inevitability of sin and a belief in the imperfection of man. The politics of eighteenth-century American independence were an expression of the influence of eighteenth-century enlightenment and the accompanying tide of idealism. American utopians articulated the belief that America could become the new garden and the new Eden in which human equality would flourish. This sentiment is written into the Declaration of Independence, and it was the product of a combination of revolutionary fervor and idealism that coincided with the interests of the mercantile pragmatists whose support is necessary if change is to occur. It is precisely this enlightened managing of idealism by the more measured, and more powerful, forces of tradition, that Wharton's novel explores.

In her critical biography of Wharton, Shari Benstock identifies the connection between Wharton's Italian novel and her view of proper government and political change:

> *The Valley of Decision* [bears] witness to Edith's curiosity about revolutionary zeal. Mass violence, however legitimate its causes, was to her the product of base instincts that once released could not easily be contained. She believed in a system in which the rich and privileged protected the poor and helpless, treating them with respect and compassion.[10]

The belief in an ordered world where the suffering of the poor and vulnerable was alleviated by acts of charity and philanthropy was one passed down by her parents, who undertook charitable works as a matter of course. Similarly, the political discourse of the circle in which she moved in Europe was that articulated by the *Times* of London, which could show compassion in its reporting of individual disasters (such as mining accidents, the sinking of the *Titanic*, and outbreaks of disease), but took a severe line on anything that smacked of insurrection (strikes, suffragist protest, and anarchist revolution). Although she had no memories of the Civil War, she had grown up in its aftermath, and the cultural, psychological, and human price paid for rebellion was still very real for Americans from North and South during the late nineteenth century.

The rhetoric of momentous events is announced in Wharton's title, which is taken from the book of Joel in the King James version of the Bible. "Multitudes, multitudes in the valley of decision: for the day of the Lord is near in the valley of decision." (Joel 3:14). The Old Testament prophet predicts the day of judgment and the welcome turn of events that this will bring, for "Then shall Jerusalem be holy" (Joel 3:17). Wharton insisted that the first part of the biblical quotation be printed in italics and separate from the title, and described the phrase "multitudes, multitudes in the valley of decision" as the motto of the book.[11]

The novel explores the nature of political judgment and decision making, and the idealistic quest for political reform. Wharton's conflicting feelings about the nature of revolutionary change and the multitudes had been signaled in *A Motor-Flight Through France*, when she passes a comment on the French Revolution: "If there are few spots in France where one more deeply resents the senseless havoc of the Revolution, there are few, where, on second thoughts, one so distinctly understands what turned the cannon on the castle."[12] The first half of *The Valley of Decision* traces the fortunes of Odo Valsecca, a boy who has been farmed out to a country village but who is actually next in line to a title and an estate. His progress toward Turin parallels the gradual disclosure of his real position in society. The progress is at first encumbered by that apparent necessity in historical novels to establish place and period by creating scenes that appear like illustrations from a child's history book (the traveling players, the dogs in the castle hall, and so on). The following passage, describing the moment when Odo is reunited with his mother, Donna Laura, as a consequence of the death of his father, illustrates this tendency, but it also demonstrates Wharton's analytical eye at work: "For the first day or two [Odo] sat unnoticed on his little stool in a corner of his mother's room, while packing-chests were dragged in, wardrobes emptied, mantua-makers consulted, and troublesome creditors dismissed with abuse, or even blows, by the servants lounging in the antechamber. . . . How any one could be in want who slept between damask curtains and lived on sweet cakes and chocolate it exceeded his fancy to conceive . . ." *VD,* 19). Though Wharton was probably aware of the model provided by George Eliot's *Romola*, which appeared in the year of her birth (1862), she said that she had not undertaken systematic research before writing this novel. Instead, she had immersed herself in the environment that forms its setting:

> The truth is that I have always found it hard to explain that gradual absorption into my pores of a myriad details—details of landscape, architecture, old furniture and eighteenth century portraits, the gossip of contemporary diarists and travellers, all vivified by repeated spring wanderings guided by Goethe and the Chevalier de Brosses, by Goldoni and Gozzi, Arthur Young, Dr. Burney and Ippolito Nievo out of which the tale grew. I did not travel and look and read with the writing of the book in mind; but my years of intimacy with the Italian eighteenth century gradually and imperceptibly fashioned the tale and compelled me to write it; and whatever its faults—and they are many—it is saturated with the atmosphere I had so long lived in.
>
> (*ABG,* 84)

In 1901 Maurice Hewlett had written an introduction to Stendhal's *La Chartreuse de Parme* for the "Masterpieces of French Romance" series edited by Edmund Gosse.[13] Wharton admired Stendhal, and there are some similarities between *Chartreuse*, with its Italian setting and Napoleonic theme and Wharton's *The Valley of Decision*, though Wharton's novel explores an earlier period of Franco-Italian interaction. Wharton loved history, but it is likely that the research for her novel was as much literary as it was historical. This is reflected in her review of Maurice Hewlett's *The Fool Errant* (1905), a novel that also had an eighteenth-century Italian setting. Detail is important, she argues, because the eighteenth century "was all in *nuances*."[14] It is a fine defense of historical realism.

In Wharton's novel Donna Laura's loss of a husband is overshadowed by distress caused by the loss of money, property, and status. The apparent coldness of women such as Donna Laura is attributed more clearly in later novels to a dependency created by the institution of marriage. Here such an analysis is disguised by the historical setting, which allows the sharp implications of Wharton's critique to be cushioned by the distance of time. It is appropriate, therefore, that the theater, acting, and disguise should hold such a prominent theme in the book,[15] which contains many operatic moments. Moreover, there is nothing particularly profound about the observation that "the need of money was somehow at the bottom of her troubles," and Wharton knows this.

In the first part of the novel the new world that is emerging, the world of ideas that elevates the body, nature, and the natural impulses, is at first glimpsed only as a radical, degenerate force. On the journey to Turin, Odo's guardian, Cantapresto, warns him of the heretical ideas he can expect to find suppressed by the king: "You are too young, doubtless, cavaliere, to have heard of the philosophers, who are raising such a pother north of the Alps: a set of madmen that, because their birth doesn't give the entrée of Versailles, are preaching that men should return to a state of nature, great ladies suckle their young like animals, and the peasantry own their land like nobles" (*VD*, 79).

Cantapresto, himself a man whose social position is quite lowly, attributes the views of these followers of the young romantic movement to their own social exclusion from the court of Versailles, and is pleased to report that the king stamps them out "like vermin."[16] This is not Odo's experience, as he comes into contact with a clandestine group called the Honey-Bees, committed to exploring and discussing the revolutionary ideas in science and politics and dedicated to the concept of Liberty. The ideas inspire him and he makes it his ambition to serve the people and to dedicate himself to their liberation from feudalism. The honeybee was the symbol later adopted by Napoleon.[17]

The Valley of Decision explores that perennial, but patrician political and philosophical question: are the people ready for freedom? In the novel, the Church and the aristocracy agree that they are not. Order, tradition, regulation, and a hierarchy are all necessary. Odo, observing the suffering of the peasantry, among whom he lived as a boy, is not so sure, and is amenable to the new ideas. The novel's second section, "The New Light," starts very precisely in 1774, two years before the American Revolution and fifteen years before the French Revolution. Odo is twenty-two, and as yet the Reformation is the only political revolution that the Western world has seen, and that did not change very much the ordering of affairs in the Piedmont part of Italy.

Bound by the possibility that he could become regent, and even inherit his cousin's dukedom, Odo does not become a political revolutionary, and lurks at the edge of the clandestine groups that meet to discuss the new ideas. His political education takes a significant turn when he hears from a priest that present evils may be explained by an understanding of history, rather than an understanding of tyranny. Individuals are the victims of their cultural past. This judgment is shown to moderate his beliefs, and a succession of disillusioning discoveries takes its toll on a will that has always been vacillating. He finds himself the target of a faction in court politics, and flees for his own safety. This is the politics of personal ambition, in which church, charlatan, and the Illuminati compete for power. Odo takes refuge in Venice, a place of carnival and masques, possessing its own intrigue and decadence, where nuns are also courtesans. He is reunited with Fulvia, the woman he has grown to love, but she, too, has been forced into a convent after the death of her father and the treachery of a publisher (who has taken her small legacy) has left her destitute.

Although Fulvia Vivaldi is often regarded as one of Wharton's less successfully realized characters, she is very interesting for a number of reasons. The daughter of Professor Vivaldi, she is an intelligent woman driven by a vision of political reform to relegate love and marriage to a second order of importance. She is represented with great sympathy and her self-sacrifice is shown to be no trifle. Few, if any, of Wharton's other women combine the qualities of ambition, intelligence, and selflessness. Lily Bart, who is aware that marriage can be a trap, nevertheless does not have another clear goal in life. Undine Spragg is ruthlessly ambitious, but for quite materialistic and blatantly self-interested reasons, and hers is not a sophisticated intelligence, rather a cultural instinct for survival. The closest parallel to Fulvia in Wharton's prewar writing is probably Justine in *The Fruit of the Tree,* which in a very different context repeats the triangular relationship of the idealistic, but wavering, man who marries a shallow wealthy woman to further a cause and finds strength and support from a poor woman he loves. This is to oversimplify the similarities, because the former duke's widow, whom Odo marries for political reasons is quite unlike Bessie. Bessie, the first wife in *The Fruit of the Tree,* initially shares some of John Amhersts's enthusiasm for reform, and the nurse Justine Brent is defined more by her belief in euthanasia than by her wider political vision. As a nurse she is cast in a role that was becoming increasingly institutionalized and respectable, not to say conventional, for women, but like Fulvia she provides strong support for an idealistic man.

In *The Valley of Decision,* it is Fulvia who is Odo's inspiration, and although the narrator is at pains to stress the relative normality in eighteenth-century Italy of her achievement of being awarded a university chair while being the duke's mistress, these are not achievements that would be regarded as normal for the women who were the contemporaries of Wharton's readers in 1902, the year in which the novel was first published. Before this resolution of her role, Odo has theatrically rescued Fulvia from a corrupt convent and is willing to renounce his claim to the dukedom so that he can follow her into exile in revolutionary France. She says no. He can do more good for his people if he becomes the benevolent and progressive duke that they deserve. Fulvia's vision of justice is spoken with great fluency and sincerity. There is no narrative sniping or irony at all. Fulvia believes in the cause, and Wharton seems intent on making sure that there is nothing here to make us question the purity and sincerity of her motives: "[Your future] belongs, as much as any slave's, to his master, to the people you are called to rule. Think for how many generations their unheeded sufferings, their unrewarded toil, have paid for the pomp and pleasure of your house! That is the debt you are called on to acquit, the wrong you are pledged to set right." (*VD,* 481–82). Odo is freshly inspired by the rightness of this idealism, even though as a program for immediate action it is less a recipe for revolution than one for benevolent despotism or noblesse oblige. The couple give each other up and Odo becomes Duke of Pianura.

Although Odo resolutely sets about his task of reform, he encounters opposition from the people whose lives he is intending to improve. His explanation is one that seems to inform the political argument of the novel, which is that good practical reforms involve the direct relief of illness and poverty, and that this cannot be brought about simply by the free distribution of enlightened ideas:

At first he had hoped to bury his personal disappointments in the task of reconstructing his little state; but on every side he felt a mute resistance to his efforts. The philosophical faction had indeed poured forth pamphlets celebrating his reforms, and comparing his reign to a Golden Age. But it was not for the philosophers that he labored; and the benefits of free speech, a free press, a secular education, did not, after all, reach those over whom his heart yearned. It was the people he longed to serve; and the people were hungry, were fever-stricken, were crushed with tithes and taxes. It was hopeless to try to reach them by the diffusion of popular knowledge. They must first be fed and clothed; and before they could be fed and clothed the chains of feudalism must be broken.

(*VD*, 524)

Odo concludes that the ideology and practice of feudalism is the enemy, but that in the Italian city-states the class that could end it did not wish to. He notes the contrast with the situation in France where those who supported and often led the revolt were indeed members of a class that had something to lose. South of the Alps there was an interest in change, but not a profound belief in the need to do so. The Renaissance had been accommodated by the Church, and as a result "The Church had never troubled the Latin consciousness" (*VD*, 525). Odo despairs at the pervasion of the belief that the priest was the person who knew best how to deal with the poor.[18]

Although Odo's despair at the blindness of the populace is made understandable, his failure is not simply attributed to the power of the Church and other leading figures to support change. The failure is the product of Odo's own strategy, one encouraged by Fulvia, which has given more attention to ideas than to practical work. This failure is highlighted by Wharton's use of the diary device, whereby the reader is suddenly presented in section 5 of book 4 "The Reward" with an "unpublished fragment" from Mr. Arthur Yonge's *Diary of his Travels in Italy in the Year 1789*.[19] The first person diary extract includes observations that are clearly designed to hammer home the wider rhetorical argument of the novel. The early entries describe Mr. Yonge's first meeting with Odo, and a visit to the estate:

(October) The 6th . . . . I cannot say that the impression his Highness produced on me was one of *happiness*. His countenance is sad, almost careworn, though with a smile of engaging sweetness; his manner affable without condescension, and open without familiarity. I am told he is oppressed by the cares of his station; and from a certain irresolution of voice and eye that bespeaks not so much weakness as a speculative cast of mind, I can believe him less fitted for active government than for the

> meditations of the closet. . . . I thought I perceived in him a sincere wish to study the welfare of his people; but was disappointed to find among his chosen associates not one practical farmer or economist, but only the casual closet–theorists that are too busy planning Utopias to think of planting turnips.
>
> The 7th. Visited his Highness's estate at Valesecca. Here he has converted a handsome seat into a school of agriculture, tearing down an immense orangery to plant mulberries, and replacing costly gardens and statuary by well-tilled fields; a good example to his wealthy subjects. Unfortunately his bailiff is not what we should call a practical farmer; and many acres of valuable ground are given up to a botanic garden, where exotic plants are grown at great expense, and rather for curiosity than use; a common error of noble agriculturalists.
>
> (*VD*, 554)

The flaw in character ("the irresolution of voice and eye") is reflected in the failure to do the work well. Like Hamlet, Odo is represented as more the scholar than the man of action, whom fate has given the chance to implement ideas that he is more at home discussing than putting into practice. His heart is in the right place, but even his appointments (such as the bailiff) are not practical men. He is a version of the charming but unreliable male dilettantes that we meet in so many of Whartons's short stories and novels set in contemporary America and Europe. He thinks too much.

By the end of the novel a rather bleak picture emerges. The "people" are now represented as the mob. Odo "begins to feel the social and political significance of those old restrictions and barriers against which early zeal had tilted" (*VD*, 636). The ideal state has become a "figment of his brain" (ibid.).

The Valley of Decision, with its empatic eighteenth century setting and deliberate absence of direct references to America (mentioned only as the site of a recent revolution of the kind that would not suit Italy) is markedly different from Wharton's other pre-World War I novels and novellas, which have a contemporary backdrop. Her first published novel is part romance, part history, and part political meditation. It reflects a fascination with history and religion, particularly the political power of the Catholic Church in general and the Jesuits in particular. The novel shows the power of intrigue and the way that it is sometimes expedient for the Church and the rulers they endorse to support liberal reform. As De Crucis, an agent for the Jesuits and a former Jesuit himself, explains:

> Nothing could be more fatal to your prospects than to have it said that you had chosen a former Jesuit as your adviser. In the present juncture of

affairs it is needful that you should appear to be in sympathy with the liberals, and that whatever reforms you attempt should seem the result of popular pressure rather than of your own free choice. Such an attitude may not flatter the sovereign's pride, and is in fact merely a higher form of expediency; but it is one which the proudest monarchs of Europe are finding themselves constrained to take if they would preserve their power and use it effectually.

(*VD*, 509–10)

This fascination with the power of Rome surfaces in later fiction such as *Madame de Treymes* and *The Custom of the Country*, but the French setting of these later novels means that nowhere else in Wharton's fiction does it feature as the political epicenter of the narrative. By the end of *The Valley of Decision*, however, the rhetorical emphasis on the more sinister and cynical maneuverings of the Church has been replaced by a more respectful attitude to the importance of faith. De Crucis is given a long speech in the final section in which he advances the case for the Church, which contains the germ of "all those humanizing energies which work together for the lifting of the race." (*VD*, 639).

Wharton claimed that she wished to present all sides of the argument with the fairness that they deserved and De Crucis's claims may not be any closer to Wharton's own beliefs than are Fulvia's, but both cases are given voice by powerful advocates of each philosophy. Coming as one of the final speeches, however, its position in the novel gives De Crucis's speech a special rhetorical status. When the sentiments are put alongside the description of the events unfolding in revolutionary France, it amounts to a clear rhetorical endorsement of a particularly reactionary argument: "The new year rose in blood and mounted to a bloodier noon. All the old defences were falling. Religion, monarchy, law, were sucked down into the whirlpool of liberated passions. Across that sanguinary scene passed, like a mocking ghost, the philosopher's vision of the perfectibility of man. Man was free at last—freer than his would-be liberators had ever dreamed of making him—and he used his freedom like a beast" (*VD*, 647).

The word "reactionary" is used with caution, because Wharton herself was not intellectually complacent. It is a word that is appropriate in relation to this novel, however, because the view that very few changes constitute progress is a view that ultimately questions the possibility of the "perfectibility of man" and the possibility of progress at all. To question the excesses of the French Revolution is not to be a reactionary, but to imply that the reign of terror and its aftermath is the model for all social change driven by the people is to move into an Orwellian skepticism of utopias so severe that it paralyzes the possibility of social change. Even Vernon Lee, the contemporary so admired by Wharton[20] that she may be the inspiration for Fulvia, knew that this was an unwarrantedly pessimistic view of humankind, and Lee concludes her otherwise very enthusiastic review of Wharton's novel by saying so.[21] Like so many of Wharton's novels, the narrative ends on a note of gloom that is at odds with the vibrancy, sharpness, and energy of so much of the writing that has preceded it. The narrator shows us the joy of living, but leaves us with the stark reminder that such joy is fleeting, as life does not end joyfully.

In arguing that Wharton's analysis of eighteenth-century Italy may appear to overemphasize the Machiavellianism of politics in a way that endorses the reactionary view that we should be skeptical of idealism and ideology, there is a risk of making the novel sound as if it possesses a rhetoric that has been overtaken and discredited by more recent thinking about politics. The reverse is true. Odo's understanding that change occurs when it serves the interests of the middle classes is one that continues to be in post-Marxist analysis the dominant historical reading of the period. Recent historians draw conclusions about the French revolution that coincide with those made by Wharton in this novel.[22] But the novel's skeptical conclusion warrants William Vance's verdict that "Wharton does not like the actuality of popular democracy, however sentimentally she can agree with the justice of liberal theories."[23]

Wharton's subject is the absence in Italy of changes that parallel those in France and it is the proclericalism of the bourgeoisie in Italy and the Church's strong alliance with the aristocracy that is precisely her point. *The Valley of Decision* may not be her best novel, but it offers striking evidence of a mediated political and historical analysis. It will do to remember this novel with its discussion of ideology when we assess her later work, for as Blake Nevius points out: "The general conclusions of the final, important chapter will be reiterated in *French Ways and their Meaning, A Motor-Flight through France,* and *A Backward Glance,* and they will be found to occupy the centre of the argument in Mrs. Wharton's subsequent novels."[24] It is an argument that favors custom and tradition over change and widening democracy.

In her fiction the politics and ethics of this novel will be repeated, but in a more contemporary setting. The failure of Odo's and Fulvia's humanitarianism will be revisited in the failed idealism of John Amherst and Justine Brent, central characters in *The Fruit of the Tree,* while the showy, frivolous aristocracy of the eighteenth century evokes the mood of the post–Civil War dynasties and their hideous Fifth Avenue mansions in *The House of Mirth.*

Ethical Questions in Novellas, 1900—1907: *The Touchstone, Sanctuary,* and *Madame de Treymes*

Although the early 1900s in America was the period of Progressive Era politics, with widespread political concerns about the power of trusts, cartels, money, monopolies, and big business in general, Wharton's novellas of the period did not engage directly with reformist politics or the issues brought to light by muckrakers in such magazines as *McClure's*. In 1903 *McClure's* was publishing Ida Tarbell's scrutiny of Standard Oil, Ray Stannard Baker's attack on labor violence, and Lincoln Steffans's "The Shame of Minneapolis." At first Wharton looked beyond these socioeconomic issues and continued to explore ethical problems of the kind favored by her good friend, the novelist Paul Bourget. Her choice of narrative subjects, however, contains its own implicit political position. The moral dilemmas faced by characters in *The Touchstone, Sanctuary,* and *Madame de Treymes* are predicated on the assumption that behavior is an individual responsibility, irrespective of context. It is a belief that is implicit in the first of these two works, but one that begins to be seriously interrogated in *Madame de Treymes*.

Success, Money, and Ethics

The Touchstone (1900) and *Sanctuary* (1903) have been characterized as sentimental,[25] this sentimentality being something Wharton left behind when she came to write her social satire, *The House of Mirth* (1905). This is a little unfair. There is satire and irony in these two works. But there is also a sense in which Wharton is always working in the tradition of the eighteenth-century sentimental novel and the cult of virtue. Those, like Lily Bart in *The House of Mirth* and Anna Leath in *The Reef,* who have the capacity to empathize and imagine the feelings of others are the virtuous characters. Moreover, the alliance of a sympathetic heart and the adherence to a strict morality were the marks of the man or woman of sentiment.

Lev Raphael[26] argues that it is time to reexamine and reassess *The Touchstone* because it offers evidence of the central influence of shame on Wharton's characters, an influence that is the key to the shaping of their psychology and behavior. Raphael's study is not a successful argument for the reevaluation of these early texts, however, because the theme of shame and guilt is so broad as to be observable in almost any novel. I make this point not to attack Raphael's study, which is inspired by Silvan Tomkins's affect theory, but to acknowledge that in asking for a reading of Wharton that acknowledges the political discourses in which her language was formed and developed, I am at no point arguing that politics is the "key" to her work.

The Touchstone is the contemporary story of a clever and successful novelist who the young Stephen Glennard seeks out in the old university town of Hillbridge. She is separated from her husband (he eventually dies) and is flattered by Glennard's attentions, sending him a succession of letters on his retreat to New York. But it is here that the narrator makes the famous comment that "Genius is of small use to a woman who does not know how to do her hair" (170) and Glennard does not return her affection. She retreats to the European mainland, and dies.

The letters are valuable, and needing money to marry a woman he does love, he overcomes his scruples and has them published. The guilt, and need for secrecy, eats away at his soul, his marriage, and his friendships. His wife Alexa discovers the truth and forgives him (his motive having been understandable), but neither of them can escape the fact that their marriage was founded on the moral betrayal of someone's memory.

Sanctuary is also based on a guilty secret, this one being less equivocal. The plot illustrates the interest in exploring complicated, carefully constructed ethical problems, of the kind favored by Bourget. In *Sanctuary* Denis Peyton inherits money from his brother, and when the mother of his dead brother's child comes to claim part of the inheritance, he conceals from the court that his brother had admitted to him that he had secretly married this woman. Her claim is dismissed, and she and the child are later found drowned in the lake on the Peyton estate. The first part of the narrative concludes with Kate Orme's decision to marry Denis, despite knowing his secret, because she believes that the only way to do some good is to ensure that she brings up a child who would never practice such deception. A child, named Dick, is born, but is only six years old when the father unexpectedly dies. Dick grows up and is trained as an architect. His friend and fellow architectural student Paul Darrow possesses talent sadly lacking in Dick, and just before he unexpectedly dies, he gives permission for Dick to use his design as a competition entry. Unlike his father, he resists the temptation to practice deception from which he can profit, and it is made clear that this is owing to his mother's good influence.

The second situation is indeed contrived, and these narratives lack the economy of the short story and the depiction of society possible in a novel. Both narratives, however, confront questions about the ethical problems posed by the need for money and success. They are not simple problems of black and white, but the ethical dilemmas posed by shades of grey. Glennard loves Alexa and she him, so his motive in selling the love letters, written by someone who is now dead, is to provide happiness for himself and for another. He has scruples and overcomes them, believing that is the correct course of action. The opposite situation arises in *Sanctuary*, where Dick need not have scruples, because both the girl he likes (Clemence Verney) and his friend Paul Darrow authorize the use of the museum design. Yet, quite rightly, he does have scruples, and perhaps because it would be easy to rationalize ignoring them, he does not. The story is a counterpoint to *The Touchstone*, because we presume that Dick will enjoy a happy future, unlike the emptiness of relationship that seems the fate of Stephen Glennard and his wife.

It is the need for success, whether material or by reputation (in a profession such as architecture the second will inevitably lead to the first) that these stories examine. The characters are vehicles for these ethical problems, but there is even in these early stories the sharp observation that characterizes so much of Wharton's later work. Each novella marks a stage in Wharton's awareness of politics. *Sanctuary*, published a year after *The Valley of Decision*, addresses the question of how a child can be shaped and influenced by a single parent. Politics may appear peripheral, but before she became a widow Kate wished Denis to be a politician and he gave it a try before failing. Kate has in the meantime set herself the task of saving her son from the moral weakness of his father and of his father's brother. It is a scientific experiment, and it is somehow appropriate that her son Dick should take up that most scientific of the arts, architecture, and set about designing a museum of sculpture for a competition. Yet neither of these novellas offer a close analysis of culture that was to emerge in *The House of Mirth*. Having put an aspect of American culture under the microscope, as we shall see, in her next novella Wharton returned to a European setting, but now that she was increasingly drawn to Paris, the setting here was to be contemporary France rather than eighteenth-century Italy. And here the clash of ideologies becomes more significant in an exploration of the relationship between religion, culture, and marriage

Madame de Treymes, *Culture, Politics, and Marriage*

Madame de Treymes, published in 1907, is a short novel set entirely in France, and it deals with what on the surface appear to be purely moral issues concerned with questions about what is honorable, what is meant by trust, and the ethics of divorce.

These are indeed matters of principle and fine judgment, but in this brief novella each is seen to be subject to the particularities of culture and history. John Durham is an American in Paris and he wishes to marry an American woman who is separated from her aristocratic and immoral French husband. Her name, Fanny de Malrive, formerly Fanny Frisbee, suggests to a modern reader an almost humorous welding of cultures, but this is quite at odds with the seriousness with which the situation is represented: she has a young son, and the husband's powerful Catholic family are, for religious reasons, against divorce. Only Madame de Treymes, Fanny's sister-in-law offers hope as the potentially sympathetic go-between, and once Durham has tried and failed to persuade Fanny to contemplate marriage, it is with the devious and shifting Madame de Treymes's negotiations with Durham that the novella is principally concerned. This is a narrative less concerned with romance than with transactions, hybridity, and negotiations.

In 1907, the date of *Madame de Treymes,* Wharton began her permanent sojourn in France, and the novel reflects issues that were specific to that country. From 1900 there was a major campaign in France to separate church and state, an aim that was finally realized in 1908. In a move that has echoes of the maneuvering in *The Valley of Decision,* though from a different quarter, French politicians from the Radical party saw anticlericalism as a way of assuaging popular ambitions. The grievances of the electorate could be steered in the direction of the clerical and feudal enemy. Devious manipulations were as ever, the stuff of politics.

But to describe Madame de Treymes as devious and manipulative is to do the narrative positioning of the text a disservice: she is a product of her culture as much as Durham is of his, as the narrative is at pains to make clear. Janet Beer has drawn attention to the way that the novel makes, through the character of Fanny, the political forces shaping cultural identity quite explicit. Fanny has seen this process working not only on herself, as an American woman who has married into a French family, but on her son, who the family has thoroughly colonized. Fanny explains the matter to Durham:

> There is nothing in your experience—in any American experience—to correspond with that far-reaching family organization, which is itself a part of the larger system, and which encloses a young man of my son's position in a network of accepted prejudices and opinions. Everything is prepared in advance—his political and religious convictions, his judgements of people, his sense of honour, his ideas of women, his whole view of life. He is taught to see vileness and corruption in everyone not of his

own way of thinking, and in every idea that does not directly serve the religious and political purposes of his class.[27]

There is nothing to suggest that this cool political analysis, which would have sounded subversive and radical if put in the mouth of a character with socialist sympathies, is not to be taken in any way other than seriously. Fanny may be a queen in the cultural game played by the chess players of French privileged class, but she is a queen who knows how she is being manipulated. While it is true that she specifically mentions the agency of the Church in shaping the mind of a boy such as her son ("the forming of the mind begins with the first consciousness"), it is the broader set of beliefs about which she is most concerned.

The novel's emphasis on cultural difference also highlights cultural ignorance. Durham's discovery of the machinations of French aristocracy offers a perspective on his own unawareness of the practices of politics and class. It provides an opportunity for a reappraisal of his reading of both France and America. He was stimulated by Fanny's increased sophistication and her use of silence where once she would have felt the need to fill the space with words. But this is not a sophistication achieved without a price, as her outburst quoted above shows.

The novel also touches briefly on the issue of missed opportunities in a manner familiar to any reader of Thomas Hardy, who Edith Wharton had met in London and whose meliorism often looks suspiciously close to determinism, a quality also discernible in Wharton's work. Why had not John Durham married Fanny Frisbee when he had the chance? In Wharton's case the answer is less important than the fact. There was an opportunity, and because it was not seized at the right time, it is difficult, if not impossible, to retrieve. It is a situation rich with the dramatic irony that Wharton was to repeat in her next novel set in France, *The Reef*.

I have already suggested that the influence of Henry James's work on Wharton, important though this was, was secondary to the model he provided of the dedicated artist together with his infectious delight in European culture and society and the consequent disparaging of America. It is now apparent that French novelists, for whom James also had a great admiration, rather than English or American, had the greatest influence on Wharton's writing during this period. Balzac and Stendhal were admired and read; in 1902 Wharton cited Stendhal's *Le Chartreuse de Parme* (1839) for comparison in her resume to William Crary Brownell of *The Valley of Decision*.[28] More contemporary, and a personal friend, was the French writer Paul Bourget, whom Wharton had met for the first time in 1893 and who, as I have been suggesting, was to have an influence on her work, not so much in terms of technique, but through his conception of the purpose of the novel. Bourget was a critic and novelist who explored sociological and psychological problems in his fiction. He was a friend of Henry James, and Bourget's later novels, such as *Un Divorce* (1904), confirm the Frenchman's deep Catholic and Royalist sympathies.

Adeline Tintner argues that a number of the novels and short stories written by Wharton before 1910 are a response to ideas in Bourget's fiction and that *Madame de Treymes* is a corrective to Bourget's *Un divorce*. Bourget was a member of the Catholic Right whose members emphasized the need for tradition and stability, for institutions and *rootedness*. In the 1890s, France had been subject to a discourse about rootedness, particularly from the novels of Maurice Barrès whose *Les déracinés* seeks to expose the alienating effects of the new scientific rationalism, a theme taken up by Bourget in his novel *Le disciple*. At the time of writing *Madame de Treymes*, Wharton does not seem to have shared this extreme conservatism, partly because she was also able to see the damaging effects on women of institutions and beliefs whose long history in this instance were insufficient to make their sinister exclusivity acceptable.

Failure of Assets and Capital in *The House of Mirth* (1905)

Between the publication of *Sanctuary* and *Madame de Treymes*, Wharton struck gold. The enormous success of *The House of Mirth*, both in terms of the number of copies sold and the critical reception, was the turning point in Edith Wharton's career. She was not just a writer, she was a famous writer, and as a famous writer she could command high payments for all her future fiction. She found the experience very gratifying.

The House of Mirth is a sustained and detailed exploration of art, image, capital, and the commodification of women. It was a departure from the historical novel form of *The Valley of Decision*, for it enters the territory of naturalism.

Recent criticism increasingly locates a discussion of the novel in the context of contemporary discourses about poverty and vanishing species. The reality of extreme urban poverty in the land of dreams was evidence of the growing social conscience in American political life during the late nineteenth century. In 1890, for example, Jacob

Riis, a Danish immigrant, published *How the Other Half Lives,* an exposé of tenement life for the poor in New York's East Side. Gavin Jones draws attention to Lily's statement in *The House of Mirth* that she knows nothing more dreadful than poverty. Jones argues that poverty should be seen as an ontological rather than an economic factor, and that Wharton is a writer "who sought to break down class differences, a writer whose exploration of female consciousness emerges from the *socioeconomic* position of women, trapped between financial dependence on men and the impoverished alternative of work."[29] I will be taking issue with the first part of this claim, but his invitation to see poverty as a "relational and shifting category," with the consequent admonition for critics who offer an essentialist take on Wharton's class interests, is timely. It also permits a reading of the novel that sees the individuals and events as metaphoric rather than realist, one that sees the depiction of Lily's fall as scientific rather than bourgeois or aristocratic. The novel's naturalism is unmistakable, but I do not think that this is because Wharton was trying to imitate Zola or Dreiser. She shares with them a belief in the power of external agencies and forces, but it leads the narrative neither in the direction of modernism or socialism. The novel is not a Wellsian analysis of forces, as in *Tono Bungay,* for example, which rejects both the old feudal aristocracy and the new crass materialism. *The House of Mirth* attempts to rescue the idea of noblesse oblige (and thus that of the Old New York aristocracy before it was corrupted by the new money) by offering a charitable view of the poor and an idealization of the woman who puts ideals above money.

The politics of the novel are complex. As part of a meditation on the importance of money and subtle gradations of class, Lily Bart represents probity in business and that sense of honor that Wharton so admired. Lily may be hopeless with money, may be extravagant and wedded to the comfort of luxury, but she not only pays her debts but also balks at using unscrupulous methods to do so. In a Dickensian moment,[30] she witnesses the fruits of her one good, charitable action when she meets the working girl Nettie Crane, now Nettie Struther, who has been "saved" by the money that allowed her to recuperate in the country when she was suffering from lung trouble.

But as throughout the novel, even this act of goodness on Lily's part is not without irony and ambiguity. The money that was spent was actually Gus Trenor's money, and apart from Bertha Dorset, Gus is the most odious character in the whole novel. And what exactly is the salvation that this act of charity has brought about? It is marriage and motherhood, clearly much preferable to premature death, but presented in a rhetorical flourish that is hardly progressive politically.

After thinking enviously that even on the cliff at the edge of the abyss it is possible for a woman to enjoy the comfort and protection of a nest, Lily concludes: "Yes, but it had taken two to build the nest, the man's faith as well as the woman's courage. . . . [Nettie's] husband's faith in her had made the renewal possible—it is so easy for a woman to become what the man she loves believes her to be!"[31]

Yet the scene in Nettie's kitchen is Lily's moment of epiphany and seems to carry much of the weight of the political rhetoric of the novel. After reflecting at length on that characteristic turn of the century—anxiety, rootlessness—Lily concludes: "All the men and women she knew were like atoms whirling away from each other in some wild centrifugal dance; her first glimpse of the continuity of life had come to her that evening in Nettie Struther's kitchen" (*HM*, 248).

There is a certain romanticised banality about this vision of new life and maternity as the missing element from civilization, the equivalent of Stephen Blackpool's recipe for the ending of class conflict in *Hard Times*,[32] but in case we are missing the point, Lily swoons into her final sleep with a drug-induced hallucination that makes her think Nettie's baby is cradled on her arm.[33]

Lily is convinced that she must fall into the abyss, the early twentieth-century term for the horrors and squalor of poverty. The novel never takes us into this territory, though its rhetoric wishes us to believe that Lily has fallen far. From the point of view of the fashionable society of which she was a member, her fall into shop work is great, and that is the point of view that is kept before us, because it represents a loss of status that Lily herself wishes always to feel. Her ambition is to return to that society, vindicated, but not at any price. Wharton's reading of privilege and wealth is complicated. It is clear that Lily's decline is caused by the need for money in the absence of marriage, and that men are everywhere the gatekeepers. It is not possible for Lily to play the stock exchange herself, so she turns to Trenor.

The possession of huge personal wealth is not seen as an objectionable thing. What is objectionable, in the novel's terms, is rapacity and ruthlessness in its pursuit or maintenance. That is why Rosedale is condemned (in a style that reflects the anti-Semitism of the period without ever questioning it) and why Mrs. Hatch and Bertha Dorset are both dangerous to Lily. Rosedale's Jewishness is foregrounded ("He had his race's accuracy in the appraisal of values, . . . with that mixture of artistic sensibility and business astuteness which characterises his race" [*HM*, 15, 16]) by the narrator, but the language of naked anti-Semitism of the kind peddled in the 1890s by the Populist movement and other groups in the United States at the end of the nineteenth century[34] is filtered through specific characters, such as Judy Trenor, who declares that Rosedale is "the same little Jew who had been served up and rejected at the social board a dozen times within her memory" (*HM*, 16). Lily, too, is described as having an "intuitive repugnance" to Rosedale, which makes her want to instinctively dispatch him to an oubliette without trial (ibid.).

As often, Wharton's inclusion of a phrase such as "without trial" (*HM*, 16) sets up just enough of a query to allow for future revelations and revisions. The novel seems to question some of the earlier narrative assumptions, though sometimes with more enthusiasm than others. The charwoman scrubbing the stairs at the Benedick is seen by Lily with all the disgust that the self-satisfied rich reserve for the poor. The woman has "a broad sallow face, slightly pitted with small-pox, and thin straw coloured hair through which her scalp shone unpleasantly" (*HM*, 13). On her second encounter with the woman, now employed by her aunt, Mrs. Peniston, Lily has no reservations about planning the dismissal of this servant, who wittingly or unwittingly seems to be exercising a power that derives from knowing that Lily has visited Selden's room unchaperoned. Lily takes her bitterness about her own dependence on society out on the servant class, uncharitably viewing her maid as someone in the same position as herself but with a more regular income (*HM*, 24). At this stage in the novel all the lower classes are lumped together as one mass, and Lily (though sometimes it seems to be a view shared by the narrator) sees them as the Other. "The char-woman, after the manner of her kind, stood with her arms folded in her shawl" (*HM*, 80) is the description that precedes the moment when she produces the parcel containing Bertha Dorset's love letters to Selden. When Lily asks the woman a question about the letters, the voice that describes the servant's response sounds as if it might be coming from beyond Lily: "The woman was unabashed by the question. She was evidently prepared to answer it, but like all her class, she had to go a long way back to make a beginning. . . ." (*HM*, 81). When Lily finds herself coming into closer contact with the intermediary class of shop and office workers, class is treated with more sensitivity and understanding. A fellow worker at the milliners offers the hand of friendship, and long before this, Lily has proved herself a popular visitor to the Girls' Club, a self-improvement organization for working women that Gerty Farish supports. Gerty describes this visit to her cousin Selden:

> She really can't bear to hurt people's feelings—it makes me so angry when I hear her called cold and conceited! The girls at the club don't call

> her that. Do you know she has been there with me twice?—yes, Lily! And you have should have seen their eyes! One of them said it was as good as a day in the country just to look at her. And she sat there, and laughed and talked with them—not a bit as if she were being *charitable* you know, but as if she liked it as much as they did.
>
> (*HM*, 105)

This conversation takes place at the *tableaux vivants* evening in the first part of the novel and provides a contrast with the decorative superficiality of the evening about to unfold with Lily winning admiration for her pose as Reynolds's *Mrs. Lloyd*. The visit to the Girls' Club is the explanation for the kindness of Nettie Struther, and the temporary comfort provided by the poor but secure kitchen of this working girl when Lily is at her lowest point. Here, Lily expresses genuine affection for this woman, her life, and her baby, an affection that contrasts with the return of bitterness that spills out when she is among her fellow workers at the millinery shop:

> Lily slipped out last among the band of liberated work-women. She did not care to be mingled in their noisy dispersal: once in the street she always felt an irresistible return to her old standpoint, an instinctive shrinking from all that was unpolished and promiscuous. In the days—how distant they now seemed!—when she had visited the Girls' Club with Gerty Farish, she had felt an enlightened interest in the working classes; but that was because she looked down on them from above, from the happy altitude of her grace and her beneficence. Now that she was on a level with them, the point of view was less interesting.
>
> (*HM*, 224)

This is honest but damning, and certainly not overturned by what the narrator allows us to read as Lily's oversentimental romanticizing of working-class family life, even though this vignette was a novelistic convention of the period that Wharton may be presenting without any irony. The scene is ambiguous.

The realization of the utter rootlessness of her own life that so distresses Lily on the evening of her death is all the more painful because it is something that she has condemned in others. Queenie Leavis draws approving attention to the narrator's dislike of meretricious modernity as represented by modish hotels, and she cites this description from the novel:

> The environment in which Lily found herself was as strange to her as its inhabitants. She was unacquainted with the world of the fashionable New York hotel—a world over-heated, over-upholstered, and over-fitted with mechanical appliances for the gratification of fantastic requirements, while the comforts of a civilized life were as unattainable as in a desert.[35]

The world of the luxury hotel, which Lily experiences firsthand when she is employed as a companion for Mrs. Norma Hatch at the Emporium Hotel, represents wealth without purpose. There are no engagements for the Emporium Hotel set to keep, so her work as Mrs. Hatch's assistant is light, but the rhetoric encourages us to see the set from which she has fallen as a group possessing some sense of social responsibility and philanthropic duty. Those who live at the Emporium live for pleasure, and the only discernible ambition is (in the case of Mrs. Hatch, who is a divorcee from out West) to gain admission to that more fashionable set. In a fine image, Wharton comments that "Lily had an odd sense of being behind the social tapestry, on the side where the threads were knotted and the loose ends hung." (*HM*, 215). The word "promiscuity," used in Charles Bowen's description of the hotel Nouveau Luxe in *The Custom of the Country* and in the description of Lily's fellow workers at the millinery shop quoted earlier, is Wharton's linguistic auto-da-fé, her signal of condemnation for all that is worst about society. Indicative of the casual, indiscriminate relations between people that she most feared, the repeated use of the term is very revealing.

The movement in *The House of Mirth* from the wealthy New York society that eventually ostracizes Lily to the working-class world that accepts her shows that Wharton did have a developed sense of the politics of class. This forms part of Lily's education in the way that it does not for another woman who refuses to conform to the rules of privileged society with its marriage conventions, Edna Pontellier in *The Awakening* (1899). Both Edna and Lily die alone, but there is an ironical contrast between the representation of the two women at the end of each novel. Even though Edna's "death" is represented as a positive act of a woman refusing to be constrained, she has been let down not only by the men around her, but by the women, too, who had seemed to promise so much in the sisterly scene on the veranda, which is presented early on in the novel. Lily dies in an irritatingly ambiguous way, with the narrative favoring the view that her death was not an act of will, but an act of misjudgment about the effects of the dose of the drug she had taken.

This ending is much debated. If Wharton believed that all novels should have a moral purpose,[36] what purpose does Lily's death have? It is Christlike in its self-sacrifice,[37] but no one is redeemed. The conclusion reflects the modern crisis of despair, which is why Q. D. Leavis did not feel able to put Wharton into the Leavises' category of "great" novelists, who offered positives rather than negatives. On the grounds that *The House of Mirth* subverts genres by mixing realism with sentimentalism, Carol Singley is happy to call the text "modernist,"[38] a category that is examined more fully in the following chapter.

It is stretching a point, but definitions of modernism have encouraged such a stretching, seeing continuities in Western culture that have convincingly challenged Virginia Woolf's claim that there was a single sea change in or around December 1910. Perhaps Wharton offers a clue in the name given to the Dorsets' Mediterranean yacht, which becomes Lily's nemesis. The boat is called the *Sabrina,* and in Milton's *Comus,* Sabrina, the victim of a revenge attack orchestrated by her father's first wife, jumps in the River Severn and drowns, but is miraculously transformed into a water nymph. Lily's death is not presented as a heroic or mythic event, however, and her demise conforms all too readily to the stereotypical death of the heroine in nineteenth-century operas and novels, from *La Bohème* to *Madame Bovary.* Society exacts a price on the woman who resists convention. At the same time, Wharton may be signaling the hypocrisy (or, if we wish to be less charitable, for commercial reasons she found it politic to conform to the conventional treatment) of the nineteenth-century belief that physical weakness in women is a sign of delicacy and spiritual cultivation. Thus, the image of the dead young woman not strong enough to cope with life is that of one who has preserved her virginity, who is safe and pure, and not sexual.[39]

Is Lily a dodo transformed, but not saved by, beauty? Kassanoff's reading of Lily's death is blunt and unsentimental ("She is more useful dead and stuffed, as it were, than alive. The messy contingencies of motherhood, Wharton seems to suggest, would compromise—indeed diminish—Lily's status as a racial icon").[40] Lily achieves a kind of perfection, therefore, in death, but without progeny the moment is also one of racial extinction. She dies with a dream of holding a baby, but it is someone's else's baby and just a dream. In a reading that privileges the novel's naturalism, Lily becomes a type, reified and doomed.

Although there is an ambiguity about Lily's death that makes it wrong to call it suicide, there is a clear case for reading the novel alongside the sociologist Émile Durkheim's 1897 study, *Le suicide.*[41] Durkheim did not share the early nineteenth-century belief that science and technology would inevitably contribute to human progress. He believed in the scientific *method,* studying "primitive" societies in Australia and elsewhere, and drawing out general laws and principles from the grouping of facts that emerged from his close observation. But in the Western world he noted how material prosperity released the harmful instincts of greed and passion. These threatened social norms, and he noted the increased rootlessness, or "anomie" of people, particularly working people, as they became alienated from the conventions and rituals of society. This is an analysis shared by Wharton, and *The House of Mirth* tracks Lily's fall as she finds in the modern world no organic community into which she can fit.

A corollary of this is the claim that Lily's apparently pointless death demonstrates that women should not be given the burden of responsibility for saving men morally in a world that has abandoned belief in salvation. The broader issue relating to the subjection of women and the need for reform across the whole of society is signaled sotto voce toward the end of *The House of Mirth*. Lily has known something approaching the solidarity of sisterhood from her brief exchange with Miss Kilroy, her fellow shop worker, and the novel offers us a glance at the issues involved in working-class factory life, which Wharton was to take as her focus in her next novel. When Lily becomes unemployed, she takes refuge one day in a little restaurant on Fifty-ninth Street, and observes a world of women, oppressed by work ("sallow" again) but also united by it, all seen as enjoying a sense of activity and purpose that contrasts with her own atrophy:

> The room was full of women and girls, all too much engaged in their rapid absorption of tea and pie to remark her entrance. A hum of shrill voices reverberated against the low ceiling, leaving Lily shut out in a little circle of silence . . . Her eyes sought the faces about her, craving a responsive glance, some sign of an intuition of her trouble. But the sallow preoccupied women, with their bags and notebooks and rolls of music, were all engrossed in their own affairs, and even those who sat by themselves were busy running over proof-sheets or devouring magazines between their hurried gulps of tea. Lily alone was stranded in a great waste of disoccupation.
>
> (*HM*, 235)

Lily is excluded from this world of work because, as she consoles herself, "[s]ince she had been brought up to be ornamental, she could hardly blame herself for failing to serve any practical purpose" (*HM*, 232), but the discovery that she cannot function even at the most basic practical level is a great blow to her self-esteem. The culture in which she had her place is the one that praised her ornamental qualities, and it is the world of Veblen's Conspicuous Consumption. Contrasting with the Fifty-ninth Street restaurant is the one presented to us in Monte Carlo: "The strident setting of the restaurant, in which their table seemed set apart in a general glare of publicity, and the presence at it of little Dabham of the 'Riviera Notes,' emphasized the ideals of a world where conspicuousness passed for distinction, and the society column had become the role of fame" (*HM*, 168).

Lily's greatest triumph was her pose as Mrs. Lloyd in the *tableau vivant,* and at the end of the novel the narrator, drawing on the discourse of Darwinism and Social Darwinism, exonerates her from any blame for willingly collaborating with the shallow values of her former society:

> Inherited tendencies had combined with early training to make her the highly specialized product she was: an organism as helpless out of its narrow range as the sea-anemone torn from the rock. She had been fashioned to adorn and delight; to what other end does nature round the rose-leaf and paint the humming bird's breast? And was it her fault that the purely decorative mission is less easily and harmoniously fulfilled among social beings than in the world of nature? That it is apt to be hampered by material necessities or complicated by moral scruples?
> (*HM*, 235)

This, more than anything, is the argument of the novel. Culture and society create values, cultivate desire, and direct behavior. At one point Lily cries out that she is tempted to tell Selden that "I am bad through and through—I want admiration, I want excitement, I want money!" and that this is her shame and the cause of her self-loathing (*HM*, 132). But the novel insists that it is society's shame that is responsible. Wharton's subject is that which a frivolous society destroys, and society is responsible for Lily's destruction because it has created a situation in which Lily has to tirelessly "work" at the daily but frivolous task of being acceptable. That has been Lily's only occupation since achieving adulthood; it is a wasteful society that squanders the talents of its women in this way. Lily's potential is never realized because she is unfit for any world outside the hothouse in which orchids and lilies are cultivated.

Although discussions of Lily as a symbol of white Anglo-Saxon purity have contributed much to a political reading of the novel, there is a danger of them overshadowing earlier important readings that focused on the Bart/Barter metonymy. The huge expansion of American capitalism and business during the Gilded Age is reflected in the discourse of the market, a discourse that Wai-Chee Dimock, in an early influential study, showed permeating the whole novel. Dimock proposed a reading whose conclusion offered an analysis worthy of Marx: "The fluidity of currencies in *The House of Mirth*, the apparently endless business possibilities, attests to the reduction of human experiences to abstract equivalents, for exchange."[42] Such rates of exchange are based on inequality. Lily gets poor returns on the "deals" throughout the novel. She gets poor return for being on the *Sabrina,* partly because it takes her time to realize exactly what the "deal" actually is. The novel shows us in this instance the way that although economic power may be in the hands of men it can be mediated and exercised by women. Bertha and Mrs. Peniston have limited means, but they are willing to speculate. Ultimately they display what Georges Bataille has identified as the hatred of expenditure that characterizes the bourgeoisie, an acquisitiveness that is their justification and raison d'être.[43] The bourgeoisie are afraid to spend and this miserliness of spirit extends to Selden, who has been gathering spiritual capital but is afraid he might have to spend it if he develops a relationship with Lily. In the language of commerce, therefore, he does not invest but remains a spectator.

Lily is the one who pays regularly, paying a high price for her visit to Selden's apartment, paying with drudgery for her stay at Bellomont, paying for her encounter with Percy Gryce, paying traumatically for "borrowing" from Gus Trenor, paying in reputation again for her travels on the *Sabrina,* paying for working for Norma Hatch at the Emporium Hotel, and paying severely for her feelings for Selden. The irony is that her behavior is at odds with a society where it is normal *not* to pay. In Dimock's reading, Lily's willingness to pay back her debts is thus a challenge to the system, which assumes that debts will not be repaid in cash. But it is an ineffectual challenge. Her rejection of the offer of a loan from Rosedale is also futile, unless in rejecting it she is consciously signaling her "refusal to live"[44] on these debased terms. In other words, she will not agree to use Bertha's letters to exercise power over Bertha, as proposed by Rosedale, for moral reason: "What Lily is rejecting is not so much the idea of revenge as the degradation of revenge in the arena of exchange."[45] Such a reading challenges the contention that Lily is a person without a moral center, possessing only a sense of identity that is taken from those surrounding her, and from being observed. I agree with Dimock here, that the presentation of Lily differs from that given in *The Custom of the Country* to Undine Spragg, who is seen as lacking any constraining moral principles. Be that as it may, Lily's gesture is futile within the context of the novel because Selden is never to be aware of it.

The novel does not offer a political solution, however. All the reforming philosophies presented in the novel are treated with an ironical skepticism. Sometimes this is direct, as in the comment on Mrs. Fisher, where campaigning is seen as a mere diversion: "Mrs. Fisher's latest hobby was municipal reform. It had been preceded by a zeal for socialism, which had in turn replaced an energetic advocacy of Christian Science" (*HM,* 39). Sometimes it is indirect, as with Selden's republic of the spirit, with its aim of freeing everyone from money, poverty, ease, anxiety, and all material chance. This is fine except that Selden spends a great deal of time in the republic of the material, "the element you disapprove of" (*HM*, 56), as Lily astutely observes. Dimock notes that his republic turns out to be less of a republic than a refined replica of the social marketplace, of which Selden is a full participating member.[46] Lily is skeptical of all political reform, asking Selden whether it isn't the case that "people who find fault with society are too apt to regard it as an end and not as a means, just as the people who despise money speak as if its only use were to be kept in bags and gloated over? Isn't it fairer to look at them both as opportunities, which may be used either stupidly or intelligently, according to the capacity of the user?" (*HM*, 56).

This perhaps reflects Wharton's own position, where it is the reform of the New York Society for the Prevention of Cruelty to Animals that had been her main social commitment during her time in the city. Lily thinks fondly of the "duties" that fashionable society recognizes, absent from the pleasure-seeking world of Mrs. Hatch (*HM*, 215). But in this novel we have not seen fashionable society very often about its duties. When Lily Bart goes to see the women at the Girls' Club, therefore, she finds herself in for something of a shock:

> Her visit to the Girls' Club had first brought her in contact with the dramatic contrast of life. She had always accepted with philosophic calm the fact that such existences as hers were pedestalled on foundations of obscure humanity. The dreary limbo of dinginess lay all around and beneath that little illuminated circle in which life reached its finest efflorescence, as the mud and sleep of a winter night enclose a hot-house filled with tropical flowers. All this was in the natural order of things, and the orchid basking in its artificially created atmosphere could round the delicate curves of its petals undisturbed by the ice on the panes.
>
> (*HM*, 119)

The stark juxtaposition of "the natural order of things" and the hothouse orchid suggests that the narrator does not see this as the natural order at all. But the narrative voice elsewhere suggests that Lily's worldview echoes that expressed in Mary Cadwalader Jones's 1894 study of Working Girls' Clubs. Mary Cadwalader Jones who was descended from a distinguished colonial family, was married to Edith's brother Frederic, and her advice to those women starting up such clubs (wealthy society women like herself) is revealing for its frank acceptance of the existing social order and the casual justification of glaring inequalities. Mrs. Frederic Jones advises that those running such clubs would be unwise to seek to disguise their own privilege from the young working women who attend: "The girls are sure to end by knowing that we keep servants, wear evening dresses, and go to the opera; and by plainly speaking of these things when necessary (the necessity will be rare) as comforts won for us by our husbands' or our fathers' intelligence and labors, we make the distinction in our way of living more one of degree than one of kind."[47]

Such complacency was alien to Edith Wharton, but it would be wrong to assume that because *The House of Mirth* ruthlessly exposes the damage that New York society can do to its members, and because it shows the readers from that world that the deprived humanity of a poor, lower class exists just off Fifth Avenue, that therefore its author had some political solutions. I fail to see evidence of the radicalism observed by critics such as Elaine Showalter (Lily must die so that working women can be born) and Elizabeth Ammons (the symbolic final image of the union of Lily and the working-class infant whose vitality provides solace for the dying woman).[48] Dimock sees a glimpse of a narrative solution in the comments on rootlessness in the paragraph that begins "Her parents had been rootless," but sees this image of the "sanctified ancestral house" as a "quintessentially aristocratic ideal."[49] The casual representation of the rooted working-class home (Nettie's) remains unexamined, and as the image of "bird's nest built on the edge of a cliff" shows is more symbolic and transcendental than real.

This absence of radicalism, however, does not prevent Wharton from questioning aspects of the assumptions that her social group took for granted.[50] It has long been noted that Wharton "had no social improvement or political agenda, and did not spend time 'doing good'; yet her sense of responsible citizenship implicitly repudiated the narrow, self-serving attitudes of her parents and friends."[51] In *The House of Mirth* we see Lily beginning to recognize her own complacency:

> [I]t is one thing to live comfortably with the abstract conception of poverty, another to be brought in contact with its human embodiments. Lily had never conceived of these victims of fate otherwise than in the mass. That the mass was composed of individual lives, innumerable separate centres of sensation, with her own eager reachings for pleasure, her own fierce revulsions from pain—that some of these bundles of feeling were clothed in shapes not so unlike her own, with eyes meant to look on gladness, and young lips shaped for love—this discovery gave Lily one of those sudden shocks of pity that sometimes decentralize a life.
>
> (*HM*, 119)

As a lowly hatmaker Lily discovers the drudgery and exhausting nature of urban work, but she does not live long enough to experience sustained poverty. She is doomed to extinction. In her next novel

Wharton decided to move beyond New York and confront the world of working-class life that is strikingly, but fleetingly, glimpsed through the windows of *The House of Mirth*. In *The Fruit of the Tree*, questions of social improvement would be interrogated more forcefully, or at least that seemed to be the original intention.

Politics, Reform and *The Fruit of the Tree* (1907)

Anyone who has read *The Fruit of the Tree* will not be totally surprised by the enthusiasm with which Edith Wharton threw herself into philanthropic work in France during the First World War. In many ways it represents a return to the theme and construction of *The Valley of Decision*, though this time with a contemporary New England setting. The central triangle is the same in that in both novels a young idealistic man marries for convenience and then finds a soul mate in another woman with whom he can never live happily. Such a description neglects the political ideas that are supported by this narrative scaffold. Ostensibly progressive, they are in fact deeply conservative.

The central character in this novel, John Amherst, is driven by a desire to improve the lot of the workers in the Westmore cotton mill. He is descended through his mother from a privileged class, though working rather implausibly as an assistant manager in the mill. In common with many philanthropists, including Wharton, he wants to change the lot of individual workers without changing the structure of society as a whole. The sanctity of the individual is to be preserved. It is an American reading of social change, but the influence of Europe is also discernible.

The period between 1900 and 1914 is one in which an increasing number of people in Europe felt that some kind of revolution was about to happen. The anticipated revolution was a social and political one rather than the military apocalypse that actually happened, but the reasons for this feeling that there was about to be a cataclysmic change are not difficult to identify. Changes in technology were taking place at a frantic pace. Workers in England and France and throughout Europe were striking for better conditions. In England suffragettes were carrying out a militant campaign that was reported in the newspapers on an almost daily basis. In America the stock market collapsed in 1907. In Paris in 1911 there were food riots. Working people were demanding a better place in this new world governed by banks, mass production, and rapid distribution. As Roger Magraw observes: "The 'real' issue in French politics in the 1900s was the relationship between the capitalist state and a growing and militant labour movement."[52]

These questions about agency and about who controls the means of production and its products (the fruit of the tree) form the subject of the novel.[53] The novel makes it clear early on that this new management clearly cannot be in the hands of the workers. Dillon, the mill worker who lost his hand, is symbolically castrated and rendered impotent politically in the very first chapter. He is a "Hand" without a "hand," and the general metonym also works as a sexual metaphor in Wharton (the "third hand" in "Beatrice Palmato"). Responsibility therefore falls on the shoulders of the enlightened responsible employer. The novel's politics offer an endorsement of noblesse oblige.

The novel first announces itself as a novel of industrial reform in the tradition of nineteenth-century social reforming novels such as *Hard Times,* and Wharton produces the novel at a time when this subject was proving very popular among American novelists. Since the death of Dickens in 1870 there had been a series of novels by American writers exploring the impact of the new industrial and commercial urban world in what Twain called the Gilded Age. William Dean Howells's *The Rise of Silas Lapham* (1885) examined the life of the self-made man who makes a fortune as a paint manufacturer. Theodore Dreiser's *Sister Carrie* (1900) examined the life of the ambitious woman, drawn from the country to the city of sweatshops and theater as if by a magnet. Frank Norris's *The Octopus* (1901) exposed the power of the railroads in the wheat-growing areas of California. The commercially astute Wharton would have noted that at the turn of the century American writing had included a number of novels with a labor reform theme,[54] from Elizabeth Stuart Phelps's *The Silent Partner* (1879) to W. D. Howells's *Annie Kilburn* (1889). The popularity of muckraking novels, exposing industrial corruption, had continued into the twentieth century, reflecting the idealism of the Progressive Era, and 1906 saw the publication of the American novelist Winston Churchill's *Coniston,* Samuel Hopkins Adams's *The Great American Fraud,* and Upton Sinclair's *The Jungle.* As Tuttleton points out, Edith Wharton's later correspondence with Upton Sinclair shows her clear opposition to socialism,[55] and her friendship and correspondence with Howells makes his *Annie Kilburn,* though published a generation earlier in 1889, a more likely immediate model for *The Fruit of the Tree.* It also has a New England setting, focuses on the laboring classes, and contains an indictment of the economic system.

The Fruit of the Tree starts as a novel of social reform, but attention then focuses on the incompatibility of husband and wife in marriage. John Amherst, the idealist, marries Bessy, the widow of the man who owned the factory, partly because she appears to share his vision of reform. After a short while it is clear that she prefers house parties,

New York, and expensive swimming pools. By then mutual disenchantment has set in, although Amherst continues with his work and dreams.

The third "issue" addressed by the novel is euthanasia, as if Wharton was reluctant to abandon the ethical issues explored in her novellas. Bessy falls from her horse, damages her spine, and is likely to be paralyzed and in great pain for the rest of her life. Should a nurse ever help a patient to die? Early in the novel Amherst expresses his belief that it would be a kindness to do so, when a factory worker is badly injured in an industrial accident. The issue is complicated by the fact that Justine, the volunteer nurse to whom he confides this belief, and who gives Bessy the drug that allows her to die, goes on to marry Amherst, though the thought of marriage was never in her mind until the death of his wife. (Or was it? She later realizes she can never be sure.)

Debates about euthanasia reached a crescendo in 1906, as Wharton worked on the manuscript, and the novel can be situated in the context of the specific debate about the use of drugs. In *The House of Mirth* Lily seeks relief and escape through drugs. In the later novel, *Ethan Frome,* Mattie Silver decides to, or is forced to, live with her pain until she dies naturally. Bessy Westmore is somewhere in between, and the issue of euthanasia is raised to make a higher political point. As Kassanoff notes, "Justine's act of euthanasia is thus deeply embedded in the novel's logic of class, for in giving the heiress the fatal drug dose, Justine seeks to restore to Bessy a measure of the integrity, personal specificity, and bodily control denied to the automatized, prosthetized Dillon."[56]

The final issue raised by the novel is the hypocrisy of the idealist who shies away from the action, which in theory he was keen to endorse. When he learns that Justine was responsible for the act of euthanasia, Amherst runs away. He later returns, there is a reconciliation, but although the final scene is a happy one, each knows too much about the other to be entirely at ease in this marriage. If the title suggests the fruit of the tree of knowledge, and the subsequent fall of humankind, then John and Justine share Adam and Eve's banishment from paradise. The final paragraph of the novel on one level provides the reader with the rhetoric of the happy ending, but the images of sunset, smoke, shadows, and marsh (albeit drained) undercut the simple innocence of such a resolution:

> "Dear," he said, "let us go out and look at the marsh we have drained."
> He turned and led her through the open doorway to the terrace above the river. The sun was setting behind the wooded slopes of Hopewood,

and the trees about the house stretched long blue shadows across the lawn. Beyond them rose the smoke of Westmore.[57]

As the issue changes, so does the focus on a particular character. Amherst is the focus for the issues of social reform, Amherst and Bessy for the incompatibility in marriage, Justine for the issue of euthanasia, and Amherst once again for the clash between idealism and practice. Amherst is the constant, however, although several critics make Justine the main character, seeing her as a New Woman: self-sufficient, intelligent, independent.

The Fruit of the Tree is a novel with a shifting focus and this is sometimes seen as a weakness. A catalogue of commentators, including R. W. B. Lewis, Cynthia Griffin Wolff, Blake Nevius, Henry James, and Millicent Bell have all been unhappy about the multitude of issues, from social reform to euthanasia, from the New Woman to marriage.[58] Some critics[59] have attempted to rescue it from this charge by arguing that women and marriage sit at the centre of the novel, and that the other issues are subsidiary. Others[60] have sought to reconcile these two positions by arguing that the social issues and the issue of marriage are complementary, with the incompatibility of John Amherst and Bessy Westmore echoing the incompatibility of Amherst's dreams of reform and the actual circumstances of manufacturing.[61] More specifically, it is the product of the inconsistency between his progressive view of society and his patriarchal view of marriage.

This multiplicity of themes have been read as differing aspects of a single issue: "The novel explores the central tension between the personal and the political—specifically, the ways in which the scientific disciplines of professional medicine, industrial management, urban planning, architecture, and even psychology sought to regulate the personal, the lives and bodies of Americans, for the benefit of the political, the body politic."[62] This view sees Wharton's subject as the newly emergent professional-managerial class, a site in this novel notable for the intersection of class and gender. Amherst and Justine are active idealists. They not only believe there should be a better, fairer society, they are committed to making it. Amherst comes from a "good" family and represents the new duties incumbent on the privileged in the twentieth century. His energy and interest in reform contrasts with the effete listlessness of Bessy's father, Mr. Langhope.

Unfortunately, Wharton's idealists seem doomed to fail. In her autobiography Wharton identifies Meredith's *The Adventures of Harry Richmond* (1871) as one of two Meredith novels whose message she understood.[63] In his study of Meredith and politics, Jack Lindsay describes the development of Harry as he moves "from romantic delusions into a positive view of the world, but who does not accept the Squire's egoist greed as a solution."[64] This is a journey made by Odo and partly made by Amherst. Progressive political activity is far preferable to apathy, and infinitely preferable to reactionary entrenched interests, but only so much can be achieved by idealism. Better to be practical, hardworking, and not too obsessed with visions or dreams that will always disappoint.

The two practical activities explored in this novel are medical nursing and engineering. Each challenges the model of enforced idleness described by Thorstein Veblen in *The Theory of the Leisure Class*[65] and reverses the gendered situation in her other imaginative writing. In much of her most well-known fiction, including *The House of Mirth*, Wharton explores the world of women who do not work and professional men who have a great deal of spare time, of socialites and nonpracticing lawyers. Here, in a quite different way from *Bunner Sisters*, which is concerned with the working poor, Wharton shows not the philanthropy of the privileged but their engagement in good work, inspired by their reading and intellects.[66] The purposeful body at work is contrasted with the useless body, though this contrast is not restricted to the issue of productivity and service to the community. Allied to this political issue is the ethical question of what to do with the bodies of those who are unable to contribute, for reasons of intellectual or physical shortcomings. It has to be remembered that eugenics was considered a respectable and progressive science during the first third of the twentieth century, as it was seen as the servant of the better society.[67] The corollary of breeding the healthy and the productive, however, is the discarding of those whose bodies are broken. Euthanasia was the subject of a 1906 essay by G. Lowes Dickinson,[68] which Wharton may have read, and in *The Fruit of the Tree* the class implications of euthanasia are brought to the fore, as Donna Campbell has noted:

> When Justine applies the same logic of euthanasia to the pain wracked and paralyzed body of Bessy Westmore that she has already applied to Dillon, the injured worker, she unwittingly exposes the class-based eugenics with which euthanasia is allied. Defined as a rich woman whom Amherst had never been able to wean from the position of social parasite, Bessy is already, according to the laws of class and consumption, a useless body. Thus Bessy's accident intensifies but does not fundamentally transform her status, a status that according to the laws of class validates the right of the rich to be useless. Through the contrasting euthanasia discussion of Dillon's and Bessy's cases, Justine exposes the unwritten and

explosive principle that science or its representatives may kill the useless body of the poor but not of the rich.[69]

The triangle of Amherst, Bessy, and Justine is another example of the triangular relationships that frequently occur in Wharton's fiction, with only a gender reversal (two men and one woman) needed to mirror Wharton's own circumstances. In that Bessy is the figure of desire, highly sexualized with her long flowing hair, and Justine the intellectual and spiritual soul mate, the triangle corresponds to the depiction of desire in *The Valley of Decision* rather than that in *Ethan Frome,* where the ironically named Zenobia ceases to be the object of desire. Justine, like Fulvia Vivaldi in *The Valley of Decision,* is the driving force behind social change, a woman practicing a profession that in the first decade of the twentieth century was just becoming respectable for women. Medical nurses rose in status as the science of healing gave medical practice more authority. On the other hand, the caring role was the deeply traditional one assigned to women. Justine, however, is an independent, freethinking person, and in many respects an embodiment of the New Woman, a figure about which Wharton had mixed feelings. The novel was originally to be called "Justine Brent," suggesting that just as the exploration of Lily Bart had formed the center of the extraordinarily successful *The House of Mirth,* so another woman-centered novel in a very different social context might repeat that success.

The change of title, to a phrase associated with Milton, the opening of *Paradise Lost* and the expulsion from Eden, is instructive. It suggests a political position that is at best ameliorative. At worst it signifies an irredeemable fall. Humans have been expelled from Eden and they will never be able to return to paradise on this earth. They can strive to make things better, but human imperfection will defeat the grandest schemes (the argument advanced in *The Valley of Decision*). Deborah Carlin sees this rather bleak message as not only the unifying feature of the novel, but as an example of its conservative message. Justine is the transgressive woman, the American Eve, who challenges medical orthodoxy by putting her belief in euthanasia into practice when Bessy is dying in agony. And with the patriarchal model of Eve before her, she accepts that she must suffer banishment for her crime and become a self-imposed exile. There is no rhetorical hymn to rebellion as there is at the end of *The Awakening,* therefore, where even though Edna is swimming to her death she is resisting external judgment and punishment from her own society. Wharton had seen what *The Awakening* had done to Kate Chopin's reputation, and perhaps as a woman with a keen awareness of the market, she knew it to be politic not to risk anything that might be regarded by her middle-class readers as subversive or offensive. But equally, the resolution of events in *The Fruit of the Tree* does offer a political reading of society, one with which women readers in particular could identify. The shortcomings of the man Justine has married are all too apparent toward the end of Wharton's novel, and the failure of men carries with it a failure of their politics. But there is also a class issue that the novel inadvertently makes. Only those with pedigree matter in this novel and what is important is what this class decides to do about the challenge from workers and the new-money middle class. The success or failure of those with pedigree is subordinate to a rhetoric that sees them as the guardians of civilized society. It is their role, and it is their duty.

Leaving Massachusetts, Leaving America

In her 1903 letter Wharton may have expressed dismay at the American culture that she always started to forget about during her stay in Europe, but once she had moved out of New York into the Berkshires, America was not too inhospitable a place for her to develop as a writer. The years 1901 to 1907 were a period during which Wharton enjoyed a clarity and breadth of vision that was blurred between 1907 and 1913 when her life underwent fundamental changes.[70] The meeting and affair with Morton Fullerton, which had an emotional, sexual, intellectual, and political significance for Edith Wharton, coincided with and may have been an important stimulus for the decision to move permanently to Europe.

Wharton had become a successful novelist in Massachusetts. *The Fruit of the Tree,* and more importantly for her reputation and income, *The House of Mirth,* had been written at The Mount. *The Custom of the Country* had been started there in 1907, though it was not to be completed and published until 1913. Her first novel to be written entirely in Paris, *Ethan Frome* (1911) had a western Massachusetts setting. Even *The Reef* (1912), though written largely in Salsomaggiore, the *terme* near Parma where she was recuperating, with a setting mainly in a French country house, conveys the interior world of the Mount. Though New York and France provided experiences that were essential to the setting and sensibility of much of her most well-known fiction, Massachusetts was essential in providing the base and foundation for her development as a serious, professional writer.

The years 1907 to 1909 were to see a hiatus in the completion of longer prose fiction, however. During this period she spent summers at The Mount and the rest of the year at the newly acquired apartment in Paris. She published a collection of short stories (*The Hermit and the Wild Woman and Other Stories*), a travel book (*A Motor-Flight Through France*), and a collection of poems (*Artemis to Actaeon and Other Verses*).[71] She also did one of the least politic, but ultimately most liberating, things in her personal life so far, in embarking on an ardent, emotional, and sexual affair with Morton Fullerton. Novel publication was briefly and temporarily suspended at a point when novel writing, as publications by Joyce, Dorothy Richardson, D. H. Lawrence, Virginia Woolf, and Proust between 1910 and 1915 were to show, was undergoing the technical and conceptual reformation that was represented by Woolf as a major challenge to writers like Wharton, whose reputation had been made in the first ten years of the twentieth century. I do not think that it is a complete coincidence that it was at this moment that Wharton gave up work on the draft of *The Custom of the Country* and embarked on two novels that show the influence of the new writing. Wharton's political and aesthetic relationship to early modernism is a key issue in the discussion of her 1910–14 writing. If the skirting of modernism ended at all in her writing career, it ended now.

3

Apart from Modernism? Mr. Proust, Mr. Bennett, and Mrs. Wharton (1910)

> Proust came of age in a world with no electricity or central heating, without rapid transit and mass communication. By 1910 he had witnessed the arrival of electric lighting, the telephone, the automobile, motion pictures, the Paris subway, and the airplane. He characterized his era as the "age of speed" and showed in *Search* how these remarkable inventions changed daily life and the way people perceived time and space.
> —William C. Carter in the introduction to *Proust: A Life*

Varieties of Modernism

Where should we position Edith Wharton in relation to modernism? Now that her work is commanding widespread critical attention, and her reputation continuing to rise, it seems an appropriate moment to ask this question. It is a defining one, but what once seemed to be an easy question to answer has now spawned confusingly divergent views, based on differing assumptions about what modernism is. The easy response to the question is that it is obvious that Wharton, despite her fondness for Proust, was opposed to most of what modernism stood for. At odds with this is a view that takes a much more liberal reading of modernism, seeing the movement as being less about technique and experiment and more about deracination and alienation.

In American readings of Wharton and modernism, which are less concerned with the European first period that was supposedly triggered "in or about December 1910" and more with the work of post–World War I expatriate writers such as Scott Fitzgerald (who visited Wharton for tea) and Hemingway, Wharton is being identified as a writer linked to "the modern," or as a modernist writer, by a growing number of critics. Two examples will illustrate this, both of which draw attention to specific technical features of Wharton's early fiction. In her 1987 essay on the *The House of Mirth,* Roslyn Dixon links technique to ideology:

> Wharton's ideological perspective suggests that she is less connected with the "Great Tradition" in literature than she is concerned with the modern French tradition leading to structuralism. In the evolution of character, she conducts an empirical assessment of the "whole" by applying Durkheim's principles; like the moderns Wharton perceives society as devoid of values and dedicated to self gratification. And like the moderns, Sartre for instance, Wharton perceives choice as the only avenue to selfhood . . .[1]

There are some big jumps here, from the novel to Durkheim (a writer Wharton was aware of and with whose views about the effects of alienation she had great sympathy), to Sartre and to structuralism, whose philosophy is not one she is likely to have shared had it been available in 1905. Dixon does not actually call Wharton a modernist, but that description is now being used to describe features of Wharton's work, almost as if the experience of the social economic pressures of the modern world (modernity) and the artistic celebration of the new uncertainty and indeterminacy (modernism) are synonymous. In her introduction to *A Historical Guide to Edith Wharton,* Carol J. Singley writes that "Edith Wharton made her mark on literary modernism," citing *Ethan Frome,* "where Wharton developed techniques to probe a character's inner consciousness and incapacitating sense of isolation. Like many other modernist writers, Wharton was an expatriate with firsthand experience of the devastating effects of war who feared for the demise of civilization itself."[2]

Terry Eagleton, in *Exiles and Émigrés,*[3] emphasized the deracination and social exile, whether as a result of choice or force of circumstances, experienced by many of the most well-known male modern writers of the first part of the twentieth century. The lives of Conrad, Lawrence, Yeats, Pound, Eliot, and Joyce, whose work forms the largely male canon of the first wave of modernism, illustrate this point. In this respect, if in no other, Wharton had something in common with such writers. She traveled ceaselessly in Europe, and even when she had established herself in France, she continued to move restlessly about the continent. In "Landscapes of Desire,"[4] however, Shari Benstock argues that Wharton remained essentially American even when living in Europe. In this sense she was radical (springing out of the roots, of which she had many) rather than *déracinée.* Millicent Bell makes a similar point. In French Wharton would have been described as *dépaysée,* which "means to be out of one's element, adrift and astray."[5] The term "expatriate" more closely describes

Wharton's actual position, because it allows for the fact, recalled by Americans with very mixed feelings, "that some of their great artists felt more at home in their skin abroad than at home."[6] In 1909 the attraction of living permanently in Paris might have been linked to the fact that it was the place where Morton Fullerton worked, but it was also more culturally stable, conservative, and nineteenth century in some of its manners than New York or other parts of America. Wharton was drawn by European intellectual traditions, its culture and its history, as were Pound and Eliot. But to those once most readily thought of as modernists has been added a group recovered by feminist and postcolonial readings of modernism such as those included in the recent *Cambridge History of Twentieth-Century English Literature*, edited by Laura Marcus and Peter Nichols, readings that have explored questions relating to gender, class, race, ethnicity, and empire. This group includes writers such as H. D., Richardson, West, Gilman, Chopin, Mew, Stein, Cather, Rhys, Larsen, Hurston, and Barnes. For the original canon of Anglo-American modernists, the legacy of the nineteenth century was something to be swept aside. Bloomsbury, whose members had grown up in the nineteenth century, saw themselves as eighteenth-century satirists and wits, honest, open, rational, and sharp, and their mission was to blow away what they saw as the deadening legacy of Victorian England.[7] Virginia Woolf, the most experimental Bloomsbury writer, did not wander far from her native England, and Proust did not wander far from his native France. Exile and deracination, therefore, are not quite adequate defining features of the new movement, though gender and sexuality respectively may have caused a feeling of cultural exile that is perhaps better defined as alienation.

What, then, of this idea of alienation? In Wharton there is alienation, but not of the *modernist* existential kind, where meaning itself is often questioned. In Wharton critics have observed a gendered alienation, in which the sense of "other" can be located at "the intersection of Wharton's modernism and portrayals of female sexuality."[8] In her essay on Wharton's "Others"[9] Dale M. Bauer develops the thesis that Wharton represents female longing for sexual connection as a form of addiction,[10] because it is mediated by a commerce-driven culture. The trope is completed by linking characters such as Lily Bart, Justine Brent, and Mattie Silver with paralysis and drugs. They thus represent the alienation that the "different" woman must inevitably experience. Similar arguments, however, have been used to associate the three respective novels in which these women appear with the naturalism of Dreiser and the realism of Howells, and it is difficult to see Wharton's treatment of female sexuality as specifically *modernist* when each woman is shown to be struggling with practical work rather than with abstractions. That is not to say that Woolf's Rachel Vinrace and Richardson's Miriam Henderson do not face practical problems, however. It is a question of emphasis and focus.

In his essay on postmodernism[11] Fredric Jameson identifies the emphasis on individualism and the privatization of style as the key feature of modernism, which is why it lends itself so readily to the parody and pastiche that is so characteristic of postmodernism:

> The great modernisms were . . . predicated on the invention of a personal, private style, as unmistakeable as your fingerprints, as incomparable as your own body. But this means that the modernist aesthetic is in some way organically linked to the conception of a unique self and private identity, a unique personality and individuality, which can be expected to generate its own unique vision of the world and to forget its own unique unmistakeable style.[12]

Elsewhere[13] Jameson locates modernism, with its belief in the autonomy of culture, historically. Far from being outside history and the society it intends to "Blast," Jameson sees it as a reflection of the second stage of capitalism. It is eventually to be absorbed and appropriated by mid-twentieth-century capitalism, and reified in universities, Hollywood, television, and multinational company headquarters. It was both revolutionary and reactionary. It seeks to create a utopia, either through the technology or systems that modernity had brought us, or through a rejection of them and an escape into the depoliticized, dehistoricized world of pure language, pure image, or pure form. Its abstraction seeks to transcend history and is sometimes a rejection of bourgeois values and sometimes a rejection of the collective masses. It is for the few, either because the few will lead humanity to the utopia, or because humanity as a whole is too stupid to understand what artists understand. Yet the canonical modernist texts, particularly the poetry of Pound and Eliot, contain an inherent contradiction and paradox. As Stan Smith explains: "The great Modernist texts return repeatedly to remotest origins for the authority to speak, seeking in Homer, Virgil, Propertius, Li Po, Dante, etc., the authorising pre-text of their discourse. In the process they appear to turn their backs upon Eliot's 'immense panorama of futility and anarchy which is contemporary history.' Yet everywhere in their work that repressed returns."[14] Smith argues that modernism's textual and historical sources need to be acknowledged "not from any antiquarian interest, but to understand how these sources are used to manufacture a profoundly contemporary configuration, making what Walter Benjamin called a 'constellation of the present with innumerable pasts."[15]

It is precisely modernism's spurning of history, in its manifestos if not in its actual practice, that irked Wharton so. This denial of history has been seen as an Oedipal desire on the part of modernists to free themselves from their Victorian parents or their Edwardian elder siblings.[16] In a stroke, manifestos such as Woolf's "Mr. Bennett and Mrs. Brown" (1924) and Forster's *Aspects of the Novel* (1927) sought to cast aside the narrowness of Victorian and Edwardian art. Such a clear repudiation of the past stemmed from a conflicting response to history and the material world. In short "[t]he Edwardians responded directly in their fiction to the events of their time; the Modernists née Georgians proclaimed themselves emancipated from history, inhabitants of a world of art governed not by the vagaries of daily events but by timeless aesthetic standards, disinterested creation, and universal human concerns."[17] Wharton objected to this sweeping aside of her generation of writers not simply because these manifestos rejected her personally (though by implication they certainly did) but because they rejected history and regarded the social novel as a vulgar form preoccupied with the things of the world. Wharton felt that they had completely missed the point.

Modernism, modern, and modernist are terms that were variously used after World War I by poets such as Laura Riding and Robert Graves and by critics such as Edmund Wilson, I. A. Richards, and F. R. Leavis[18] to describe a process that Virginia Woolf traced to its beginnings in 1910, that Wilson traces to its beginnings in the 1890s, and that more recent studies[19] trace back to Nietzsche and romanticism.[20] Stan Smith insists that, ironically, the trend known as modernism was keen on establishing its own history, and that it stands in a dual relation to its own time:

> On the one hand it expressed the age's will to power, to recuperating like Eliot's Tradition "all the past," in an act of cultural conservatism which identifies with the triumphal processions of the victors. On the other hand, its fractured discourses and interrupted narratives figure the reality of an historical order of exploitation founded in the inequalities of class, race, nation and gender, in exclusion, privilege and, ultimately, massacre.[21]

The influence of America and Americans was great, but it was not created by America. It is important, however, to be precise about how the term is being used, becaue otherwise it ceases to have any useful purpose. As practiced by writers modernism is inextricably linked to the fragmentation of perception that resulted from photography, the cinema, underground travel, and the reconceptualization of time, especially as advanced by Bergson. In the 1890s the philosopher Henri Bergson had asked questions about the scientific description of time as an objective, external entity. Time, he pointed out, was experienced differently in different places by different people. In his 1889 study *Essai sur les données immédiates de la conscience* Bergson discussed the effect and experience of time on the consciousness. In 1896 he developed this thesis, discussing in *Matière et mémoire* the effect of memory. Central to his argument was the idea of duration, which meant that time is experienced subjectively at different rates, and the belief that the Newtonian sequentiality of the mechanical model of time and the universe was inadequate as an account of the functioning of time. Einstein was to supply the physics and mathematics that confirmed the need to revise the concept of time, publishing in 1905 his essay "On the Electrodynamics of Moving Bodies." Clocks could strike the same hour in different places at different times and still be right. Relativity theory was born.

Such an erosion of the idea of objective time was a challenge to middle-class assumptions about the ordering of the universe, an assumption as firmly rooted in France as it was in England. The universality of time supported the case for a universality of imperial order, and science was the handmaiden in this ordered world.

> Bourgeois culture presumed the objectivity of time. Newtonian physics assumed that, for a given way of measuring time, each event could have only one time associated with it. Events having the same time were said to be "simultaneous." A Paris conference of 1912 accepted Greenwich Mean Time as the basis for world time and set up the 24 time zones we know today. Global time was implemented at 10 a.m. on 1 July 1913, when the Eiffel Tower sent the first time signal transmitted around the world. It was assumed that this represented absolute, objective time and this was anchored in science.[22]

But novelists, following in the footsteps of Bergson, Einstein, and William James, challenged this assumption. Proust, who had a family connection with Bergson, began a long series of novels that amounted to a meditation on time. Virginia Woolf also applied the new theories to the practice of writing. In her own famous reflection on modern fiction, she rejected the way realism, with its attention to surface detail, had tried to depict time.

> Look within and life, it seems, is very far from being "like this." Examine for a moment an ordinary mind on an ordinary day. The mind receives a myriad impressions—trivial, fantastic, evanescent, or engraved with the

sharpness of steel. From all sides they come, an incessant shower of innumerable atoms. . . . Life is not a series of gig lamps symmetrically arranged; life is a luminous halo, a semi-transparent envelope surrounding us from the beginning of consciousness to the end. Is it not the task of the novelist to convey this varying, this unknown and uncircumscribed spirit, whatever aberration or complexity it may display, with as little mixture of the alien and external as possible?[23]

The modern scientific language of "atoms" is contrasted with the antiquated image of the soon to be obsolete "gig lamps." The existence of the atom had been shown in X-rays produced by Friedrich, Knipping, and Laue in 1912 and by Bragg in 1913, confirming Perrin's 1908 interpretation of the "Brownian movement" of particles, which were constantly in motion. From the nineteenth century on, discussion of the electron and the discovery of radioactivity made atomic theory a vibrant topic, and Einstein's 1905 theory of molecule movement was the inspiration for Perrin's research. Atoms were exciting new realities in the early modernist period, and Woolf's image of a "shower of innumerable atoms" reflects this modern scientific discourse and its application to culture. Elsewhere in her writing Woolf displays her own Victorian roots, but here she is recalling an important change in aesthetics, perception, and writing that occurred during the period that coincided with Edith Wharton's permanent transfer to Europe.

Although developments in technology such as film, telephone, wireless, and automobile appeared almost simultaneously in the United States and Europe, the political and cultural changes that occurred during the Belle Époque, the name given in Europe to the twenty-five years before the outbreak of World War I, were more noticeable in England and France than they would have been in America. There was more to change, for one thing. The class structure, the inequalities in pay, houses, education, and medical provision and the immense weight of Victorianism created a social pressure cooker that many thought would end with an explosion. In England the shocks caused by the widespread strikes, the presence of anarchists, the militancy of the suffragettes, the sinking of the *Titanic*, the arrival of the Russian ballet, and the sight of planes flying around the capital seemed to confirm that a cultural volcano was on the verge of exploding, causing despair among some. E. M. Forster writes of this changing world: "It is coming quickly, and if I live to be old I shall see the sky as pestilential as the roads. I have been born at the end of the age of peace and can't expect to feel anything but despair. Science, instead of freeing man—the Greeks nearly freed him by right feeling—is enslaving him to machines . . . Man may get a new and perhaps a greater soul for the new condition. But such a soul as mine will be crushed out."[24]

In England Wharton was cushioned from some of these changes by the protected circles in which she moved. But the privileged class was beset by anxiety. Servants were becoming harder to find as office work offered women more tolerable conditions of service. There were fears of the mass of people rising up from the abyss into which social conditions had consigned them. There were fears that an educated working class is a dangerous working class. There were fears that the nation was degenerating, and that the ruling class was becoming effete. Baden-Powell, the English hero of Mafeking, wished to breed a nation of strong men and strong leaders and the Boy Scouts sought to realize this ambition. But if even schoolchildren were going on strike (as they did in 1911), then the revolution could not be far away.

In France, where Edith Wharton came to live by 1907, many of these anxieties and events were duplicated, though less dramatically. There were strikes and calls from the socialists and the syndicalists, the new movement of trade unionists, for better wages and working conditions. Because the Church exercised such a powerful influence, the suffragist campaign was more muted than in England, but other social trends were more pronounced. There was a decline in the birth rate and a rise in alcoholism among the working class.[25] Nevertheless, an economy that continued to be predominantly rural, despite the growth of France as an industrial power, disguised some of the more pronounced effects of factory production and class inequality observable in Britain. The standard of living had risen for both peasantry and bourgeoisie, while the old aristocracy had largely lost their social and political importance.[26] More and more they began to mix and merge with the bourgeoisie, who dominated this period:

> [M]any of them married into the families of industrialists and businessmen, and some even took to business themselves. It was the industrialists and business men who most frequently bought their chateaux and their collections of furniture or works of art. The great banking and industrial families were still more influential than before. After the British it was the French financiers who were the bankers of the world. The amenities and pleasures provided for the wealthy increased. Yachting and racing joined hunting among the main sports, while fishing, shooting and dancing remained popular with all classes and football and cycling races aroused intense enthusiasm. The manners of the richer bourgeoisie were aped by the *petite bourgeoisie* but the distinguishing mark between them, according to one historian, was the absence of a *salon* or drawing room in the *petit bourgeois'* home.[27]

Cultural change was dominated by bourgeoisie taste. There was an enormous increase in the numbers of journals, magazines, and books. Writers enjoyed a high status. In the nineteenth century, romanticism had been replaced by realism as the dominant form of narrative fiction, and by the end of the century the "scientific" naturalism of Zola had taken realism one step further toward clinical observation of human behavior and its causes. There was an inevitable reaction: the novels of Paul Bourget, such as the antipositivist *Le Disciple* (1889), represent one response, while the poetry of the Symbolists with its theory of the musicality of poetry represents another. The nationalism of Bourget confronted the internationalism of Anatole France, and, later, the writing about writing that characterized modernists such as Proust. In many respects changes in writing trailed behind those in painting, so that the impressionism of mid-nineteenth-century painting only percolated into writing after 1900, by which time impressionism had been succeeded by postimpressionism, cubism, and futurism. It was Ford Madox Ford, James Joyce, and Virginia Woolf who were to respond in their writing to the breakthrough painters had made.

If there were similarities between the circumstances in England and France, there were also differences that made Wharton's adopted country more amenable to change. Martin Green emphasizes the political importance of the identification with the modern in both countries, even though its reception may have differed in each case:

> Modernism has never been fully welcomed or acclimatized in England, and its reflection in literature is partial and easily overlooked. But it is important. . . . because it is one of the major ways artists have disaffiliated themselves from the ruling class, and therefore from imperialism. (Because it also disaffiliated them from the working class its political character is nevertheless ambiguous.) In France, at least according to French critics, the writers/readers renounced their social allegiances in the second half of the nineteenth century.[28]

Wharton was never to make such a renunciation, however.

Looking Backward

By the time *A Backward Glance* was published in 1934 Edith Wharton had come to distance herself from the first wave of modernism. Her autobiography suggests that she felt betrayed by developments in writing that were made possible by the assaults on the barriers made by her own generation of late Victorians and Edwardians. The betrayal was twofold. The new generation of modernist writers lumped novelists such as Wharton and Galsworthy together and regarded them as the old guard. Wharton in turn says that the newer writers had taken experiment and subject matter too far. Wharton's postwar view accords with the judgment made by an early critic of Dorothy Richardson who declared that her *Pointed Roofs* was the product of an unsound mind and that in Miriam Henderson the reader is presented with the same "egoistic consciousness and self absorption" that we find in the journal of a neuropath.[29] Wharton sums up her response to similar tendencies in the new fiction she has read: "The amusing thing about this turn of the wheel is that we who fought the good fight are now jeered at as the prigs and prudes who barred the way to complete expression—as perhaps we should have tried to do, had we known it was to cause creative art to be abandoned for pathology!" (*ABG*, 84).

In the essay that opens *The Writing of Fiction* (1925) Wharton questions the originality of the style of writing that ten years before had been regarded by Virginia Woolf and even the otherwise dismissive anonymous reviewer of *Pointed Roofs*, as new, definitive, and different:[30]

> The stream of consciousness method differs from the slice of life in noting mental as well as visual reactions, but resembles it in setting them down just as they come, with a deliberate disregard of their relevance in the particular case, or rather with the assumption that their very unsorted abundance constitutes the author's subject.
>
> The attempt to note down every half-aware stirring of thought and sensation, the automatic reactions to every passing impression, is not as new as its present exponents appear to think. It has been used by most of the greatest novelists, not as an end in itself, but as it happened to serve their general design: as when their object was to portray a mind in one of those moments of acute mental stress when it records with meaningless precision a series of disconnected impressions.[31]

The disparaging tone, with its strong sense of disapproval, is apparent here and earlier in Wharton's essay where she is at pains to emphasize how it was the French writers of the nineteenth century, such as Stendhal and Balzac, who were the real pioneers. They possessed a mastery of technique that she finds sorely lacking in the writing of many of her contemporaries: "The distrust of technique and the fear of being unoriginal—both symptoms of a certain lack of creative abundance—are in truth leading to pure anarchy in fiction, and one is almost tempted to say that in certain schools formlessness is now regarded as the first condition of form."[32] The new writing, therefore, makes a virtue of the condition and perception that reflects mental stress. Wharton rejects, in effect, the claim made in Woolf's essay on modern literature that the new experimental writing is a more accurate rendition of life as perceived and experienced by the individual's consciousness. The preoccupation with psychology will lead to anarchy. Pejorative words like "mental stress" and "anarchy" convey Wharton's desire to distance herself from the new writing that is exciting the next generation, who in her view exhibit an unwelcome immaturity in drawing a line through everything that is past: "Another unsettling element in modern art is that common symptom of immaturity, the dread of doing what has been done before: for though one of the instincts of youth is imitation, another, equally imperious, is that of fiercely guarding against it."[33] Wharton's belief in logic, clarity, and the need to shape the artistic material is evident from her chosen epigraph for *The Writing of Fiction*, a quotation from Thomas Traherne: "Order the beauty even of Beauty."

For reasons such as this Edith Wharton has the reputation for being decidedly antimodernist, reverting finally to a set of attitudes that are distinctly unpleasant: "Many of the least agreeable features of her later period—the deepening intolerance, the reactionary hauteur, the abrasive anti-modernism—surface even more virulently in her critical work, while making immitigably explicit the regressive and rather unappetizing social preconceptions on which so much of Wharton's judgement ultimately rests."[34] Frederick Wegener, whose remark this is, is even more severe in his discussion of Wharton's "'anti-modernist' aesthetic" in his essay in *A Forward Glance*[35] where he argues that Wharton's antimodernist statements cannot simply be traced to the 1925 review that compared Wharton's *The Mother's Recompense* to Virginia Woolf's *Mrs. Dalloway*, the experimental technique of the latter making Wharton's novel look tired and old-fashioned. Instead, they are the product of a much more profound political Brahmanism. Drawing largely on Wharton's 1927 essay, "The Great American Novel," a diatribe against the impact of America on thought, art, and social behavior, Wegener sees clear parallels between Wharton's lofty disparaging remarks about the populace's rush to acquire plumbing and modern material conveniences and her denunciation of the "shortcut" experimental techniques favored by modernist writers.[36] What they have in common is a standardization, whereas art comes from variety:

> America has indeed deliberately dedicated herself to other ideals. . . . As she has reduced the English to a mere instrument of utility, so had she reduced relations between human beings to a dead level of vapid benev-

olence, and the whole of life to a small house with modern plumbing, heating, a garage, a motor, a telephone and a lawn undivided from one's neighbor's.[37]

Modernist writers were bad writers because they lacked education and chose unsuitable subject matter such as "the rudimentary characters"[38] from the "least developed classes" (her own subject in *Ethan Frome*, but mediated through an educated narrator). Only cultivated people should be writers, while a "long course of cinema obviousness and tabloid culture has rendered the majority of readers insensible to allusiveness and to irony."[39] In her two late studies of modern writing, "Tendencies in Modern Fiction" and "Permanent Values in Modern Fiction," both published in 1934,[40] Wharton expresses a similar argument more moderately, saying that writers such as Woolf, Lawrence, Faulkner, Katherine Mansfield, and Joyce should not reject the past, should not be impatient with existing syntax, and should not take shortcuts to the establishment of character. A development along the lines of the naturalism of Sinclair Lewis and Theodore Dreiser is the way forward for the new novelists. Shari Benstock, in discussing Wharton's friendship with Louis Gillet, a museum curator who came to know and admire Joyce, emphasizes her rejection of the new work that was appearing:

> Edith's letters to Gillet make no mention of Joyce, the modern writer whose work she disliked more strongly than any other—although she spared no kind words for D. H. Lawrence, William Faulkner, T. S. Eliot or Virginia Woolf. . . . Trusting Gillet's opinion on literary matters, and unaware that he had changed his mind about Joyce's *Ulysses*, Edith shared her opinions on modern writing and often asked about avant-garde French writers—for example, her Riviera neighbor Paul Valéry, one of the most important experimenters in poetry in the early years of this [*sic*] century. "I don't like Valéry's writing," she said. "When you have a free moment, please tell me how he impressed you."[41]

Wharton is thus charged with a deep-rooted bigotry and narrow-mindedness in her post–World War I comments. At the same time, as we have seen, other, more recent critics have regarded Wharton's writing as groundbreaking and reclaimed her as a "modernist." In her editor's introduction to *A Historical Guide to Edith Wharton*, Carol J. Singley is happy to classify Wharton as a modernist, a view supported by more than one essayist in that collection.[42] Elsewhere, in her essay on *A Son at the Front*, Judith L. Sensibar presents this 1923 novel set in World War I as a rewriting of the masculinist tradition, in which Wharton confronts (incestuous) homoeroticism in a pioneering way. In making her argument, Sensibar has no qualms about grouping Wharton with modernist writers: "To my knowledge, of all the early Modernists, only Edith Wharton has attempted to explore such complicated erotic terrain."[43] This is a view that the editors of *Wretched Exotic*, the collection of essays on Edith Wharton in Europe, which includes Sensibar's study, endorse: "Sensibar demonstrates that Wharton, far from being insensitive to the issues that the literary Modernists raised, actually preceded them with the novel's critique of a homophobic world of male dominance."[44]

In all this there is a shift from a view that sees Wharton writing against a background of modernism, but in opposition to it, and one that positions her in the mainstream of the movement. It is worth pointing out that the editors of *Wretched Exotic* are more cautious than their contributor, in that they do not actually bracket Wharton with "literary Modernists" as does Sensibar. Yet she is not alone among the essayist in *Wretched Exotic* in encouraging the belief that if the net is spread wide enough, it will encompass both Wharton and significant modernist writers. Susan Goodman's account of "Edith Wharton's Inner Circle"[45] emphasizes the following:

> Paul Bourget's membership in the French Academy and Berenson's court at I Tatti in Florence provided the inner circle with a legion of power acquaintances. The literary figures surrounding the group—to give a cursory list—included Joseph Conrad, Ford Madox Ford, H. G. Wells, Stephen Crane, Edmund Gosse, Charles du Bos, André Gide, Marcel Proust, Virginia Woolf, Anna de Noailles (Claud Silvé), Lytton Strachey, Sinclair Lewis, F. Scott Fitzgerald and Jean Cocteau.[46]

But it is important to distinguish between those whom Wharton met (such as H. G. Wells), those (such as Bourget) whose penchant for contriving moral dilemmas in fiction allegedly influenced her own narrative technique,[47] and those with whom she had no contact whatsoever (such as Virginia Woolf).

Elsewhere in this collection of essays there are more persuasive, more cautious arguments for a reevaluation of Wharton's relationship with modernism. In "Landscapes of Desire" there is a call for a reappraisal of Wharton's relationship to "the modern," while acknowledging that such a reappraisal has to bypass Wharton's own objections to the "NEW":

> The "Modern" is a difficult category to summarize and define, no less so at the end of the twentieth century than it was during the years of its rise to cultural prominence. Until quite recently we were not encouraged to think of Edith Wharton as a "modern." The cultural, social, and political

range of the term "modern," despite its global claims, was too narrow to include her. By social class and upbringing, by her cultural interests and aesthetic principles, by the very ease which she engaged European life, she did not fit the modern. Indeed, she represented all that the young fauves hoped to overthrow . . . She has for so long been seen as anomalous in literary history, *passée* in Paris during years of cultural tumult, unable, and also unwilling, to shift gears and respond to the call MAKE IT NEW, that to theorize Edith Wharton as a modern is a direct challenge to those who make and shape literary history.[48]

Wharton's position on what we now call modernism was complex, as was the movement. On the eve of the Postimpressionist exhibition, she went to an exhibition of paintings by Ford Madox Brown, who by 1909 could hardly be regarded as an overly abstract or challengingly new artist. Nevertheless, Wharton did not approve of the work: "There is a curious exhibition of Ford Madox Brown's pictures in London. What a strange unnatural phase of art."[49] In the same letter she reports that she intends to bid at Christie's for a painting by Richard Parkes Bonington, the English romantic painter from Nottingham, best known for his landscapes and historical scenes.[50] On the other hand, in 1915 she approached Stravinsky for a contribution to *The Book of the Homeless*.[51] She expressed disgust at what she saw as the pornography of Joyce's *Ulysses*, yet admired Proust's impressionism. The early volumes of Proust in her personal library are "closely marked."[52]

Wharton and Proust

In 1906 Edith Wharton came to live in the Faubourg St. Germain on the Left Bank in Paris. At the same time, in the same district, Proust began his chronicle of the salon life that Wharton wished to live, and which was about to disappear. What she came to cherish, because it contained all the formal certainties of upper-class American life with none of the philistinism, Proust sought to satirize. Yet they were both outsiders, required to nurture a secret that was officially unacceptable. For Wharton it was the breakdown of her marriage and her imminent affair with Fullerton; for Proust it was his homosexuality. They had in common their dedication to writing, their belief in the cultivation of superior taste, and their loneliness. Both were inspired by Ruskin and architecture, and, a fact that seems a little strange until the explanation is given: both preferred to do their writing in bed.[53] Each saw admirable qualities in the society that they sought to satirize. Wharton, in *A Backward Glance*, sees no irony in condemning the "littleness" in Proust produced by his fondness for the company of dukes and duchesses, in the midst of an autobiography that is a wistful paean for the socially exclusive Old New York society and eliteness of Parisian salon life with its litany of aristocratic names:

> His greatness lay in his art, his littleness in the quality of his social admirations. But in this, after all, he merely exemplified the tendency not infrequent in novelists of manners—Balzac and Thackeray among them, to be dazzled by contact with the very society they satirize. It is true that *pour comprendre il faut aimer* this seeming inconsistency may, in some, be a deep necessity of the creative imagination.[54]

Wharton claimed credit for alerting James, by then an elderly, ill man, to Proust's work. Her account of James's response is revealing of her own attitude to modernism.[55] After reading two pages of the first volume of *A la recherche du temps perdu* Wharton felt herself to be "in the hands of a master, and was presently trembling with excitement which only genius can communicate." She acts, swiftly: "I sent the book immediately to James, and his letter to me shows how deeply it impressed him. James, at that time, was already an old man and, as I have said, his literary judgments had long been hampered by his increasing pre-occupations with the structure of the novel and his unwillingness to concede that the vital centre (when there was any) could lie elsewhere."[56]

Wharton follows this story about Proust with one about Lawrence, two writers who sit under the broad umbrella called modernism. She suggests she responded favorably to the vitality in Lawrence's writing, but reports that James is impatient with writers who do not pay attention to the stern demands of form and structure. James's own novels, however, particularly the later ones, such as *The Wings of the Dove* (1902), *The Ambassadors* (1903), and *The Golden Bowl* (1904), with their detailed rendering of the finer detail of psychology, perception, and sensibility, are themselves closely linked to modernism, as Malcolm Bradbury is keen to emphasize. Writers such as Virginia Woolf, Gertrude Stein, and Dorothy Richardson acknowledged his importance for the development of the novel, even if they did not consider him "one of us": "His works, they saw, offered a double vision of fiction; they carried realism onward into modernism, and restored modernism to its origins in realism."[57]

Did Edith Wharton appreciate that her beloved Henry James was seen as transitional in the move from Victorian fiction to the modernism and practices she later condemned? She was as close to James as anyone could be and would have approached with the utmost respect every one of his novels published after their close friendship began. Nevertheless she expresses reservations that this preoccupation with form could have the effect of excluding "life" from art (the argument James had with Wells), though Wharton remained loyal to an emphasis on the importance of form and structure in narrative fiction. One of the crucial questions to address in seeking to establish Wharton's relationship with modernism is the extent to which she could see and acknowledge the achievement of those who wished to move in a different direction, achievements that Conrad and the later wave of modernists had seen in James, and that James had seen in Proust. Wharton's comments on Proust and Lawrence suggest that she *was* alert to the possibilities being opened up by the next generation of writers. She never expressed a willingness to follow them (a refusal to imitate that may be regarded as a strength, however, rather than a weakness), but that is not to say that she did not absorb their influence. On the other hand, her own reported impatience with the difficulty of the later James style, and her apparent silence on the work of Joyce, Ford, Virginia Woolf, and Dorothy Richardson does not suggest a sympathy with modernism as a whole. Yet she is not unaware of their work and Benstock offers a revealing description of Wharton's own response to the criticism that her 1925 novel, *The Mother's Recompense*, was unambitious:

> In the London *Saturday Review*, Gerald Bullett described *The Mother's Recompense* as a "well-staged drama in which the expected always happens." Comparing it to Virginia Woolf's new novel *Mrs. Dalloway*, he called Woolf a "brilliant experimentalist," while Edith Wharton was "content to practice good craftsmanship without enlarging" the scope of the novel as a genre. Edith agreed that it was an "old-fashioned novel." She was not trying to follow the new methods ("as May Sinclair so pantingly and anxiously does"), she wrote to John Hugh: "My heroine belongs to the day when scruples existed."[58]

Ostensibly Wharton's comment resonates with some of the pompous Olympian majesty of a Lady Bracknell, and seems to equate experiment with want of moral purpose. In 1925 Wharton was sixty-three and either ignored or dismissed by the generation of modernist writers who had followed her. In Virginia Woolf's essay "American Fiction" she was grouped with Henry James, and though these writers' achievements were acknowledged by Woolf, ultimately her verdict was that "[t]hey do not give us anything we have not got already."[59] The position was reinforced by the fact that contemporary writers such as Pound did not recognize James as an important link between their work and the writing of the nineteenth century. Pound was contemptuous of James, as was Ford Madox Ford. They both considered him bound up in his own insularity, impervious to external thought, and overfussy. The fact that Wharton and James inhabited the salon world of Paris made them products of an era that had passed. On the other hand, Woolf herself was not uncomplicated in her own reaction to what are now seen as the key works of modernism. She, the scourge of the generation of Edwardian writers epitomized by Arnold Bennett, nevertheless was unpersuaded by the experimental method evident in the opening chapters of *Ulysses*.[60] She disparages Joyce's work almost as much as Wharton did. The period creates some unexpected alliances and paradoxes.

REALISM, NATURALISM, SYMBOLISM, VORTICISM . . . AND FAITH

In some discussions of the nineteenth-century changes of perception, which anticipated some aspects of modernism, the origins of these changes is traced back to classicism and romanticism and the beginnings of modernity.[61] If romanticism is a reaction to the ordered, rational world of the early and mid-eighteenth century, a reaction that privileges the individual's imagination above the needs of society, then realism represents the return of the values of materiality, of the values of the middle class, of documentary newspaper reporting and the importance of marriage, class, dress, and status in the bourgeois world. The bourgeois materialism that provides the surface for much realism was itself to lead to its own eclipse. The technology that we associate with modernity, including such developments as the train, telegraphy, photography, the automobile, the underground, and the cinema changed the way the world was perceived. In particular it changed the way the world was *seen*. In *Techniques of the Observer* Jonathan Crary discusses the way that late twentieth century cultural criticism has influenced the way that we now regard nineteenth-century modernity:

> The early work of Jean Baudrillard details some of the conditions of this new terrain in which a nineteenth-century observer was situated. For Baudrillard, one of the crucial consequences of the bourgeois political revolutions at the end of the 1700s was the ideological force that animated the myths of rights of man, the right to equality, and to happiness. In the nineteenth century, for the first time, observable proof became needed in order to demonstrate that happiness and equality had in fact been attained. Happiness had to be "*measurable* in terms of objects and signs," something that would be evident to the eye in terms of "visible criteria." Several decades earlier, Walter Benjamin had also written about

the role of the commodity in generating a "phantasmagoria of equality." Thus modernity is inseparable from on one hand a remaking of the observer, and on the other a proliferation of circulating signs and objects whose effects coincide with their visuality, or what Adorno calls *Anschaulichkeit*.[62]

Edith Wharton would have grown up with an awareness of such inventions as the stereoscope, the phantasmagoric effects of the magic lantern, and the phenakistiscope. If realistic, three-dimensional effects could be achieved by the stereoscope, and ghostly effects during a phantasmagoria display, what did that say about realism? Such questions were, understandably, to have a much more immediate impact on painting and visual representation than on writing, and they permeated fiction more slowly. In any case, though as a young reader in the 1870s and 1880s Edith Jones read widely, much fiction was banned from the Jones household because of the supposedly bohemian character of the authors.

Wharton's own pre–World War I writing preserves many of the characteristics of realism, and it is not surprising that Meredith's 1870 novel, *Harry Richmond*, was among her favorites, as were the works of Trollope. But she is also sympathetic to the aims of naturalist writers like Zola, and both *The House of Mirth* and *The Fruit of the Tree* bear witness to this influence. And there are some short pieces of fiction by Wharton, such as "The Valley of Childish Things" notable for their impressionistic style, written in response, perhaps, to changes in aesthetic perception.

In the 1890s an inevitable reaction set in to the deterministic and scientific philosophy that underpinned naturalism. Symbolism in poetry, music, and the visual arts carried over into novel writing, and the following description of the music of Debussy could apply just as well to Wharton's stories "The Fulness of Life" and "Ogrin the Hermit," with their dreamlike, visionary qualities: "*L'Aprés-midi* does not so much go somewhere as weave a spell or evoke a place of magic and sensuality, a sleepy summer's day and a satyr's joys. The specificities and concreteness of realism disappear; the material world exists no longer for itself (if at all) but only to suggest other, deeper truths."[63]

Yet Wharton was not seduced by the lure of an aestheticism that many of her male friends found attractive. She liked the romanticism of Poe and Nietzsche, but was not satisfied with a movement that declared "art for art's sake." Wharton felt that architecture, art, and fiction should always have some moral purpose. In her eyes, aestheticism was identified with decadence. In any case, it was a male world from which women seemed to be excluded except as the subject of art, or as its consumers. Wharton's early fiction shows that she was not unsympathetic to the use of legend, folk tale, and faerie in her writing, something that characterized a strand of late-Victorian art from the Pre-Raphaelites to Beardsley and art nouveau, and reveals a resistance to modernity. As Singley points out, this was certainly the case with a solid Victorian such as Charles Kingsley, whose interest in fairy tales, Greek stories, and history was linked by the need for a moral purpose in them all.[64] The difference, according to Singley, is that Wharton treated such allegorizing with a certain measure of irony. Lily Bart is not really Sleeping Beauty, Zenobia not really the Wicked Witch. Wharton's ghosts are not ghosts, but impressions. The religious strand in Wharton made myth and folklore attractive, in poems such as *Artemis to Actaeon,* for example, as a device for signaling the Emersonian transcendental, but the rational, scientific part of her found the new sciences of psychology and anthropology attractive. The paradox was that Wharton felt she could embrace them, but she did not like it when liberal theology attempted to so.[65]

Important to Wharton's intellectual development was George Santayana, the Spanish philosopher who was exactly the same age as Wharton and brought up in Boston.[66] He was educated at Harvard, where he was a professor of philosophy from 1889–1912, and like Wharton moved from the United States to live in Europe, first in France and England, and then in Italy. His *The Life of Reason,* published in 1905, argued that the true purpose of reason is not in idealist dreams but in logical activity that takes account of facts. Santayana's interests were in art and Christianity[67] and in 1900 he had published *The Poetry of Christian Dogma,* a study that rejected both Calvinism and transcendentalism. Wharton has annotated her copy of his later work, *The Life of Reason,*[68] but while she could respond favorably to his intellectual skepticism, she would not completely abandon her belief in the ineffable. She could not travel with the materialists because she was willing to believe in something beyond the material. She could not travel with esoteric transcendentalists because they became anti-intellectual and scornful of science and reason. That is why *The Imitation of Christ* by Thomas à Kempis was so attractive. It had a place for reason, but argued that there are certain mysteries to which it is futile to apply reason. Wharton owned a leather-bound copy, much annotated and much read.[69] She has marked the following in her edition[70]: "God's salvation is a mystery that cannot be discussed, explained or defined."

Wharton's debate with religion and science reflects the widespread nineteenth-century debate on the same subject, reflected not least in the fashion for religious novels. It is important to remember that Wharton entered the period of early modernism as a person already forty years old and steeped in late-Victorian discourses and debates. As younger men and women, Joyce, Lawrence, Woolf, and Gertrude Stein had much less baggage to jettison.

❖

Vorticism was the name given by Wyndham Lewis to a movement that corresponded closely to the most aggressive and celebratory form of what was later called modernism, and at the very moment of its arrival, Wharton seems to take a backward-looking move in her fiction. In 1910, the year in which Virginia Woolf said "human character changed,"[71] Edith Wharton published a collection of stories with the positively Edwardian term "ghosts" in the title. One reading of this would be the most simple. Wharton was too conservative to change. She was too old to change.

There is another possibility. If Wharton's work does stand apart from the experimental literary modernism of Woolf, Joyce, and Gertrude Stein, it is possible that what she rejected was not the experimental character but the retreat from the connection between art and wider society. In other words, it is the political, ultimately bourgeois, message of Anglo-American modernism that she disliked, fearing that the fragmentation of representation anticipated and fostered a fragmentation in society as a whole (which it did). Her chosen subjects, in the books published between 1910 and 1914, of class, New England rural tragedy, ghosts, new money, French tradition, and Old New York society have a social dimension that put her at odds with modernism, but as Fredric Jameson has made clear, modernism marks an end to collectivism in art:

> [P]erhaps the immense fragmentation and privatization of modern literature—its explosion into a host of distinct private styles and mannerism—foreshadows deeper and more general tendencies in social life as a whole. Supposing that modern art and modernism—far from being a kind of specialized aesthetic curiosity—actually anticipated social developments along these lines; supposing that in the decades since the emergence of the great modern styles, society has itself begun to fragment in this way, each group coming to speak a curious private language of its own, each profession developing its private code or idiolect, and finally each individual coming to be a kind of linguistic island, separate from everyone else? But then in that case, the very possibility of any linguistic norm in terms of which one could ridicule private languages and idiosyncratic styles would vanish, and we would have nothing but stylistic diversity and heterogeneity.[72]

Art, in Edith Wharton's fiction, is never elevated above the social. And it would be wrong to equate this belief in the virtues and importance of the social with a simplistic belief in the importance of society. That society had sought to stifle Wharton's desire and in Europe its national politics, run by the traditional governing class, was to be responsible for the rapidly approaching war. In neither case did she retreat into individualism, but in her practice as a writer and as a war worker demonstrated an alternative to fragmentation and the preoccupation with self.

The Politics of Modernism

What were the politics of modernism? It is a key question, and it is one that cannot be given a simple answer because modernism was not a single movement with a single founder like Quakerism or Shakerism. Even if we concentrate on early modernism as a category, it contains its own schisms. The magazine *Blast*, edited by Pound and Wyndham Lewis, attacked the reactionary element in British life, which it felt was represented by the Bloomsbury group. Unlike them it "advocated total acceptance of the machine age, and a mechanical, geometrical and non-representational approach to art in imitation of Cubism and Futurism."[73]

Modernism was not recognized as a movement until after the period with which we are concerned, and to Edith Wharton what we now call modernism would only be recognized in its separate, specific forms. She was startled into wonder by Stravinsky's *Le sacre du printemps*.[74] She admired Proust's first novel. She disliked "the cult of the self" that she saw practiced in Joyce and Lawrence. She was appalled by what she regarded as the crude obscenity of some of the subject matter of the new writing.

Modernism was not consistent and contained its own contradictions. Those contradictions can often be traced back to the writings of Nietzsche. As Raymond Williams pointed out, there are revolutionary, socialist strands in modernism and some modernist artists such as Myakovsky, Picasso, Silone, and Brecht became direct supporters of communism.[75] Others, such as Marinetti, Pound, and Wyndham Lewis moved toward a sympathy for fascism. The antibourgeois stance of modernism could provide the stepping stone to utterly antagonistic positions, or to the opposite sides of the same ideological rock. On the one hand the politics of communism and fascism were joined in their common elevation of the group above the contemptible bourgeois model of individualism, and some artists flirted with the idea of putting their work at the service of the communist or fascist revolution. Such was the political volatility that some artists moved from one ideological pole to the other.

Raymond Williams illustrates these contradictions by referring to the case of August Strindberg, whose sixty-third birthday was celebrated in Stockholm in 1912 with a procession of the Stockholm Workers Commune. Revolutionary anthems were sung and red flags were everywhere. Yet twenty or so years earlier, the mutual admiration between Nietzsche and Strindberg suggested a very different kind of revolution, driven by a very different kind of ideology, one that celebrated the leadership of the strong and wise.[76]

The issues of gender and power are not incidental in the attraction of Nietzsche for many male modernists. Nietzsche provided a rationale for a pose that allowed male artists to redefine themselves as both masculine and artists, thus rejecting the model of the androgynous aesthete of the 1890s. Nietzsche offered the rhetoric of testosterone.[77]

Based in France as she was Wharton was distanced from this more linguistically violent manifestation of modernism, distinct from its vorticist and Anglo-American manifestation in England, its futurist manifestation in Italy. Similarly, Strindberg's Sweden and Nietzsche's Germany seemed some distance away. Shari Benstock argues that Wharton did not reject the modern just because it was new, but "was far more interested in the aesthetics of the visual (architecture and landscape) than in literary theory."[78] Her literary tastes had been shaped during her childhood and youth, and she was skeptical of what she saw as sudden new fashions.

Wharton, unsurprisingly, was not alone among intelligent readers in regarding the new experimental writing with a skeptical eye. In 1931, when the second wave of modernism was under way, a rather disdainful review of *The Waves* distinguished between the serious and the fashionable end of modernism, and looked back to the origins of the movement before World War I:

> The word "modern" has more significance today than it probably ever had before. No century can have been so conscious of its difference from other centuries as the twentieth. To go into this consciousness, this "modernism," would require a great deal of space; but if we confine ourselves to the arts, and to a very brief glance at them, we observe, beginning several years ago, a considerable number of clever people—not necessarily artists—who nevertheless desired to "express themselves." (Some began in poetry or painting and ended in advertising or lampshades.) They were much too ingenious, too renascent, to be content with the art forms that they found. Change, unconventionality, experiment were in the air. In literature, in prose, the old novel form displeased them. They wanted "new forms." It irked them to be confined to realistic narration, which precluded a language like that of the Elizabethans, which they

envied. . . . In *The Waves* we see what happens to an amiable talent that lacks an inner drive; we see virtuosity that has finally become disconnected from inspiration, virtuosity therefore that has lost its original charm and turned into a formula; we see a torrent of imagery because the imagist tap has been left running. In *Ulysses* we see a genuine work of art. It has nothing to do with the tea-room modernism that we have been discussing.[79]

Wharton would have agreed with this assessment of Woolf, but included Joyce in a similarly disparaged category.[80] At the time that these two writers were beginning their journey into experimental prose, Edith Wharton was using a very nineteenth-century subject to confront the questions about perception, consciousness, and psychology that the new century had started to pose. It certainly made her look very distant from the practices of modernism.

THE SPECTER OF THE UNCONSCIOUS: *Tales of Men and Ghosts* (1910)

> Since then he had been walking with a ghost: the miserable ghost of his illusion.
> —*The Custom of the Country*

Freud's 1915 essay "Repression" describes the haunting effect of that which is repressed, which returns, ghostlike, and has to be repeatedly exorcised: "The process of repression is not to be regarded as an event which takes place *once,* the results of which are permanent, as when some living thing has been killed and from that time onward is dead; repression demands a persistent expenditure of force, and if this were to cease the success of the repression would be jeopardised, so that a fresh act of repression would be necessary."[81] The repressed unconscious is not like some "living thing" that can be put to death. It is specterlike, but with the important difference that this ghost is not outside the body, but inside the mind. Edith Wharton would have been familiar with the new ideas about the workings of the mind, not least because she knew William James through his brother Henry. William James, like many of his contemporaries, took a broad view of the field of psychology and was a founding member of the Society for Psychical Research" and became its president from 1894–95. His study of the religious mind, *Varieties of Religious Experience,* published in 1902, was much admired. Edith Wharton was less impressed. Perhaps Wharton's antipathy was partly inspired by jealousy of Henry James's devotion to his older brother, or perhaps there was another, more ideological reason: "[A]long with the jealousy, there was a more purely intellectual aversion: the Enlightenment side of Edith Wharton was offended by William James's modernist philosophical flexibility."[82] Wharton was adamant that reason is something that *cannot* be blurred.

Henry James had employed the devices of the ghost story in *The Turn of the Screw* (1898), but it has long been argued[83] "that there are no ghosts in *The Turn of the Screw*, and the horrifying apparitions seen by the governess and by her alone are hallucinations in the tormented mind of a sexually repressed woman."[84] Ghosts in narratives can be regarded as manifestations of the decentered "unhomely," a word that is the more literal translation from the German of the Freudian concept known more familiarly as the "uncanny." In his 1919 essay on the uncanny[85] Freud describes a supernatural story from *Strand Magazine* that he read during the war, in which a young couple see strange shapes and smell strange smells at night, after examining a curiously shaped table with carvings of crocodiles on it. The strangeness of the table conjures up the crocodiles.[86]

Nicholas Royle[87] sees the concept of the uncanny as central to the philosophical debates about modernity, citing Heidegger's thesis that the ordinary is extraordinary,[88] and that the feeling of being not-at-home in the world is the characteristic feature of the human condition. Invented in the eighteenth-century age of reason and enlightenment, the concept of the uncanny marks the baffling boundaries of the rational. Kristeva has argued in *Strangers to Ourselves*[89] that Freud's 1919 essay changes the way we regard politics and ethics, as we experience and see the foreignness of ourselves. And as Cixous has demonstrated, the uncanny conjures up the sense of being doubled that is allied to writing and to reading, when we write and read another self. For Cixous.[90] Freud's essay is less an essay than a theoretical novel. Poe, Dostoevski, and Kafka all explore the uncanny. Royle considers Knut Hamsun's *Hunger*, a novel of performed madness, in which the writer hero eats his own text to stave off hunger. It is the first modernist novel, he claims. Bohemian hunger is not a subject that Wharton writes about with much sympathy, and when she seems to be wanting to, as in *Hudson River Bracketed* (1929) and *The Gods Arrive* (1932), the rhetoric verges on melodrama.

In another part of his essay[91] Freud refers to the fascination with the concept of the evil eye, which had been studied by the Hamburg oculist Seligman in 1910. One of the most well-known stories in *Tales of Men and Ghosts* is "The Eyes," first published in *Scribner's Magazine* in 1910. Culwin, the host and narrator of the story within the story, begins by telling of his stay near New York with his aunt, who had known Washington Irving. She lived "not far from Irvington, in a damp Gothic villa"[92] A cousin, Alice Nowell, is supplied to copy the book he is writing. There is a hint of some flirtation, but Culwin regards Alice as a dull, plain girl and announces his intention to leave for Europe. She kisses him, he feels guilty, and they become engaged. He sees the eyes for the first time, and the description anticipates aspects of Freud's 1919 essay:

> [T]he sensation of being thus gazed at was far from pleasant, and you might suppose that my first impulse would have been to jump out of bed and hurl myself on the invisible figure attached to the eyes. But it wasn't—my impulse was simply to lie still . . . I can't say whether this was due to an immediate sense of the uncanny nature of the apparition— to the certainty that if I did jump out of bed I should hurl myself on nothing—or merely to the benumbing effects of the eyes themselves.
> (*CS, 1891–1910*, 810)

He leaves the house and the country because of the eyes and goes to England and Rome. Although he has effectively abandoned Alice, she remains in touch, and one day in Rome her cousin Gilbert Noyes, himself a would-be writer, appears. Culwin enjoys his company and appearance, and there is more than a hint of homoeroticism in the description of the relationship. But then history repeats itself as Culwin, at the last moment, cannot bring himself to say what a bad writer the boy is. Having been "kind" to him, the eyes appear and continue to appear for some time. They only disappear when he finally brings it upon himself to tell the truth. Noyes leaves, takes a job as a clerk in a consulate in China, and becomes fat and married. The story returns to the present, and Culwin is seen to have the very eyes that he has been describing.

The fear of the "evil eye" is an ancient one, and is founded on the belief that some people have the power to send noxious substances darting from their eyes, which will lead to the destruction of whatever is the subject of their gaze. Freud explains this belief as follows:

> There never seems to have been any doubt about the source of this dread. Whoever possesses something that is at once valuable and fragile is afraid of other people's envy, in so far as he projects on to them the envy he would have felt in their place. A feeling like this betrays itself by a look even though it is not put into words; and when a man is prominent owing to noticeable, and particularly owing to unattractive attributes, other people are ready to believe that his envy is rising to a more than usual degree of intensity and this intensity will convert it into effective action.

What is feared is thus a secret intention of doing harm, and certain signs are taken to mean that that intention has the necessary power at its command.[93]

Mr. Andrew Culwin, who is both the subject and object of the gaze, is presented as a man of unattractive attributes: "'He can never have looked like anything but a bundle of sticks,' Murchard had once said of him. 'Or a phosphorescent log, rather,' some one else amended; and we recognized the happiness of this description of his small squat trunk, with the red blink of the eyes in a face like mottled bark." (*CS, 1891–1910,* 811). From the beginning he is defined as a "spectator, a humorous, detached observer of the immense muddled variety show of life. . . . who cowered gnome-like among his cushions, dissembling himself in a protective cloud of smoke."[94] In his narrative he likens himself to "the trustful spectator who has given his gold watch to the conjurer, and doesn't know in what shape he'll get it back when the trick is over."[95] This preoccupation with the act of seeing and observing corresponds to the reassessment of the ways of looking that had been brought about by photography, painting, and the cinema. Wharton herself was keenly interested in the visual representation of landscapes, gardens, and architecture and the aesthetics of visual perception.

In her story Wharton enters the territory explored by psychoanalysis (even though "The Eyes" has all the trappings of a traditional story of the supernatural) by making the eyes disembodied. They are finally revealed to be a projection of Culwin's own eyes, something he had half suspected.[96] They are thus the product of his repressed guilt, most obviously feelings about his own deceit of others, but more interestingly perhaps, his own deceit of himself if the homoerotic element is there to suggest the repression of his own sexuality. Terry Castle has shown how the "overindulgence in poetic or erotic fancies" prompts "the appearance of spectral forms."[97] Society has attempted the regulation of desire through religion (as shown in *The Turn of the Screw*), through clinical psychoanalysis (as shown by Freud's case studies), and through self-regulation (as discussed by Foucault in *The History of Sexuality* and *Discipline and Punish*). "The Eyes" is a story of self-regulation in which the controlling gaze of the panopticon has been internalized, but returns to the surface through the relating of the narrative. At the end of the story the "eyes," which at first seemed temporary and eventually driven from his experience, have their permanent, indelible place on his face. He is his own nightmare.

After the war Wharton was dismissive of Freudian analysis, and lumped it with occultism as a form of specious nonsense. In a 1922 letter to Bernard and Mary Berenson, she sends a note of recommendation for a young woman, Philomenè de Lévis-Mirepoix. The note reveals Wharton's enthusiasm for intellectual rigor and clear thinking:

> The more you see of her, the more you will both like her; & both you and Mary can do so much to carry on the kind of mental training which you saw her need of last year, that I want to give you a reminder. The pity is that, as you saw her, her charming eager helpless intelligence has not been left empty, but filled with third rate flashy rubbish of the kind that most enervates the mental muscles—"occultism," the Sar Perladan mediums ("after all there *is* something in it"), vital fluids, & all the lyre—or the lie! . . . But something can be done—& is still, I'm sure, worth doing!—Above all, please ask Mary not to befuddle her with Freudianism and all its jargon. She'd take to it like a duck to—sewerage. And what she wants is to develop the *conscious,* & not grub after the sub-conscious. She wants to be taught first to see, to attend, to reflect.[98]

It may appear surprising, therefore, that with her "self-declared role as the priestess of reason"[99] and her impatience with those who were skeptical about the value of scientific knowledge, that Wharton should be so interested in the idea of ghosts. It is even more surprising when we consider the relationship between the belief in ghosts, mysticism, and the feminine. The Theosophy movement, which had been founded by Madame Blavatsky, who outlined its beliefs in *The Secret Doctrine* (1888), had its origins in the seances conducted by Helena Petrovna Blavatsky, in which she claimed to receive mystic messages from her Eastern Mahatmas. When Blavatsky died in 1891, the leadership was taken up by Annie Besant, and in her study, *The Divine Feminine,* Joy Dixon shows how many active suffragists and feminists became involved in the movement, which offered a distinctly "feminine" form of spirituality.[100] Theosophy appealed to many women, as it "made explicit connections between ancient wisdom and feminine, maternal power, and between European scientific rationalism and patriarchal rule."[101] It produced a discourse that informed the experimental novels of May Sinclair and Dorothy Richardson, who saw their feminist, mystical, and artistic beliefs as complementary.

Such a cocktail of feminism, mysticism, and antirationalist spirituality was no doubt anathema to Edith Wharton, whose skepticism would not have been tempered by the fact that in 1885 the Society for Psychical Research, which the unadmired (by Edith Wharton)

William James had helped found, had declared Madame Blavatsky an imposter (even though my enemy's enemy is sometimes my friend). Wharton does not seem to have been convinced by the possibility that the world was entering a New Age, and that Eastern religious wisdom was the salvation that the materialist and industrialized West was looking for. Even the fact that Theosophy drew on the rhetoric of Darwinism, seeing human development subject to evolutionary stages did not make it more acceptable. The "discovery" and launching of Juddu Krishnamurti in 1909 may have attracted widespread interest in the claim that a new world teacher had been discovered, but Wharton seems to have remained immune.

This resistance to the lure of esoteric occultism by someone ready to believe in ghosts is less paradoxical when we consider how Wharton defined her interest in the supernatural. In the preface to *Ghosts,* her final collection of stories, Wharton claims that it is less a question of belief and more a question of certain kinds of experience. Ultimately she defines it as a narrative question:

> "Do you believe in ghosts?" is the pointless question often addressed by those who are incapable of feeling ghostly influences to—I will not say the *ghost-seer,* always a rare bird, but—the *ghost-feeler,* the person sensible of the invisible currents of being in certain places and at certain hours.
>
> The celebrated reply (I forget whose): "No, I don't believe in ghosts, but I'm afraid of them," is much more than the cheap paradox it seems to many. To "believe" in that sense, is a conscious act of the intellect, and it is in the warm darkness of the pre-natal fluid far below our conscious reason that the faculty dwells with which we apprehend the ghosts we may not be endowed with the gift of seeing.... The doctor who said that there are no diseases, only patients would probably agree that there no ghosts, but only tellers of ghost-stories, since what provides a shudder for one leaves another peacefully tepid.[102]

What interests Wharton, therefore, is the representation of a kind of experience that is not normally visible. It is a psychological subject with which she is most concerned, and in this respect we are heading off in the wrong direction if we think of these stories as essentially about the supernatural, or primarily an opportunity to write about her personal life.[103] They are about observable effects. This subtle difference takes her less far from modernism than the description "ghost story" might lead us to imagine. In employing elements of the gothic, Wharton was using a genre that had long shown itself useful as a form for exploring the taboo.[104] The gothic can be seen as the corollary to the Enlightenment, not as its antithesis. It applies reason to the irrational. Wharton's later, post–World War I ghost stories take on a deliberately parodic form, combining comic elements with metafiction references.[105] The genre was versatile.

Although the collection of ten short stories was published in 1910 with the title *Tales of Men and Ghosts,* the stories themselves had appeared in magazines during the preceding years, years during which Edith Wharton's affair with Fullerton began and ended. The immediate impact of that affair is evident in the last of the ten stories (as published in *Tales of Men and Ghosts*), "The Letters," which explore not ghosts, but the meaning of reading.

The central character is a young governess, Lizzie West, working in France but failing to win over her protégée. The mother of the child is a virtual invalid, addicted to the consumption of light novels (and drugs?), but the father, a painter called Vincent Deering, not only listens sympathetically to Lizzie's confession of failure, he awakens a passion by kissing her: "They kissed each other—there was the new fact" (*CS, 1891–1910,* 863). What Vincent and Lizzie principally seem to share is a sense of disappointment in their failure to achieve success as artists. Deering has known passing success, but his work now goes unrecognized. His marriage, too, is a failure. Then his wife dies, and he moves to America with his daughter. At first he responds regularly to Lizzie's letters but then the replies dry up.

That would be a sense of disappointment and loss with which to end the story, but then events take another turn. Lizzie inherits some money and escapes the world of teaching. Deering returns from America and tells her he was moved by her letters but could not reply because he was poor. Despite being virtually engaged, she not only believes him but marries him. Three years into the marriage she discovers the unopened letters in a bag. Again, the expected end is not forthcoming. A terrible change takes place in her feelings, but she finally settles for acceptance of a lesser, but singular love.

The power and importance of letters is an important theme in the two novels that were to follow. In *The Reef* Anna's failure to respond to his letters is George Darrow's excuse for his affair with Sophy Viner; in *The Custom of the Country* Ralph Marvell longs for letters from Undine but they come less and less frequently. Letters between lovers are sites for the mingling of language and desire, which is the force that drives the novel itself. They are artifacts that betoken the power of language to move, engage, inspire, delight. Their absence or unread status is a denial of language and a denial of feeling. To learn that writing has been unread is the ultimate betrayal: to learn that spoken words describing the power of the (unread) letters amounted itself to fiction is to rip the veil from the possibility of emptiness that is the obverse of the power of language.

Reason and Modernism

Does the appearance of such a collection of stories as *Tales of Men and Ghosts* at a time when Woolf, Joyce, Lawrence, Proust, Gertrude Stein, May Sinclair, Djuna Barnes, and Dorothy Richardson were producing such different, experimental writing indicate that Wharton shut her eyes to experiment? I think not. Virginia Woolf, D. H. Lawrence, and James Joyce all explored aspects of haunting or the supernatural in their shorter fiction.[106] As for Wharton, short stories such as "Full Circle" and "The Daunt Diana" (1909), "The Eyes," "The Legend," and "The Letters" (1910) all deal with psychological subjects, and often the uncanny element is provided by the ghostliness of letters and writing.

Wharton's next two novels were her most experimental in that form and questions about showing and telling guided the writing. *Ethan Frome*, though very different from Ford Madox Ford's *The Good Soldier*, is an exploration of impressions with a possibly unreliable narrator. *The Reef* is an exercise in point of view that controls the focus and limits the action. They are not stream of consciousness novels, but they would not have been out of place in *Blast*, even though that magazine, true to its name, blasted all the values with which Wharton publicly identified. They are the most self-consciously artistic of her novels. Finally, it is just possible that the "Beatrice Palmato" outline and extract was a conscious effort to confront and experiment with the explicitness of modern writing with its frank treatment of sexuality that she found so difficult in Joyce.

Furthermore, we should not be swept along by a reading of the period driven by her contemporaries who claimed to be in the vanguard of modernism; in late twentieth- and early twenty-first-century discussions of the relationship between realism and modernism, the former has frequently had its champions, Fredric Jameson being one of the most influential.[107] Now it is true, as Jameson points out, that some criticism of modernism is the product of a postmodernist perspective, which far from favoring a return to realism, celebrates irony and the undermining of all forms of representation. It therefore has little in common with Wharton's position. She, like modernist writers, is very serious about her art.[108]

At the heart of any discussion of Edith Wharton's relation to modernism sits her complex relation to rationality and its corollary, the transcendent.[109] The relationship between the rational changing philosophical meanings of the word "transcendent" is an issue not only characterlzled by paradox and contradiction, but one that is explored thoroughly in her fiction. Is the transcendent like the sublime? Does it go beyond the real, as in the mystical sense, or is it a term more accurately used to describe the way that we experience the phenomenon of the world, in the Kantian sense? Wharton's sharp, practical mind favored the latter, but her sense of fear, the Furies, and the religious allowed her to give a sympathetic hearing to the former.

As Singley reminds us, Wharton was a keen advocate of rationality at a time when women's femininity was defined by their distance from reason. She had no formal education but read widely and voraciously, her reading including works of philosophy and scientific theory. In a single exuberant letter to Morton Fullerton, Wharton makes passing reference to works by Locke, Dépéret, Kellog, and Delage, works that contain interpretations and commentaries on such issues as heredity and evolution. Wharton feels it necessary to downplay her intelligence, however, coyly asking Fullerton if he knows Delage's *L'Hérédité:* "And if you do, could I understand it, even in bits?"[110]

Later in this letter she speaks of the "poor dear maligned Goddess of Reason," which, quoting from Milton's *Comus,* she likens to the much-slandered philosophy, a subject

> Not harsh and crabbèd, as dull fools suppose
> But musical as is Apollo's lute[111]

That this was difficult territory for a woman is made clear in Wharton's short story "The Pelican" (1898) where a woman gives lectures on subjects ranging from Keats and Ruskin to Theosophy and evolution to fund her son's education. The male narrator presents her as foolish, and there is a caustic description of the awfulness of her lectures. This may have been Wharton's way of disguising commitment to something that she knew was the subject of male prejudice. In 1925 Wharton called herself, only half mockingly and fully aware of the paradox, the "priestess of the Life of Reason."[112]

Reason, Religion, and Transcendentalism

On the other hand, Wharton's advocacy of reason never extinguished her latent sense of the spiritual and her acknowledgment of the limits of reason. By the end of her life, her library contained more books on religious subjects than on any other, and included a much-marked copy of *The Imitation of Christ* by Thomas à Kempis. Toward the end of this influential celebration of the devotional, imitative Christian life, Thomas à Kempis insists on the limitation of the powers of reason:

> Human reason is weak, and may be deceiving; but true faith cannot be deceived.
> All reason and natural investigation ought to follow, and not precede or infringe upon it.
> For faith and love are here most especially predominant and operate by occult ways in the most holy and super-excelling Sacrament.
> God, the eternal and immense, of power infinite, doth things great and inscrutable in heaven and in earth; and there is no searching out His wonderful works.
> If the works of God were such that could easily be comprehended by human reason, they could neither be called wonderful or unspeakable.[113]

Wharton's comment that one of the few things that she disliked about England was the fact that you were required to attend church every Sunday may suggest a secular outlook, but that is far from the case. Wharton's lifelong dialogue with religion is traceable to her adolescent infatuation with the Reverend Dr. Washburn, the father of her close friend Emelyn Washburn. Edith Jones was thirteen, and for the next three years her friend's father became the object of an adolescent crush. A father figure who combined spirituality with learning, Wharton's infatuation, in Singley's view, resulted in the eroticization of religion and a possible source of the incest theme, which surfaces in a number of Wharton's works. The fascination with religion and its erotic power is clearly marked in the short stories, "The Hermit and the Wild Woman" (1906) and "The Duchess at Prayer" (1900), and the sacred and the profane intermingle throughout her first published novel, *The Valley of Decision*, where, for example, the object of desire is a nun.

It would be wrong to suggest that religion was simply an outlet for suppressed sexuality. It was a source of intellectual inquiry for Wharton, as she subjected herself to the full spectrum of Christian doctrine, from Calvinism to Catholicism. The same Edith Wharton who could describe herself as the priestess of reason (a phrase that contains its own paradox) and who could express a keen interest in anthropology, engineering, and the biological sciences could also see the virtues of the transcendental romanticism of Emerson and the other transcendentalists. It is the transcendentalist in Whitman that made him such an attractive poet, and the discovery of Nietzsche led her to recognize the passionate celebration of life and the joyous assertiveness of both men. Wharton sought out this assertiveness throughout her life, and although men such as Egerton Winthrop, Walter Berry, Paul Bourget, Henry James, and Bernard Berenson, who were her intellectual companions between 1900 and World War I, expanded her aesthetic, philosophical, and literary knowledge, they all disappointed her when it came to moral strength, none more so than Fullerton, who completely failed her. Fullerton, like Teddy Wharton and Henry James, leaned on her at a time when she would have appreciated someone on whom she could lean.

At the time of the first wave of modernism, 1908–15, Wharton's transcendentalism was submerged beneath her impatience with thinking that was woolly and imprecise, as some of the offshoots of transcendentalism could be. As Carol Singley has pointed out, Wharton's early short story "The Angel at the Grave" (1901) is one that anticipates this paradoxical territory. Paulina Anson is the granddaughter of a famous transcendentalist, Orestes Anson. She is the custodian of his papers and house, and dedicated to the writing of his biography. By the time it is complete no one is interested in him anymore, seeing him only as a friend of Emerson or a correspondent of Hawthorne. Orestes' transcendentalism is mocked by the narrator, as his name suggests, but then a young man visits the faithful granddaughter and reveals that her father was indeed an eminent man, but his eminence lies in his pioneering work on the subject of *evolution,* as one of his papers shows. She has not been the angel at the mouth of an empty tomb after all. Her dedication has been justified, and she feels as though "youth had touched her on the lips."[114]

It is possible to read "The Angel at the Grave" as a coded rejection of William James's pragmatism, which had been influenced by Emerson's philosophy.[115] Wharton, as has been noted, disliked William James, seeing in his *Principles of Psychology* (1890) and *The Will to Deliver* (1897) an anti-intellectualism that brought him close to Bergson. It was precisely this strand of antirationalism that contributed to the aesthetics of modernism, with its celebration of the sensation, the vision, the epiphany, the artistic revelation of beauty or the terrible. Conrad, Lawrence, and Virginia Woolf in literature and Picasso, Van Gogh, and Gauguin in painting explore the atavistic and the primitive, myth and symbol, the affective and the individual. Wharton was suspicious of this aesthetic turn, seeing it as regressive and preoccupied with the abnormal and the pathological. She did not dismiss the next generation as artists, but was critical of what she saw as an absence of moral purpose, of form and of concern with society as a whole. In 1921, at the beginning of the second wave of modernism, she wrote of Proust's *Sodome et Gomorrhe:* "The last Proust is really amazing, but I think he has fourvoyé himself in a subject that can't lead anywhere in art, & belongs only to pathology. What a pity he didn't devote himself to the abnormalities of the normal, which offer a wide enough & untilled enough field, heaven knows."[116] Part

3: APART FROM MODERNISM? 113

of her antipathy springs from her dislike of any sympathetic treatment of homosexuality. In her more measured 1934 reassessment of Proust's achievement Wharton identified both his strengths and his weaknesses:

> Genius he had, and to a prodigious degree, Fortune had perhaps endowed him more lavishly with natural gifts than any French writer of fiction since Balzac. If he had known how to use them as the far less lavishly gifted Flaubert used his—and the "Education Sentimentale" offers many a valuable points of comparison—Proust might have been the new Balzac, the great master he just failed of becoming.
> As the years pass, and my view of him falls more and more into perspective, I find it but little changed in its main lines. I thought then, and I think now, that his intellectual speculations hampered his genius as a story teller, and that the mist of Bergsonian metaphysics, which now and then thickens to a fog, not only impedes the progress of his tale, but frequently blurs the vivid faces of his protagonists.[117]

In this reappraisal of Proust Wharton stresses the importance of character. That is what Proust remembers, she claims, and that is his achievement. Her assessment of his work as marking the end of a movement, rather than the beginning of a new one, was prescient in the sense that many now see modernism as the conclusion of nineteenth-century movements such as romanticism (transferred to the city). Wharton reconsiders the shock of the new, and sees its reputation as misleading: "When 'Du Côté de chez Swann' gave us its first electrical shock I suppose we all thought: 'Here is an innovator! Here is new wine in a new bottle!' But, though there is a certain sense in which genius is always new, the great originators draw as much from the past as from the present—and Proust was no exception. Indeed it is truer to say of him—though few would have said it when his first volumes appeared—that he ends the long and magnificent line of nineteenth century novelists, than he opens a new era. Even his method, new as it seemed at first, is only a somewhat careless combination of the traditional terms of fiction.[118]

In saying this Wharton was confirming the view expressed in *The Writing of Fiction* (1925) that Proust, who "ten or twelve years ago seemed to many an almost unintelligible innovator" has been transferred to "his rightful place in the great line of classic tradition."[119] This is the preliminary, however, for an attack on the kind of experimental writing Wharton does not like, where innovation is seen as a product emanating from those lacking in cultural resource: "It is as much the lack of general culture as of original vision which makes so many of the younger novelists, in Europe and America, attach undue importance to trifling innovations. Original vision is never much afraid of using accepted forms; and only the cultivated intelligence escapes the danger of regarding as intrinsically new what may be a mere superficial change, or the reversion to a discarded trick of technique."[120]

I have called Wharton's comment that Proust marks the summation rather than the beginning of a movement as prescient. It is also a very convenient view for a much older novelist (Edith Wharton was seventy-two), concerned that her work was now looking old-fashioned and backward-looking, to hold. In finally discounting Proust's method as "a somewhat careless combination of the traditional forms of fiction"[121] and as a practice hampered by the mists of Bergsonian metaphysics, Wharton's remarks sound complacent. It does not confront what novelists such as Proust, Joyce, and Woolf were trying to do. In this sense Wharton is at odds with modernism. But in recognizing the achievement of Proust, and in acknowledging approvingly that he was more interested in the inward drama of life than in its outward accidents,"[122] Wharton takes up a complex position on the subject of new French writing.

In her 1925 essay on Proust Edith Wharton dwelt at greater length on Proust's experimental technique, and though she finds much to praise, most notably his dedication to the discipline of writing,[123] her enthusiasm is for a Proust that she wishes to reclaim as part of a longer French tradition. She thus plays down his association with experimental modernism:

> If at first Proust seemed so revolutionary it was partly because of his desultory manner and parenthetical syntax, and chiefly because of the shifting emphasis resulting from his personal sense of values. The points on which Proust lays the greatest stress are often those inmost tremors, waverings, and contradictions which the conventions of fiction have hitherto subordinated to more generalized truths and more rapid effects. Proust bends over them with unwearied attention. No one else has carried as far the analysis of half-conscious states of mind, obscure associations of thought and gelatinous fluctuations of mood; but long and closely as he dwells on them he never loses himself in the submarine jungle in which his lantern gropes. Though he arrives at this object in so roundabout way, that object is always to report the conscious, purposive conduct of his characters. In this respect he is distinctly to be classed among those whom the jargon of recent philosophy has labelled "behaviourists" because they believe that the proper study of mankind is man's conscious and purposive behaviour rather than its dim unfathomable source. Proust is in truth the aware and eager inheritor of two great formulas: that of Racine in his psychology, that of Saint-Simon in its

anecdotic and discursive illustration. In both respects he is deliberately traditional.[124]

Again, such remarks, which steer the reader of Proust in the direction of society rather than introspection, can be seen as self-serving. By citing Racine and Saint-Simon, Wharton is evoking a tradition that she would wish to be acknowledged in her own work. It may well be that it is the shared ability of Racine, Saint-Simon, and Proust to realize and evaluate character that explains her decision to group Proust with writers with whom she herself had been compared. She and the most highly regarded new French writer are engaged in a shared practice of novel writing. But in identifying modernism's preoccupation with what she regards as "the unfathomable sources" and suggesting that in Proust's case at least (she does not attempt to reclaim other writers in this way) there is a clear moral lantern shining a beam into this "submarine jungle," to use her striking image, her observation, however self-interested, is one that is vindicated by more recent historicist readings of modernism in general and Proust in particular. Although Proust's novel begins and ends as a meditation on time, and in the first volume published in 1913 is preoccupied with the workings of the mind and the operation of memory, as it progresses it provides a complex commentary on politics, as Malcolm Bowie[125] has shown. The narrator offers satirical readings of class, the bourgeoise, the aristocracy, anti-Semitism, the Dreyfusards and the anti-Dreyfusards, feudal order and artistic disorder, and many other political matters relevant to turn of the century France. As Bowie says, the positions are often contradictory, everything seems to be negotiable and up for mediation, and the political argument seems often to be one that counsels despair. But the subject of politics and the analysis of society is a central feature of this work, as it is in Saint-Simon's *Mémoires* and Racine's plays.

The irony has not gone unnoticed that this sequence of narratives most credited with taking the novel forward begins and continues as a long reminiscence. It opens with a hugely sentimental fondness for times that have past, not just the treasured bedtime mother's kiss, but the village of Combrai as it was in the last century when the child was growing up and the intensity of feeling that was then possible. Bowie comments on how everything in the novel seems to serve this purpose:

> [W]orkers, and especially family servants, are of interest to the narrator for what they tell of the past. They are embodiments of folk wisdom. They are a living link with feudalism and their language, for all its mala-

propisms and faults of grammar, is a philological treasure house, a rich layer of sedimented medieval forms. Through Françoise, or the street-traders whose cries echo in the opening pages of *La Prisonnière*, an otherwise lost antiquity continues to speak.[126]

Although in the novel as a whole there are passing references to the world of machines and the twentieth century ("certain workers have the glamour of modernity about them: electricians, mechanics, telephonists and employees in the rapidly expanding aviation industry are participants in a huge technological revolution . . . and are seen collectively by the narrator as standard bearers for enterprise and invention'[127]), the first volume, *Du côté de chez Swann* (1913), is rural, in a village dominated by the Church and its rituals and an elderly aunt. The impressionistic style was new, but the pace is nineteenth century rather than twentieth. The emphasis on the slow, languid pleasures of reading contrasts with the celebration of the speed of the machine and the instant moving images of the cinema, celebrated by the futurists. In subject matter both Proust and Edith Wharton look back to an earlier era, but in method and politics they differ.

There are few glimpses in Wharton of workers being alive "to the poetry of the new."[128] When glimpsed, they are seen as downtrodden victims of an uncontrolled system. She does not present the reader with the complexity of Proust's critical view of class society, where capitalist employers replace repression with the creation of needs, excitement, and new identities, so that the workers now crave the new products and enjoy the new machines. I am not suggesting that Proust is the H. G. Wells of *Tono Bungay* (1909), but merely suggesting that he possessed a breadth of vision, an intensely comic vision at times,[129] that made him amenable to Wharton and admired by her.

Wharton approved of the concern of experimental writers to get beneath the surface of things. But she did not approve of what she saw as a flight from analysis to the patrolling of the transcendental or subliminal unconscious through metaphysics. Carol Singley notes that such a development flew in the face of the logic and reason that underpinned clear thinking, clear writing, and clear behavior. In *A Backward Glance* Wharton identified the profound effect that early encounters with books on logic and philosophy had on her:

> [T]he books which made the strongest impression on me—doubtless because they reached a part of mind that no one had thought of arousing—were two shabby volumes une'arthed among my brother's college text-books: an abridgement of Sir William Hamilton's "History of Philosophy" and a totally forgotten work called "Coppée's Elements of

Logic." This first introduction to the technique of thinking developed the bony structure about which my vague gelatinous musings could cling and take shape; and Darwin, and Pascal, Hamilton and Coppée ranked foremost among my Awakeners.[130]

If Coppée's *Elements of Logic* was the antidote to William James's pragmatism, it was also partly responsible for her coolheaded approach to modernist experiment. Edith Wharton was too much the Yankee and product of Old New York society to be drawn into the net of aestheticism, and having resisted the lure of this prelude to modernism she could also resist the more extravagant charms of modernism itself. Scientific thinking and antisentimental philosophy became her guards against writing of the kind that women had to dissociate themselves from, whether it be the "silly novels" by "lady novelists" that so irritated George Eliot, or the novel of experiment that earned Dorothy Richardson such critical opprobrium. Wharton's position on art was shaped by her belief that the fact that reason cannot explain everything in the world is no excuse for resorting to imprecision, a position endorsed by George Santayana in 1905. In Wharton's 1904 short story "The Descent of Man," she is scathing about the gullibility of the reading public. Professor Linyard, a scientist who has taken early retirement, submits to the publishers a work of soft, hazy, transcendental pseudoscience intended as a parody. The book becomes a bestseller, the "skit" on current scientific mumbo jumbo not having been recognized as such by either the publishers or the reading public. The professor intends his next work to be a serious scientific work, but needing money to fund his son's lavish expenses, agrees to write a sequel to "The Vital Thing," in a similar vein. The narrative voice makes it clear that this is a betrayal of the serious purpose that should always characterize writing.

Apart from Modernism?

At the beginning of this discussion of Wharton's relationship to modernism it was necessary to illustrate some of Wharton's observations by ranging well beyond my chosen emphasis on the writing that was produced before 1915. There is a strand in Wharton's postwar critical work that is virulently antidemocratic and antimaterialist. But so were certain parts of modernism itself and that cannot be taken as evidence of antimodernism. Some parts of the essays by Wharton that Wegener cites could have been written by D. H. Lawrence or T. S. Eliot, while others are not so far from the antiglobal capitalist rhetoric of the present day:

> America's sedentary days are long since past. The whole world has become a vast escalator, and Ford motors and Gillette razors have bound together the uttermost parts of the earth. The universal infiltration of our American plumbing, dentistry, and vocabulary has reduced the globe to a playing—field for our people; and Americans have been the first to profit by the new facilities of communication which are so largely their own invention and promotion. We have, in fact, internationalized the earth, to the deep detriment of its picturesqueness, and of many far more important things; but the deed is done, the consequences are in operation. . . .[131]

I would not want to dehistoricize this by claiming it is uncannily prescient of American-owned multinational companies and their influence, because Wharton's fondness for a hierarchical society underpins much of her dissatisfaction with the modern. What she did not suspect was the extent to which many of the modernist writers she came to disparage shared her dissatisfaction with mass culture, and how the 1920s and 30s would see intellectual alliances between Southern Fugitives, T. S. Eliot and F. R. Leavis, all wishing to preserve literary traditions while welcoming certain kinds of artistic innovation. Modernist writers, in the main, were opposed to industrial and consumer culture, which is why in England the critic and influential Cambridge tutor F. R. Leavis found it so easy to champion D. H. Lawrence. Yet in their belief in an object correlative, and in the autonomy of art, she would have parted company from them. Art could not stand outside the society that spawned it. Wharton is always the novelist of wider social and economic forces. That may distinguish her from Eliot and Pound (though even that is questionable) but not from novelists such as Lawrence, the Joyce of *Dubliners* and *Ulysses,* and the Ford Madox Ford of *The Good Soldier.*

In calling for a more positive reading of Wharton's relation to modernism I am speaking of the prewar Wharton and her relation to the first wave of that movement, that is, the writing that appeared before 1915. This was before Virginia Woolf and James Joyce published their most well-known works in the 1920s, and before Proust completed *À la recherche du temps perdu* in 1927. It is not before cubism, but it is before the most striking work of Picasso, and before surrealism and the development of Dada. It is certainly before Faulkner, Hemingway, and F. Scott Fitzgerald, whom American criticism sometimes places collectively under the umbrella "modernists." On the other hand, Gertrude Stein's salon, which was not so very far from Wharton's Paris home, flourished in the years 1908–13. Although there seems to have been no direct contact between these two American women, Wharton's close friend Bernard Berenson frequented Stein's salon and would have provided a bridge between the bohemian and the sedate.[132] Class, age, sexual orientation, and religion separated the two women writers, however, and though Berenson may have provided Wharton with reports and gossip, there is no evidence that she used this bridge to find out about this nearby modernist hothouse for herself.

How, then, should we situate the fiction produced by Edith Wharton during these prewar years? There is clearly no point in pretending that Wharton rides the tide of early modernism and closely identifies with any of its writers. She had no contact with any of them and there is no evidence of their influence on her writing between 1910 and 1913. Instead, is it possible to see her works apart from what has gone before and apart from what was to follow? Perhaps in so doing we can read her work, not in relation to the modernism movement, but in relation to the development of art that was to lead to modernism. In other words, instead of concluding that Wharton was apart from modernism, as if there is a simple binary equation, is it worth considering the question, apart from self-conscious modernism (or to be more precise, the self-conscious NEW), what other kinds of writing were there? We might assume that in Virginia Woolf's later analysis, Arnold Bennett and Edith Wharton would have been classed in the same group, because they were both social realists more interested in the functioning of society and the material world than the world of the spirit and the mind.[133] But I do not think that Wharton has more in common with Bennett than with Lawrence, for example, or Ford Madox Ford, though *The Custom of the Country* bears some comparison with *Clayhanger* or *The Old Wives' Tale*. Apart from the difference in country and class, there is a difference in the chronicling of material detail, observed faithfully and fully by Bennett but much less so by Wharton who, with the exception of *The Custom of the Country*,[134] does not dwell on long descriptions of dress and interiors. Is it helpful to see *Ethan Frome* as a spare tale with a modernist character, told by an uncertain narrator like Dowell in *The Good Soldier?* One characteristic of modernism is that it draws attention to its construction, like the Eiffel Tower, a monument that shares the girder structure of the Statue of Liberty, also made in Paris. But whereas the statue conceals the iron inner structure, the Eiffel Tower makes a virtue of exposing it. *The Good Soldier* is much admired as a complex, impressionistic work and it is discussed in the context of impressionism and modernism, not least because Ford Madox Ford sits at the center of the publication of much early modernist fiction in England. It will prove instructive to reassess *Ethan Frome* in a similar way, but not with the purpose of proving that it really ought to be called a modernist work.

There seems little doubt that Wharton's argument with modernism concerned a basic disagreement about the function of the novel.[135] Wharton did not object to the open treatment of the taboo bourgeois subjects such as abortion, sexuality, adultery, and illegitimacy. She was not a prude. But she did insist on the ethical role of literature. All novels should have a purpose. They should be neither "entertainments" nor should they be art for art's sake. To regard literary modernism as a form of writing without purpose is to misread it, however. It may often be self-referential, abstract, and contemptuous of the need for a wider audience, but the generation of early modernists were in earnest and fervent of purpose. If we ignore the photographs of the Bloomsbury set lounging about like aesthetes in their gardens and concentrate instead on Woolf's activity as a writer, if we consider the earnest moral agenda of Lawrence or Joyce (holding a mirror up to Dublin in *Dubliners*), then the charge of ethical indifference collapses. These writers wanted to show something that their contemporaries had concealed, whether this was ways of seeing human behavior, psychology, or sexuality.

The contemporary debate about the new writing defined itself as a debate about "character." In "Mr. Bennett and Mrs. Brown" Virginia Woolf refers to Arnold Bennett's claim that capturing character is more important to a novelist than the plot, matters of style, or an originality of outlook. Woolf agrees that character is important, and that is "to express character . . . that the form of novels. . . . has evolved."[136] She does not approve of novels that preach doctrines or celebrate the British Empire. But she argues that Bennett, Wells, and Galsworthy fail to capture character because they are either preoccupied with the houses the character lives in (Bennett's eponymous Hilda of *Hilda Lessways* [1911] is taken to task on this count), a utopian alternative, or the injustice of society. Woolf seeks to depoliticize the novel on the grounds that Edwardian novelists fail in their presentation of character, and are like boot makers extolling the virtues of watches.

There is a curious paradox in Woolf's essay. It is usually assumed that when Woolf says that "In or about December 1910 human character changed," what she means is that there was a change in the representation of life in art, as demonstrated by the Postimpressionist exhibition held in London at that time. But Woolf's illustration is by way of the famous (or infamous) reference to the change of behavior in "one's cook,"[137] who is now on far more familiar terms with her employer than was her Victorian predecessor. Woolf refers to a social change, which the novel must reflect, and does not seem so enthusiastic about the Russian novel (which would dive into Mrs.

Brown's soul) or the French novel (which would discuss her as a type) or the *Ulysses* of James Joyce (charged with indecency, though this indecency is the understandable product of impatience). In 1910 Woolf's own most experimental novels were yet to be published, so she is not alluding to the body of her own work. Although, as we have seen, she shared with Edith Wharton a reservation about Joyce and an apparent belief in the importance of character, she differs from Wharton in her enthusiasm for the sound of the metaphorical ax chopping down everything that is old, a sound that is welcome unless you wish to sleep, Woolf observes tartly. She also parts company from Woolf in the apparent relegation of the social, the political, and the material to the status of the dross of writing. In this Woolf shares the view of Proust's writer/narrator, that his Sunday vacation walks with his family "remain for me linked with many of the little incidents of that one of all the divers lives along whose parallel lines we are moved, which is the most abundant in sudden reverses of fortune, the richest in episodes; I mean the life of the mind."[138]

If Georgian, or modernist writing, is to be defined as writing which was preoccupied with the life of the mind, Edith Wharton was not a modernist writer. She admired Proust's 1913 novel, which she read (in French) in the year in which it appeared,[139] but she was not driven to write to capture the fleeting moment, as Proust's narrator reveals in his account of the need to record the impression of the three steeples, ever changing their position as the coach returns to Combrai, a situation in which writing so "relieved my mind of the obsession of the steeples, and of the mystery they concealed" that he began to sing for joy.[140] Wharton's writing, however, should be read in relation to the practices and ideas that influenced modernism. This may encourage a rereading of some of the most unlikely works. If Wharton's study of ghosts and men can be read symbolically as a study of the repressed, influenced in part by James's *The Turn of the Screw*, then this would show Wharton to be responding to contemporary questions about and experiences of perception, uncertainty, and the unconscious. She may not have acknowledged Freud as an influence, but these are Freudian, and ultimately modernist questions. Wharton's work cannot be regarded as a variation of modernism because that makes the word so elastic as to become loose and imprecise. She offers an alternative that addresses important twentieth-century questions about society, politics, and power, which modernists sometimes overlooked. Wharton's alternative to modernism includes the "ghost stories" that are described by the Lewises, borrowing from William James, as the product of Wharton's "feminine mystical mind"[141] which the "scientific-academic mind" of Wharton the rationalist was unable to silence and repress. It is a big leap from the 1910 publication *Tales of Men and Ghosts* to the recognizable practices of modernism, however. Human character has not changed in these stories. *Ethan Frome,* however, Wharton's next complete and very different novel, which returned to these questions about society with a framing device that it shares with *The Turn of the Screw,* was a departure from anything she had written before. Its structure and method bridges part of that gap with modernism, and makes it possible to move from one to the other with a step rather than a leap. For some critics it is the novel that has actually crossed the bridge, and is an example of the new writing practices of modernism itself.

In their influential text on European modernism, Bradbury and McFarlane identified four great preoccupations in the modernist novel, providing reference points that survive the broadening and questioning of the canon that subsequent examinations of race, gender, sexuality and engines have allowed.[142] One is the "preoccupation with the complexities of its own form," the second and third are "the representation of inward states of consciousness with a sense of nihilistic disorder behind the ordered surface of life and reality," and the fourth is the freeing of narrative from the demands of an "onerous plot."[143] *Ethan Frome* is the pre–World War I Wharton novel that comes closest to exhibiting these features, and it is the one that critics have been most willing to describe as "modernist." In 1911 Edith Wharton published a piece of fiction that was very different from anything she had written before.

4
Ethan Frome, Modernism, and a Political Argument (1911)

> In 1887 [Louis Poubelle, the Paris Prefect of Police] sought to organise the thousands of workers who came looking for jobs in the Town Hall Square. He wanted this to take place inside, out of sight, and subsidised the first Bourse. Inspired by the Communard Jean Allemane and by the young anarchist journalist Fernand Pelloutier, workers insisted on their right to run the Bourses themselves. They thus created a unique French institution, not only a place to look for jobs, but a space for political development, further training and unions. By 1907 there were 157 Bourses.
> —Charles Sowerwine, *France since 1870: Culture, Politics and Society*

Paralysis and Entropy

Ethan Frome, written in Paris, echoes contemporary European debates and anxieties about health, history, and social decline as well as concerns about intellectual, emotional, and national paralysis. Jennie Kassanoff has drawn attention to the class dislocation, illness, and sterility revealed in the final revelatory tableau in the novella, when the narrator sees the crippled, dependent Mattie and the childless, drug-ministering Zenobia for the first time.[1] The terrible sleighing accident has transformed the formerly vibrant Mattie Silver into another version of the lifeless Fromes,. and drugs signify her fall. Her father inherited a thriving drug business, but it collapsed and Mattie's parents died. Unlike Lily Bart, Mattie is condemned to survive her own confrontation with death and wither into a terrible old age.

Wharton had written the original version of the story that was to become *Ethan Frome* in French as an exercise in 1907. Three years earlier James Joyce had completed "Eveline," later to be published in *Dubliners* in 1914.[2] Both Joyce's short story and Wharton's novella explore dreams of escape that are unrealized because of a disastrous combination of crushing social constraints and the failure to experience the full passion of love. Both end with a terrible epiphany.

Though these parallels can be discussed in relation to contemporary commercial and religious pressures (shop-keeping, Protestant land speculation, and Catholicism in Ireland, shop-keeping, industrialization, and Puritanism in Massachusetts), I would first like to follow up the earlier discussion of modernism by considering each text in relation to the label "modernist" to see whether the very different directions taken in their later writing by Joyce and Wharton are anticipated in these works from the early modernist period.

Joyce's Eveline is a nineteen-year-old Dubliner who dreams of escape from her violent drunken father and the bullying female supervisor in the store where she works. The home setting is one of poverty and bleakness. Eveline sits by a window where the "odour of dusty cretonne"[3] invades the nostrils, inactive, allowing the thoughts of her present and past life to drift through her mind. There are some pleasant memories of her father in a playful, friendly mood, but there is also a terrible warning of what might be her own future, as she recalls her mother's life, "a life of commonplace sacrifices closing in final craziness."[4] She dreams of running away with Frank, a sailor who wants her to elope with him to "Buenos Ayres." She keeps the appointment at the docks, but at the last minute suffers a failure of nerve. Her failure to join Frank on the ship is explained partly by a promise to keep the family home together, but most of all it is explained by a failure to feel, a failure that is attributed by Joyce to the paralyzing effect of a culture that inhibits thought and feeling.

What is striking in this story is the way Joyce reveals this. He does not tell us. He shows us by rendering the description of Eveline's world in her own language through free indirect discourse. The method itself is not new (Jane Austen uses a form of it all the time) but it is the way that Joyce shows the paralyzing effect of conventional, repeated, and stale forms of language that Eveline has absorbed that is different, as the narrator moves in and out of Eveline's idiom. The narrative deftly moves into the conventionality of both cliché and euphemism without reverting to direct speech. Eveline thinks of what they might say at the store "when they found out she had run away with a fellow,"[5] and how her father "was usually fairly bad of a Saturday night."[6] Most revealingly the poverty of her thought is shown by the way she thinks of her possible escape only in the cliché of romantic novels: "Escape! She must escape! Frank would save her. . . . Frank would take her in his arms, fold her in his arms. He would save her."[7] Yet when the moment comes she finds escape impossible and stands at the barrier with a white face "passive, like a helpless animal. Her eyes gave him no sign of love or farewell or recognition."[8]

Mattie Silver also finds escape impossible, and after the sleighing accident she, too, is likened to a "little animal twittering" (under the snow). Wharton is similarly interested in showing how culture and circumstances trap people, especially women. But Joyce is particularly keen to demonstrate how the cause of this entrapment can be traced to language, and in so doing he shows us the inescapable tentacles of that language. Wharton, particularly in this novel and its successor, *The Reef*, is equally interested in showing us how cultural forces work on us. Moreover, both *Ethan Frome* and *The Reef* deploy an impressionistic use of language. Later in this chapter I will be exploring the complex way in which Wharton does this in *Ethan Frome* through the eyes of a speculative, unreliable narrator. But I think we can see enough in "Eveline" of Joyce's interest in rendering the detail of consciousness through its specific languages to prepare us for later developments in his work, most immediately (in *Blast* in 1915) the paragraphs rendered in the language of babyhood and early childhood at the start of *A Portrait of the Artist as a Young Man*. It is in his primary desire to show the relationship of language to perception that makes Joyce most clearly a "modernist" writer. The language in which Eveline conceptualizes the world makes her the person she is.

In *Ethan Frome* there is a tension between the focus on Ethan, Mattie, and Zenobia as "types" of those living in rural poverty and the distilled focus on the leisurely, professional engineer whose impressions we rely on for this narrative. It is recognized that *Ethan Frome* can be read as a narrative about narrating, a quality that would seem to qualify it for the label "modernist," or even "postmodernist." But though the narrative method greatly interests Wharton, she never lets go of her primary concern, which is not the abstraction of consciousness or self-reflexivity but the impact of social and economic pressure on human behavior.

In this respect Wharton's novella has more in common with another contemporary story of entropy and paralysis, E. M. Forster's 1909 short story "The Machine Stops," unlikely as that may seem. Forster's story is set in a future in which the world is running down and human beings have virtually no physical or emotional contact with one another. They live underground in individual cells like insects and communicate via speaking tubes. Forster's target is technology and the dehumanization of the human race. It is the debilitating presence of technology that contributes to the paralysis of human will in "The Machine Stops," whereas in *Ethan Frome* it is the absence of technology that is partly the problem (Frome's old-fashioned sawmill technology and his failure to pursue a course in physics is contrasted with the engineer-narrator's expertise and successful profession). But despite these differences both Forster and Wharton see the novel as an artistic form of rhetoric rather than a potentially abstract form of art. As a result both occupy the border territory of modernism because their dialogue is not just with the mind, but with the behavior shaped by the individual's relationship to society, class, and economics. Another way of illustrating this is to emphasize that Wharton's novel has more in common with the technique of Conrad's *Heart of Darkness* (1899)[9] than it does with the language experiments of Gertrude Stein's *Tender Buttons* (1914). Conrad's novel shares with Wharton's an investigation into meaning through a narrator trying to make sense of the world's ambiguities.[10] The instability and uncertainty of knowledge is characteristic of the epistemological question raised by modernist fiction, as is the fragmentary way in which that "knowledge" is presented as an impression rather than a fact. But whereas Marlow's fascination with Kurtz ends with a revelation of the horror of the emptiness at the heart of the soul, in *Ethan Frome* the engineer's preoccupation is with Frome's history, and the revelation at the end is not a revelation of a "universe without meaning" but one of hopelessness. Its focus is domestic and on the poverty and selfishness that destroys hope in this isolated small society. That is why I am not persuaded by writers such as Linda Costanzo Cahir and Carol J. Singley who identify *Ethan Frome* as an unambiguously modernist work either because it confronts a kind of alienation, or because it has a "modernist message" that paradise cannot be regained, or because it has an unreliable narrator.[11] Such a verdict assumes that modernism and modernity are synonymous, and ignores the politics of the aesthetic assumptions that underpin modernism. Unlike Gertrude Stein, her neighbor in Paris, Wharton did not believe that good art would emerge from the assumption that sometimes language *should* be about itself. It is worth considering Stein's *Tender Buttons* (1911) for a moment, a work published by Stein in the same year as *Ethan Frome,* as it illustrates a conception of the "new" writing that explains Wharton's rejection of this form of modernism.

Stein experimented with language in ways that show the influence of the ideas of William James and Bergson about consciousness and time. The experiments have been described as scientific, and surreal rather than cubist.[12] The title *Tender Buttons* must be metaphoric, but what the metaphor stands for (a nipple? an absurdity?) remains deliberately obscure. The prose writing is in a form which abandons

4: *ETHAN FROME,* MODERNISM, AND A POLITICAL ARGUMENT   127

narrative, attacks denotation, and is not "explained" by Stein's description of it as poetry. The starting point may be an everyday object, but the "still life" studies of objects frequently defy shared understanding or communication:

A CARAFE, THAT IS A BLIND GLASS

> A kind in glass and a cousin, a spectacle and nothing strange a single hurt color and an arrangement in system to pointing. All this and not ordinary, not unordered in not resembling. The difference is spreading.[13]

The effect is similar to that of aphasia and anticipates the randomness of automatic writing, be it that of the Dadaists or Burrough's "cut-up" method. In such later instances the aim of the writing was to bypass rationality and order, a purpose Wharton regarded as evidence of insanity. Stein retained the belief that the artist had a special role in disclosing the essence of perception (and thus did not regard her "art" as a correspondence to a meaningless world) but in David Lodge's words, Stein's artistic aim in 1911 "was to eliminate the human altogether, because the human carried with it ineradicable vestiges of time as a continuum rather than as a continuous present."[14] Wharton believed that the desirability of such an elimination could be conceived only by someone who felt herself to be apart from society. Cubist philosophy, whether applied to writing or painting, produced an art that Wharton fundamentally rejected.

I am not suggesting that Stein's language experiments represent the essence of modernism, for modernism took many forms, but that it is useful to regard them as occupying the other side of a line that Wharton would not cross. That line is the perceived limit that separates an aesthetic that seeks to stay within the social and human world from one that sees art as something that transcends society. These stem from contrasting and irreconcilable political assumptions, and only one side of the line provided the geography that would take modernism to the conclusion that it reached after World War I. It was not Wharton's side of the line that provided this territory.

The different politics that underpin *Ethan Frome* and separate it from *Tender Buttons* are crucial, and to assist an understanding of these politics it is helpful to consider Edith Wharton's intellectual relationship with Morton Fullerton, a man whose political influence is often overlooked because he was also Wharton's onetime lover. His political thought had arguably a greater influence on Wharton than that of the politically experienced close friend, Walter Berry, not least because Fullerton was as much a critic as an agent of the status quo.

And Fullerton published books in which, in other circumstances, Wharton might not have taken keen interest.

A Political Triangle

The relationship between Edith Wharton, Henry James, and Morton Fullerton is sometimes discussed as a complex triangle of transferred eroticism, with Wharton as James's surrogate acting out an *amour* with Fullerton, with James as voyeur and with Fullerton as Wharton's sexual surrogate for the "inner circle" of male companions who were so easily distracted by beautiful women such as Sybil Cutting.[15] Alongside such discussion comes an awareness of the professional, literary nature of this triangle, with James advising Wharton about her work and Wharton advising Fullerton about his. What is often underplayed is the extent to which this was a triangle that supplied a site for a reading of global politics, the special field of Fullerton the journalist. To trace this process, we must go back twenty-one years.

Fullerton's study "English and Americans," which had just appeared in two parts in the *Fortnightly Review*,[16] is referred to in a February 1890 letter to Fullerton from James, who promises that the article will be the subject of discussion when they meet.[17] The letter provides evidence that James was a reader of the *Fortnightly Review*, a journal that concerned itself with international affairs and historical and literary topics, featuring articles such as "Europe and the Annexation of Bosnia Herzogovena."[18] Though the literary subject matter was only part of its remit, its contributors during the first fifteen years of the twentieth century reads like a roll call of Edwardian writing and included Maeterlinck, Max Nordau, Belloc, Gissing, Gosse, Swinburne, Edward Garnett, Galsworthy, Violet Hunt, May Sinclair, Arthur Ransome, H. G. Wells,[19] Ford Madox Hueffer, Havelock Ellis, G. K. Chesterton, E. F. Benson, Thomas Hardy, Eden Philpotts, and Ezra Pound.

Fullerton's article, which was to be included in *Patriotism and Science* three years later,[20] offers a genial analysis of English conservatism and gradualism, showing how the English are flattered by praise from Americans, and have a long experience of making subtle concessions to change when necessary as the means of avoiding revolution and rebellion. It offers an analysis of the temperaments of the two countries, a subject that forms the center of so much of James's fiction. The novelist's letters to Fullerton show that he is a reader of the *Times*, for whom Fullerton worked as a journalist, first in London and then in Paris. James had a low opinion of the newspaper, redolent as it was of the less attractive features of the British mind: "The British mind is the most wondrous thing in nature—unspeakable, immeasurable, awful. And to see it bare its mounded riches to the heavens and the nations with childlike confidence—over the placid water closet of *The Times,* as it were, is to see an unforgettable thing."[21]

James would probably have advised Fullerton on his first book publication, *In Cairo* (1891), in which Fullerton uses the term that has later been applied in a description of Wharton's position in Europe when she decided to settle there: "And to be *dépaysee,* as Frenchmen sometimes say in a word untranslatable in English by one equally precise, is for travellers such a common experience of pain."[22] Although largely an impressionistic travel guide for the Englishman (or American) abroad, *In Cairo* provides evidence of Fullerton's interest in national cultures, an interest that was to be informed by stays in Paris and Spain. In his *Times* reports, and in his essays, Fullerton offered a perspective on international relations that Walter Berry, who also knew Egypt as an international judge, would have provided a much narrower insight into. As we know from Wharton's opinion of James's later works, liking the person does not automatically lead to an interest and sympathy in his/her writing, but with Fullerton there is ample evidence of this interest from Wharton, who was a careful and shrewd reader of his work. An eye and ear for a polished style may have been her specialty, but in reading Fullerton for style she would have encountered ideas about states, power, and imperialism that contributed to her political awareness. In considering what it means to be an American in France, or in England, Wharton decided to confront the fundamental question of American identity. James had advised her to "do America," but though she had followed his advice and examined American Old New York society and Massachusetts industry, there was an older European America, that of the rural poor, that she had yet to address.

Edith Wharton started and completed *Ethan Frome* in Paris, and at first it is difficult to see any connection between the novel's account of life in rural Massachusetts and the French city in which it was written.[23] Wharton tells us a great deal about one important aspect of her Paris life of this period, and that is her immersion in the life of the salon, but the world of the artist, flourishing though it was in the decade or so of the belle époque, is totally divorced from the life of a struggling sawmill owner in the hard winter of the New England woods. Gertrude Stein's *Three Lives* and Diaghilev's Ballets Russes may have signaled the rising modernist temperature in Paris in 1909 as Wharton wrote, but her tale concerns a place in which there is no room for art. The world of strikes, of new technology, and the French argument about the separation of church and state, also seem distant from the world of her novel. In France the political rhetoric was antimilitarist, pacifist, and internationalist, and it must be remembered that on the eve of World War I France had a socialist government. The rise of Germany produced a fear fueled by the memory of the defeat of 1870, so that the common foes of capitalism and Germany were synonymous. The years 1904 to 1914 may have been the years of the entente cordiale, but they were also the years of the alliance with Russia, a country plunging into revolution. Such politics appear alien to the world inhabited by Edith Wharton.

Yet French culture and its attitude to modernism provided an endorsement of many of the attitudes to art, social organization, and tradition that had by 1911 become second nature to Wharton. Paris may have been the city in which Stravinsksy's *The Rite of Spring* and cubism made their appearance, but each met with huge opposition from the forces of reaction and tradition. The antiauthoritarianism of the artist-rebels earned them the condemnation of a French cultural hegemony that prided itself on the authority of the state. There was such a tremendous reaction from the conservative and establishment elements in French society, stimulated by the fear of anarchy (for such was the perceived outcome of the strikes and art that the rebellious factions fermented) that there was a flight into classicism and nationalism. Cubists (partly because of Picasso) were described as *métèques* or "damned foreigners," and their art as "anti-French." Eric Cahm[24] identifies the three central values in classical French culture with which modernism collided, and each of these values had a sympathetic ally in Wharton. The first of these, says Cahm, is "the concept of harmonious order in cultural and political affairs, an order which can be achieved by the voluntary, or enforced, adherence of the individual to norms laid down from above." The second is the "unshakeable adherence to reason" and the third is the vision of man in universal rather than individual terms.

Paris was a creative city that fostered the performance of the new, but would draw the line (the line that Wharton would never cross) when "the new" seemed to promise anarchy. It is precisely this experience of a separate confident culture, with its own strong and specific sense of history, identity, and cultural assumptions that permitted Wharton to reassess in her 1911 novel an aspect of her own history and identity as an American. Wharton's imaginative visit to her subject from the urban sophistication of establishment Paris parallels the journey made by her narrator from his world to that of Ethan's. It is a journey to the very heart of the myth of American identity.

METAFICTION AND THE POLITICS OF AMERICAN IDENTITY

One of the reasons the philosopher Richard Rorty claims to prefer poetry and the novel to philosophy and the discourse of reason is that prose fiction in general, and the novel in particular, can incorporate a multiplicity of discourses, and is capable of weaving into a text its own metadiscourse.[25] Rorty is not simply alluding to metafiction, which explicitly draws attention to its own process of composition, but to fiction as an intrinsically dialogic form, as described by Bakhtin.[26]

Among other things *Ethan Frome* is a story about storytelling. Its subject is the art of narration itself, or more precisely the fleshing out of the narrative from the scant facts available to the narrator. This is not without irony: New England Puritanism, with which the early inhabitants of Starkfield are associated (in the original manuscript Starkfield is located in Vermont, but this has been crossed out by Wharton and replaced with the word Massachusetts), regarded art as artifice and at odds with "truth." This is a novel that is as much metatextual as intertextual. The important and unusual lines of dots that precede the main narrative signal entry into a constructed world, and do so in a very deliberate way. And if this text invites the reader to speculate on the nature of storytelling, it also invites a consideration of myth making—for in presenting the world of rural New England, the novel invites a questioning of the foundation myth of America itself.

It does so by contrasting the rural poor, who are the late nineteenth-century inheritors of the land peopled by the Pilgrim Fathers, with the modern American world that has left them behind. Such a contrast is effected by engaging with the new discourse of the modern world, empirical science. It is significant that this study of America was written in Europe, which the colonists had left behind at the beginning of the age of scientific technology. *Ethan Frome* was written in Wharton's Paris apartment, and between the successful commercial year of 1905 and the disastrous personal year of 1913 Wharton spent long periods away from her Massachusetts home, moving regularly between France and England.[27] During this period, debates about knowledge and the expansion of education crossed the channel and centered on the question "what kind of learning is appropriate for the nation's children in the twentieth century?" Was a classical arts education to be superseded by the need for a knowledge of science and the needs of industry? All these questions are harnessed to empire, because for France, England, and America the acquisition of new colonial territory required engineers to domesticate it and an educated civil service to manage it.

EDUCATION, ENGINEERING, AND EMPIRE

In the nineteenth century there had been a battle over which discourse should sit at the center of the curriculum in schools in England, with modernizers like Huxley arguing for science and classicists like Thomas Arnold arguing for literature. In England, by 1911 literary study was sensing signs of victory: the English Association had been established in 1906 and literary study was enjoying growing prestige. The *Times Literary Supplement* appeared as an additional section in the *Times*. Literature was enjoying a prestige and a circulation that it had not known before.

The curriculum subject English defined itself largely in opposition to science, and there are glimpses of this dialectic between art and science in *Ethan Frome*. The narrator may be a storyteller through enforced idleness, but he is an engineer and scientist by inclination and profession. Ethan borrows the narrator's book on popular science—the narrator recalls that it may have been a book on developments in biochemistry—and the moment signals an early foreshadowing of the idea of the dream-not-realized. Although the relationship between science and the novel has been well documented in discussions of British and Irish novels such as *Frankenstein, Dracula,* and *Dr. Jekyll and Mr. Hyde,* the emphasis on the gothic is often at the expense of the detail of the scientific discourse with which the narrative events contest. It is a mistake to see science as just another ingredient in the recipe of fiction.

In France the debates about science and education had raged no less fiercely. French Catholic schools, with their antirationalist ethos, were arguably responsible for diverting influential "elites" away from industry and science while the abstract training of the École Polytechnique led to a disdainful view of "practical" engineers.[28]

Such debates, about practicality and abstraction, engineering and science, touch on this 1911 novel, and were more developed in France than they were in New England America where practical ability had always assumed prominence. These debates should be mapped against the perspective on political life that Fullerton introduced and the relationship of this perspective to Durkheim's pessimistic sociological reading of material progress that was touched on in chapter 2.[29] In *The House of Mirth* Wharton had traced a world in which a woman is adrift in a culture that seems to have lost all sense of value.

4: *ETHAN FROME,* MODERNISM, AND A POLITICAL ARGUMENT 133

In *The Fruit of the Tree* Wharton had moved her focus to the industrial world and depicted an attempt to apply an idealistic and philanthropic vision to the world of factory work, as Robert Owen had done in the nineteenth century. Both novels conclude on a pessimistic note, with an argument that coincides with Durkheim's view, published in 1895 and widely disseminated by 1911, that selfishness undermines progress in the late nineteenth-century world of Western industrialism. Science and technology, which others thought could advance human evolution, was not doing so.

A more recent French essay that contributed to contemporary debates about politics, philosophy, and culture in 1910–11 was Georges Sorel's *Réflexions sur la violence* (1908), which attacked the idea of inevitable progress and argued for the positive, even creative role of myth and violence in the historical progress. Sorel had trained as a civil engineer until 1892, but then abandoned this career to become a revolutionary syndicalist when he discovered Marxism in 1893. He defended Dreyfus with a passion, but in all other respects his socialist ideas would have been anathema to Wharton. His argument that resistance to the state's coercive force, a power often abused by the state, was the creative historical role of violence had a Nietzschean ring to it, however, that might indirectly have had a bearing on Wharton's decision to draw on a fatal sledding accident reported in the local Lenox newspaper in 1904 and make the pivotal moment in her 1911 narrative Ethan's attempt to end his own social entrapment with a dramatic act of self-inflicted violence. This is not a matter of Wharton reading Sorel but of his ideas informing a discourse that Wharton absorbed, the cultural process demonstrated by Kassanoff in her discussion of *The Fruit of the Tree*.[30]

In 1893 Fullerton had published *Patriotism and Science,* a book whose final section on "Democracy" has as its starting point the claim that "equality of political rights, and an inequality in social conditions is the great peril of the modern democracies."[31] This observation, made by Emile de Laveleye,[32] is acknowledged by Fullerton to be a fine axiom, but in his view it is one that takes us nowhere. The crucial question is the one that asks how social inequality can best be ended: "Are there no discernible causes tending to the extinction of, or else the taming in the savagery in, inequality of conditions?"[33] Fullerton provides one simple but unamplified answer. Science will forward the move toward social equality and therefore there must be scientific advance at prodigious speed. It was a view that still commanded considerable support in the early 1890s.

Wharton was interested in, and knowledgeable about, the sciences of evolution, anthropology, and sociology. They were consistent with her belief in the need for laws, order, and form in art. It is not this, but Fullerton's call for the removal of inequalities in society that challenged two assumptions that informed Wharton's thinking. It challenged the assumption that inequality is a necessary evil, because for art to survive a privileged leisure class must survive. It also challenges the assumption, an assumption to which Wharton subscribed, that the material progress brought about by science is ruining humanity. Fullerton does not call for radical political change, but he argues that the class system needs to be eroded, if not abolished altogether, if democracy is to survive. He notes that the search for equality is "instanced everywhere in the rise of socialism."[34] Everywhere in the West there is evidence of what he calls the "laic" movement, the modern spirit expressed in the impulses that make the temper of a person resentful of authority. Matthew Arnold's "Philistines," he observes, have been overtaken. Theirs was a tendency toward conservation that acted as a brake on change. Science exerted a force that released that brake.

Ethan Frome is set in rural Massachusetts in a world that has been influenced by science and technology. The railroad has replaced the stagecoach, there is electricity, and there are new brick buildings in Starkfield. Inscribed in this novel are debates about technological determinism,[35] the belief that changes in technology provide the dominant force in society and exert a far greater influence on societies and their processes than anything else. Ethan's sawmill is water driven, and water-driven sawmills were being phased out in the 1830s, long before the setting of this novel (which is in the age of electricity). Ethan is all too aware of the opportunities he has missed. He wanted to be an engineer and had taken a year's course at a technical college in Worcester. Kate Gschwend argues that Mattie, too, is unable to adapt to modern methods. She has an unsuccessful past as a stenographer and as an assistant in a department store. One reading of this narrative, therefore, is that their failure to adapt is indicative of a psychological paralysis, and that this is then confirmed by their physical infirmities, caused by their sledge disaster. This reading would support Fullerton's call for the need for all to embrace the developments offered by science and technology, as the engineer-narrator clearly has.

The problem with this is that Starkfield as a whole has not been bypassed by change, yet the benefits are not unequivocal. Harmon Gow was the stage-driver before the trolley arrived, and the coming of the railroad has not made the town any more communitylike than it was before. In fact the new business methods in the new brick grocery store may make it more efficient, but the old store had a more human face. These observations match Durkheim's view that technological change can lead to a disintegration of the moral fabric of society. As for the narrator himself, he represents a similar ambiguity, an engineer/scientist engaged in the artistic practice of imaginative story construction.

The figure of the engineer is an important trope in Wharton's work and one that often signifies colonial enterprise.[36] He is a new professional "type" in America and elsewhere, and invariably a commanding figure. His mystique made him a cultural hero,[37] and magazines such as *McClure's, Century, Harper's,* and *Scribner's* (the magazine to which Wharton contributed regularly) frequently published at the turn of the century articles about engineers and their awe-inspiring achievements. Conquering nature was a central part of the imperial project, and the triumph of the engineer over the land and sea parallels the triumph of American imperialism over its rivals. Frederick Wegener sees traces of the discourse of imperialism in the language used by the engineer narrator in *Ethan Frome,* where Ethan is described with the eye of the occupying colonial power. The narrator's first description of Ethan is that he is the "most striking figure in Starkfield. . . . It was not so much his great height that marked him, for the 'natives' were easily singled out by their lank longitude from the stockier foreign breed."[38] Wegener notes that the narrator's perspective "resembles that of a detached colonial explorer recording the practices and inhabitants of an alien tribal culture."[39]

The narrator is thus more French intellectual than no-nonsense practical Yankee. His language, however, shares something in common with the discourse of the ethnographer, which is how the tone of the detached narrative voice in Wharton's novel, *The Custom of the Country,* has been read, as we shall see in chapter 6. But the rhetoric of imperialism is something that Wharton would have been familiar with, following closely as she did the essays by Morton Fullerton published in the *National Review* between 1910 and 1911. Fullerton approved of American expansionism, taking the subject beyond the vision of a well-known work by one of Wharton's contacts in the Rue du Varenne during 1906–7, Archibald Coolidge. Coolidge's *The United States as a World Power,*[40] published in 1908, sees U.S. imperialism as an extension of Manifest Destiny and this would have met with the approval of what Wegener describes as Wharton's "imperial sensibility."[41] She had, as noted earlier, described herself, only half ironically, as a "rabid imperialist." Wegener notes that "the socially and intellectually conservative disposition of Wharton's circle in the Faubourg Saint Germain" came close to representing "the entire proimperialist elite of the *belle époque.*"[42] In other words, there is indeed a connection between the politics of *Ethan Frome* and the discourses Wharton was hearing in the city in which it was written. But the imperialist voice is only one aspect of the novel.

Intertexuality, History, and the Formative Function of Literature

A reader who approaches *Ethan Frome* having read novels from the mid-nineteenth century and the New England fiction of dark romanticism, whether the Brontës or Hawthorne, will immediately recognize Wharton's homage to these earlier fictions. The framing devices tap into the genre of dark romanticism, but she stops short of employing more sensational gothic machinery, which even in her ghost stories she avoids. As noted earlier Henry James had provided a model of how to use the uncanny for an exploration of the psychological in *The Turn of the Screw* (1898). In *Ethan Frome*, however, the only ghosts are the ghosts of memory and those recollections of former selves and earlier happiness.

Successful intertextuality does not signify limitation or derivation, and in deliberately including elements that remind us of texts with foregrounded troubled narrators (Lockwood in *Wuthering Heights*, the narrator in *The Blithedale Romance*), the novel offers a historical, but uncertain reading of behavior. Like such novels as *Wuthering Heights* and *The Scarlet Letter*, which use the gothic-derived features of dark romanticism as devices that permit the subversion of conventional moral practice and behavior (adultery versus marriage in each case), *Ethan Frome* uses literary allusion to challenge the normative message of the bourgeois realist novel that marriage is always best. At the same time the novel seems to act as a commentary on the American Dream.

To demonstrate this point it is useful to be reminded of the features of American character identified by J. Hector St. Jean de Crèvecoeur in *Letters from an American Farmer* (1782),[43] features that include openness, the absence of class, the appetite for work, and the belief in success and the optimism that was central to this formation of a new political identity. They contrast with the dark sense of foreboding that informs many of Hawthorne's novels. Such an atmosphere of gloom questions the shining optimism of the American Dream, and Hawthorne is the New England writer above all others who steers Wharton from the light of the city to the darkness of the human soul. In entering this landscape, Wharton was revisiting the preindustrial world.

Ethan Frome pays homage to Hawthorne in a number of ways. Like *The Scarlet Letter, Ethan Frome* is an exploration of the effects of concealment, but there is no Hester Prynne figure in Starkfield. Mattie, who initially holds promise as the passionate woman, lover, and liberator, ends up a more shrunken figure than Zeena, defeated by her physical injury in a way that contrasts with Hester's subversion of her badge of humiliation and punishment. In another, passing Hawthorne allusion, Zenobia Frome is clearly the antithesis of Zenobia in *The Blithedale Romance,* a woman who becomes the object of the narrator Coverdale's voyeuristic and fetishistic description, as in a moment of sexual reverie he constructs in his imagination her ample body unclothed and subjects it to his gaze. As for the legendary Zenobia, queen of Palmyra and ruler of the eastern Roman Empire for a time, Wharton's powerless New Englander could not be more of a contrast. Zenobia of Syria married a Roman senator and lived at Tivoli. Roman writers refer to her energy, her dark beauty, and her pleasure in luxury. The Zenobia allusion is deliberate in its irony, and it is likely that Wharton had both the original Zenobia and Hawthorne's character in mind when she chose the name to replace the one of Ann that appears in the French exercise written in 1907, for as a child Edith Newbold Jones had a direct link with the world of Hawthorne. At the age of thirteen Edith had met Emelyn Washburn, a young woman of nineteen, who was the daughter of Emerson's cousin and so part of the Concord circle. From Emelyn Wharton is likely to have learned of Margaret Fuller, on whom Hawthorne's Zenobia is clearly based, and there is a mischievous archness in making the Zenobia of *Ethan Frome* so frail, cold, and asexual. Hawthorne could dissect American Puritanism, but recognized the power of life that the Puritans struggled to suppress. The Puritans themselves, ironically, were a passionate group. They were passionate about religion and good works, if fearful about sexuality and art. In Hawthorne they are seen to be prospering, so that when in *Ethan Frome* Wharton confronts failure, poverty, and marriage her interrogation of America is an explicitly political act.

This Massachusetts novel also interacts with a later Wharton text, *Summer* (1917). *Ethan Frome* was called *Hiver* in its French form, just as *Summer* was called a "hot Ethan" by Edith Wharton herself. The parallels are obvious, in the setting, the sense of entrapment, the theme of illicit love. But in *Summer* everything is again in reverse, this time in reverse to the situation in *Ethan Frome*. It is warm summer to Ethan's winter, it is the woman who is trapped by men and not the other way around, and the sexual desire is released in passionate meetings in an abandoned house. If *Ethan Frome* is harsh realism, *Summer* has properties we associate with Hawthorne's reading of romance: the dark symbolic Mountain with its sinful people, the ambiguity of its "sinners," such as lawyer Royall, the moments of festivity that end in disappointment, the sense of a harsh judgmental community that is almost eager for the exposure of sin on which its bigotry and narrow self-righteousness can feed. Even the summer is tinged with the promise of autumn, and the fleeting nature of pleasure is made clear.

Any consideration of the relationship of Wharton to Hawthorne will also need to consider a reading of *Ethan Frome* as allegory or cautionary tale, with the moral purpose that Wharton thought essential. The role of the narrative in the formation of the reader-subject is well established. Shotter (1989) has argued that the function of language is to provide constraints that are formative and not, primarily, communicative. Thus, for example, the concept of the ownership and possession of property is not just part of the currency of dialogue, it also shapes identity and behavior.[44]

It is no coincidence that Wharton was writing at a time when it was being argued in support of the teaching of English in schools and universities that literature can teach us how to live. Narratives may not originally have had a normative function, but they readily serve this purpose. Gilbert and Gubar make this connection when they describe *Ethan Frome* as an investigation into the laws of culture "and the anti-romantic family romances that may have ultimately determined those laws."[45] In this sense *Ethan Frome* asks to be read as a cautionary narrative, a *Blithedale Romance* without the wryness. The warning concerns the crushing consequences of residual Puritanism, commercial change, and rural poverty. This anti-Puritanical reading takes the rhetorical slant of the novel to be that if we suppress our passions, we become discontented and suicidal. But equally the rhetoric can be interpreted as a warning about the consequences of transgression, of indulging the passions and deliberately straying from the path, when that path teaches duty, with commitment to work and commercial activity as the only acceptable channel for the passions. So, analogously, Wharton shows how the personal constraint of living within the bounds of a loveless marriage is translated into the oppression and cruelty of the constraints of an enclosed world.

The novel is ambiguous in its presentation of the individual's dream of escape through illicit romance. But more fundamentally it shows the limitation on behavior imposed by real poverty, the theme introduced in 'Bunner Sisters,' sidestepped in *The Valley of Decision* and *The Fruit of the Tree*, and only partially confronted at the end of *The House of Mirth*, as Gavin Jones has shown. An anonymous contemporary critic saw *Ethan Frome* as an argument for socialism in that if a crew of wrecked sailors were washed up on a desert island, society would not expect them to endure their fate.[46] The narrative supports a number of contradictory readings: the rhetoric condemns the traditions that deny the possibility of pleasure, but is also harsh on those who are tempted to turn their backs on tradition. It exposes the paradoxes in the construction of Puritan identity.

In the absence of support from society at large, such oppression and the self-regulatory sacrifice that we find in the novel is the product of the need to survive and endure a harsh landscape, and there is a displacement of the hardness bred by the climate and remoteness into the hardness of personal relations. Like Lockwood in *Wuthering Heights*, the narrator becomes increasingly shocked by the brutality of the people into whose story he has intruded. But Wharton's novel also shows traces of another Brontë novel, *Jane Eyre*. In *Ethan Frome* there is a similar dark secret concerning a marriage made in hope turning horribly into a marriage in name only, the discovery of which causes Jane Eyre to flee. Eventually, when Rochester is maimed and in need of her, Jane returns, but there is no such happy ending for Ethan or for Mattie. All have learned to crush their feelings, rather like the women in the story of self-denial written more than ten years earlier, 'Bunner Sisters.' And in the emphasis on the repressed, the abject, and the denial of the yearning for illicit pleasure, the narrative examines the New England "origins" of America and the Puritan territory of sublimated desire.

The Politics of Sexuality: Desire, Transgression, and Power

Desire is often defined as a discursive practice: it can be just as culturally specific as gender or sexual practice and, as Catherine Belsey notes,[47] it is not one of the "givens."[48] Desire for the unobtainable, for the Lacanian "lack," may be discussed in terms of transgression, a process that has the effect of throwing the norms of gender boundaries and sexual orientation into relief, or the displacement that occurs when desire is articulated in relation to objects.

Plato identified desire as the sign of imperfection, the longing for something outside the soul, a longing that materializes in the form of the body. The perfect, winged soul desires nothing outside itself, and the loss of wings causes the soul to fall into materiality. For Aristotle there are differing types of desire: the active, rational, controlled desire and the natural desire associated with passivity. These are not necessarily gendered, but have lent themselves to a binary that corresponds to cultural constructions of gender, and they can be deconstructed through a reading of the transgressive, be it incest, insanity, or moral starvation. The incest theme is explored more fully in *Summer*, but Ethan and Mattie *are* related, and the crippling of the transgressive Ethan and Mattie is suggestive of the blinding of Oedipus, whose very name draws attention to his lameness. The commodification of desire is also hinted at earlier, when at the dance Mattie passed down the line of men, and Ethan fears that he has lost her to Denis Eady, son of the ambitious and prosperous Irish grocer Michael Eady.

Earlier I suggested that the principal character in the text is not Ethan but the narrator, whom we may read as a signifier of the lack that propels desire. He has no lover (as far as we can tell), he has no work (for the duration of the winter), and he has no involvement with events other than to speculate on them. He relies on others to drive him around, to feed and amuse him. He is dependent on Ethan. He is the watcher/listener and in his writing there is a sense of the priest listening to and reporting the confession of the New England community.

In *The Second Sex*[49] Simone de Beauvoir emphasizes the link between Puritanism and the fear of sexuality, while in *The History of Sexuality*, Foucault (1986) describes confession as one of the discourses of sexual practice, especially in Western Christianity. Although the act of confession is something we associate with Roman Catholicism, the drive to expose in court sexual desires and adultery was one of the significant practices of early Puritanism, as the Salem witch trials demonstrated. Furthermore, the zeal with which confession was pursued, and the absorption of the sexual energies into the quarrying and detective practices of the inquisitor, suggests a sublimation of desire in cases of so-called possession, ranging from Catholic Loudun to Protestant Salem. The narrator in *Ethan Frome* is very clearly acting out the role of the inquisitor, and like the inquisitors in cases of witchcraft, it is up to him to put a construction on the story from the evidence available. Moreover, all such stories are at root stories of an alleged sexual relationship, and in Foucault's terms provide an opportunity to talk openly and at length about that which is usually considered forbidden; such impropriety requires silence.

Although not attracted to any of the living members of the triangle of Mattie, Zeena, and Ethan, the narrator *is* drawn to the romance of the young Mattie and the young Ethan, and makes their story his own (we do not know if his version corresponds to the events). But just as Lockwood—and we noted how consciously Wharton drew parallels between the remoteness of her setting and the remoteness of the moors in *Wuthering Heights*—is interrupted in his interest in the surviving Cathy when he realizes that she is attracted to Hareton, so the narrator in *Ethan Frome* experiences a great shock when he discovers that the young desirable Mattie, last visualized in language suggestive of a rush of sexual ecstasy as they slide with gathering speed down the hill toward "death" with Mattie locked between Ethan's legs, is now merely the bitter invalid who sits paralyzed at the Frome table.

Desire is inextricably linked to power, or its lack. In their discussion of schizoanalysis and literature Deleuze and Guattari (1975) argue that desire *is* power. In 1908, three years before the completion of *Ethan Frome*, Havelock Ellis's *Studies in the Psychology of Sex: Sexual Inversion* was published, and although restricted to the medical profession in America after legal proceedings against the first volume in the series (1897), this and other books by Ellis, such as *Man and Woman* (1894), were extremely well known. Ellis (like Deleuze and Guattari) was influenced by Nietzsche, and his "sexology" is informed by a theory of the male will to power and female masochism.

In *Ethan Frome* it is Zeena who enjoys the triumph of power. This power comes from "caring" and from nursing, and it was in the role of "nurse" that she first met Ethan. Once again there are echoes of Brontë, as Jane Eyre's first contact with Rochester is through nursing him when he has fallen from his horse, and Jane eventually marries him as nurse/wife to care for him in his blindness. In such a context the inequalities of power between men and women are removed, and men submit to the temporary power of the nurse. This is the only outlet for power that Zeena has, however, and when no one else seems to need her nursing, she turns her nursing power on to herself. But in the end she has two adults to nurse, though in the way that she is realized imaginatively by Wharton, she falls a little short of becoming the phallic woman, the "powerful and dominating humiliator" (Kaplan 1991).

In psychoanalytical terms the hegemonic effect of patriarchy is that the repression of the feminine is acted out by women. So Zeena's hatred of Mattie is not simply the corollary of her desire for Ethan and the hatred of the insecure or the usurped for her (potential) rival, it is the hatred of one sex for its own. Mattie represents the feminine of dreams, she is forgetful and dreamy, and stands for a particular kind of female aesthetic. Ethan, a dreamer himself, responds to this: "He had always been more sensitive than the people around him to the appeal of natural beauty."

What strikes many readers is the rhetoric of loss—the cooling of desire through lack, as represented by the loss of movement (paralysis and lameness) and property. These are linked when Frome looks at his reduced farmhouse, when an association of ideas caused him "to see in the diminished dwelling the image of his own shrunken body."[50]

These are sentiments that run counter to the more canonical construction of American identity that celebrates desire and fulfillment, achievement and success in pursuit of the American Dream. Countering this unquestionably powerful sense of lack and deprivation there is another less obvious rhetoric. This is the production of new images through desire, which creates a new object for itself and gains access to that object. As Wharton had written passionately to Fullerton in the period immediately preceding the writing of *Ethan Frome*: "All the ghosts of the old kisses come back, Darling, and live again in the one I send you tonight."[51]

The mingling of death and pleasure, of love and ghosts should not be surprising when we consider that she was in the middle of writing a series of ghost stories. Earlier that year, in June 1908, in a letter to Morton Fullerton that seems to foreshadow the ending of *Ethan Frome*, she had described her reactions when she heard that the motor had crashed into a tree: "I felt the wish that I had been in it, and smashed with it and nothing left of all this disquiet but 'coeur arrête.'"[52]

When *Tales of Men and Ghosts* was finished in June 1910 Edith Wharton began work on *Ethan Frome*, drawing on a sketch she had done as an exercise when she was learning French in Paris three years before. The plot predates the actual affair with Fullerton, but not their meeting in the city where he was employed as an assistant to the Paris correspondent for the *Times*. The writing that had commenced in June was interrupted by her own illness and the need to care for Teddy during the autumn of 1910, but was completed following a six-week uninterrupted burst starting in January 1911. So it was a winter composition, produced in the aftermath of nursing her husband, with no prospect of a reunion with Fullerton in sight. The novel is informed by this sense of gloom.

The differences between the 1907 French version and the full narrative are not as substantial as one might imagine, except in one important respect. The triangular relationship remains the same: a married sawmill owner, the young female relative that he loves, his sickly wife that she works for as a servant. The drive toward death is there, described very explicitly in the French version:

> The harsh, stubborn willpower, which led the first inhabitants of New England into these wildernesses, has made their descendants creatures of

passion and self-denial. Strong religious faith has left behind a flavour of martyrdom, and a type of implacable uprightness which master the most violent emotions. But the drab, monotonous life, a long history of wasted life and repressed instincts, too often led to a mortal sadness, a loathing for life, even among women and the healthy, which sometimes extended to melancholy and madness.

(Unpublished translation)[53]

But Mattie and Hart at least kiss and allow the passion to be expressed, however fleetingly: "He abruptly put his arms around her, pulled her towards him, and kissed her trembling lips. . . . He had a great desire to look into her eyes one last time" (unpublished translation). The kiss is immediately followed by a feeling of gloom, which the narrator identifies as endemic, in the longer paragraph that was just quoted. But there is a positive side to this self-denial that the narrator also acknowledges, for what holds Hart back is actually a virtue, an act of altruism: "He would have liked to speak, to tell her about his tender feelings and his despair; but a generosity held him back. Since he could do nothing for her, since his love could be nothing but a source of misery and suffering for her, it was better to keep quiet, to brace himself this last attack on his senses and his heart" (unpublished translation).

Although the rhetoric of the text encourages us to read this as a noble action ("a generosity held him back"), this reading is immediately subverted by the succeeding paragraph, which speaks of harsh stubborn willpower and the crippling effects of self-denial. The text reveals an inner dialogue, a dialectic on the subject of duty, pleasure, and sacrifice, while the published version seems to conclude with a verdict on the side of duty.

One of the more obvious changes is in the names. Mattie remains the same, but Anna becomes Zeena and Hart becomes Ethan Frome, Hart being a little too obvious, and Anna not sufficiently allusive. The most significant plot difference between the two texts is the inclusion of the sledging crash, and its consequences, in the published version. The sense of squander and waste in the 1907 French version at least allows the reader to hope that Anna might really be ill and the situation resolved through her merciful death, or that Mattie might suddenly see a way of escaping into a world where there is no scandal, a hope expressed by Archer in *The Age of Innocence*. In that novel Ellen Olenska dismisses Archer's hope as fantasy, but in *Ethan Frome* hope is extinguished through showing as well as telling. In the final scene Mattie is revealed to be as bitter and twisted as Zeena—and it is by taking the narrative forward twenty years that Wharton crushes us in a way that we are spared in *The Age of Innocence*, where Archer does not enter the building to see the Madame Olenska that it is now too late for him to be with.

But the most significant difference of all between the two versions is the framing device of the narrator, who consciously weaves his own tale based on the information that is available to him. The novel is sometimes criticized for moving from the narrator's viewpoint into that of the characters in ways that the narrator said would not be done. But the narrator reminds us constantly of what he is doing, and as noted earlier, this text explores and exhibits the way that desire expressed through writing constructs its own subject and object. This is not modernism, but it has the self-consciousness of modernism, another characteristic of which is the uncertainty and unreliability of the observer, and the way in which desire and narration are refracted through the prism of consciousness.

Freud is the modernist presence that seems to hover over *Ethan Frome*, and many critics have discussed Freudian themes. Gloria Erlich explores the consequences, for a sexual education, of multiple mothering, where the child's affection is divided between mother and one or more nanny figures. In Erlich's reading, the consequence of this for Wharton's fantasy life is "the displacement of her sexuality onto words and books."[54] Applied to *Ethan Frome* Erlich's theory would mean that the narrator's construction of this tale of failed adultery is a fantasy that is the site of transferred, thwarted desire. Carol Wershoven discusses the figure of the female intruder whose arrival in Wharton's novels results in a questioning of the society into which she makes her entrance, a questioning she herself articulates or that she forces others to confront. Clearly Mattie is less perceptive and less enigmatic than Ellen Olenska or Lily Bart, but to Wershoven *Ethan Frome* is the archetypal Wharton novel: "It is the essential conflict, the recurring motif, of the woman who is at once more vital, braver, and more receptive to all of life than the society she must confront or challenge."[55]

Wershoven goes on to argue that *Ethan Frome*, like *The Valley of Decision* (1902), exposes the "warping and distortion of personalities through imprisonment in a static, nightmare world."[56] It is a novel of destruction, arguing for the terrible consequences of the paralysis of desire. Wharton may not have liked the extinction of desire that she encountered in *The Wings of the Dove*, Henry James's 1902 novel with its own triangular relationship, but she had written her own novel of destruction in which not only the situation but the telling of it has become the subject. It is not so very far from the method practiced in Ford Madox Ford's *The Good Soldier*, whose impressionism acts as a convenient bridge between realism and modernism.

4: *ETHAN FROME,* MODERNISM, AND A POLITICAL ARGUMENT   145

Gender, Capitalism, and the American Dream: Mask and Masquerade

Ethan Frome was written in the immediate aftermath of the affair with Morton Fullerton and for some critics there is a clear link between text and autobiography; "*Ethan Frome* is one of Edith Wharton's rare compositions told in the first person, and the tale seems to exorcise her worst fears in a 'vision' of the life she might have had if she had not escaped from her marriage and the life that accompanied it."[57] In her published autobiography, however, Wharton chose not to mention the Fullerton relationship, drawing attention instead to other aspects of the text's origins. The cool, detached language of her account of the novel in *A Backward Glance,*,[58] like the text of *Ethan Frome* itself, is an act of concealment. There is no mention of the (unrealized) sexual triangle that appears to be the subject of the narrative. This is also true of the narrative method itself. At first we see only the mysterious limping Ethan, and there are hints that the limping is linked to a secret subject about which the Starkfield people are reluctant to speak. But when they do speak, they confirm Bakhtin's dictum (1986) that we say, and what we say says something more, only it is what they do *not* say that says something more. Their reticence and relative silence is a patriarchal, Puritan silence, and the landscape is cold and masculine. Ethan is associated with that landscape: "He seemed a part of the mute melancholy landscape, an incarnation of its frozen woe, with all that was warm and sentient in him fast bound below the surface.... I simply felt that he lived in a depth of moral isolation too remote for casual access and I had the sense that his loneliness was not mainly the result of his personal plight, tragic as I guessed that to be, but had in it ... the profound accumulated cold of many Starkfield winters."

As I noted earlier, Elizabeth Ammons argues that Wharton's distancing narrative technique reveals fear of being classed as emotional and feminine at a time when woman were struggling to achieve equal status with male novelists. Ammons notes that "by the turn of the century the battle over white male ownership of the high art novel in the United States had come to a head."[59] In 1911, the year in which *Ethan Frome* was published, Charlotte Perkins Gilman's essay "Men and Art" had appeared in *The Man Made World*[60] pointing to the major difference between "art" and "Art," the former being what women produce and the latter what men reserved for themselves. Wharton, who had met and befriended Henry James, was determined to be recognized as a serious Artist with an uppercase A. Her separation from other women can be read as a "self-defensive attempt to secure her status as an artist in a male dominated world by separating herself from 'feminine' fiction—that is allegedly soft, second-rate work."[61]

This distancing was not as striking as that practiced by her contemporary Willa Cather who denigrated female writers partly to mask her own lesbianism, but in both cases there is a similar paradox. The rhetoric of Edith Wharton's personal statements about gender, the New Woman, and feminism collides with the rhetoric of much of her fiction.[62] On the one hand she is dismissive of women who were campaigning for the vote or more education. In *A Backward Glance*, as we shall see, she writes that women are made for procreation and for pleasure, and that the kitchen is women's natural domain. Wharton preferred the company of men, and when visiting England sought out from her own sex not Mrs. Pankhurst, but Mrs. Humphry Ward, a novelist and public figure well known for her hostility to the women's suffrage campaign. This public antipathy to the woman's movement cannot be explained as the immature prejudices of an unformed New England debutante. The woman of letters is ridiculed in "Xingu," published in 1911, the same year as *Ethan Frome*, when Edith Wharton was nearly fifty. On the surface Edith Wharton was a figure reassuring to the anxious Edwardian male: a wealthy, attractive woman who willingly accepted the conventional man-woman relationship and did not form solidarity alliances with her own sex. No public feminist or suffragette she.

Yet in her New York fiction Wharton offers the reader sustained critiques of the feminization of women and the construction of that "femininity." The "ladies" that she satirically dismembers in *The Custom of the Country* (1913) are formed by a culture that commodifies women. Kaplan (1988) and Gilbert and Gubar (1989) have each noted the similarity between Wharton's representation of the position of married women in her fiction and the views advanced by Thorstein Veblen, whose *Theory of the Leisure Class* was published in 1899 and very widely read. Veblen argued that in a capitalist economy bourgeois women may no longer be the obvious drudge and chattel of the man, but as symbols of their husband's wealth and power through their conspicuous consumption they continued to enact the role of servant, whose main function is to enhance and glorify the master through the public and ceremonial consumption of the goods that his wealth produces. For Veblen marriage is "an archaic institution," but as a cultural determinist, he offers no alternative to it. Similarly, Edith Wharton, despite being a contemporary of Edward Carpenter, William Morris, Charlotte Perkins Gilman,

Havelock Ellis, Olive Schreiner, and Kate Chopin was too rooted in the traditions of the New York business aristocracy to propose alternatives.

Wharton's novels, like Jane Austen's, are severe in her treatment of those who stray from the path. In *The House of Mirth*, *The Custom of the Country*, and *The Age of Innocence* the reader is presented with a series of clinical case studies illustrating the way that women of whatever intelligence or independence of mind are shaped by the laws of their culture. In this sense, *Ethan Frome* is part of Edith Wharton's much larger project, but in this novel everything, including gender, is presented in reverse. Wharton locates her narrative in the world of the rural poor rather than the urban rich, and both title and focalization seem to suggest that it is the man who is more trapped than the women.

Is this just an artistic sleight of hand or evidence that she believed that for every Lily there was an Ethan, and that money rather than gender and desire lies at the root of the problem? In other words, society should not make the independence of women its priority because that not only would not solve society's problems, it would create new ones. Wharton's *public* utterances on the role of women remained consistently conservative. In her autobiography *A Backward Glance* she fondly recalls the skill of the female cooks who produced wonderful dishes for her to eat when she was still a child.

> I have lingered over these details because they formed a part—a most important and honourable part—of that ancient curriculum of housekeeping which, as least in Anglo-Saxon countries, was so soon to be swept aside by the "montrous regiment" of the emancipated: young women taught by their elders to despise the kitchen and the linen room, and to substitute the acquiring of University degrees for the more complex art of civilised living. The movement began when I was young, and now that I am old, and have watched it and noted its results, I mourn more than ever the extinction of the household arts. Cold storage, deplorable though it is, has done far less harm to the home than the Higher Education.
>
> *ABG* (1993), 41

If the voice is partly ironical and arch, it is also trenchant and reactionary, addressing and reassuring two sets of readers at the same time. The support for traditional customs cannot be explained by saying that the majority of women of her class and generation would have held such views. Wharton was fully aware of the power and success of those with dissenting voices such as Charlotte Perkins Gilman. Gilman's poem attacking the antiSuffragists, begins:

>   Fashionable women in luxurious homes
>   With men to feed them, clothe them, pay their bills

and it concludes

>   ... traitors are they all
>   To great Democracy and Womanhood[63]

Yet Edith Wharton was perfectly able to see the limitations of the attitudes of aristocratic societies such as the one in which she grew up. In *A Backward Glance,* only a few pages after expressing disapproval of the women's movement, she describes the attitudes of her parents and their group to writers:

> [M]y parents and their group, though they held literature in great esteem, stood in nervous dread of those who produced it. . . . As for Herman Melville, a cousin of the Van Rensselaers, and qualified by birth to figure in the best society, he was doubtless excluded from it by his deplorable Bohemianism, for I never heard his name mentioned or saw one of his books. Banished probably for the same reason (as) Poe, that drunken and demoralised Baltimorean. . . . I cannot hope to render the tone in which my mother pronounced the names of such unfortunates, or on the other hand, that of Mrs. Beecher Stowe, who was so "common" yet so successful. On the whole, my mother doubtless thought, it would be simpler if people one might be exposed to meeting would refrain from meddling with literature. . . . I am sure the chief element in their reluctance to encounter the literary was an awe struck dread of the intellectual effort that might be required of them.
>
> *(ABG,* 46)

With its sociologically presented setting *Ethan Frome* simultaneously offers a political reading of suppressed femininity and inadequate masculinity. If the gender of the principals is reversed, then something more recognizable emerges, as in the negative taken from a photograph of the Turin Shroud. In this reversing process the narrator is a woman who has time on her hands, has a scientific mind, which, not being put to good use, amuses itself with storytelling and speculation. In her construction of the story there is an iteration of the speculative: rather than things being thus, they "seem[ed]" or "felt" a particular way. The narrator learns of a triangle of relationships, which in cross-gendering becomes a woman (Ethan/Edith) married to a sickly man (Zeena/Teddy), but attracted (partly in her imagination) to another man (Mattie/Morton). The sense of this is not to read the life into the art, but to examine the possibility that Wharton was only in a position to explore the painful consequence of suppressed deferred sexual feelings when those feelings had been directly experienced through a simultaneous articulation in language. For Wolff "*Ethan Frome* deals with the tragic and sterile renunciation of sexuality"[64] and the suppression of the sexual could be represented adequately when Wharton had transgressed and enjoyed the pleasures of transgression as defined by the social discourse of her class.

In this sense the lesson applies equally to men and women. If Ethan the character is read at face value as a representation of masculinity, he embodies, figuratively and literally, turn of the century anxieties about degeneration and the feminization of the male. As a hardworking New Englander he seems as remote from the fin de siècle aesthete as it is possible to be, but in his preference for sensation, the imagined and the dreamed over action and decision making, he signifies a weakness and an effeteness that was troubling to late-Victorian and Edwardian constructions of masculinity: "He let the vision possess him as they climbed the hill to the house. He was never so happy with her as when he abandoned himself to these dreams."[65] But as Wolff points out, this dream is soon to be replaced by a nightmare of having to look after two embittered and cold women.

The nightmare vision will define the rest of his life. This is perhaps the lesson to the narrator; it is certainly intended as a lesson for the reader. It is better to strive for the real, if limited, possibilities for happiness, for the phantom of ideal rapture may well lead to a reality of unrelenting despair.[66] But what then of moral duty to follow despair?

In Max Nordau's pseudoscientific theory of degeneration (1895)[67] the mystical and the aesthetic are symptoms of effeminacy in the masculine and are to be crushed. Ethan is punished because he is neither strong enough to kill himself nor to escape. Using Gilbert and Gubar's categories, he is one of Wharton's many "Not-men." Gilbert and Gubar quote from Olive Schreiner's 1899 essay "The Woman Question": "[O]nly an effete and inactive male can ultimately be produced by an effete and inactive womanhood."[68] This description may more readily fit some of Wharton's wealthy, passive New York society males such as Newland Archer, in that Ethan is too poor to be inactive, but it is clear that the more inactive Zeena becomes, the more ineffectual Ethan becomes too.

Read again in terms of gender reversal, the narrator may be seen as signifying the oppressiveness of marriage, as Ethan is trapped in a loveless marriage, a marriage he entered only for companionship. Duty and society prevent Ethan/Edith from abandoning that marriage, and at that same time it reads him as indecisive and compliant. His role is to care for others, his duty is to care for others, as caring roles were (and often still are) constructed as something to which women were more constitutionally suited. If Ethan/Edith fails in his duty she fails as a woman, she ceases to be a woman, and in this novel, she has been assigned the status of a not-woman. The importance of duty and the need to sacrifice personal pleasure if such pleasure is achieved at the expense of someone else's suffering, is a recurrent theme in Wharton, as the turning point of *The Age of Innocence* demonstrates. Such an allegiance to a moral principle is not simply the product of class (for Wharton) or religion (the New Englanders in *Ethan Frome*). It was being reinforced by Nordau himself as an evolutionary imperative:

> Progress is possible only by the growth of knowledge; but this is the task of consciousness and judgment, not of instinct. The march of progress is characterised by the expansion of consciousness and the contraction of the unconscious; the strengthening of will and the weakening of impulsions, the increase of self-responsibility and the repression of reckless egoism. . . . And he who who places pleasures above discipline, and impulse above self-restraint, wishes not for progress, but for retrogression to the most primitive animality.[69]

Michael Millgate makes a similar point in his discussion of *The Age of Innocence:* "What faces Newland and Ellen . . . is not a simple question of conforming or not conforming, but a much more difficult problem of fundamental morality; what keeps them apart at those moments when they seem closest to flight is Ellen's clear recognition that happiness cannot be built on the suffering of others."[70]

It would be wrong to ignore the more general social and class point, however. In this text *all* the characters are trapped within and by the expectation of their culture: Mattie is represented as a servant who is forced to quit without notice, Zeena as a drudge of a wife who is constantly ill, Ethan as a man who has to work long hours to support the Frome household. And for this reason we should not be too eager to find in *Ethan Frome* confirmation of a performative reading of gender: as Joan Copjec argues in *Read My Desire* (1995), sex may not be prediscursive, but unlike class and race, it cannot be explained simply as a product of signification, cannot be reduced to a discursive construction, and therefore cannot be deconstructed in the same way as class and race.

By the conclusion of *Ethan Frome*, the three principals are either wounded or confined. Although (ironically and remarkably) Zeena seems to have made something of a recovery; her obsession with her own health continues as she continues subscribing to the medical journals that the narrator sees Ethan collect from the the post office. Ethan hobbles, symbolically castrated and gelded by the sled crash and its outcome, with not even the consolation of any suggestion of the romance of the wounded artist Philoctetes to soften the awfulness of his fate. There is nothing comforting in this novel.

Philosophy, Religion, and Dream

Students often comment on the bleakness of *Ethan Frome* and there is no doubt that the final vignette presents us with a scene chilling enough to have come from the frozen Lake of Cocytus, the ninth circle of hell in Dante's *Inferno*. Harold Bloom[71] sees the novel's austere character as a consequence of a stoicism and asceticism that links Wharton and Ethan to Nietzsche[72] and Schopenhauer:

> Like Wharton, Ethan has an immense capacity for suffering, and an overwhelming sense of reality; indeed like Edith Wharton, he has too strong a sense of what was to be the Freudian reality principle.
> Though an exact contemporary of Freud, Edith Wharton showed no interest in him, but she became an emphatic Nietzschean, and Ethan Frome manifests both a Nietzschean perspectivism, and an ascetic intensity that I suspect goes back to a reading of Schopenhauer, Nietzsche's precursor. What fails in Ethan, and in his beloved Mattie, is precisely what Schopenhauer urged us to overcome, the Will to Live, though suicide was hardly a Schopenhauerian solution.[73]

I think there is more of an ambiguity about the sledding accident than this comment suggests, but the incident can be read as the couple's tacit decision that life is not worth continuing, and that they might as well just submit themselves to the sled ride to see what happens. Such fatalism, which informs the outlook of all those who live at Starkfield, is attributed by Bloom to Wharton's Emersonian heritage. Carol J. Singley sees the novel as marking an important staging post in Wharton's personal journey through Christianity. Brought up in the formal, ritualized Episcopalian faith, she moved in the latter part of her life toward Catholicism, but in between shared an outlook that had much in common with Calvinism. Her first attempt at autobiography, "Life and I," reveals a Calvinistic tendency, Singley argues. In "Life and I" Wharton reports: "I had . . . worked out of my inner mind a rigid rule of absolute, unmitigated truth-telling, the least imperceptible deviation from which would inevitably be punished by the dark Power I knew as God."[74]

Wharton recalls how, as a child of six or seven, she amused her fellow pupils by saying that the mother of their dancing teacher looked like an old goat. So guilty did she feel about having said this publicly, that she confessed it to her teacher and was bewildered when instead of being commended for her honesty she was roundly admonished. Her sense of guilt was increased. "It is difficult to imagine how the sternest Presbyterian training could have produced differing or more depressing results. I was indeed 'God-intoxicated,' in the medical sense of the word."[75]

Ethan Frome is notable for what is absent in Starkfield, for whom the word "community" is a misleading epithet. The absence of heat reflects the absence of love. The absence of conversation reflects the absence of inquiry. In the nineteenth century women such as Margaret Fuller and Charlotte Perkins Gilman had tried to recuperate the tradition of the mother-goddess, the Greek goddesses, and the matriarchy. Such a presence is absent from this novel. *Ethan Frome* can be seen as both a Calvinist novel and a modernist allegory set in an unredeemed and unredeemable universe.[76] There will be punishment for any pleasure, especially illicit pleasure. This makes sense, but Singley's argument that Calvinism and modernism share the same pessimistic view of the universe, because they share the same view of human limitation, seems a rather loose link. Singley, rephrasing an argument she has taken from Daniel J. Schneider,[77] explains that a loss of faith in God led to a pessimism in which faith in reform became a pipe dream. This is certainly the anxiety expressed in Arnold's poem "Dover Beach," but it ignores the rhetoric of socialism, or of early twentieth-century imperialism. Modernism pays debt to neither of these rhetorical positions, however, and the bleak conclusion of *Dubliners, The Good Soldier, Sons and Lovers, Prufrock, The Voyage Out,* and *Metamorphosis* do indicate a level of despair about the human condition. The revelation seen by the narrator of *Ethan Frome* of three ruined lives is a terrible moment, offering no hope.

Such a bleak rhetoric can alienate some readers. When I prepared an edition of *Ethan Frome* for teaching purposes, I knew it would be helpful to start on a positive note. Apart from raising questions about gender, poverty, and desire, what else was the text doing? The starting point in the seminar room could certainly have been a discussion of such issues as loneliness and entrapment, constructions of duty and pleasure and the choice that has to be made between them, and the mystery that the narrative establishes in the opening paragraphs. But if we consider how this very American story had been written from the distance of Europe, it can be useful to see *Ethan Frome* as an interrogation of the American Dream, the "original" story told of

4: *ETHAN FROME,* MODERNISM, AND A POLITICAL ARGUMENT   153

America, the one that overlooks the history and culture of Native Americans. It is the story celebrated on Thanksgiving Day, when the successful beginnings of the Pilgrim "Fathers" colony is commemorated, and with it the beginning of the Dream. In such a postcolonial reading the novel can be seen to be the dark shadow of the American Dream, as Ethan's dream of escape ends up as perpetual nightmare and stasis. From the distance of Paris the Europeanized Edith Wharton was able to review and reread America, and this politicization of Wharton would have been impossible without the transatlantic perspective. Europeanization provided not only a cultural, but also a political education. As Fullerton himself had noted of another political change, in which defamiliarization led to fresh insight: "Until Voltaire had got to know England by his travels and friendships, he was not Voltaire."[78]

How modernist a novel is Ethan Frome? One way of answering this question is by looking at what have been seen as the defining qualities of modernist writing. David Lodge[79] identifies modernist fiction as writing that possesses specific qualities. It is "experimental or innovatory in form," and is "much concerned with consciousness," particularly with the working of the subconscious or unconscious. It has no real beginning because it plunges straight into the stream of experience, its ending being similarly "open" and inconclusive. The fourth characteristic is its use of symbol, archetypes, repetition with variation, and other devices that replace the traditional structuring device of plot. Finally, the modernist novel abandons chronological order and the reassuring figure of the reliable narrator.

Matched against this *Ethan Frome* scores approximately three out of five, scoring half out of one for most of these features, but a full mark for the last. It is concerned with experiment, though the precedents of James and Conrad make it not completely innovatory. It is concerned with consiousness, perception, and impression, though not so much with the subconscious. It plunges straight into the action, but it ends with a scene that provides resolution to the mystery that the narrative set up. It certainly has an unreliable narrator, and plays with chronology.

It is easy to see why *Ethan Frome* is regarded as Wharton's most modernist work. Although the setting is rural rather than urban, it possesses many of the other qualities that we associate with modernism. There is uncertainty about the story itself, there is a hero who is anything but heroic, there is a landscape that is as much psychological as real. As Martin Halliwell argues, the "moral paralysis" identified by Trilling makes the novel a "powerful expression of modernity."[80] This paralysis is a failure of will and a moral inertia, what Halliwell calls the "condition of demoralisation" that is characteristic of both fin de siècle American naturalism and European decadence. Wharton's sojourn in Europe may have meant that she was exposed to both traditions, but as I will show in the next chapter, this did not mean that she was ready to absorb the ideology of the aesthetes or embark on the modernist mapping of the alienated consciousness. Ethan is denied the possibility of introspection, but if he could recover his will, it would not best be used to dive into his own soul. In this respect Ethan is in the same position as Joyce's Eveline, a young woman whose poverty and social position denies her the luxury of angst. Whereas by the end of *Dubliners* Joyce, through Gabriel Conroy, prepares us for Stephen Dedalus, whose representation in *A Portrait of the Artist as a Young Man* does involve a dive into the subconscious, Wharton did not continue in the direction in which the modernist apparatus of *Ethan Frome* seemed to be leading. Instead, in her next novel Wharton rejected a further exploration of solipsism and once again visited the situation of the erotic triangle. This menage, however, is acted out in circumstances in which for a brief moment the forces of social restraint are suspended and fleeting desire can be satisfied. Wharton's judgment is damning, for the metaphor she provides for lurking power of the subconscious is that of a hidden, wrecking, underwater reef.

5
Vulgarity, Bohemia, and *The Reef* (1912)

> If you shall chance, Camillo, to visit Bohemia, on the like occasion whereon my services are now on foot, you shall see, as I have said, great difference betwixt our Bohemia and your Sicilia.
> —*The Winter's Tale* 1.1.1–4

> He never loses himself in the submarine jungle in which he gropes.
> —Edith Wharton on Proust

So far I have been arguing that one of the main obstacles that prevented Wharton from identifying with the new writing that became known as literary modernism was her anxiety about its political implications. In this chapter I wish to show how this tendency is manifest in the rejection of bohemian ideology with which she felt the new writing was associated. It is a rejection that is enacted in her 1912 novel *The Reef*, which links a lack of commitment and discrimination in behavior to a similar lack in art. Both practices lead to a vulgarity that Wharton found unacceptable.

America: "Eating bananas for breakfast"

Edith Wharton's reservations about American culture are well documented. Her decision in 1911 to make France her permanent base suggests not only her fondness for the congenial society in that country, but also her increasing alienation from the United States. Such a disillusionment with the country of her birth had a long genesis. As she records in "Life and I,"[1] she was only four years old when she left America, and she did not return to live until she was ten. Her childhood response to this return was one of disappointment and dismay:

> I was keenly interested in this change in our existence, but I shall never forget the bitter disappointment produced by the first impressions of my

native country. I was only ten years old, but I had been fed on beauty since babyhood, & my first thought was: *"How ugly it is!"* I have never since thought otherwise or felt otherwise than as an exile in America; & that this is no retrospective delusion is proved by the fact that I used to dream at frequent intervals that we were going back to Europe, & to wake from this dream in a state of exhilaration which the reality turned to deep depression.[2]

This is not to underestimate the importance of her decision to make The Mount her home, endorsed by the wishes of her new husband for whom Europe had limited attractions. Wharton found the time at The Mount very productive, for it was there that she wrote the early novels that established her reputation.[3] It was in Massachusetts that she established herself as a writer, and the period she spent in the great house at Lenox was an important period in her (self-) education. Free from the constraints of her parents, who were not interested in learning, she was able to build a library and read extensively. Her childhood, youth, and early marriage may have been spent mainly in Europe, New York, and Newport, but her professional life begins to take shape in no small measure owing to the refuge that was The Mount. That experience of country house living informs the 1912 novel *The Reef*, even though by then Wharton was spending much of the year in the Paris apartment that replaced the one that she and Teddy had leased. The setting for *The Reef* may be France, but the French house and its park feature largely as a backdrop, and all the principal characters are American.

Yet these are not Americans of the kind she had derided in a 1904 letter to Sara Norton, when a breakdown of the "motor" caused her to spend the night in a hotel in Petersham, Massachusetts:

But I must avoid the subject of America—for I have been spending my first night in an American "Summer hotel," & I despair at the Republic! Such dreariness, such whining sallow women, such utter absence of the amenities, such crass food, crass manners, crass landscape!! And, mind you, it is a new & fashionable hotel. What a horror it is for a whole nation to be developing without the sense of beauty, & eating bananas for breakfast.[4]

Wharton's friend and mentor, the Harvard art historian Charles Eliot Norton, complained of the real cultural threat posed by the new vulgarity, a sentiment echoed by Wharton in 1905 when, as Jennie Kassanoff has noted, she remarked that "a handful of vulgar people, bent on spending and enjoying . . . may become an engine of destruction" because of the disillusionment they cause.[5] Although Wharton's fiction reveals an acknowledgment of the energy and excitement that new-money Americans bring with them, their crassness and lack of refinement is what she was to emphasize in *The Custom of the Country*, the novel that straddles *The Reef*, started as it was in 1908 but not completed and published until 1913.[6] In that novel she gives full rein to her feelings about this "engine" of destruction, and returns to the setting and style that characterized the successful *The House of Mirth*.

The Reef is a more experimental novel than its successor and like *Ethan Frome*, shows the influence of the contemporary theories of impressionism practiced in their novels by writers such as Conrad, whose work she came to admire,[7] and Ford Madox Ford. But though in common with *The Good Soldier*, it provides a study of an attractive male who has a sexual secret, it has nothing like the intricate formal structure caused by the incessant time shifts in Ford's novel. Wharton dispensed with the figure of the tentative and uncertain narrator she had used to such good effect in *Ethan Frome*. The novel provides a different kind of experiment in exploring in detail the psychology of Anna Leath and her "rival" Sophy Viner, but Wharton still wished her novel to be a place in which she could explore a central ethical problem in relationships in the manner favored by the utterly premodernist novelist, Paul Bourget.

In *The Reef* Wharton examines a series of conundrums about sexual behavior and convention that were exercising even the kind of Americans whose company she valued, and which her recent affair with Morton Fullerton had thrown into sharp relief. The novel has things to say about passion, sex, and female purity. It explores the implication of self-denial and restraint for women. Using the euphemism made popular by Grant Allen's novel,[8] it is about men who do, women who do, and women who don't. It is a novel about ownership, both the ownership of property and sexual ownership, of belonging and being possessed. It examines that issue that was central to Wharton's experience, the value and purpose of pain, renunciation, and suffering, illustrating through Sophy and Anna what Gloria Erlich calls the "difference between 'renovating anguish' and 'sterile misery.'"[9] More abstractly, it explores the elision of time, unfolding a situation in which the past comes to have a devastating impact on the present. Politically it looks down into the reef and sees an abyss.

Europe, and France in particular, seemingly offered safe anchorage for those who shared the traditions and tastes that Wharton had inherited from her family. Europe, she believed, could be relied upon to resist the worst excesses of American popular culture. The conservative classes still appeared to be the ruling classes, and unlike the banana-eating hotel guests in America, knew how to conduct themselves.

There was, however, another aspect of European life that offered its own challenge to her values and beliefs. Despite her deep conservatism, this perceived threat was not, as might be imagined, burgeoning French political radicalism. In Paris in 1908 she would not have been unaware of the anticapitalist, pacifist, and internationalist rhetoric of the French government debates. But Wharton did not come into direct contact with socialism, a movement whose politicians did not gain access to her inner circle. As a writer, however, she occasionally had contact with those at the fringes of that troubling world known as bohemia (Bernard Berenson, the art critic, was a friend who attended Gertrude Stein's salon and Proust was a neighbor whose work she later championed), and a debate about bohemia is explored not only in her post–World War I novels, such as *The Gods Arrive*, but also in her earlier fiction, especially *The Reef* (1912). Wharton's world was too ordered to admit any direct experience of the bohemian lifestyle that had become fashionable in late nineteenth-century Paris. Instead, it was the implications of bohemian ideology, with its celebration of rootlessness, that she found unsettling. The idea that was particularly troubling was the possibility that in literature the bohemian and the modern were one and the same thing and that the accommodation of bohemian values by her artistic peers might be just as threatening to the ordered, civilized life as the vulgar march of materialism, which bohemianism supposedly opposed.

Bohemia and "Deplorable Bohemianism"

> Holmes, who loathed every form of society with his whole Bohemian soul, remained in our lodgings in Baker Street, buried among his old books, and alternating from week to week between cocaine and ambition. . . .[10]

In the extract from *A Backward Glance* quoted earlier, Wharton concludes that Herman Melville, who was qualified by birth "to figure in the best society" and whose work she came to admire, was excluded from her parents' library on the grounds of his "deplorable Bohemianism," a reputation that also accounted for the banishment of the books of Edgar Allan Poe.[11]

As Virginia Nicholson, granddaughter of Vanessa Bell, explains in her study of the avant-garde minority led by the Bloomsbury group, the origins of the term "bohemian" are complex:

> We now translate the French word "Bohémien" as "gypsy," but the original Boii were refugees from the area known until recently as Czechoslovakia. From the early days of the Roman empire until the Middle Ages,

waves of these displaced people fled to western Europe. Many of them, it appears, threw in their lot with disreputable groups of wandering minstrels. . . . When the first genuine Romanies appeared in France from central Europe with their nomadic habits, they were identified with the previous arrivals, and by the late 16th century all gypsies were indiscriminately labelled Bohemian, regardless of their exact origin. Right from the start, the country of Bohemia was located wherever its inhabitants were to be found.[12]

The lifestyle associated with these wanderers from Moravia, Romania, Bohemia, and Czechoslovakia eventually became identified with the antibourgeois, anti-intellectual lifestyle of the group that became known as the romantic avant-garde. The shifting, rootless life of the artist, the separation of the artist from the community, the resistance to the materialism, Puritanism, and industrialization of Victorian society, all contributed to the unconventional character of this lifestyle, however conventional that unconventionality later became. But there are problems with the concept itself, as Rosemary Hill points out: "The whole idea of the bohemian is slippery to the grip of an organizing mind. The *OED* [*Oxford English Dictionary*] sense a certain impropriety in the word itself, concluding its definition on a note of exasperation: 'Used with much more latitude, with or without reference to morals.'"[13] Hill is less exasperated than the *OED*, and says that Bohemia may not have a mappable geography, consistent sociology, or specific economy, but it does have a history. The political earthquake of the French Revolution supplied the fissures in which bohemians could live, often in the ruins of the ancien régime. They were often from the dispossessed, lower-middle-class artisan classes.

By the late nineteenth century, thanks to Henry Mürger's *Scenes of Bohemian Life,* Victor Hugo's *Les Miserables,* Baudelaire's *flaneur,* Wildes's French *Salome,* and George du Maurier's enormously popular 1894 novel *Trilby,* in which Svengali controls the model Trilby's singing voice, the word "bohemian" conveyed an image of the world in which poor artists, vegetarians, lotus eaters, and the inhabitants of the demimonde intermingle and defy convention. It was a world made vivid by the life story of Rimbaud, whose wanderings took him from Paris, to London, and to North Africa, places that also attracted Wharton. Although Rimbaud went to very different districts from the ones frequented by Edith Wharton, as a serious writer interested in the work of other serious writers she was familiar with his work and life, and with the dual character of bohemia itself. On the one hand the word conjured up images of urban squalor, drugs, violence, and decadence, which Wharton, having grown up in an environment hostile to bohemia (as the comments about Melville and Poe showed) would have found unsavory and unwelcome. On the other, in the late-Victorian and Edwardian period in England "bohemia" was a playful, somewhat fashionable concept treated lightly, for example, by Kenneth Grahame, author of *The Wind in the Willows*, in his essay "A Bohemian in Exile." The essay celebrates an image of rural gypsy wandering that Wharton, a great wanderer herself, could comfortably identify with.[14] It need not signify anything too radical.

Wharton was nevertheless uneasy about the contemporary flirtation with bohemianism. It would be an exaggeration to say that the subject became her preoccupation, but *The Reef*, which among other things is an exploration of the consequences of what happens when bohemia confronts Old World society, is a novel that shows that its range of meanings fascinated her. This uneasy fascination is unsurprising. With Henry James she shared an admiration for the writing of George Sand, and George Sand's early lifestyle (like George Eliot's) presented a challenge to Wharton's Old New York assumptions about correct behavior and female virtue. Wharton confronts the issue when she goes to visit Sand's house at Nohant, in a visit that made Henry James so envious he persuaded her to make a second "motor-flight through France" the following year, this time with James in the passenger seat. In the published book Wharton makes clear in a reference, whose surprising juxtaposition may not be intentionally ironical, her view of the free unions and other irregularities that went on in this house during Sand's occupation of it during the 1830s, "the too intimate servants in that household—which calls to mind 'Wildfell Hall.'"[15]

Ann Brontë's novel is more a nightmare of drinking and violence than it is an orgy of sexual license (although there are indeed illicit liaisons), but Wharton consoles herself with the thought that the French house itself had a reforming influence on the bohemian behavior practiced there, unlike its fictional counterpart:

> And so one may, not too fancifully, recognize in it the image of those grave ideals to which George Sand gradually conformed the passionate experiment of her life; may even indulge one's self by imagining that an old house so marked in its very plainness, its conformity, must have exerted, over a mind as sensitive as hers, an unperceived but persistent influence, giving her that centralizing weight of association and habit which is too often lacking in modern character.[16]

The contrasting influence of old house and bohemia is a feature of two later novels by Wharton. Vance Weston, the writer whose life forms the subject of her post–World War I novel sequence, *Hudson River Bracketed* (1929) and *The Gods Arrive* (1932), comes into close contact with bohemia in New York, Paris, and London, and bohemian artists are seen to be shallow and (like Weston at this worst) self-absorbed and unable to complete their work. Only a good woman can rescue them. Halo Tarrant, who was Vance's muse in the first of novel, settles for being his mother-figure in the second. She sees through the shallowness of bohemia, and knows that what both she and Vance really value is structure, tradition, and a good house like the Willows, the setting for the reunion of Vance and Halo, who at the close of the two-novel sequence is expecting his child. The Willows in these later novels assumes an almost mystical quality reminiscent of Howards End, and provides the recuperative environment that Givré, the chateau in *The Reef,* signally fails to supply.

In *Edith Wharton's Brave New Politics* Dale M. Bauer discusses *The Reef*'s dialogue with bohemia in the context of politics and class. Darrow's error is having sex with someone from the servant class. At the same time, bohemianism represents the anarchy of free love politics. Bauer quotes Darrow's familiarity with "ladies" and with women who were not ladies, and his avoidance of the bohemian class, that "intermediate society which attempts to conciliate both theories of life."[17] The thoughts are given as Darrow's, but the voice seems to be that of the narrator, who applauds the sincerity and clarity of a world in which women are either "irreproachable" or sexually available and there is no confusion about which is which. It is the unsettling ambiguity of bohemianism that is marked out for disapproval, as a "cheaper convention" than the other two.[18] We glimpse the world of English bohemia in London at the house of Mrs. Murrett, and of American bohemia in France in the account of the Farlows, whose name suggests the depths to which they are prepared to sink, and for whom Wharton reserves a paragraph of her typically crushing satire. Darrow learns about them from Sophy:

> The Farlows themselves—he a painter, she a "magazine writer"—rose before him in all their incorruptible simplicity: an elderly New England couple, with vague yearnings for enfranchisement, who lived in Paris as if it were a Massachusetts suburb, and dwelt hopefully on the "higher side" of the Gallic nature. With equal vividness she set before him the component figures of the circle from which Mrs. Farlow drew the "Inner Glimpses of French Life" appearing over her name in a leading New England journal: the Roumanian lady who had sent them tickets for her tragedy, an elderly French gentleman who, on the strength of a week's stay at Folkestone, translated English fiction for the provincial press, a lady from Wichita, Kansas, who advocated free love and the abolition of the corset, a clergyman's widow from Torquay who had written an "'English Ladies' Guide to Foreign Galleries" and a Russian sculptor who lived on nuts and

was "almost certainly" an anarchist. It was this nucleus, and its outer ring of musical architectural and other American students, which posed successively to Mrs. Farlow's versatile fancy as a centre of "University Life," a "Salon of the Faubourg St. Germain," a "Group of Parisian 'Intellectuals,'" or a "Cross-section of Montmartre" . . .

(*TR* 40)

Many aspects of life are lumped together here. Some, like free love, vegetarianism, and political activism are very characteristic of bohemian society, but Wharton seems to have taken the opportunity to take potshots at some subjects, such as a guide to foreign galleries written by a clergyman's widow from Torquay, which sound anything but bohemian, unless this is a veiled reference to erotic art. The point is that Mrs. Farlow's indiscriminate lumping together of such diverse beliefs is itself an indictment of bohemian outlook.

Unsurprisingly the idea of bohemia as the playground of poor artists, starving in Parisian garrets, was regarded much more romantically by artists themselves. In 1893 Puccini announced his intention to base his next opera on Henry Mürger's novel *Scènes de la vie Bohème*, though he soon discovered that a rival composer, Leoncavallo, had already started to write his own *Bohème*. Both completed their works, but though Puccini's made the greater impact, it initially received a cool reception when it was first performed in Turin in February 1896. *La Bohème*, however, with its sentimental and romantic picture of bohemian lowlife, soon began to win an audience and provide a popular image of bohemianism. The death of Mimi, the transgressively sexual but fragile, beautiful woman, conformed to that operatic convention of the death of the heroine, a convention that permitted a Victorian audience to confront their own taboos. There are easy sexual unions in *La Bohème* and no one to express disapproval. Puccini had adapted Mürger's Mimi, who is much harder and more ruthless, abandoning Rudolfo after six months in search of richer patrons. Puccini's Mimi goes to church and treasures her prayer book. In Puccini's opera Mimi becomes central, reflecting that fin de siècle fascination with the poor tragic heroine with a sexual history. Such women as Mimi inspire the poet, the musician, the painter, and the philosopher, and the love and desire that they inspire is shown as a higher thing, kindling hope and dreams in a cold winter environment in which poverty means that there is no heat and no food, only passion and the erotic charge of the body.

Mürger's *La Vie de Bohème* is the book given to Philip Carey in Somerset Maugham's 1915 novel of bohemian life, *Of Human Bondage*, and it inspires Carey to go to Paris and live this life. When Wharton was writing *The Reef*, therefore, this enduringly popular image of artistic life already had a history of over sixty years, influencing writers as different as Conan Doyle and Proust. Mürger's work was originally written as a series of sketches for a magazine, *Le Corsaire,* and published between 1845 and 1849 and then later gathered together to form the play, *La vie de Bohème.* Mürger had originally not seen himself as either a playwright or a novelist. His original ambition had been to be a poet, but the subject of poor artists proved very popular and was read as a politically incisive study, employing elements of realism and impressionism. Puccini's opera may lack the political edge, but it was an innovative piece of opera, much plainer and simpler in its content than the public was used to. Puccini also had an eye for the market, and as John Steane has noted, the length of the arias often coincided with the length of the new ten-inch 78-rpm gramophone records.[19]

Edith Wharton, whose father was a lover of opera, though she herself attended only occasionally,[20] touches on the world of student-artists in *Sanctuary,* as this is the circle in which moves Dick Peyton, the young apprentice architect who has entered a competition to design a museum of sculpture: "To his visitors' requests to be shown his plans for the competition, Peyton had opposed a laughing refusal, enforced by the presence of two fellow-architects, young men with lingering traces of the Beaux Arts in their costume and vocabulary, who stood about in Gavarni[21] attitudes and dazzled the ladies by allusions to fenestration and entasis."[22] A long way from Paris of the 1830s, this is the light world of Puccini's version of bohemia, and although we are to meet that lightness of tone in *The Reef* in the account of life in Mrs. Murrett's house, we do not encounter the poverty, cold, and hunger that is so central to Mürger and Puccini.

A fear expressed in *The Reef* is that chateau-life France sometimes shows itself just as tolerant of the loose behavior that is normally associated with the pervasive influence of bohemianism in the Latin Quarter of Paris. The verdict is that of Adelaide Painter, who in the condescending fashion of the expatriate imperialist looks down on the people native to the country she has decided to occupy. She assesses the likely consequences if Owen, Anna's stepson, is parted from Sophy, her daughter's governess, and forced to marry someone considered more suitable: "You might hustle him into that kind of marriage; I daresay you could—but if I know Owen the natural thing would happen before the first baby was weaned. . . . Do you think it would be odious of him to return to his real love when he'd been forcibly parted from her? At any rate, it is what your French friends do, every one of them! Only they don't generally have the grace to go back to an old love" (*TR,* 217). Adelaide Painter is presented in a number of contrasting lights, and it is unclear how we are to read her. At first she is a figure of fun, the stereotyped expatriate Francophobe who is more American than Americans who still live in the United States. But she is seen as direct and efficient, and Anna seems happy to have her as an ally. She describes Adelaide's views in a light and airy fashion: "She detests the French so that she'd back up Owen even if she knew something—or knew too much—of Miss Viner. She somehow regards the match as a protest against the corruption of European morals" (*TR*, 219). At times this attack on decadent Europe seems part of a Protestant, anti-Catholic agenda. At times it seems part of a more specific American belief in the superiority of New York society, which is both more moral and more energetic. There is the same ambiguity about Europe, and Americans in Europe, that we find in a Henry James novel such as *Daisy Miller*, where Daisy is cut by her fellow Americans but most fully understood by an Italian. It is clear that Daisy's unconventional behavior is misread as bohemianism, when it is really the product of a directness and freshness that higher society finds embarrassing and unacceptable.

We see bohemia at its most unsettling through the eyes of Anna Leath when she goes to visit Sophy Viner's sister Laura at the end of the novel, but it is through the American, Sophy Viner herself, that we have the novel's most cautionary message about the descent that can follow from experimenting with bohemian ways, a descent that begins in a very specific place.

Chelsea

Sophy Viner spent five years in London, in what Darrow recalls as "the awful house in Chelsea," as "one of the dumb appendages of the shrieking inescapable Mrs. Murrett" (*TR*, 15). Chelsea has long been associated with bohemianism, and in the late Victorian period achieved a certain notoriety as the place in which such colorful residents as Whistler and Oscar Wilde were seen to live an extravagantly bohemian lifestyle. Cheyne Row and Cheyne Walk were particularly favored by writers and artists in the Victorian and Edwardian periods. George Eliot, Whistler, and Turner had all occupied houses in Cheyne Walk, as had Dante Gabriel Rossetti, one of the leading poets and painters in the Pre-Raphaelite movement. Cheyne Row, which is just off Cheyne Walk, had been the home of Thomas Carlyle[23] (for forty-seven years), Oscar Wilde, and John Singer Sargent. Chelsea is also the setting for the first consummation of the "free union" initiated by Herminia Barton, who is *The Woman Who Did* in the novel by

Grant Allen that caused a great scandal when it appeared in 1895: "A week later [Alan] knocked timidly one evening at the door of a most little workman-looking cottage, down a small side street in the backwastes of Chelsea. . . . [W]ithin it was as dainty as Morris wall-papers and merino hangings and a delicate feminine taste in form and colour could make it. Keats and Shelley lined the shelves; Rossetti's wan maidens gazed unearthly from the over-mantel."[24] Although Herminia teaches at the "Carlyle Place Girls' School," there is a social divide between this and Bower Lane, the working-class street in which she lives. Both rich employer and poor neighbors share the conventional disapproval of the Shelleyan free union, which begins as the unmarried Herminia, dressed in a white gown with a white rose in her hair, ceremonially takes the chosen man to her bed.

Chelsea had particular quaint pockets of bohemianism, and a reassuringly safe picture emerged in Arthur Ransome's study *Bohemia in London* (1907). Ransome assures his readers that "Bohemia is only a stage in man's life, except in the case of fools and a very few others."[25] It is a life for young people, and for young men as "even the maddest cigarette-smoking art student, when she has married her painter, takes him away from bohemia, which is, as perhaps she knows without thinking of it, not the place for bringing up a family. The woman is always for stability and order; a precarious, haphazard, irregular, unhealthy existence has none of the compensations for her that it holds out to the husband."[26]

Ransome lived in Chelsea, supported by the income from the newspaper that published his reviews and articles. His historic survey, which takes in the Chelsea of Leigh Hunt, Lamb, Carlyle, Swinburne, Meredith, and members of the Pre-Raphaelite Brotherhood, offers a tourist's guide, in which the excesses are limited to daring dress, exuberance, and a little drinking. Though he shares Allen's utterly conventional views about the role of women, there is no hint that Chelsea and bohemia might be places of sexual freedom and decadence. Yet by 1909 it was a place frequented by the epitome of British bohemeniasm, the painter Augustus John, who was as well known for his string of lovers and traveling around Britain in a gypsy caravan as for his art.

Perhaps the most immediate reason why this district was in the forefront of Wharton's mind at this time was that Henry James, who was hardly a bohemian but who had written about the decadence of bohemian life in *The Ambassadors* (1903), wrote and lived there. In January 1912 James was struggling to write his autobiography *A Small Boy and Others*, and had rented "a couple of small and sequestered rooms in the depths of Chelsea" to which he repaired each morning to write, staying each day until two.[27] "I apply myself to my effort every morning at a little *repaire* in the depths of Chelsea, a couple of little rooms that I have secured for quiet & concentration—to which our blest taxi whirls me from hence every morning at ten o'clock, & where I meet my amanuensis."[28] Traveling by taxi from the Reform Club to rooms where he would dictate to a typist may not seem the essence of bohemian life, but it is artistic environment that is important, as is shown by this letter to Mary Cadwalader Jones, in which James again emphasizes the modest size of the rooms: "I have a couple of very modest and sequestered little rooms in the dim depths of Chelsea..............London sins of course always by excess."[29] Chelsea had been the setting for the bohemian party in which Kate Croy meets Merton Densher in *The Wings of the Dove* (1902).[30]

The ellipsis in James's letter is his own, allowing the word "Chelsea" to sink in before supplying a characteristically playful verdict on his new environment, which he clearly found congenial. In September James found a five-bedroom flat on the fifth floor of 21 Carlyle Mansions in Cheyne Walk, and liked it and its price sufficiently to take out a lease that began in January 1913. By then Wharton had finished *The Reef*, which she had worked on intensively during a "rest cure" in Salsomaggiore, northern Italy, in mid-May 1912. By June she had completed two-thirds of the manuscript, which she sent to Fullerton for his comments, as she hesitated before writing the key scene in which Anna learns of Darrow's affair with Sophy.[31] Wharton did not visit Henry James in London until July, when they went on a number of excursions (when she departed in mid-August he spoke of his relief that the greatest "whirligig . . . known to the 'Annals of Man'" was now motoring in the Auvergne.[32] Although Wharton's previous significant visit to London had been in December 1911, when she met John Singer Sargent to discuss the proposed charcoal portrait of Henry James, she regularly corresponded with James, and during the writing of *The Reef* in the spring and summer of 1912 would have been aware of his Chelsea connections. However, her letter of November 27, 1911 to Charles Scribner[33] suggests that she had already started work on the *The Reef* by then, and the meeting with Sargent in his Tite Street studio the following month may have triggered thoughts of the world of bohemia, and scandal, though Sargent's reputation for scandalous painting had long since passed. Tite Street is in Chelsea, a few minutes away from Cheyne Walk, and his studio had been Whistler's.

Sophy Viner is thus placed in the context of Chelsea's reputation for bohemian society, but like Vance Weston in *The Gods Arrive*, she is not yet "corrupted" by it. "How could such a face have been merged in the Murrett mob?" muses Darrow, who imagines Sophy in a ruff, with a rose behind her ear, taking part in an Italian comedy (*TR,* 16). Such an observation, however, may be interpreted as a consciously superficial reading of Sophy, a repetition of the kind of projection of male fantasy that was visited on Lily Bart by Selden in *The House of Mirth.* It is a projection very evident in *The Woman Who Did,* where Herminia is described as wearing "a curious oriental-looking navy-blue robe of some some soft woollen stuff, that fell in natural folds and set off to the utmost the lissom grace of her rounded figure" and having a "free and vigorous English girl's body."[34] Herminia, advanced as she is in her views on "free unions" is emphatically distinguished by the narrator from the group of New Women who reject motherhood as well as marriage. Grant Allen's Herminia is an invention who allows the narrator to reassert conventional views on the childbearing role of women:

> Every good woman is by nature a mother, and finds best in maternity her social and moral salvation. She shall be saved in child-bearing. Herminia was far removed indeed from that blatant and decadent set of "advanced women" who talk as though motherhood were a disgrace and a burden, instead of being, as it is, the full realization of woman's faculties, the natural outlet for woman's wealth of emotion.[35]

Though inclined in her later, post–World War I comments to favor "traditional" roles for women, Wharton would have allowed herself a smile at the description of female placidity in the narrator's earlier claim that "[d]eep down in the very roots of the idea of sex we come on that prime antithesis—the male, active and aggressive; the female, sedentary, passive, and receptive."[36] What is revealing, however, is how even those texts with apparently radical antibourgeois ideas could maintain essentialist ideas about sexual difference.

Much has been made of Sophy's first name, signifying wisdom, and her last, signifying the pleasures of the sybaritic life.[37] This duality seems to stand for an internal tension, as the competing elements of mind and refinement and body and sensual pleasure wrestle for supremacy in her life. At first the finer elements seem to triumph. She escapes the "dreadful" house in which she has been a "reader" for five years, following a quarrel with Mrs. Murrett. Darrow having assumed she is Mrs. Murrett's niece, Sophy says that she can imagine nothing worse. He shares her judgment, regarding the Murrett household as a "blurred tapestry" (*TR,* 17). It is a place of crystal-gazing and hypnotism, visited by "Mademoiselle—and Professor Didymus and the Polish Countess" (*TR,* 18). It has provided Sophy with her only education after boarding school, and it has not been a good one. But she is not yet damned. Following her outburst at the unfairness of a culture in which Lady Ulrica, for no apparent reason that Sophy can fathom, had been given the privileges of clothes, admiration, yachting, and Paris, while she, Sophy, has the drudgery of straightening accounts, seeing the dogs get their sulfur, and copying visiting lists, Darrow concludes that she "had stuff in her." At this early stage in the novel Sophy is determined to turn envy into achievement and seems another incarnation of Lily Bart, though crucially lacking the "capital" that is Lily's striking beauty.

Other glimpses of Sophy, however, suggest a woman that the narrative is unsure about. Her indiscreet reference to Lady Ulrica never daring to "un—," because she is an assembled beauty who came apart like a puzzle, makes her blush with a mixture of envy and realization. For Lady Ulrica to remove her clothes before a lover would be to reveal the falseness that was hers "from head to foot," in Sophy's phrase. Thus Sophy teased Jimmy Dance, who had been convinced that Darrow and Lady Ulrica were lovers (*TR*, 18). The indiscretion of Sophy's comment is signaled by the narrator's refusal to write down the second part of the word that Sophy breaks in two. It is indelicate in mixed company to talk about women undressing. A code has been broken.

The account of Sophy's upbringing, the tale of an orphan who loses even the small inheritance that her guardian had been promising, is a story of neglect and adult indifference. The Farlows, the bohemian Farlows, with whom Sophy has been staying after her traveling companion in Europe elopes with an American "matineé idol," find her a place with the "turbid" Mrs. Murrett, in the belief that the Chelsea house is the last of the salons. It is not, but Sophy endures her five years there with a "light hearted philosophy" that Darrow finds appealing. Lady Ulrica notwithstanding, Darrow does not generally approve of women who are clearly neither ladies nor of the "other kind." He is suspicious of the "third type" who shelter behind the privileges of one class to conceal the customs of another. But Sophy falls into the category "girl," and Darrow's judgment is that "her experience had made her free without hardness and self-assured without assertiveness" (*TR*, 27). In that rather double-edged phrase, she has been acquainted with "the real business of living" (ibid.). Later, however, during the ten days they spend together in Paris, Darrow's impressions of Sophy are more critical. He notices how bored she is by art galleries and ideas, and that it is the "story" that interests her most when they go to see a play. Her description of her own sense of independence begins to irritate him, and the rhetoric here seems to be the narrator's as much as it is Darrow's:

"Besides," she rambled on, 'I'm not so sure that I believe in marriage. You see I'm all for self-development and the chance to live one's life. I'm awfully modern, you know."

It was just when she proclaimed herself most awfully modern that she struck him as most helplessly backward; yet the moment after, without any bravado, or apparent desire to assume an attitude, she would propound some social axiom which could have been gathered only in the bitter soil of experience.

(*TR*, 62)

The combination of annoyance and admiration is typical of the ambiguous way in which Sophy is presented to us through Darrow's eyes. She is described in terms that emphasize her insubstantiality: "She hung about him like a leaf on the meeting cross-currents, that the next ripple may sweep forward or whirl back. Then she flung up her head with the odd boyish movement habitual to her in moments of excitement" (*TR*, 72). This is the second reference to Sophy's boyishness (the allusion is also made when she is first introduced) and it may be of no significance. Most biographical accounts of the relationship between Wharton and Fullerton tend to assume that Wharton was ignorant of his bisexuality. It would be a mistake, therefore, to suggest that this is a coded reference to a particular kind of homoerotic sexual relationship, given that Sophy reappears in the text and becomes engaged quite conventionally to Owen. Furthermore the "boyish" look, with bobbed hair and shapeless smock dresses, was becoming fashionable with some young women, as we can see from contemporary photographs of Dorothy Brett, Carrington, and others from the pre–World War I Slade Art College set. The epicene look clearly intrigued Wharton. In *The Custom of the Country* the Princess Estradina is described as bohemian in her dress, having traces of artificial color in her hair and mauve powder on her face. She has a "boyish" aspect and the "gait of a baker's boy balancing his basket."[38] But this androgyny is not intended to suggest a straightforward Sapphic inclination. The text is ambiguous. The princess is separated from a husband and has two daughters.

But if the boyishness of Sophy in *The Reef* is not there to suggest the taboo of homosexuality, there is another transgression that is frequently being hinted at. Sophy is in her early twenties, Darrow, thirty-seven and nearly old enough to be her father. In Victorian and Edwardian Europe such an age difference between lovers was neither unusual nor remarkable (Edith's husband was thirteen years her senior and middle-aged men often married very young women). The text frequently reminds us, however, that in Darrow's eyes Sophy is very young indeed: "Her behaviour had all the indecision and awkwardness of inexperience. It showed that she was a child after all; and all that he could do—all he had ever meant to do—was to give her a child's holiday to look back to" (*TR*, 72). This does not prevent Darrow, who shares a first name with Edith Wharton's father, from taking Sophy to his bed, however, and in the presentation of this betrayal of trust there is more than a little of the rhetoric of the fatherly role in *Lolita*. To Sophy it is an adventure that she is willing to embark on. We are told, both by Darrow and by Sophy herself, that there was no persuasion. On the other hand, there is nothing of the proud assertiveness and "principle" that characterizes the strong-willed Herminia in *The Woman Who Did*. The willingness to enter a "free union" may be similar, but the constant reference to her childlike relation to Darrow is suggestive of the incest theme that is traceable in *Ethan Frome, Summer,* and the much-discussed fragment from "Beatrice Palmato." It is a theme to which we shall return.

The depiction of Sophy is too complex for her to stand simply as a metonym for bohemia. It is true that she behaves in a way characteristic of the uncommitted artist in abandoning her ambitions to be an actor. This apparent dilettantism, a trait that irked Wharton in life, makes it less surprising that Candace Waid in her discussion of Wharton's use of the myth of Persephone does not discuss Sophy, even though she superficially matches the image of the woman artist who has visited the underworld and leaves an ineradicable impression on those who remain above. She has tasted of the pomegranate seeds of eroticism, and the death of her parents cause her to be prematurely separated from her mother. Like the rival women haunted by the letters from their husband's previous lovers (in *The Touchstone*, and in the "Pomegranate Seed"),[39] Anna is haunted by the knowledge that Darrow and Sophy have been lovers, and envies the knowledge and experience of sexual fulfilment and freedom that Sophy seems to have. The novel's description of Sophy even confirms the observation made by Waid that these Persephones are to all intents and purposes ghosts, and thus provide a link with (and an explanation for) the ghost story genre that so interested Wharton. Sophy is pale and ghostlike when we last see her: "Sophy Viner appeared almost immediately, dressed for departure, her little bag on her arm. She was still pale to the point of haggardness, but with a light upon her that struck Anna with surprise." (*TR*, 278). There is a price to pay for this descent into the underworld, as well as a reward, and if elsewhere Wharton shows that the price is worth the reward, and that the artist has to suffer for her art, that is not the final message here.

It is perhaps for this reason that Waid does not cite this novel as evidence of Wharton's exploration of the power of women. As in

Ethan Frome, no one escapes from the penalty exacted for a moment of erotic pleasure. The downfall of the three central characters has all the inevitability of classical tragedy, with disaster the consequence of their own earlier behavior. Thus the novel's Racinian reputation, established by Henry James. But if Sophy is not bohemia, it is bohemia that has programmed her to enjoy ten day's pleasure with Darrow, with no worries about the consequences. Had she not, in the judgment of the narrative, felt free from constraints, then the prospect of a reasonably happy marriage to Owen could later have been realized. Darrow, too, has shown weakness, and his pursuit of Lady Ulrica in the Chelsea house is intended to show that he has also been drawn to this corrupting world. For it is the corrosive effect of bohemian practice that the rhetoric of Wharton's novels warns against. The novels show bohemian values as patriarchal and damaging, assigning women, in Hermione Lee's words, the role of "muses, models or mistresses."[40] Wharton delays the full exposure of these corrosive and corrupting effects until the end with the final scene revealing to us the full vulgarity of Sophy's sister in Paris.

Paris

The horror of bohemia is brought to the fore in the closing scene in which Anna visits Sophy's sister in an attempt to discover Sophy's whereabouts. Laura McTarvie-Birch is a singer who lives in the Hôtel Chicago near the Place de l'Etoile. Each of these names carries its own significant allusion. The Place de l'Etoile is the site of the Arc de Triomphe, but the moments that follow are to be anything but triumphant. Moreover, the Place is named after the star of destiny (important streets radiate out from it) so there is further irony in the name of the location. Although the district is highly fashionable, the hotel has the name of a midwestern city, and in Wharton the Midwest is the place from which bad women come.[41] The occupation "singer" seems to be offered as a euphemism for a woman of loose morals,[42] and we are told that Laura has experienced the "vicissitudes" of the much married. Her current married name is suggestive of the practices of sadomasochistic prostitution, for she is identified as "Mrs. Birch" throughout her conversation with Anna. Laura is now living with her current lover, Jimmy Brance, a man who is dealt with in the usual merciless way reserved by Wharton for those who have met with her disapproval: "Anna was still wondering when and in what conjunction of circumstances the much-married Laura had acquired a partner so conspicuous for his personal charms, when the young man returned to announce 'She says it's all right, if you don't mind seeing her in bed" (*TR*, 364).

We have met Jimmy Brance before, of course. He was a regular enough visitor at Mrs. Murrett's house for Sophy Viner to have been on familiar terms with him and he is a reminder of that awful place (awful to all the "respectable" characters in *The Reef*). The concluding scene of the novel is not such an odd digression if we see Jimmy Brance as a convenient analepsis,[43] making the reader return to the world of Mrs. Murrett, to realize the inevitable trajectory down the slippery slope whose mouth opens up in that world.

For if the presentation of the Paris hotel occupants were not enough to make clear the moral, the interior is described with a level of detail that has been absent in most of the preceding narrative, and the function of this detail is to show us dinginess, corruption, and vulgarity that is suggested by Mrs. Birch's pink bed, her caramel-eating pink dog, and the lurid appearance of the pink curtains and immense pink powder puff. The bedroom is "dim, untidy" and "scented" and the reader has been prepared for this unedifying scene by the description of the journey through the interior of the hotel. The "hesitating" lift carries Anna up past a succession of "shabby landings." The passage along which she then walks smells of "sea-going luggage," an indicator of transience, while the narrow sitting room into which she is admitted reeks with the strong smell of tobacco. In this room, with its "faded roses" and "devastated breakfast tray" Anna is inspected by a silent, "short, swarthy" man, presumably a money-lender, who assesses Anna in material, commercial terms: "Under his gaze she had the sense of being minutely catalogued and valued; and the impression, when he finally rose and moved toward the door, of having been accepted as a better guarantee than he had had any reason to hope for" *TR*, 363). The point of this depiction of the squalid world that Laura inhabits is to show us Sophy's inevitable future, and the inevitable future of all who engage in casual relationships. Most disturbingly, Laura's fate, which is linked to Sophy's, is presented as a matter of genetics: "In the roseate penumbra of the bed-curtains she presented to Anna's startled gaze an odd chromo-like resemblance to Sophy Viner, or a suggestion, rather, of what Sophy Viner might, with the years and in spite of the powder-puff, become" (*TR*, 365). Anna's horror of the powder puff is signaled in an earlier scene when Sophy appears with traces of powder on her face. The cheapness and vulgarity of this causes Anna to recoil until she realizes that Sophy has been trying to mask the fact that she has been crying. Even so it is a reminder of Sophy's earlier ambition to be an actress, a thought that horrifies Madame de Chantelle when she imagines the "unspeakable" people that Sophy has probably been mixed up with.⁴⁴ But in this final scene we learn that Sophy has gone to accompany the vulgar Mrs. Murrett to India, and her return to the netherworld is guaranteed.

This damning indictment and rejection of bohemian values and the world that Sophy inhabits comes as something of a surprise, because right up until this final scene the narrative has been wavering between an anxiety about, and an understanding of, a mode of sexual behavior that is outlawed in Old New York society. There seems to be an understanding that terms like "bohemian" and "modern" are used extremely loosely, and are relative. In Wharton's next novel, *The Custom of the Country*, bohemianism is treated fairly lightly, as something fashionable, like literature. At one point Undine thinks it would be nice to be married to an artist, and encourages Ralph to take up his novel again: "She already saw herself, as the wife of a celebrated author, wearing 'artistic' dresses and doing the drawing-room over with Gothic tapestries and dim lights in altar candlesticks."⁴⁵ Bohemianism in *The Custom of the Country* is equated with cosmopolitanism and the exchange of tradition for the modern in Parisian society: "Madame de Trézac . . . [threw] off the most sacred observance of her past. She took up Madame Adelschein, she entertained the James J. Rollivers, she resuscitated Creole dishes, she patronized negro melodists, she abandoned her weekly teas for impromptu afternoon dances, and the prim drawing room in which dowagers had droned echoed with a cosmopolitan hubbub."⁴⁶ In *The Reef*, where the treatment is also sometimes lightly satirical, Madame de Chantelle observes signs of dangerous radicalism in Anna: "Don't think, please, that I'm casting the least reflection on Anna, or showing any want of sympathy for her, when I say that I consider her partly responsible for what's happened. Anna is 'modern'—I believe that's what it's called when you read unsettling books and admire hideous pictures (*TR*, 190).

Not for a moment is this assessment meant to be taken seriously, but it does seem to be part of a long process of social reevaluation for Anna. The recognition of the power of passion and desire that comes to the awakened Anna seems to promise an epiphany. It perhaps does, but the sight that Anna sees before her in the Hôtel Chicago confirms the rightness of her decision to give Darrow up. We do not know that she does so, because Sophy's absence means that the announcement is not made, but in the rhetoric of the novel the honorable intention was to save Sophy and not to marry a man who has dallied with the attractions of the demimonde. The experience has led Anna to a fresh understanding of the complexities of the world, but as far as Anna is concerned, to understand is not to accept. In this respect, she is like Kate Orme in *Sanctuary*, a woman driven to action because she can see the dangers of nonintervention. The rhetoric of the novel wishes the reader to accept Anna's political view of society and human behavior, just as it does Kate's, and the observation Janet Beer makes about Denis Peyton and Kate could equally apply to Anna and George Darrow:

> There is a peculiar inversion of innocence and experience in process here; Denis, who "knew about these things!" is less capable of understanding the worst human terrors because his failures of imagination protect him from comprehension of "moral darkness." So, the young woman who has been carefully safeguarded from too much knowledge of the world; "—such things are kept from girls"—is the one capable of plumbing the depths of the "abyss" because she has been nurtured to reverberate to every nuance of the moral "labyrinths" that lead away from the points at which she encounters, in her imagination, the complexities of the outside world.[47]

I do not think that Darrow is shown to be quite so obtuse as Peyton. He has intelligence and a developed aesthetic sense, and he seems to be far more successful at this job than Denis ever is. But the argument of *The Reef* seems to be that for all George's masculine knowledge of the ways of the world, he is not a good judge of the consequences of action. For all of Anna's lack of experience of the reef, she is aware of its dangers because she can imagine sinking into the "submarine jungle" that would be the consequence of the moral collision. Only if that is the case can the otherwise odd concluding episode of the novel be vindicated. The contemporary fear of the extinction of humankind, encouraged by Herbert Spencer's speculation that as humans degenerated other species would become dominant, was reflected in stories in which ants or cephalopods replace us. The particular origin of the underworld/abyss metaphor, which haunted so many Edwardian writers, can be traced to one such story, H. G. Wells's "In the Abyss" (1896), a tale of a diver discovering a civilization of reptilian bipeds who live in a city below the sea.[48] The message is that there are others waiting to take over if we lower our guard. The fear of the abyss and the anxiety about the degeneration of human civilization was a prevalent one in 1912, and it is a very pertinent fear with which to end a novel whose title is *The Reef*, a place where some of the gaudy creatures are very poisonous.

RACINE, BERGSON, AND THE LIFE OF PASSION

An emphasis on these anxieties about bohemia would seem to be at odds with Blake Nevius's claim that Wharton wanted the best of both worlds, "that of old New York and that of Bohemia," and that her "republic of the spirit," as outlined by Selden in *The House of Mirth*, accommodates a compromise between the two.[49] This verdict is true only if we accept the respectable, dilettante version of bohemia, the one described by Arthur Ransome in *Bohemia in London*, as a legitimate version of an imprecise term. Can the rich be bohemian? The cases of Lord Byron, and (much nearer Wharton's time) of Lady Ottoline Morrell[50] would seem to suggest that wealth is not a barrier. This being so, two things become clear. The artistically inclined, materially comfortable characters who feature in Wharton's 1910–13 fiction can be associated with bohemia, though they are not poor, and the rejection of bohemia in *The Reef* is a rejection of Bohemia's manners and morals, not its art. It is only after 1915 that she questions its art.

Although Wharton was unhappy about the final appearance of *The Reef*,[51] Henry James admired this novel more than any other. In a letter to Howard Sturgis written on 10 December 1912 he wrote: "I think she is very wonderful to have been able to write the exquisite 'Reef' (for I told her that what is finest in The Reef to be really exquisite, and haven't scrupled to try inordinately to encourage her by putting that faith in the most emphatic way."[52] Earlier, on December 4, he had written to Wharton: "Anna is really of Racine, and one presently begins to feel her throughout as an Eriphyle or a Bérénice."[53]

In this same letter Henry James praises Wharton for having shed the latent influence of George Eliot, and having found her own voice in this novel, which is "stronger, firmer and finer" than those that have gone before. James's comment that *The Reef* is Edith Wharton's Racinian novel would have been pleasing to Edith Wharton for a number of reasons. Racine was a much-admired dramatist of the classical era of French drama, and like James, Wharton had a high regard for the French literary tradition. As a dramatist of ideas, whose concentration on character and the exclusion of all material extraneous to the main theme, he represented a writer of tragedies who kept to the unities and took great care with the structuring of form. These qualities were highly valued by Wharton, and her novel announces a five-book structure that corresponds to the five-act structure of tragedy.

If these Racinian qualities seem to place the novel in a tradition of late seventeenth-century classical drama, greatly distant from twentieth-century theater, its Racinian theme bridges the centuries. As Margaret Forster points out: "Central to the majority of [Racine's] tragedies is a perception of the blind folly of human passion, continually enslaved to the pursuit of its object and destined always to be unsatisfied."[54] Wharton was fully aware of this idea in her beloved Keats, where the moment of pursuit is captured and frozen on the frieze of the Grecian Urn, and it is another concept that anticipates Lacan's idea of the Other, always unattainable, always unreachable and unrealizable. In the imagery of the novel, it is the cup from which Darrow drinks a deep draught of pleasure, only to find the source of the spring tainted (*TR*, 255), an image made even more explicit when Anna seems to offer her beauty "held up like a cup to his lips, but as he stooped to it a darkness seemed to fall between them" (*TR*, 268). Better sometimes to accept the dream for what it is, and not become a slave to it. But in Keats the vision of the Grecian Urn also suggests a fear of sexuality and an equation of sexual experience with violence, with the garlanded heifer being taken to be sacrificed, amid the "mad pursuit," the "maidens loth," the "struggle to escape" and "the wild ecstasy." The lover can never kiss his beloved, but he will always have his love and never will she fade. It is a "Cold Pastoral," but for Keats there are the consolations of abstract, unspoiled, eternal Beauty. Panting love remains forever undisappointed: "unheard" melodies are sweeter.

Wharton's novel engages with a central question that had exercised Western culture after the first great wave of romanticism had swept across Europe. How is life to be understood, and how is life to be experienced? As an intellectual question this has political ramifications, because if Racine was right and passion enslaves, then reason, logic, and science are the tools by which human beings can liberate themselves, and a political model founded on order, rules, and laws is to be preferred to the alternative, which is anarchy and barbarism. But what if the romantics, including her cherished Keats, were right in identifying something that can only be understood through the experience of the sublime, something that transcends reason? What if truth *is* beauty? What if reason is efficient but cold, while the very uncontained and disordered nature of passion and feeling is what brings a fulfillment to life, through the experience of the threat of obliteration that is at the the heart of the sublime, or the energy and action celebrated by Georges Sorel? The idea of "Life" is a recurrent and very important one to Wharton. In the early years of her marriage to Teddy, the short story "The Fulness of Life," had chronicled the absence of passion in a marriage. Her passionate poem written at the height of the affair with Fullerton had been called "Life" and the fragment of the abandoned first draft of chapter 1 of her autobiography was called "Life and I." In *The Reef,* the narrative takes us back to Anna's youth in New York society and the hopes that she then had: "Some day she would find the magic bridge between West Fifty-fifth street and life; once or twice she had even fancied that the clue was in her hand. The first time was when she had met young Darrow. She recalled even now the stir of the encounter. But his passion swept over her like wind that shakes the roof of the forest without reaching its still glades or rippling its hidden pools" (*TR*, 88). Anna had wondered how she could have been so cold in his presence, and in the dead of night would get up to try new ways of doing her hair. But when next in his company it would be the same as before: "[A]s soon as he reappeared her head straightened itself on her slim neck and she sped her little shafts of irony, or flew her little kites of erudition, while hot and cold waves swept over her, and the things she really wanted to say choked in her throat and burned the palms of her hands" (*TR*, 89).

But there is no great mystery about this behavior, or about this struggle. Earlier in the same chapter Anna recalls how as a girl she envied other girls their intimacy, what she calls the "freemasonry" between them. These young women "seemingly unaware of her world of hidden beauty, were yet possessed of some vital secret which escaped her" (*TR*, 87). In all of this there are echoes of Bergson's élan vital, the driving life force described by Bergson (who was a great influence on the later Sorel) in his 1907 work *L'Évolution créatrice*, published in English as *Creative Evolution* in 1911. Wharton was an avid reader of Bergson during her early years in Paris,[55] when his reputation was at its highest. He was most well known for the concept of duration, and his belief that time was a reality, and at first it may appear odd that Wharton was so interested in his philosophy. Yet Wharton would no doubt have wanted to know what it was about Bergson that caused such widespread interest, and the challenge that he posed to her belief in the need for reason, logic, and order may well have been part of the attraction. Bergson was not a proponent of mysticism, but he did believe that certain kinds of knowledge can only be gained directly and intuitively, without the machinery of concept, symbol, and the operation of the intellect. In *Creative Evolution* Bergson argues that because evolution presses human beings to triumph in what is essentially a material world, all those faculties, such as reason, science, and language, which allow Homo sapiens to dominate that world, have been developed, but at the expense of intuition and direct understanding. It is important to recognize that for humans to evolve the élan vital must be understood as including this intuitive element, which must be acknowledged and cherished. Such a view would explain to Wharton this sense she had that for all intelligence and intellectual faculties sometimes seemingly unremarkable people had an ability, a directness, an intuition about what to do in any given circumstance that she did not possess. This, then, would parallel in the novel the "vital secret which escaped [Anna]." But it is not that this element is missing in her, it is rather that it has been suppressed by the values of the society in which she has been reared. Anna feels a sense of exclusion, and this "deepened the reserve which made envious mothers cite her as a model of lady-like repression' (*TR*, 86). This repression of feeling is characteristic of her upbringing: "Sometimes, with a sense of groping in a topsy-turvy universe, Anna had wondered why everybody about her seemed to ignore all the passions and sensations which formed the stuff of great poetry and memorable action. In a community composed entirely of people like her parents and her parents' friends she did not see how the magnificent things one read about could ever have happened. She was sure that if anything of the kind had occurred in her immediate circle her mother would have consulted the family clergyman, and her father perhaps even have rung up the police" (*TR*, 87).

Bauer points out how twice Wharton refers to the "police" as a central metaphor for the control of passions and sensation in Anna's world. Much later in the novel, Anna has her eyes opened by events and now "looked back with melancholy derision on her old conception of life, as a kind of well-lit and well-policed suburb to dark places one need never know about. Here there were dark places, in her own bosom, and henceforth she would always have to traverse them to reach the beings she loved best!" (*TR*, 353).

In her fiction Wharton's narrator frequently observes how significant environment is in determining behavior and perception. Anna's hesitancy and silence on sexual subjects contrasts with Sophy's frankness, which surprises Darrow when Sophy wants to know more about a famous actress: "[T]he next moment [she] was questioning him about Cerdine's theatrical situation and her private history. On the latter point some of her enquiries were of a kind that it is not in the habit of young girls to make, or even to know how to make; but her apparent unconsciousness of the fact seemed rather to reflect on her past associates than on herself" (*TR*, 49).

There is a similar argument in James's *Daisy Miller*, but Daisy's provincial New York State background explains her apparent forwardness. Though there is the predictable urban sophisticate's patronage of provincial life, Winterbourne's judgment of Daisy is seen to be flawed, and there is nothing to say that she is anything but "innocent," even if her innocence amounts in the rhetoric of the novel to a disastrous naïveté. Darrow, like Winterbourne, is the male dilettante, the American who has become jaded, perhaps, through being too long in Europe. Early on in the novel he is seen to possess a world-weary manner, which is shared by his acquaintances:

> It was wonderfully pleasant to be able to give such pleasure. Darrow was not rich, but it was almost impossible for him to picture the state of persons with tastes and perceptions like his own, to whom an evening at the theatre was an unattainable indulgence. There floated through his mind an answer of Mrs Leath's to his enquiry whether she had seen the play in question. "No. I meant to, of course, but one is so overwhelmed with things, in Paris. And then I'm rather sick of Cerdine—one is always dragged to see her"
> That, among the people he frequented, was the usual attitude towards such opportunities. There were too many, they were a nuisance, one had to defend one's self! He even remembered wondering, at the moment, whether to a really fine taste the exceptional thing could ever become indifferent through habit; whether the appetite for beauty was so soon dulled that it could be kept alive only by privation.
>
> (*TR*, 33)

But if Darrow is a counterpart to Winterbourne, Sophy is no Daisy. She mixes with people with advanced views and she has no inhibitions about sleeping with Darrow. She is neither misunderstood, nor are we asked to believe that she is taken advantage of. She simply follows her passion and her sense of adventure to whatever goals they seem to lead her. Darrow's impression is of a "girl" willing to enjoy a brief sexual encounter in the Paris springtime, a moment of mutual pleasure without any long-term consequences. In the Edwardian period this was the male view of sex that was challenged by such texts as Christabel Pankhurst's *The Great Scourge and How to End It* (1913). Here it is a view held and practiced by a woman. Ultimately Wharton's novel endorses the view that there is no such thing as harmless, casual sex, but this conclusion is reached only after many readings of "a free union" have been examined.

SOCIETY, CONVENTIONS AND THE POLICING OF DESIRE

In one respect *The Reef* seems to signal that it will pick up the baton of *Ethan Frome*. The name of the French country house, Givré, suggests the freezing world of rime and hoarfrost. We move rapidly from the spring of the opening scene to the autumn at Givré, and although there is no snow and ice, there is much rain. It is as if they are underwater in this French house by the river, where umbrellas and outer coats are a necessity. The mood echoes that of *Bleak House*, where in Chesney Wold, a great house in Lincolnshire, England, a couple are to be separated by the discovery of an affair that the young Lady Dedlock had before she married. Here too the rain drenches the grounds, and there is an atmosphere of suspicion and surveillance. In *The Reef,* the rain and Sophy's tattered umbrella bring Darrow and Sophy together at Dover, and it conspires to bring them, when they walk together under Darrow's umbrella, to the injured child in the lodge house.

Yet Wharton's title, threatening though it may be, also suggests the warmth and life of the tropical sea. For there is an ambiguity in the notion of a reef. Ships may perish on its hidden dangers, but it can also provide protection and shelter to those who move inside it. The novel is as much an exploration of that protective world of custom and convention as it is of the damaging effects of the unyielding barrier of hard coral and the wreckage this may cause. Many ships go down in this novel, but Anna navigates her way back to the calm waters of the lagoon. At the risk of overextending the metaphor, Anna has dived down to see the inhabitants and forms of the reef and she does not like what she sees there. This feeling is true not only of her concluding journey into the bohemian world of Laura Birch, but of earlier moments, as when she feels that in allowing herself to stay in Darrow's room she is repeating the experience of other women he has known, or in the description of Adelaide Painter, who is the only one who feels comfortable at a moment of high tension in the house: "Miss Painter alone seemed not only unaffected by the general perturbation but as tightly sealed up in her unconsciousness of it as a diver in his bell" (*TR,* 226). Here the underwater world is one that can only be entered safely by those who are sealed from its dangers. Adelaide Painter is presented as a ridiculous woman in many ways, but her practicality and reliability are features that both Darrow and Anna acknowledge, and benefit from. For all his greater sophistication and intelligence, Darrow is not able to descend to the exotic and return to the surface unharmed: "It was Darrow's instinct, in difficult moments, to go straight to the bottom of the difficulty; but he had never before had to make so dark a dive as this, and for the moment he shivered on the brink" (*TR,* 153). But the movement of the water is sirenlike and seductive: "He felt again the sweep of the secret tides, and all his fears went down in them" (*TR,* 156). In this "sea" environment, which is associated with the women who dominate this novel, Darrow is out of his depth.

The reef, like desire, is both a place of delight and danger. To Marilyn French, the reef on which we founder is passion, but it is at the center of life itself.[56] It is the hidden nature of the reef, like the suppression of desire, that is its fascination. Anna is a woman who has been educated to suppress her passions, but to what end? Darrow questions the very values that he had felt were under threat at the Chelsea house of Mrs. Murrett. Perhaps Chelsea has its good points after all, if it can foster the directness and openness of a Sophy, who is such a contrast to the more respectable Anna:

> The reflection set him wondering whether the "sheltered" girl's upbringing might not unfit her for all subsequent contact with life. How much nearer to it had Mrs. Leath been brought by marriage and motherhood, and the passage of fourteen years? What were all her reticences and evasions but the results of the deadening process of forming a "lady"? The freshness he had marvelled at was like the unnatural whiteness of flowers forced in the dark.
>
> (*TR*, 29)

This is a damning indictment of the effect on young women of the values of respectable society. But how is Sophy really to be read? In Singley's view she represents both wisdom and the female principle of the Old Testament, and she is the victim in this narrative. Her fate is an indictment of a society that will not allow women to be open, passionate, sexual, and spontaneous. It is a society that controls women because it fears them. Bauer takes a very different line, seeing Sophy as the embodiment of all that Wharton distrusted in the New Woman.[57] The "freedom" which is on display in the last chapter is shown to be sex, which is mercenary, tawdry, and prostitutional. Certainly the narrative is not kind to Sophy in the flashback, which gives Darrow's view of the circumstance in which he and Sophy became lovers. "She hadn't a drop of poetry in her" Darrow recalls (*TR*, 262), and he is dissuaded from taking her to the Louvre because "when he had tried looking at pictures with her she had first so persistently admired the worst things, and then so frankly lapsed into indifference, that he had no wish to repeat the experiment" (*TR*, 263).

If there is an ambiguity about Sophy, there is no less an ambiguity about Anna. The reticence and evasions that Darrow finds so frustrating, and that Anna herself is so very conscious of, are not the product of a coldness and absence of feeling, though this is the impression that can easily be given. Anna is possessed by a passion that she struggles to control. Its suppression is usually successful, but when released, it is an overwhelmingly erotic force:

> The sense of power she had been aware of in talking to Darrow came back with tenfold force. She felt like testing him by the most fantastic exactions, and at the same moment she longed to humble herself before him,

> to make herself the shadow and echo of his mood. She wanted to linger with him in a world of fancy and yet to walk at his side in the world of fact. She wanted him to feel her power and yet to love her for her ignorance and humility. She felt like a slave, and a goddess, and girl in her teens . . .
> (*TR*, 125)

As so very often, the ellipsis seems to signal a move toward the ineffability of desire and the unspeakable character of the erotic: "They paced the paths between the trees, found a moldy Temple of Love on an islet among reed and plantain, and sitting on a bench in the stable yard, watched the pigeons circling against the sunset over their cot of patterned brick. Then the motor flew on into the dusk . . ." (*TR*, 127). Anna and Darrow are at their most intimate in this part of the novel, and as often in Wharton the hand becomes the part of the body that stands for eroticization: "[H]e mused on the enjoyment there would always be in the mere fact of watching her hands as they moved about among the tea-things . . ." (ibid.). The ellipses lead the reader to speculate on what meanings or events have not been expressed, and translate the banal into the suggestive. Elsewhere the ellipses suggest moments of romantic transcendence, when physical intimacy is presented in terms of a journey toward the celestial: "He recalled every detail of her face, the fine veinings of the temples, the bluish-brown shadows in her upper lids, and the way the reflections of two stars seemed to form and break up in her eyes when he held her close to him . . ." (*TR*, 130). Sometimes the ellipses serve as an observation of the passion of emotional struggle, not between the two lovers, but within Anna, where jealousy and passion compete with pride and decorum as she asks Darrow delicate but insistent questions about the night at the Paris theater when he encountered Owen. They also suggest the male vanity, which, being the object of desire, can stimulate: "Yes! It was worth a good deal to watch that fight between her instinct and her intelligence, and know one's self the object of the struggle . . ." (*TR*, ibid.).

The ellipses can also stand for the seething emotions and whirling of thoughts that a secret sexual history can generate when that history threatens to surface in a way that would prove disastrous. Darrow finds himself being questioned about Sophy by Owen, and the situation threatens to move beyond the control of Darrow's skills in diplomacy: "His sensations were too swift and swarming to be disentangled. He had an almost physical sense of struggling for air, of battling helplessly with material obstructions, as though the russet covert through which he trudged were the heart of a maleficent jungle . . ." (*TR*, 144). But most of all the ellipses seem to stand for moments of erotic and physical intimacy, which are so sublime as to defy the spoken or written word. One of the final clusters is, ironically, when Darrow is recalling his affair with Sophy and the moments that led to the beginning of their sexual relationship:

> She had said: "I wonder what your feeling for me was?" and he found himself wondering too . . .
> [S]he had committed the fatal error of saying that she could see he was unhappy, and entreating him to tell her why . . .
> Darrow felt as if he has clasped a tree and a nymph had bloomed from it . . .
> [T]he summer wind stirred in the trees, and close by, between the nearest branches and the brim of his tilted hat, a slight white figure gathered up all the floating threads of joy . . .
> [T]he thought had made the air seem warmer and the sun more vivid on her hair . . .
> (*TR*, 261–62)

And so it continues, each step taking them a little bit nearer the bedroom in which they pass a wet afternoon, because Sophy is bored by paintings and the tedious cinematograph show lasts only an hour. The romantic moment by the stream is replaced by a tawdry episode in a rainy city, but that does not dispel the erotic charge that this prolonged analepsis carries with it.

This erotic charge is given an additional frisson by the fact that it is told in retrospect, on the eve of the proposed marriage between Anna and Darrow and Owen and Sophy that would make Darrow Sophy's father-in-law. The difference between their ages, she "owning" to twenty-four and Darrow to thirty-seven, was noted earlier as something unremarkable in the Edwardian and early Georgian period, but it becomes more explicitly a relationship with incestuous overtones given subsequent events, and this aggravates the already considerable transgression in society's eyes of sexual intercourse between two unmarried people, the woman being the greater transgressor. In an act of incest, however, the older person is perceived to be the more responsible, and therefore more transgressive.

The theme of incest is announced when they first arrive in Paris and attend the theater, Sophy draws to Darrow's attention that *Oedipe* is playing at the Français and Darrow says that they should go to see it together. As he sits alongside Sophy and thinks briefly of Anna, his manner to the younger woman becomes "fraternal" and "almost fatherly" (*TR*, 53). Yet back at the hotel desire and a sense of the erotic reemerge as he imagines her removing her clothes in her nearby room:" [T]hrough the fumes of his cigar his imagination continued to follow her to and fro, traced the curve of her slim young arms as she raised them to undo her hair, pictured the sliding down of her dress to her waist and then to the knees, and the whiteness of her feet as she slipped across the floor to bed . . ." (*TR*, 57). Next day they do indeed go to see *Oedipe* at the Théâtre Français, and once again the jaded Darrow struggles to understand Sophy's excitement. For him it is a dull, stale production and the poetry of the play is missing. But to Sophy it is thrilling even though, as he loftily concludes, "her education had evidently not comprised a course in Greek literature" (*TR*, 60). A moment later he understands what she is seeing, and what he is unable to see. For Sophy the play is not literature, it is that elusive element that counts for so much in Wharton, it is "life" itself. "[S]he saw it as he had never seen it: as life" (*TR*, ibid.). Such a thought makes him briefly aware of all theories of art and stagecraft that he normally brought to bear on his judgments, and how artificial this was in comparison with Sophy's directness. But although his realization seems to be presented as a moment of envy, it is immediately qualified by a sense of danger: "When she talked to him about 'life'— the word was often on her lips—she seemed to him like a child playing with a tiger's cub; and he said to himself that some day the child would grow up—and so would the tiger" (*TR*, 61).

This is not the first reference to Sophy as a "child." It is one of many that reinforce the sense of an incestuous relationship. In a telling early moment in Paris Darrow, Pygmalion-like, imagines Sophy as "a terra-cotta statuette, some young image of grace hardly more than sketched in the clay" (*TR*, 72). This image fades as he imagines how inexperienced she must be (despite five years at Mrs. Murrett's). Her behavior is awkward and indecisive: "It showed that she was child after all; and all he could do—all he had ever meant to do—was to give her a child's holiday to look back to" (*TR*, ibid.). Later in the novel, when they meet again at Givré, even though in the interval they have slept together, he continues to see childlike qualities: "He transmitted his instructions with mechanical precision, and she answered in the same tone, repeating his words with the intensity of attention of a child not quite sure of understanding" (*TR*, 198). He calls her "My poor child" (*TR*, 205), and Anna's appeal to Darrow to be supportive of "her daughter-in-law" reminds us of what in family terms Sophy will become if she marries Owen (*TR*, 221). "Poor child—you poor child!" Darrow says, when Sophy reveals to Darrow that she is afraid of being with Owen because "I want to keep you all to myself." But Anna, too, speaks to Sophy in these terms: "Goodnight, dear child," she said impulsively, and drew the girl to her kiss" (*TR*, 228). In all of this the adult–child relationship is constructed, even if in years Sophy is not really a child. The incest is thus a linguistic and metaphoric one, rather than an actual one, but the persistence of the language and the metaphor is too striking to be accidental.

It is appropriate that this novel, which explores the transgressive, should do so within the strict frame of a formal structure. The five-part drama, the central unity of place and unity of character all echoes the conventions of classical tragedy. It is matched by a formal symmetry, of both time, setting, and character. The world of Mrs. Murrett evoked in the opening pages returns in the concluding ones. There are symmetries of relationship. Anna wishes to rescue Darrow from what she sees as the dangerous clutches of the "silly" Kitty Mayne, but fails to express her own feelings adequately. Darrow is attracted to Anna Summers, but is too distracted to prevent her from accepting Fraser Leath as a husband. With a cruelty of fate that would do justice to Thomas Hardy, there is a glimpse of a second chance, before that too is snatched away. Symmetry extends to setting, and the architecture of Givré, a house that reflects the character of her husband Fraser Leath, whose mask of bohemianism covers a conventional and ordered mind. His face is a "symmetrical blond mask" (*TR*, 93), and in the first years of Anna's marriage "the sober symmetry of Givré suggested only her husband's neatly balanced mind" (ibid.). In Leath the formal and the unconventional meet: "He exacted a rigid conformity to his rules of non-conformity" (ibid.). He represents the hypocrisy of sham bohemianism. He professes liberal views, but bows to his mother's strict Catholic code when it comes to social behavior, because it is very agreeable to have access through his mother to the heights of French Catholic society. Social politics thus governs personal politics, whether knowingly or not. Leath initially offered Anna the perfect compromise of the questioning insider that he seemed to be:

> The subversiveness of Mr. Leath's opinions was enhanced by the distinction of his appearance and the reserve of his manners. He was like the anarchist with a gardenia in his buttonhole who figures in the higher melodrama. Every word, every allusion, every note of his agreeably-modulated voice, gave Anna a glimpse of a society at once freer and finer, which observed the traditional forms but had discarded the underlying prejudices; whereas the world she knew had discarded many of the form and kept almost all the prejudices.
>
> (*TR*, 92)

The concern with form, which was also noticeable in *Ethan Frome*, allows Wharton to construct textual boundaries within which the paradox of controlled transgression is possible. Wharton is able to explore the taboo, the dissident, the outlawed in a context that will allow judgment, suffering, and the rediscovery of the perimeter fence of order to restore stability to an otherwise anarchic world. The novel allows the writer a space in which to confront and experiment with otherwise forbidden behavior, safely behind the veil of fiction. I do not think there is any dishonesty or pretense in this. In her novels Wharton the writer really did loosen the ties that bound her politically, and ran with ideologies and philosophies whose company she could not normally keep. In *The Reef* Wharton explores what it means to be uninhibited and she allows herself to imagine what happens if there are no restraints, no barriers. But the novel finally introduces a barrier of its own, in which the ellipses that have signaled passion and pleasure now signal its opposite. There is a succession of chilling reflections: "[T]he inevitable conclusion was that both must go, and she be left in the desert of a sorrow without memories . . ." (*TR*, 300). "She would not have had Sophy Viner live the hours she was living now . . ." (*TR*, 302). There is a momentary lapse, but Anna's understanding of "life" brings down the curtain: "If life was like that, then the sooner one got used to it the better . . . But no! Life was not like that" (ibid.). And there is a return to the ellipsis that signals the extremes of suffering, likened to the mortification brought about by religious asceticism, which has its own perverse attraction: "No 'spiritual exercise' devised by the discipline of piety could have been more torturing; but its very cruelty attracted her. She wanted to wear herself out with new pains" (*TR*, 303).

Yet Anna allows herself one night of sexual pleasure with Darrow, which makes her conclude that she can never give him up. But the physical tie, powerful though it is, is not enough. Anna has lost her faith in Darrow and cannot bring herself to marry him. In a telling moment Darrow insists that Sophy did not become his lover because she is an emancipated woman who believes in and acts on the "new theories" (*TR*, 290). She is not to be cast as "the woman who did" for principled reasons. Anna's response suggests that such principles would at least have amounted to an "excuse"; without even that, the affair is even more inexcusable. It is the ephemeral, transient nature of the relationship that Anna finds so threatening. Passion and desire need to be policed, otherwise society crumbles.

The Reef and Global Politics

In an earlier work[58] I rather rashly claimed that it would be difficult to argue that Wharton's fiction from 1910–13 was manifestly in-

5: VULGARITY, BOHEMIA, AND *THE REEF*

formed by the social unrest in Europe and the global politics of the period. On the surface, *The Reef* seems to present politics lightly, as a mere diversion in society conversation that moves easily from international events to the price of beverages:

> [Adelaide Painter] talked of the lateness of her train, of an impending crisis in international politics, of the difficulty of buying English tea in Paris and of the enormities of which French servants were capable; and her views on these subjects were enunciated with a uniformity of emphasis implying complete unconsciousness of any difference in their interest and importance.
>
> (*TR*, 211)

The narrator's comment makes clear that this lack of discrimination is a sign of her foolishness. As some readings have shown,[59] *The Reef* is most decidedly a novel in which internationalism is a theme, and the fact that the setting is for the most part a French country house a few hours outside Paris should not disguise the way that the discussion of the complicated entanglement of relationships is presented in the context of a discourse of diplomacy, spying, and national difference. The setting is France but all the principal characters are American. Some are Americans living permanently in France (Anna), others are visiting (Darrow), yet others come to France during vacation time while they study at Harvard and Oxford (Owen), while others are moving to France for an apparently long stay (Sophy). Surrounding these are other expatriate Americans who live in France (the Farlows) but continue their American links, or remain unaffected by the move (Adelaide Painter, who will always be from South Braintree, outside Boston) or have assumed French manners and a French name (Madame de Chantelle, a name which may or may not be intended to anticipate or contrast with the singing Laura). By the end of the novel each of the four Americans involved in the complicated central relationship of Sophy-Darrow-Anna-Owen-Sophy) is pledged to undertake a journey to yet another country, a journey that we never see them make or that we know they are not going to embark on. Sophy has left for Brindisi en route for a journey to India. Darrow and Anna, who rediscovered one another at a dinner at the American Embassy in London, were at one point committed to a journey to South America as man and wife, but Anna finally rejects the possibility of marriage. Owen is on the eve of a long visit to Spain, to obliterate the pain caused by Sophy's severing of their engagement.

Darrow's occupation of diplomat at the American Embassy in London provides a detail which takes the novel beyond the issue of exile and the American abroad, the theme so thoroughly examined by Henry James. Darrow's diplomacy becomes a metaphor for questions about dissembling, authenticity, and trust. He is a resourceful diplomat who always knows how to say the right thing. Anna is reassured whenever he is present. He smoothes over difficulties. He is tactful. He is described as an "active young diplomatist" (*TR*, 9). But ultimately these attractive qualities and skills amount to nothing in his relationship with Anna, because though he can always rekindle her desire, he can never make up for the breach of trust that she feels he has committed. It is not that she judges his action in an unforgiving manner (although she admits to unbearable feelings of jealousy), it is more that she feels his behavior has corrupted her, and that it runs the risk of corrupting her daughter Effie. The world of politics and international diplomacy is thus depicted as a flawed world, because it is a world without integrity. It thrives on the practice of surveillance, of secrecy, of concealment. The novel centers on an act of concealment and the destructive effects of the discovery of that concealment. All are blasted by it. Sophy is driven back to a life with Mrs. Murrett. Owen is a shattered man who cannot bear to have the light on. Anna looks forward to a life of loneliness and disappointment. Darrow loses the opportunity to marry a woman he loved and lost as a young man, and his reputation is irreparably damaged in the circles in which Anna moves. Anna feels that she and Darrow have been irrevocably tarnished by events, and the image is a political one: "To her proud directness it was degrading to think that they had been living together like enemies, who spy upon each other's movements" (*TR*, 300).

Because the setting swiftly moves (by the third chapter) to France, and remains there throughout the remainder of the novel, and because the words on the page are without accent, it is easy for the European reader to forget that, peripheral servants notwithstanding, there are no French people in *The Reef*. In this respect it has the sensibility of imperialism, where the colonial power spends all of its time socially with its own ruling class. It would be wrong to say that this is also the sensibility of the novel of imperialism, because such novels as *A Passage to India* (1924) or more contemporary narratives such as Conrad's short story "Karain,"[60] do have "native" characters at the centre. In any case, Americans are not occupying France as a colonial power. They are, nevertheless, in a position to lead very separate lives. In *The Reef* the French as a nation are only discussed once, and that by the unreformed American with the extravagant name betokening queenship, Australia, and decoration, perhaps, rather than art. Anna describes the formidable Adelaide Painter thus: "She detests the French so that she'd back up Owen even if she knew nothing—or knew too much—of Miss Viner. She somehow regards the match a protest against the corruption of European morals' (*TR*, 219). This report, and Anna's success at winning Adelaide Painter's support for the proposed marriage of Owen and Sophy, provokes Darrow into an admiring comment that reminds the reader of his occupation: "What a tactician you are! You make me feel that I hardly know the rudiments of diplomacy!" (*TR*, ibid.).

During the year in which she was writing *The Reef*, Edith Wharton was also reading and commenting on Fullerton's study of international politics, *Problems of Power*. As a widely traveled person she did not need a book to provide her with an international perspective, but Wharton's journeys brought her into contact with governments primarily when their agents could help her unlock doors that would otherwise be closed to her, as we see in *The Cruise of the Vanadis*, for example. The object of travel was to see art and architecture, gardens and scenery. Wharton's novel forces the reader's attention on government, international relations, and the way that economic interest drives not only western societies, but the whole imperial project. With some qualifications, Bauer sees parallels between the arguments in Fullerton's political study and in Wharton's novel:

> Wharton's plot about Darrow's responsibility in his affair with Viner parallels Fullerton's concern about the plotting of international relations. Both were concerned with the "blundering alchemy" which resulted in applying social engineering (or Manifest Destiny) to intimate or international affairs. Granted, Fullerton's call for a greater diplomacy with South America is not the same as Wharton's call for sexual integrity in *The Reef*, but the two situations share a similar imperative: an argument against self-absorbed and egotistical affairs, international or sexual.[61]

She goes further, seeing the "open door" that permits Darrow and Sophy to begin their affair as analogous to the American "open door" policy in international relations. This is clever, but perhaps stretching things a little. Her suggestion that the South American posting of Darrow (and Anna, if they had married) can be linked to Fullerton's discussion in *Problems of Power* of the opening of the Panama Canal is more plausible. There is a crude, but just tenable, parallel between Fullerton's argument that the Panama Canal will have a profound impact on the orientation of geopolitical relationships, as this part of the world becomes America's Mediterranean, and the Darrow-Sophy affair. If Fullerton's book is a wake-up call to America to cease preoccupation with domestic affairs, which makes its expansionism stumbling and blind, in Wharton's novel Anna receives a wake-up when the discovery of the affair between Sophy and Darrow causes her to reassess male and female sexual relations. But I would not want to overstate the parallel between the international and the sexual politics because the sequence of writing makes such a connection questionable.

The evidence suggests that Wharton's novel was under way well before she first saw drafts of Fullerton's book, originally to be called *Internationalities*. Marion Mainwaring describes Fullerton's sojourn in Luxembourg and Wharton's letters to him there.[62] These letters are dated May 1913, but 1913 must be a mistake for 1912 was when Wharton was recuperating at Salsomaggiore. Wharton, therefore, had the shape and subject matter of the novel in place before she read Fullerton's study of international politics, but that is not to say that it did not contribute to the treatment, as Wharton revised her work. I have no doubt that the continuing intellectual contact with Fullerton and the experience of reading his work did play an important part in the development of Wharton's political awareness, but I think that this is more noticeable in Wharton's next novel, *The Custom of the Country*, which Wharton resumed after completing *The Reef*. It must always be remembered, however, that Fullerton's knowledge of and interest in international politics was not a radical's interest. He worked for that most establishment of English newspapers (as it was then) the *Times*, he was an apostle of Theodore Roosevelt's brand of imperialism, and he seems to have had little time for the causes of popular political resistance. In a discussion of the recent civil unrest and strikes in France he makes his own robustly conservative position clear in a footnote:

> Unrest, social disorder, is, of course, a general phenomenon. It is becoming manifest throughout the world in proportion as that social order, which it is the business of the State to preserve, and which is the necessary condition of the normal working of the laws that have hitherto determined the economic organism of our modern civilization, is being imperilled both by the weakness of Governments (sentimentalism, humanitarianism, indiscipline, revolutionary idealism) and by the tyranny of Governments (state intervention and state socialism, demagogic legislation, inspired by mystical notions of solidarity, privileges accorded to Syndicalism).[63]

Socialism, syndicalism, and bohemianism were all bedfellows in the eyes of traditionalists, and there is nothing in Fullerton to challenge Wharton's reservations about bohemia and "modern" thinking. Yet in his analysis of France, Fullerton is at pains not to blame the people. Rather, the villain is a system of government instituted in 1875 in the Constitution of the Third Republic, whose main purpose was to see the restoration of the monarchy. This has proved to be a totally unsuitable model of government to manage the needs of a modern democracy. *Problems of Power* reflects the widespread anxiety that the West is on the brink of revolution. Fullerton makes the point that even the United States is not immune from this anxiety. There had been an attempted revolution in Russia in 1905. France and Britain were beset with strikes. How should society cope with demands of the modern world? Fullerton comes down firmly on the side of the authority of government and the value of imperialism:

> British policy under the direction of Mr. Lloyd George tended to lack proportion; it became a policy of parochialism. The Imperial Idea seemed to have vanished from the brains of British politicians. Englishmen had forced on them a prolonged constitutional crisis, which would have been worse than futile if it had not happily served the purpose of arousing the bewilderment and the dismay of the Dominions, and thereby contributing . . . to save England from an insular grave.[64]

Thus speaks Fullerton, confidently advising empires how to manage their fates, while leaving human wreckage in the wake of his own personal relations. The irony in all this must have struck Wharton, and it perhaps explains the irony in making the accomplished diplomat George Darrow unable to manage personal relations with the same skill with which he manages international ones.

The Reef and Society Politics

If *The Reef* finds clear fault with the politics of bohemianism and the politics of international relations, it presents a more ambiguous reading of those at the top of the social hierarchy in both New England and France. Darrow is placed as the descendant of a noble New York family, the Everards of Albany, and Madame de Chantelle, the former Mrs. Leath senior, is impressed by the fact that his grandmother was an Everard. The mother of Fraser Leith is at one step removed from the city society that is presented in *The House of Mirth*. She has taken the next step of all those who pride themselves on their European pedigree and have pretensions toward the aristocracy. She has married into French aristocracy, and adopted its Catholicism. She has back numbers of the *Catholic Weekly* distributed about her room, and exhibits "pious indignation" if she suspects any slur on her adopted creed (*TR*, 217).

The politics of Old New York society, transplanted into France, may be the target of some gentle satire, as the old-fashioned Madame de Chantelle, an American who begins by saying, "They tell me things are very much changed in America . . . Of course in my youth there *was* a Society" (*TR*, 135) is presented initially as a familiar caricature, stuck in the 1860s in terms of dress and values. Lucretia Mary (Lucretia was Wharton's mother's name) has lived among "Traditions" and has no wish to return to her country of birth where she would be confronted by those "dreadful views of marriage" and the source of the "Anarchist" influence on servants and the working class. Such views are presented tolerantly, so much so that Darrow listens "with a lazy sense of well-being" (*TR*, 136). In a very revealing insight into his political values, we are told that in the present context "Madame de Chantelle's discourse seemed not out of place. He could understand that, in the long run, the atmosphere of Givré might be suffocating; but in his present mood its very limitations had a grace" *TR*, 136). Darrow is not wealthy, and sees that his membership of the diplomatic profession is well received by Madame de Chantelle, who does not see it as a humdrum job, but a "Career" (*TR*, 137) in which he is either negotiating treaties or seducing duchesses. Even his being "ordered" to South America is seen in a romantic light of a "young soldier charged to lead a forlorn hope" (*TR*, 138). Yet Darrow has chosen this occupation for sociological, rather than for social reasons, we are told, and does not intend to stay with it forever (*TR*, 137). For now it is convenient and he takes a rather practical, calculating delight in the possibility of "possessing" Anna as his wife. She would be a very fine accessory and good for his career. "[S]he was the kind of woman with whom one would like to be seen in public" (*TR*, 130). Ironically Anna does not appreciate the regard in which he holds her public image. She is self-conscious about her appearance, feeling that her forehead is too high, her eyes too small, and her hands not small enough (*TR*, 122). Her face can look too pale, there are shadows about her eyes, and her hat flattens her hair.

Though Anna's susceptibility to what she sees as Darrow's charm means that of the two he is the one given the more indulgent presentation, neither is a romanticized beauty. There is a plain, rather than tragic ordinariness about them, despite the privileged circle in which they move. It is hard to disagree with Gloria Erlich's verdict that "Anna Leath, to whom renunciation comes all too easily, demands an unreasonable degree of sexual purity from the man she plans to marry"[65] Darrow's mistake is not in trying to shuttle between society and bohemia, but in doing so without appreciating what it could cost him if Anna ever found out. He miscalculates what society's fetishization of sexual purity in women can do to women reared as Anna has been. Yet there is a tragic irony in the circumstances that bring about the revelation. This is not so much the operation of fate in bringing

Sophy to Givré, but the impossibility of the options that Darrow is then faced with. To be honorable to Sophy, Darrow must deceive Anna. To be honest with Anna would be to betray Sophy. This is a Racinian situation, where deception and tragedy are inevitable. But it is not a grand tragedy. There is a meanness about Darrow's reading of class and society. When asked about his contact with Sophy, he belittles her with the remark "She was a secretary, or something of the sort, in the background of a house where I used to dine" (*TR*, 143), and this cannot be excused on the grounds that he is simply trying to protect her. He is a diminished hero, an appropriately disappointing figure for the period of J. Alfred Prufrock, a modern world in which Darrow's and Sophy's sexual encounter is preceded by an hour at the cinema.

Perhaps it is this suggestion of ordinariness that makes it feasible that Owen, the heir to Givré, could make an acceptable marriage to his stepsister's governess. James wondered about the sociology of the novel, and though Jane Eyre marries her employer in Charlotte Brontë's novel, Yorkshire is not country house France, close to fashionable Paris. Does the novel argue for the dangers of such class-hopping marriages, or is its early rhetoric an enthusiastic endorsement of the way that love can bridge the social divide, and ought to be approved by those who would hitherto have condemned it? The ambiguity of events is indicative of an indecision and uncertainty on the part of the narrative, which is rather hastily resolved in one way when it could just as consistently have been resolved in the very opposite.

Resisting Decadence

In singling out *The Reef* for special praise Henry James did not set the pattern for later criticism, which has seen the book as flawed in its representation of Anna and Sophy Viner. Michael Millgate echoed the verdict of much mid-twentieth-century criticism that the novel was psychologically unconvincing and a little too theatrical in its contrivances:

> [Some later critics] have felt that the persistence of Edith Wharton's exploration of the central situation only succeeds in inflating it beyond all reasonable proportion—that a woman as mature as Anna Leath is supposed to be would not experience quite such perturbation at the discovery that the man she is about to take as her second husband has had an affair with the girl, governess to her young daughter, whom her son intends to marry. Considered in the abstract, the situation may seem too

reminiscent of the "well-made play," all too deliberately contrived; but the real judgement must be of the situation as it is handled in the novel itself, and here the smallness of the central group, and the closeness and multifariousness of the relationship between them, is productive of genuine anguish and of convincing moral tension. Where Edith Wharton can be criticized is in her attempted resolution of these tensions. She seems not to play entirely fair with her character or with her readers, so that we are left with a certain sense of ambiguity about our own, and the author's feelings towards nearly all the characters, and especially towards Sophy Viner, the governess, whose final actions are splendidly magnanimous but whose strength of personality appears ultimately in doubt.[66]

There is an irony in the fact that although it is Anna who comes to dominate this novel, Anna in many ways is the Wharton that the author ceased to be some ten years earlier. Anna is bound to the idea of the house, and feels the pull of the house when she is running toward Darrow. She has been largely confined to the house ever since her marriage. She has not had an extramarital relationship.

Sophy, whom we probably think of as the threat to Wharton's world, because she seems to be a threat to the older woman's life, and Wharton was a mature woman when she wrote *The Reef* (she was approaching fifty), is actually not unlike Wharton in her wandering lifestyle, which has taken her from America to London, Paris, and then finally India. She has had a short-lived affair, which has to be concealed. Yet the point that Millgate makes applies to the representation of the two women. Sophy is always the outsider and never given a point of view. The odds are stacked against her. She disappears at the end, and of the three central characters it is only Anna who is left in France.

What explains Wharton's decision not to set *The Reef* in Paris, the city in which she was living? Could this be something to do with her unresolved feelings about French culture, where the bohemian not only sat alongside the world of the salon, it sometimes overlapped? It is odd that Sophy is initially presented as being in search of the world of the stage and excitement, but that this is eclipsed by the circumstances that bring her to Givré. A country house setting allows Wharton to limit and control her characters in the manner favored by detective novel writers. Perhaps the title Givré even alludes to the fabled world of Shakespeare's *The Winter's Tale*, another story of jealousy set in a pre-Christian Sicilia and Bohemia. In *The Reef* we do not have to see the outside world, the French world. Did Wharton feel that it would be presumptuous to write about French life? The self-denying ordinance allows her to present the reader with two American women who represent two different aspects of the American abroad. In Sophy we have the adventurer, the American who sees Europe as a more sophisticated and more exciting playground for her dramatic ambitions. In Anna we have the colonial governor's wife, the American who has settled in the country in which her husband's wealth allowed him the freedom to do as he pleased. We are not told the source of his money, but his taste in art and literature suggests a man who has not had to concern himself with business or industry. For all his apparent subversion (a subversion that does not make the jump from belief to practice), Fraser seems to be yet another product of Old New York society and yet another of the dilettantes that Wharton seems to find so trying. In none of these cases do we see characters interacting with the French. They own its land and buy its arts, but they do not seem to integrate with the natives.

In *The Reef* Wharton seems to be on the brink of rejecting the idea of the need for a "police-state over desire." Anna regrets the ignorance and unpreparedness that such a repressive social practice causes in women like herself. The former "Miss Summers" is now herself more cold and wintry. Yet the novel ends with what seems to be a warning about what will happen if there are no controls, no restrictions on sexual behavior. Such a fear partly reflects the legacy of late nineteenth-century anxieties about syphilis, anxieties reflected in the creation of such femme fatale figures as Salome. Dale M. Bauer has commented on the way that open sexual expression is frequently represented as a form of addiction in Wharton's fiction.[67]

Ultimately the fear of bohemia is a fear that unsupervised desire leads to decadence. In 1905 the opera *Salome,* with music by Richard Strauss, was performed. The opera, based on Wilde's banned play of 1893, presented the male audience with the fascinating spectacle of the nightmare of the predatory, sexualized woman. Salome dances and unveils herself in front of her father, whose incestuous gaze signals one kind of decadence. More terrifyingly she is brought the decapitated head of Iokanaan, better known as John the Baptist, and kisses it with all the lustful pleasure of the triumphant lover. Wilde's *Salome,* with illustrations by Aubrey Beardsley, had appeared in a New York edition in 1909, and in Wilde's text the fascination with incest is made clear. The prophet has declared that Herod's marriage to Herodias was incestuous, and to complicate matters Salome knows why she has such power over the Tetrarch: "It is strange that the husband of my mother looks at me like that. I know what it means. Of a truth I know it too well."[68] The opera in particular, with its lush, romantic music and oriental setting, panders to male fantasy and to the male gaze. Freud had written of the gaze, and the way that when the male child sees female genitalia he is able to imagine his own castration.

Salome acts out that fear symbolically, and the fear of female sexuality is so great that Salome, like Mimi in *La Bohème*, must die in the final scene. In Beardsley's illustration, "The Dancer's Reward," the head of the prophet appears on the silver charger, which itself is supported by a phallic-looking column complete with genital hairs.

In *The Reef* a slightly different anxiety about decadence finally reasserts itself. Anna finally seems to judge bohemia as synonymous with a decadence that degrades women, an argument that Bram Dijkstra advances to explain the preoccupation with "fantasies of feminine evil" in fin de siècle painting, where depictions of female homosexuality, masturbation, bestiality, vampirism, rape, madness, and death, all legitimized by their classical or mythological setting, bear witness to the pervasion of misogyny in the male artistic imagination.[69] Bauer sees a corollary between this and Fullerton's enthusiasm for empire, and more particularly his call to America to recognize its moral responsibilities as an international power.[70] At the crucial moment, the rhetoric of *The Reef* abandons the new perspectives that it has been exploring through Anna, and it and she revert to her familiar reliance on the wisdom of social correctness, for otherwise the winged Furies will exercise their inevitable justice. Until that ending, *The Reef* has promised to be the most politically unorthodox of Wharton's novels, but I do not think that the ending should be regarded as a failure of nerve. If she had ended *The House of Mirth* with one late Victorian convention, the virgin suicide, she resists the other one, evident in *La Bohème* and *The Woman Who Did*, in which the transgressive woman is transformed by death into the martyr/victim. Sophy remains offstage, in flight but alive. What is unresolved, is whether the ending represents a conscious recommitment to orthodox values that coincided with those with which Wharton had been brought up, or whether Anna's response to the final scene is presented to confirm the overwhelming power of social conditioning, something that Wharton explores much more ruthlessly in her next novel, *The Custom of the Country*. The rhetoric of that novel suggests the triumph of orthodoxy.

6
John Jay Chapman, "Social Order and Restraints": *The Custom of the Country* (1913)

> "Politics," to Undine, had always been like a kind of back-kitchen to business—the place where the refuse was thrown and the doubtful messes were brewed. As a drawing room topic, and one to provoke disinterested sentiments, it had the hollowness of Fourth of July orations, and her mind wandered in spite of the desire to appear informed and competent.
> —Edith Wharton from *The Custom of the Country*

> The first surprise is to find the place on the whole, so much more—shall one say?—dignified and decent, so much more conscious of social order and restraints, than the early years of the life led in it.
> —Edith Wharton on George Sand's house at Nohant from *A Motor-Flight Through France*

IN DECIDING TO RESUME WORK ON *THE CUSTOM OF THE COUNTRY* Edith Wharton was abandoning her creative excursion into the modernist hinterland of impressionism and perceptual ambiguity. Instead, she was returning to the kind of naturalistic novel that allowed her to diagnose a clear type rather than embark on the untangling of a bundle of perceptions. The move had much to recommend it. There was plenty still to mine from the gold-yielding subject of New York society and its manners. This was a subject she knew intimately, it was a subject that had brought her success, and it was a subject that Henry James recommended to her. At the same time she would be writing against James's work, for her sharpness, her satire, and her flair for biting literary scorn could be given full play, and James had recommended that she keep these in check. Not only would the rise of Undine Spragg provide her with a subject that allowed her to write free from the complication of the personal parallels that the situations in *Ethan Frome* and *The Reef* introduced, she would write a Condition of America novel that would match the energy and anger of a Condition of England novel such as Wells's *Tono Bungay*. She could resist again James's advice that New York be her subject by bringing Undine to Europe. Finally in making the decision to continue and complete this subject, she could examine once again a situation that fascinated her, a society in transition. This had been her subject in *The Valley of Decision* and *The House of Mirth*, and with its analysis of the impact of new money on old values (a Balzacian theme), it was to be the subject of the novel that deserves to be regarded as Wharton's tour de force.

As I have been arguing, there was a temperamental inevitability about this decision, arising from her beliefs about society and the belief that the way that the world ought to be managed was a subject never to be neglected by those who enjoyed privilege and status. Nevertheless, in asserting that it was difficult to be a modernist writer if one's temperament was aristocratic, the obvious exceptions and objections have to be acknowledged. The first is straightforward. D. H. Lawrence believed in an aristocracy of intellect, but felt that this could be realized only in an island community, an idea that would never have appealed to Wharton. Apart from nationality, the class difference (as a miner's son Lawrence certainly did not enjoy privilege and status) meant that these two writers came at the idea of cultural aristocracy from very different directions and positions. Wharton numbered establishment politicians among her friends. She did not want to tear the whole of established society up and start again or live simply with a few kindred spirits. That was far too bohemian.

The one contemporary writer who possessed something of her ideological outlook and social position was Ford Madox Ford, who styled himself a "Tory Revolutionary." The politics espoused by Ford resisted the tidal flow of capitalism and labor reform. He was opposed to the new, popular education, which in his view produced a new kind of illiteracy, and felt that only the artist could provide in surrogate form the experience and insight that the modern world now denied modern man and woman. He was wedded to what was rapidly becoming an outmoded Toryism with a conservative, hierarchical view of the world, but was an example of that long tradition of eccentric, anarchic Tories. In *The Good Soldier* (1915), he produced one of the most adventurous and exquisite experiments in impressionism of the early modernist period. His Toryism did not preclude experiment, but his politics were a corollary of his William Morris and Pre-Raphaelite family roots, and in "On the Function of the Arts in the Republic" they are extrapolated as a kind of feudal utopianism that was never entertained by Wharton.[1] His bohemian lifestyle, serial relationships and lack of roots put him beyond her own social pale, and his editorial record of providing unceasing encouragement to new, experimental writers would have been adduced as evidence of his artistic promiscuity. Wharton did not find the obscurity and self-consciousness of the new forms of writing attractive, whether from bohemians or close friends (in 1904 she had written of Henry James that "his books of the last years I can't read, much as I delight in the man").[2] Wharton turned instead to her former style, a writing practice that involved a marriage of social realism and naturalism. Ford Madox Ford's experiences in World War I undoubtedly influenced the direction his writing took after 1915, where the Tietjens series show less of the French influence and more of the Russian. In Wharton's case the change and rejection of modernist practice occurred before 1914, confirming that her preferred subject was society and not the soul. If she could regard James as a novelist of manners, then there was no reason why she should not so regard herself.

In the two springs of 1906 and 1907 Edith Wharton explored France in her motor car, first with Teddy and her brother Harry, and then in 1907 with Teddy and Henry James. Out of these explorations came *A Motor-Flight Through France*, published in 1908, the year in which she began work on *The Custom of The Country*. It is clear that *A Motor-Flight Through France*, though primarily about the architecture and landscape of a France that could be newly discovered by the freedom of the automobile, reveals much about the model of society that Wharton was most sympathetic to, and it explains why France, rather than the United States, England, or Italy became the place in which she established her home. It also explains the tone and rhetoric of the second half of the novel.

Despite, or perhaps because of her keen sense of history, in *A Motor-Flight Through France* Wharton does not readily associate the early-twentieth-century France that she sees with Revolution. The Revolution happened over a hundred years earlier, and what is most attractive for Wharton is the old France that seems to have endured despite the many changes: "In France everything speaks of long familiar intercourse between the earth and its inhabitants, every field has a name, a history, a distinct place of its own in the village polity, every blade of grass is there by an old feudal right which has long since dispossessed the worthless aboriginal weed."[3] This is not an unusual view to find at the beginning of the twentieth century, where the very technology that was providing access to the open road and rural communities was threatening to destroy them. So it is that the very motor car that to Wharton is "restoring the romance of travel" (*MFTF,* 5) is the villain in *The Wind in the Willows* (1908), as in *Howards End* (1910). Toad's car is a dangerous intrusion into the landscape, while the Wilcoxes' car covers the village with dust. Wharton, Grahame, and

Forster all share this vision of the organic community, however, a nostalgic preference taken up by Leavis and Eliot.

For Wharton, the position is more complex. She favors not just customs and traditions with a long pedigree, but *French* customs. *A Motor-Flight Through France* is a celebration of what she sees as the enduring quality of French manners and French social life, what she calls, in phrases the first of which she has italicized for emphasis "*an intelligent acceptance of given conditions*" and a "fitting into the pattern." (*MFTF,* 28). The qualities that she singles out for praise reveal much of Wharton's own political values. Dignity, restraint, order, social acquiescence, decorum—all of these are features of a stable society, a contented society, one that is not ruffled by conflict and an infatuation for the new. Yet Wharton is perfectly aware of French history, of the passion of the French and the turmoil that the country has witnessed. It is precisely because it has this history and yet has preserved those features of life that she sees fast disappearing in America that she romanticizes it in the way she does. She admires in particular "That insistence on civic dignity and comeliness so miraculously maintained, through every torment of political passion, every change of social conviction, by a people resolutely addressed to the intelligent enjoyment of living." (*MFTF,* 29). Wharton shares Henry James's indictment in *The American Scene* of the absence of castles in the United States, which to Wharton "is a country where the last new grain-elevator or office building is the only monument that receives homage from the surrounding architecture" (*MFTF,* 32). France is so attractive because the way of life seems to endorse her own assumptions about the correct political ordering of relationships and behavior, and the importance of good aesthetic judgment. Wharton makes this point repeatedly through this largely enthusiastic travel book: "One can only salute once again the invincible French passion for form and fitness, and . . . happy is the race to whom these things are essentials" (*MFTF,* 97).

This was the kind of reverential attitude that infuriated another American, John Jay Chapman, whose second marriage to Elizabeth Chanler, "Daisy" Chanler's sister, brought him into contact with Wharton. Chapman was a privileged iconoclast, an American George Orwell who showed that while it was possible to attack the upper class from inside, the emotional and political schizophrenia this induced was never easy to resolve. Chapman came from a New England family with impeccable roots, and had been to Harvard. He was a man of impulse and dramatic gesture. Experiencing remorse for thrashing a man who had been pestering the woman who was eventually to be his first wife, he had thrust his hand into the fire and burned it so badly it had to be amputated. During his lifetime he produced a considerable body of work, including literary criticism, political analysis, a periodical called *The Nursery,* biographical studies, satire, and polemic. The collected works cover half a shelf at the Widener Library at Harvard and were gathered together for publication at the suggestion of Edmund Wilson. Despite this prolific output, he remains largely forgotten, perhaps because of his later unpleasant anti-Catholicism and links to Ku Klux Klan publications.

Chapman had turned on his alma mater in an article published in 1909 that attacked Harvard for giving its name to a five-foot shelf publication "The Harvard Classics," to be published by Colliers.[4] He felt the whole project was a betrayal of what a university should stand for arguing that "[i]t required a very peculiar juncture of influences between our educational world and the commercial world to produce 'The Harvard Classics.'" The project, in Chapman's view, was a symptom of a wider malaise in which Harvard was being run along business lines by businessmen. It was selling itself as a club for life, and thus appealing to the self-interest of the youth in the country. Chapman likens Harvard's approach to that of a baseball club, and concludes that learning is not safe if left exclusively in the hands of businessmen. There must be scholars on the governing body, and these must include scientists. Yet Chapman argues that the university should not be in league with business because it should not be involved in wider projects that require money. For Harvard to support this form of popular education is to abandon its true mission. In this instance his patrician belief in the purity of learning was a view that coincided with Wharton's own.[5]

Wharton comments on this article in an undated letter to Sara Norton, almost certainly written in 1909. Sara Norton had sent the article to her friend, who begins her reply by assuming that Sarah will be in sympathy with Chapman's sentiments, which would probably have been shared by Charles Eliot Norton, Sara's father, who was the distinguished Harvard professor so exercised about the decline of quality and the spread of vulgarity. Wharton goes on to say: "Bayard Cutting . . . thinks JC much too destructive and doesn't moreover, agree with his view of what Harvard's 'mission' should be. And still, I'm unconvinced."[6] Chapman, however, could not reciprocate, and became impatient with Wharton's writing, though he had wanted to be sympathetic. He had read *The House of Mirth* in eager anticipation of seeing it rip apart the New York social set that he loathed, but was disappointed to find no redeeming characters in it.[7] Following his visit to Wharton in Paris, Chapman wrote "La Vie Parisienne," an attack on expatriate Americans, especially those who stay in exile in France and never return. In a letter to his son[8] Chapman said that it was Wharton who triggered this polemic, published in *Greek Genius and Other Essays* in 1915.[9] The essay is interesting as an analysis that offers a commentary on the implied political position of the narrators in both *The Reef* and *The Custom of the Country*. Chapman begins by saying how seductive Paris is to all nationalities, particularly Americans. There are three categories of American "victims." First there are the Vulgarians, who as Hovey[10] points out, want the world's goods and find that they can get more for their money in Paris than elsewhere. They are open, frank, and an embarrassment to the other two groups. This group is absent in *The Reef*, which is only partly set in Paris, but is represented by Elmer Moffatt, Undine's first (and fourth) husband in *The Custom of the Country*. Chapman's second category is the Naturally Noble. These Americans believe they are noble themselves and so they are in love with Europe's social glamour. Chapman's characteristic style captures their behavior: "[A] gentle radiation of influence causes the Natural Noble from America to purr and rub himself against the knees of the great—yea even against the chairs and the wainscoting."[11]

The final category is made up of what Chapman calls the Inner Templars. These Americans are broadly democratic in their social sympathies, but are overawed by European civilization. The Inner Templar thinks that he is seeing life and experiencing art, but he is not. Chapman says that this group is detached "from the great dynamic of life," that they are "dried leaves" and have contact not with art but with what Chapman calls the excrescence of art. They are less alive than the manufacturer they ridicule in their novels, and they need to go back to the United States, not stay in Europe. If Wharton herself is the target here, then so is Anna Leath in *The Reef*. Wharton is alert to this criticism and signals it in *The Custom of the Country*, where the narrator offers the reader such a ruthless commentary on Undine's invasion of French culture. It is left to a Frenchman, de Chelles, to launch the most ferocious attack on American society in the speech that begins "You come among us from a country we don't know, and can't imagine, a country you care for so little that before you've been a day in ours you've forgotten the very house you were born in—if it wasn't torn down before you knew it!" (*CC*, 341). It is unlikely that as Wharton wrote this onslaught, aimed at Undine, she felt entirely immune from the charges leveled at the invading Americans, however different Undine is meant to be from her creator. Wharton's developed sense of irony makes such a thought almost impossible.

The Custom of the Country, published in 1913, turned out to be Wharton's last novel before World War I, though it is misleading historically to think of it in these terms and it should not influence the way we read it. It is a fine novel but its completion, its form, and its style show that Wharton had made a decision not to move in the direction that the new experimental fiction was taking. Wharton was not unknown to abandon work that displeased her. The novel's completion after a long gestation and investment of effort and its appearance in the same year that saw the publication of D. H. Lawrence's *Sons and Lovers,* Alain Fournier's *Le grand mealnes,* and Proust's *Du côté de chez Swann* suggests that Wharton had parted company with modernism *before* the interruption of World War I.

If *The Custom of the Country* is like these three European novels in being a bildungsroman, it differs from them radically in offering an anthropological study rather than a psychoanalysis of its subject. Kassanoff's analysis seems particuraly applicable here, for Undine Spragg is even more of a specimen under the microscope than Lily Bart, though unlike Lily she is not an endangered species. Undine is one of the terrible engines of destruction that horrified Wharton and, what is worse, she stands as a metaphor for the future.

Kenneth Clark, who came to know Wharton well after being introduced to her by Bernard Berenson, for whom Clark worked in Italy in 1926, judged it to be one of her best stories, along with *Summer* and *The House of Mirth,* all of which are "based on disillusion and a sense of the cruelty of life."[12] This verdict comes from Clark's autobiography *Another Part of the Wood,* in which he asserts that "*The Custom of the Country* was considered so cynical[13] by the Nobel Committee that they finally refused to give her the Nobel Prize for literature."[14] That this novel, which is not always considered one of Wharton's best, should be in contention for this prestigious award may appear surprising, but it is a novel whose very remorselessness makes it remarkable. Undine Spragg, a young woman whose physical beauty contrasts with her name, comes to New York from the midwest with her parents bent on conquest. She is ruthlessly ambitious, setting herself new goals every time she achieves an old one, resulting in a succession of advantageous marriages, which ultimately disappoint her. She represents the triumph of no single category in Chapman's typology, because she possesses a quality that they seem to lack: Undine is dangerous because she is infinitely adaptable.

The Problems of Power and Beauty

It should not be forgotten that *The Custom of the Country* was remarkably modern in the subject on which it focuses and in the treatment of that subject. In the United States the turn of the century was the age of the great trusts, the self-made men who had become captains of industry, and their great empires of wealth, property, and product. In America the rise and fall of the self-made businessman had been depicted in *The Rise of Silas Lapham* (1885). In England, as noted earlier, it was the subject of H. G. Wells's *Tono Bungay* (1909). Lapham's fall is caused by his integrity, George Ponderevo's by his lack of it. *The Custom of the Country* differs from both of these novels in not requiring its central character to fall (only be balked) but most strikingly in having as its ascendant tycoon a woman who advances through the metaphorical trust empires of marriage. The fact that her power derives from something as insubstantial and ephemeral as beauty differs little from the fact that Uncle Ponderevo makes his fortune from a quack elixir, the Tono Bungay of the tile. This tonic, like beauty, is a surrogate for "portables" such as gold or diamonds, and like money is extremely valuable so long as everyone desires to possess it. These issues were not entirely ignored by modernists. Power was something that the vorticist strand of modernism admired, but the crassness of materialism was something that both Bloomsbury and the vorticists scorned. But tenuous parallels such as this do not make *The Custom of the Country* a modernist novel, however much it may be a novel of modernity. It is driven by social and political anger, not angst.

The puzzling attraction of the novel has been skillfully historicized by Nancy Bentley in *The Ethnography of Manners*.[15] Bentley locates Wharton's pre–World War I novels in the context of debates about ethnography, degeneration, and civilization and savagery. Edwardian anxieties about degeneration were projected onto the emergence of the New Woman and expressed as fears that women were regressing to a barbarian state. Male anthropologists such as James Weir had described with scarcely concealed horror the practice of polyandry, whereby a woman once married could take on as many additional sexual partners as she wished, with the consequence that paternity was almost impossible to establish. The rising divorce rate, particularly among women in America, gave rise to concerns that women were reverting to the state of savagery. As Bentley notes: "'Degeneration' is a feminine drive: given political agency, women become essentially barbaric and will pull modern American society back with them toward the 'abyss' of prehistoric culture."[16]

Locating the novel in the context of this ethnographic discourse Bentley then makes two important points. *The Custom of the Country* is not a novel that fails in its analysis of business (which is rarely glimpsed directly), because its real subject is the *business of divorce*. The popularity of divorce, which according to Bentley rose nearly

2,000 percent between 1860 and 1929,[17] meant the proliferation of marriage, and the novel strikingly represents marriage "as the 'real business' of American life." Women are the agents in this business, "buying" husbands that they now have the power to exchange. That this is recent development is signaled by the reference to *The Hound of the Baskervilles* on the opening page, a novel published in 1902, only ten years before the publication of *The Custom of the Country*. Even the reading of popular novels is shown to be a transient thing. When Marvell next visits the Stentorian, the book has disappeared, to be replaced by a magazine.

Bentley's second important observation takes us, astutely, to the world of museums and waxworks, where "primitive" women in particular were displayed in the form of wax effigies, often naked to demonstrate some feature of anatomy. The natural extension of this was the case of Sarah Bartmann, known as the "Hottentot Venus," who was displayed in a live traveling show. This exhibiting of women as specimens is one key aspect of the contemporary interest in anthropology. Related to this was the belief that primitive people showed their lack of sophistication by privileging imitation as the way of influencing the world. To help a woman through labor, the Dayak magician would imitate the throes of labor and birth, in the belief that this would help her. As Bentley notes, one of the arguments of Sir James Frazer's influential *The Golden Bough* is that "the savage imitates the world; civilized man acts upon it and transforms it."[18]

In *The House of Mirth* Lily Bart achieves her greatest moment of triumph in the imitative show of the *tableau vivant*. But she refuses to compromise her values and principles, and will not marry for money alone. She has the opportunity, but passes it by. When she could rescue herself from the gossip that is damaging her reputation, she refuses to do so, because it would involve blackmail. By sticking to her beliefs, she drives herself into a cul-de-sac, and death is the only narrative release. Bertha Dorset is the survivor, and it is now commonplace to see the heroine of *The Custom of the Country* as the more complete anthropological study of the type that is Bertha.

Like Bertha and Lily, Undine Spragg also possesses the central asset of beauty, and she is quite prepared to be decorative, when need be. One way of reading her is as the wax mannequin of primitive, degenerate woman come to life. In fact her image is reproduced and seen by thousands, whether it is in the form of the painting by Popple displaying her pearls and body, or the society photographs that appear in magazines and newspapers. But these are detached from her, in a way that Lily's posing as Mrs. Reynolds was not. More importantly, Undine is willing to trade in marriage in a ruthless way. Before the novel opens she has already been through one marriage and divorce, and the novel chronicles a succession of alliances designed to further her ambitions. She has an energy and determination missing in Lily.

Bentley argues that the rhetoric shows that this energy may be dangerous, but it is an energy for which Old New York has no answer and on which New York thrives. If Undine is initially the anthropological object, Ralph is the anthropologist who believes that he can cultivate this specimen. Yet in Italy he learns that his wife's imitation of sophistication will always remain an imitation. She is bored by literature and European art and architecture. Ralph realizes that his cause is hopeless. He has misjudged Undine's motivation and his eventual irrelevance to her long-term ambition. As Bentley points out, he becomes a museum specimen himself. Even the chorus character/sociologist Bowen, who stands back to offer a verdict on Ralph's failure, does so from the perspective of the very meretriciousness that he bemoans, working as he does for the Parisian Diamond Company.

The novel's politics and tone may have cost it the prize in 1927 if Clark can be believed, but as an analysis of ambition, materialism, and the power of money, it is as astute and prophetic as the book that Morton Fullerton had been working on during the years in which *The Custom of the Country* was being written.

Money, not Modernism

In 1913 Morton Fullerton published *Problems of Power*, which had the subtitle *A Study of International Politics from Sadowa to Kirk-Kilissé*, but whose theme of power provides the links with Wharton's novel. There are three main arguments in this work, the first of which is philosophical. Fullerton begins claiming that "No philosophy of history is possible."[19] Instead, the best that can be hoped for is an art of history. The second argument is that the destiny of the world at the beginning of the twentieth century is being worked out in blind obedience to the will of two nineteenth-century creators, Napoleon and Bismarck, and that the world is on the brink of something cataclysmic:

> "When God wipes out," says Bossuet, "he is getting ready to write. *'Quand Dieu efface c'est qu'il se prépare à écrire.'*"
> During the last ten years the Eternal would seem to have been preparing what one of his vice-regents, the German Chancellor, recently called "the policy of the clean slate." . . . Modern Europe is working out its

destiny in blind obedience to the will of its two demiurgic creators, Napoleon and Bismarck.[20]

The prescience of the image of "wip(ing) out" seems particularly insightful because of our knowledge of the events that followed August 1914, but it is fair to say that there was a widespread feeling that immense change was about to take place in Europe, though most people anticipated social revolution rather than world war.

Fullerton's third argument, which is by far the most interesting and surprising, seems to fly in the face of his first. For in the second chapter (of book 1), which is entitled "Economic Interests and the Development of States," he advances the theory that money is the key of history. Other chapter titles in book 1 indicate the importance he attached to this theory of history. Chapter 4 is entitled "Economic Conditions and Modern Political Evolution" and chapter 5, "The Survival of Modern States in Spite of the Corrosive Action of Economic Facts." Fullerton grapples with the paradox that developments in trade and economics have an internationalizing effect, so that corporations stretch beyond national borders and continents, with the survival of a strong nationalism in the management of political affairs. It is an issue taken up in book 3, whose theme is "Economic Factors Affecting the Political Attitude of Modern States," where in chapter 2 he examines modern idealism and the migration of labor. Karl Marx had been instrumental in contributing to the ideal of working-class solidarity, which was internationalist and employed a rhetoric that was anticapitalist, antinationalist, antireligious, and antigovernment. Such idealism, argues Fullerton, has been made to look foolish by the movement of international labor, Italians emigrating to the United States being but one example. Fullerton then examines "German Commercial Expansionism" and the "Industrial and Financial Organization of France" (two of his chapter titles), before discussing the politico-economic relations between the two countries. His conclusion that politics is always driven by finance does not lead to any arguments in favor of change. His is an analysis without predictions or recommendations. He is unable to decide whether the policy of German expansion will be resolved in peace or war, saying that the readers can simply take their pick.

The bulk of the remaining parts of the book is concerned with international relations, which Fullerton the journalist has observed at close quarters. Fullerton examines and discusses the rise to power of the United States (in "The Case of the United States," which emphasizes the role that Theodore Roosevelt has played in this rise), and in "The Case of Europe" he explores the sequence and consequence of events since the Franco-German war. He writes at length about the grouping of powers in Europe, the Triple Entente, and spheres of influence from the Mediterranean to the Far East. Fullerton praises French stability that has survived the Dreyfus case and sees France as the most stable country in Europe, benefiting as it now does from the gradual separation of church and state. He discusses the Balkan question, Agadir, and British domestic politics. Despite his earlier rather airy remarks about the prospects for war, Fullerton acknowledges that the peace of the world depends on Germany: "There are, no doubt, many indications that the German rulers may eventually come to regard a war as the sole solution for the life and death economic problems with which they are confronted."[21] Fullerton describes in this section Germany's feeling of encirclement and traces the existence of a feeling of grievance that the world owes it something in the call of iron and the 'Nietzschean forms of metaphysical and mystical imperialism."[22] He exhorts Germany to cease her bluff and bluster, and to accept that 'no nation in the world is capable of contemplating an attack on her.'[23] Fullerton ends his study by pointing out that the opening of the Panama Canal has caused a shift in the center of geographical gravity from the Mediterranean to the Caribbean. The United States is now a key international player, and for the sake of the peace of the world there should therefore be a Franco-Anglo-American.

I have outlined the contents of this book in some detail because it is a book that Wharton read in manuscript form and whose style she influenced. Dale M. Bauer comments on the significance of this intellectual cross-fertilization in *Edith Wharton's Brave New Politics*,[24] but she does so, as noted earlier, in relation to Wharton's novel *The Reef*, likening the Open Door Policy discussed by Fullerton to the "open door" of the connecting hotel rooms that permits Darrow's affair with Sophy Viner to begin (Anna Leath's door having been metaphorically shut in his face). "Wharton offers no critique of Fullerton's politics," writes Bauer, "but her own work offers a glimpse of the private dimensions paralleling international policy."[25] For reasons of chronology I raised doubts about the relevance of this evidence for a reading of *The Reef*, but I fully agree with Bauer when she notes the more general importance of "an exchange which began with her intellectual responses to Fullerton and developed in her tireless work for World War I charities and, eventually, into a new attitude toward writing fiction."[26] This new attitude might more properly be described as a confirmation of an older attitude. It is an attitude that moves away from the perceived solipsism of the modern and toward a commitment to the more important social, sociological, and ethical purpose of the rhetoric of fiction.

There are three themes in *Problems of Power* that have a close bearing on Wharton's 1913 novel, *The Custom of the Country*. Fullerton's analysis of the power of money and of public opinion accords with the subject matter of this later novel, with its study of Undine's pursuit of money and status, with Undine Spragg standing as a metonymy for national ambition, as her initials suggest. Fullerton writes that "money has been the key that generally unlocks the problems of history."[27] In his very first chapter he offers a striking description of the power of banks and trusts, on whom nations are increasingly dependent:

> Behind the façade of Governments two occult powers are now determining the destinies of the world. . . . One of these is the disseminated wealth of Democracy, canalized both by the plutocratic oligarchy of the Bankers (*la Haute Finance*), whose clients, the Modern States, apply to them for immense loans, and by the great manufacturers and mining proprietors, who tend to be actuated solely by economic interest, and who often combine in international trusts, the operations of which are merely hampered by patriotic questions of national policy and national honor.[28]

The "merely hampered" is the keynote here, and it is one that resounds in Wharton's 1913 novel about a woman who is often hampered but never thwarted (the ambassadorial impasse at the end notwithstanding) in the novel. Fullerton was concerned with an international canvas, however, and the way that economics is now played out on the imperial stage. The closure of the Dardanelles by Turkey, which denied ships access to the Black Sea, caused the imperial powers to see how small states could jeopardize international trade, and this observation has been translated into the legitimatization of the great powers' right to intervene in such cases.

Fullerton's comments on the striking changes to the United States would have reinforced Wharton's decisions to make France her permanent home. He notes that in the period 1890–1910, the United States had changed far more than England or France. It was both an architectural change, and a political one. America had its skyscrapers, and it had a sense of unity of purpose that now transcended its earlier individualism. There was a new imperialism dawning, and he teasingly likens the great houses gathered near Lenox, where The Mount was located, to the villas built out of their capital by the patrician ancient Romans. By 1913, The Mount had been sold, and Wharton was to make very few return trips to the United States.

The final aspect of Fullerton's book that has a bearing on *The Custom of the Country* is his discussion of France in book 2, chapter 3.[29] The Dreyfus case had split France, and Fullerton saw that split dividing those who believed in a strong state from those who believed in the supremacy of the rights of the individual. The anti-Dreyfusards tended to believe in a powerful, centralized state, and such a state could be the excuse for repression and anti-Semitism. Its supporters believed in the central importance of authority, and they tended to be Catholic. Opposing them were those who supported Dreyfus because they believed in liberty and the rights of the individual. They were believers in free thought, and they tended to be Protestant. Wharton may have preferred the relative conservatism of France, but she was neither a Catholic nor an anti-Dreyfusard. The darker side of this strand in French life had been brought out in *Madame de Treymes* and in *The Reef*, and it was to surface in her 1913 novel.

Both Wharton and Fullerton were interested in the issue of power, in its theory and practice. Emotionally and physically Fullerton exercised power through the sexual hold he had on men and women, although sometimes he found that he needed others to bail him out. He wrote about the power exercised by the imperial powers, and here he was an observer. Wharton was interested in the power exercised by institutions and societies, and for her this was a matter well described by anthropologists rather than politicians. Both views agree that human behavior is governed by laws, and the detached tone with which Undine's progress is chronicled has been likened by Millicent Bell to that used by an ethnologist.[30]

But perhaps the most interesting link between the themes of *Problems of Power* and Wharton's novel is the anxiety that they both express about what happens when the wrong kind of people exert influence, because what governs the populace at large is selfishness.

> [T]he clamor of the populace, or the tumult of the mob, armed by the humanitarianism of our special form of Christian civilization, possesses, in the devices of universal suffrage and parliamentary government, sure instruments for the immediate and frequently selfish utilization of the wealth of the community, and for the satisfaction of party interests and class appetites in injudicious and often antinational ways.
>
> England has been, for the last few years, a very beautiful instance of these truths. The accession to power of an humanitarian doctrinaire liberalism, with radicalistic roots and demagogic leanings, the surrender of England's destinies to a Cabinet dominated by public men mystically inflamed with a "holy" passion for the improvement of the masses . . . provided an excellent object-lesson of the unadaptability to self-respecting democratic society of the purely representative form of government.[31]

Fullerton then quotes approvingly from an address given by Lord Morley, chancellor of Manchester University, in June 1913, which describes, in Fullerton's words, "the faults of ardent spirits who take to politics in a stirring age. Lord Morley attacks those idealists who get carried away with their own vision and substitute aspiration for 'reasoned scrutiny.'" The Liberal government of Asquith and Lloyd George is what both writers have in mind, a government that was committed to a program of land reform and social legislation.

It is not enough to assume that because Wharton had been close to Fullerton, and because she now willingly read and commented on his book, that she shared these views. But in her letters to him, nowhere does she take exception to the argument, even where it does not rely on an intimate knowledge of the detail of international politics but a more general view of government, people, and reform. Moreover, his belief in the evident selfishness of uncontrolled ambition and the weakness of those who should be in authority is echoed in the central theme of *The Custom of the Country*.

Houses, Customs, and Domestic Politics

In the half century following Wharton's death, *The Custom of the Country* was singled out for particular praise. In her essay "Henry James's Heiress," Q. D. Leavis identifies the novel as "undoubtedly her masterpiece"[32] while Harold Bloom, some fifty years later, argues that 'it is likely to seem, some day, Wharton's strongest achievement, though I find it rather an unpleasant novel to read."[33] Wharton's study of an ambitious woman's rise to power caused some readers to conclude that Undine is a monster, but others (often women) have rejected this epithet.[34] Michael Millgate concludes that Edith Wharton's "obvious hatred" of Undine Spragg diminishes the novel's credibility.[35] A broader view suggests she is no more of a monster than Napoleon and Bismarck. The difference is that these leaders are able to enjoy power on the international, political stage, whereas Undine's theater of war is the marriage circle, whether in the United States or France. The two almost conjoin at the end of the novel, but Undine is thwarted from becoming an ambassador's wife because her history of divorces disqualifies her husband from being offered such a post. It is not exactly perishing by the sword she has lived by, but that is the kind of effect with which Wharton wishes to conclude the narrative. I do not think that the reader is meant to enjoy her frustration, nor to relish it as a kind of just reward for her earlier behavior. It is just a stepping off point that denies Undine final triumph, but avoids the decline and death that was the fate of the less ambitious Lily Bart. There is nothing to say that she will not overcome this obstacle in the way that she has overcome all others. We are not meant to be reassured (unless we seek reassurance).

The novel had a long gestation. Begun in 1908, it was still not complete when serialization began in 1913. It is easy to speculate on what the difficulty might have been. Most obviously this period coincides with Wharton's separation from Teddy and her eventual divorce. Emotionally stressful as this was, there was also the question of other preoccupations. Wharton's affair with Fullerton took place at this time, as did her tending of the ailing Henry James. But equally the problem could have been an artistic one. Persuaded that she should return to the world of Old New York for her subject matter, there was a danger of replicating themes in *The House of Mirth,* and it is clear that in some ways Undine continues what might have been the Bertha Dorset story, or that the marriage between Undine and Ralph Marvell shows what might have happened if Lawrence Selden had married the image that was his version of Lily Bart. Undine has Lily's beauty and ambition, though not her moral scruples.

There is also the issue of geography and sexual politics, both of which are raised in Charlotte Perkins Gilman's 1898 study, *Women and Economics.* Gilman argues that society's emphasis on sex-distinction makes women passive, dependent on men, and useful only for their sex function. Her analysis of women's social position could be a description of the early formation of Undine: "[T]he consuming female, debarred from any free productions, unable to estimate the labour involved in the making of what she so lightly destroys, and her consumption limited mainly to those things which minister to physical pleasure, creating a market for sensuous decoration and personal ornament, for all that is luxurious and enervation, and for a false and capricious vanity in such supplies, which operates as a deadly check to true industry and true art."[36] Observing this new kind of American woman, at a time when suffragist protest in England and France was seen by her acquaintance Mrs. Humphry Ward as the product of "consuming" females, Wharton was able to benefit from the detached perception of geographical distance that residence in Paris gave her. In Gilman's pithy observation: "Social conditions, like individual conditions, become familiar by use and cease to be observed. This is the reason why it is so much easier to criticize the customs of other persons or of other nations than one's own . . . The Englishman coming to America is much more struck by America's political corruption and in the earnest desire to serve his brother, he tells us all about it. That which he has at home he does not observe because he is used to it."[37]

Related to this is Perkins Gilman's description of the importance of the home. In her essay "The 'Hotel Spirit' "[38] Betsy Klimasmith draws attention to the way that Gilman argued that people are shaped by the settings they inhabit, and that they should therefore take care in shaping them. This argument is to be found in both *Women and Economics* and in her later study *The Home* (1903). Perkins Gilman believed that cities that provided architecture that allowed such things as shared kitchens would be good for the development of women, as would shared child care.

Edith Wharton would have disagreed with both these proposals, but she shared Perkins Gilman's assessment of the political and social factors that operated through the historical evolution of the home. Wharton's first two books had described the decoration, architecture, and gardens of the kind she recommended to the wealthy, leisured class of which she was a member. Her 1897 study *The Decoration of Houses,* written jointly with Ogden Codman Jr., included the following observation: "It is a fact recognised by political economists that changes, in manners and customs, no matter under what form of government, usually originates with the wealthy or aristocratic minority and are thence transmitted to the other classes. Thus the bourgeois of one generation lives more like the aristocrat of another generation than like his own predecessors."[39] Wharton and Codman discuss the social function of the Roman house, which so influenced the kind of Italian Renaissance architecture that the authors favor, particularly that which appeared after the beginning of the sixteenth century. The Romans emphasized the importance of public life, in the forum and in public baths and in the street, and this is reflected in the importance of loggias, salons, and galleries in Renaissance houses. It was the "[d]angers and barbarities of feudalism" that fostered the idea in England and France of the house as somewhere private. Consistent with Wharton's beliefs, the authors then call for scientific methods to be applied to the decoration of houses, just as they are applied to architecture. Similar principles inform her 1904 study of *Italian Villas and Their Gardens.*[40] Here there is an emphasis on the social function of Italian gardens, which are places to be lived in. The paths are designed so that two or three people can walk abreast, a civilized and attractive quality.

The relevance of this discussion of the social conditioning produced by the architectural environment is that the Italian palaces and hilltop architecture so favored by Ralph are lifeless, empty places for Undine, whose "natural" environment is the hotel, the 'promiscuous' hotel in Wharton's eyes. So Ralph and Undine move rapidly at her request to the Swiss Hotel at St. Moritz, where the shallow people that Ralph clearly loathes gather happily. It is the falseness of public intercourse that is presented here. A hotel is not a graceful or civilized place in Wharton's novels. Undine is rootless and irresponsible. She is not bohemian, because bohemianism was associated with poverty, but she lives the rootless life of the bohemian. She has no base, no home, because she has no responsibilities. The chateau in France becomes a place of terrible boredom for her. She wants the glitter of noblesse, without any of its obligations. That is the verdict of the novel that so damns her. The narrator hates her as much as the narrator of Eudora Welty's, *The Optimist's Daughter* (another American indictment of the failure of the parvenu to *feel*) hates Wanda Fay.

VULGAR CUSTOMS

What is "the custom of the country" to which the title of Edith Wharton's novel refers? According to the narrator it is the practice in American marriages of excluding women from a discussion of men's business affairs. During a discussion of the failure of so many American marriages—a discussion that is really concerned with the new-money marriages that seem to be particularly short-lived—one of the characters remarks: "Why haven't we taught our women to take an interest in our work? Simply because we don't take enough interest in them" (*CC*, 129). The speaker is Bowen, a friend of the well-established Dagonets and Marvells, who represent the upper echelons of Old New York, and he is keen to emphasize the particular marital problem that has provoked this discussion, the fault with Ralph Marvell, who is Undine Spragg's current husband, but with "the genus he belongs to: homo sapiens, Americanus" (*CC*, ibid.).

In this, and in Bowen's succeeding exposition, the reader is given the essence of Thorstein Veblen's argument, developed in *The Theory of the Leisured Class* (1899)[41] and well aired in twentieth-century criticism of the novel, that bourgeois women in capitalism are primarily vehicles for the display of conspicuous consumption. This is because the decorative, leisured, and handsomely dressed woman married to a wealthy man enhances his prestige and announces his success much more visibly and publicly than he can do himself, since he is shut up in the boardroom or office most of the day, making the money. Women such as Undine collaborate willingly in this only because the culture gives them no other outlet for their talents and their energies.

Wharton often seems less forgiving, regarding such promiscuity as a form of prostitution. "[S]exual relationships are routinely described as business contracts, in which the language of economics is substituted for the language of passion."[42] Peggy Anne McNamara's comment is made about the novels of Henry James, but the fact that it could be applied with equal appropriateness to *The House of Mirth* or *The Custom of the Country* is indicative of the extent to which Wharton's novels are recognized as providing a commentary on the economic forces that drive the twentieth century and undermine the traditional hierarchies.[43] Contemporary reviewers—and the sheer volume of contemporary reviews indicate the immense reputation of Edith Wharton on both sides of the Atlantic by 1913—saw the novel as a sharp commentary on society and more specifically the ease of divorce in America (the custom of the country), the vulgarity of new money, the power of beauty, and the ability of money to corrupt. One reviewer compared Undine (unfavorably) with Becky Sharp in *Vanity Fair*, but the majority of the reviews were favorable.[44]

Wharton's title[45] also alludes to a play of the same name by Fletcher and Massinger (1619)[46] in which the duke of the country has the right to sleep with virgins on their wedding night, a custom no less rooted in patriarchal privilege and gender distortion than the American custom of excluding women from the business of the world. It is a bawdy play, derived from the *Persiles y Sigismunda* of Cervantes, and the action takes place in Italy, Portugal, and in a brothel. The sustained misogyny, in which nearly all the women are represented as capricious, materialistic, lustful, and dishonest finds echoes in the charge that Wharton's novel is the one in which she reveals most forthrightly her hatred of women. In Wharton's case, the charge seems to miss the point that Wharton's subject in the novel is the construction of women, not any generalizations about essentialist behavior.

Fletcher and Massinger's *The Custom of the Country* may have provided only a useful title. The play itself does not really explore its initial theme, that the corrosive effect of a dishonorable custom corrupts all marriages and all society, beyond the opening scenes. Lisbon, to which Arnoldo and Zenocia are taken, has its own decadence as represented by the wealthy temptress Hippolyta and the women who visit Sulpitia's brothel and exhaust the men with their sexual demands. Arnoldo and Zenocia remain pure throughout, and a number of corrupt characters experience startling reformations at the end. It could be argued that Count Clodio's decision to discontinue the "custom" shows that good triumphs, but the quickness of change throughout suggests a superficiality of belief that could easily be reversed. If Undine has an equivalent in this play it can only be Hippolyta who is wealthy and beautiful, who is determined to get what she wants, and who is used to exercising her control over men. In the end perhaps the title is enough: it refers to the exercise of power through sex and in Wharton's world of New York society, although it can never be shown to operate in the bawdy way that was possible in a seventeenth-century English play, the only things that women are allowed to trade in are their bodies. As Cynthia Griffin Wolff argues, in a world where everything, including women, is reduced to goods, marriage and divorce become matters of buying and bartering. Prostitution is the practice of the marketplace in the sphere of sexual relations, and both play and novel ask questions about the similarity between marriage and prostitution.

The phrase "the custom of the country,"[47] also appears in Charlotte Perkins Gilman's 1898 study, *Women and Economics*.[48] "Marriage is a form of sex-union recognized and sanctioned by society. It is a relation between two or more persons, according to the custom of the country."[49] The quotation does not end here, however, and continues: ". . . according to the custom of the country, and involves mutual obligations. Although made by us an economic relation, it is not essentially so, and will exist in much higher fulfilment after the economic phase is outgrown."[50] Gilman saw the late nineteenth-century economic dependency of women as a phase, which changes in the relationship between the sexes will eventually bring to an end. Her view opposed that of male anthropologists who saw changes in the status of women as regressive. Undine, who seems to bypass this dependency by freely trading in her beauty, seems to be monster to Lily Bart's martyr, to use Bentley's phrase. Why did Wharton decide to make this figure the subject of her novel?

There are several other literary precedents for the story of Undine Spragg.[51] Becky Sharp is the most often cited (Elaine Showalter argues that Undine lacks Becky's wit and perceptiveness),[52] partly because Wharton was such an admirer of Thackeray, and *Vanity Fair* has always been one of the most popular nineteenth-century English novels in America). R. W. B. Lewis claimed[53] that *The Custom of the Country* owes more than a little to Robert Grant's *Unleavened Bread*, which Wharton praises in a letter to Grant written in 1900.[54] The depiction of Lisbeth in Balzac's *Cousin Bette* provided a precedent that Wharton, an admirer of Balzac's novels, would have known. Like Undine, Lisbeth's single-mindedness and deceit is linked to her origins and her "untamed Corsican nature."[55] The ambitious Rosamond Vincy in *Middlemarch* supplied yet another model of female ruthlessness, and all of these characters reflect a type that was to return in the following decades in novels, most famously in the figure of Scarlett O'Hara in *Gone with the Wind*. As Showalter points out, Scarlett is made to suffer along the road in ways in which Undine never does. This may be a shortcoming of the novel, but equally it may be an important element in the novel's argument that the exclusion of women from business results inevitably in such unreformed behavior, because unlike Scarlett, Undine never runs a business. It is not so much that Undine is the female Elmer Moffatt; it is that Elmer is the male Undine, possessing direct economic and political power, and an ugliness of aspect that power makes unimportant. Showalter discusses the possibility that such speculation takes us in the wrong direction, however, and that we should see Undine not so much in relation to Elmer, but more in relation to Wharton. The sustained contempt and scorn that the narrative voice expresses for Undine perhaps conceals (or reveals) the latent fear of the author that she herself may be a little bit more American, a little bit more naturally cold and scheming than she would care to admit. In this argument Undine becomes Wharton's alter ego, rather than a monster.

The vulgarity of new money is represented relentlessly, and as I suggested earlier critics such as Michael Millgate have suggested that the novel is flawed because it is governed by the narrator's contempt or even hatred for Undine Spragg. Undine, however, has the redeeming feature of flexibility and social intelligence: it is her parents who are the subject of the most withering remarks, especially in chapter 21 at the beginning of book 3, when Ralph goes to visit his parents-in-law with his grandson while Undine is playing the fashionable set in Paris. Mrs. Spragg is the target for some particularly venomous remarks:

> As for Mrs. Spragg, her son-in-law could not remember having had a sustained conversation with her since the distant day when he had first called at the Stentorian, and had been "entertained" in Undine's absence by her astonished mother. The shock of that encounter had moved Mrs. Spragg to eloquence; but Ralph's entrance into the family, without making him seem less of a stranger, appeared once for all to have relieved her of the obligation of finding something to say to him.
> (*CC*, 198)

The hostility that is glimpsed in this part of the novel, and elsewhere, is usually kept in check, but does suggest a failure at times to move outside the narrative viewpoint of Wharton's class, though it could be argued that as events are seen through Ralph's eyes she is representing that view. Yet Ralph in many ways is shown as being more understanding than this, so there is a note of discord in such sections. They seem to reveal a contempt for the people, rather than the culture that has created them.

The final judgment of Undine is damning, though it is not on the grounds of her serial relationships, her love of material things, or her lack of culture. She is judged because she fails as a mother and shows no affection for her son. Unlike the classical undines, who could acquire a soul by bearing a child, Undine Spragg is not transformed through motherhood. The consequence of polyandry are that the child is not to know his father, and if his mother does not care, then he is seen to be a sad little creature. Wharton herself was going through a divorce at the time of completing this novel, but she never remarried, dedicating herself instead to war work and writing rather than the easy material profit that a wealthy husband would have brought.

Consideration of the classical undines, together with their sisters, the sirens and seductive water nymphs, steers the reader toward the tragic story of Ralph Marvell, who imagines himself as a Perseus coming to rescue Andromeda from entrapment in material society, but finally realizes that she does not want to be rescued. Undine's full name, however, takes us in another direction. She had been named after an artificial hair-waving product, the commercial French waver "Undine," and she signifies the very world of the economic "invaders" that Ralph wished to rescue her from. She is also a Spragg, a word whose many meanings, as Candace Waid has made clear, include a prop used in mining and a piece of wood used to hold a wheel in place.[56] It is not an inappropriate name for someone who would colloquially be described as a gold digger. Her initials, moreover, which appear in silver on the pigeon-blood writing paper that she has discovered is fashionable, signal that she is named by Wharton to represent those aspects of American life that she saw as most rampant. If Ralph believes that the new can be made more refined by the old, the narrative says otherwise. It is replete with warnings. Beware the new money, beware the new woman, beware the new American, and beware the new politics, it seems to be saying. The monster consumption will devour society, and will devour art and tradition, just as an alliance of Moffatt and Undine possesses and strips out the de Chelles tapestries from the chateau, importing them to a Parisian apartment and turning history into decoration. Most of all beware the new vulgarity. The problem is that the word "vulgar" comes from the Latin word "vulgus" meaning ordinary people or the public, and in condemning the vulgar the novel can be seen not simply as an attack on crass materialism, but as an assault on egalitarianism and democracy. That is a very political rhetoric, and it does not do justice to the novel to suggest that this is a conflation sustained from first chapter to last. But it is the rhetorical position of the final chapters of *The Custom of the Country*, as it is in *The House of Mirth* and *The Reef*, and it is the conclusion that leaves the final, lasting impression.

The Engines of Destruction: Business, Politics, and Modernism

It is quite possible to read *The Custom of the Country* allegorically, a reading that accommodates the charge that Undine is a one-dimensional character, or that politics and business are not very well developed in the novel, and can be regarded as something of an irrelevance. I have already suggested that Undine can be seen as a metonym for American imperial ambition, but I do not wish to argue that this is all she is, or that the novel in this respect is like *Hard Times*, more fable than economic and political analysis. It is a legitimate argument, however, that sees Wharton using business much as Trollope uses the Anglican Church as a setting for an exploration of ambition and the search for power. Stephen Orgel argues that it is precisely out of this Victorian literary tradition that Wharton writes, though he cites later Trollope models such as *The Way We Live Now* rather than the Barchester Chronicles.[57]

At the same time, Orgel argues that Wharton's novel is a work of alienation. In *The Custom of the Country*, Old New York society is shown to be moribund and doomed well before the world war that some assume Wharton considered to be its death knell. The narrator may be sympathetic to Ralph, but he is shown to be a weak and helpless man, however good as a father or husband he may have promised to be. The narrator's greater alienation is from the world of new money, however, and this is demonstrated by the persistent distancing technique of using quotation marks around new terms, habits, and practices, such as a Virginia "resort" or an "exclusive" hotel with its "guests." The language of the new-moneyed society is treated as a foreign language, to be spoken with detachment. This is the alienated voice of the socially disapproving rather than the alienated voice of modernist fiction, but in their belief in exclusivity (whether aesthetic, as the "antennae of the race" to use Pound's term, or social), the two have much in common. In the case of *The Custom of the Country*, however, the narrator's lofty condescension sometimes looks blunter than it really is, as when Undine's mind is described "as destitute of beauty and mystery as the prairie schoolhouse in which she had been educated." At first glance this appears to be saying that the absence of intellectual subtlety is the consequence of a simple education, but the narrator isn't quite making this point. Such moments can be clumsy, however, and there are others when we are clearly to feel contempt for Undine's crassness and ignorance, and the behavior of her friends. At St. Moritz these friends attend "hot, promiscuous balls," and especial disdain is reserved (albeit through Ralph) for Mrs. Harvey Shallum, a "showy Parisianized figure" (*CC*, 98): "Mrs. Shallum grated on his taste, but she was as open to inspection as a shop-window, and he was sure that time would teach his wife the cheapness of what she had to show." (*CC*, 100). Less open to inspection is the world of high finance. Orgel also argues that the "American world of capitalist enterprise," the "world of business and politics" is nearly as opaque to Wharton as it is to Undine, mainly because it is a "masculine world."[58] Wharton may not have been an insider, who mixed with businessmen and knew the culture of the marketplace and the deal at firsthand, but she identifies its practices with an acuity that should not be underestimated:

> As Ralph pushed the bolts behind him, and passed into the hall, with dark mahogany doors and the quiet "Dutch interior" effect of its black and white marble paving, he said to himself that what Popple called society was really just like the houses it lived in: a muddle of misapplied ornament over a thin steel shell of utility. The steel shell was built up in Wall Street, social trimmings were hastily added in Fifth Avenue; and the union between them was as monstrous and factitious, as unlike the gradual homogenous growth which flowers in what other countries know as society, as that between the Blois gargoyles on Peter Van Degen's roof and the skeleton walls supporting them.
>
> (*CC*, 47)

Ralph knows that he is repeating the Dagonet view of the society in which Popple is the society painter whose very name has a baublelike ring to it, and Van Degen is the representative of the "invading race" who threaten the Dagonet "aborigines." The narrator, too, undermines the authority of this view by drawing attention to the "Dutch interior" effect. The quotation marks signal the artifice and imitative nature of those who like to think of themselves as established society. They import their style, from Europe rather than Wall Street. Packed also into this short paragraph are allusions to the steel empire of Carnegie, to an organic model of society, and to the skeleton of girders that contrast with this living "growth." The narrator allows Ralph to have a "loftier" awareness of the inadequacy of his relatives' rhetoric, for he has mixed with the "Invaders," and in a phrase very similar to the one used by de Chelles in his complaint about Americans in France, recognized that through contact with the "indigenous," the Invaders "spoke the same language as his, though on their lips it had often so different a meaning." (*CC*, 50–51).

The fact that to Undine "politics" (and as the quotation at the head of this chapter shows the word in the sentence is enclosed by the distancing device of quotation marks), had always "been like a back-kitchen to business" (*CC*, 59), and had the emptiness of Fourth of July speeches should not be read as a dismissal of the subject, because it is precisely the corrupt alliance between politicians and businessmen (men as they exclusively were) that the novel shows us. It is Representative James J. Rolliver who is a key player in Apex affairs, where the Driscolls have "got all the street railroads in their pocket" (*CC*, 82) and now want the water supply as well. As Mr. Spragg reminds Moffatt, he and Rolliver always stood together, and he fiddles with his Masonic emblem as he recalls the subject. Businessman, masonry, and state politics are all intertwined in murky practices: "Undine suspected that his breach with his old political ally, the Representative Rolliver who had seen him though the muddiest reaches of the Pure Water Move, was not unconnected with his failure to get a footing in Wall Street." (*CC*, 148). In contrast, Ralph believes (naively, as it turns out) in business practice in which "decent men . . deal with each other decently" (*CC*, 163) and it must not be forgotten that "financial incorruptibility" (*ABG*, 16) was one of the chief qualities that justified the existence of the old society in Wharton's mind. But just as he has married into this new world of financial corruptibility when he thought, as Undine did, that his wife was marrying into his world, so other alliances are being formed. Moffatt announces to Undine that Indiana Frusk has managed a transaction by which she has neatly become Senator Rolliver's wife. She has parted from Millard Binch quite easily, but it has cost Rolliver "nearly a million to mislay Mrs. R" (*CC*, 170).

The new trade in marriages is dealt with satirically. De Chelles wonders why Americans need to marry, since Undine can spend time in Paris so far apart from her husband. "Oh, it still has its uses. One couldn't be divorced without it" is Bowen's reply, Bowen who is cast in the role of the sociologist observing social change (*CC*, 174, 176). "Couples were unpairing and pairing again with an ease and rapidity that encouraged Undine to bide her time," (*CC*, 180), we are told, but she does not wait very long before bringing divorce proceedings against Ralph. The market in divorces provides ready material for newspapers and society papers read by the "unshaven." There are some penalties—Indiana's divorce and remarriage required her to keep out of certain states—but Indiana herself bridles at the thought that there is anything vulgar in it, charging that the world of married men and mistresses that form the subject of French plays is the real vulgarity, a comment that has its effect on the latent Puritanism of Undine, fresh from an affair with a married man. Further satire, this time of a blunter kind, is evident in the names (Apex, Ararat Investigation, Indiana Frusk),[59] which endorse the distancing, allegorizing effect, as if Wharton wishes this part of the novel to be treated as some kind of deus ex machina, with these shabby gods supported by obvious strings.

As with all of the pre-1914 novels it is possible to read *The Custom of the Country* as a commentary on marriage that draws on Wharton's own experience. Ralph imagines his fellow victims in the drowning of marriage (*CC*, 141), and it is easy to see Ralph in the position of an Edith Wharton who has married a handsome, but shallow Teddy Wharton and then realized the mistake. It can be read as a study of a new kind of woman who successfully trades in marriage in a society in which divorce is more readily tolerated. The novel even conjures up reminders of the bohemian world that *The Reef* had rejected. Undine refers to novels that sound very much like Grant Allen's *The Woman Who Did*, discussed in the previous chapter: "In the 'powerful' novels which Popple was fond of lending her she had met with increasing frequency the type of heroine who scorns to love clandestinely, and proclaims the sanctity of passion and the moral duty of obeying its call" (*CC*, 229).

There is thus a strong case for reading the novel both allegorically, as a study of power and ambition that corresponds to those qualities of an emerging America, and as a Swiftian satire on the triumph of the marketplace. The global character of American influence is shown by the way that the "habit of imitating the imitation," the characteristic of the kind of shallow society the novel inveighs against, has been exported to France. The chapter that begins with the letter heading "The Parisian Diamond Company—Anglo American Branch" offers Bowen's view of the international society that American commercial success has helped to create: "[It was] a phantom 'society,' with all the rules, smirks, gestures of its model, but evoked out of promiscuity and incoherence, while the other had been the product of continuity and choice" (*CC*, 171).

This is a statement remarkable for its own political assumptions, but equally interesting is de Chelles's comment that such a "society" is a kind of "superior Bohemia," as he and Bowen disagree over whether or not this modern manifestation is the direct result of feudalism. Although Bowen is presented as more astute than other members of the "aboriginal" society, and de Chelles is described as far superior to his English, aristocratic counterpart,[60] both are compromised and outdone by the new economic forces. Yet neither of them are beyond reproach themselves. Bowen judges the superficiality of society, but works for a diamond company. De Chelles affectionately scorns the frequency of divorce in American society, but uses his newly found interest in a political career as a cover for a series of illicit assignations.

Politics may be the cover for adultery, or for financial corruption. The last we hear of Rolliver is that he is "in Congress now" and in Moffatt's pocket. Moffatt has triumphed and seals his success by remarrying Undine. The handling of politics, economics, and commerce should be recognized in the most devastating of Wharton's novels. In it she announces her rejection of modernism, because Undine and modernism lack moral conscience and social duty.

The Custom of the Country is a critique of selfishness and self-absorption. Undine stands for the selfish materialism of new money, but in a conflation that should not surprise us, Undine stands for the preoccupation with self that threatens to destroy art. The condemnation of a behavior that fails to imagine the feelings of others is the theme that drives the novel, and it is the theme of every chapter. In the center of the novel, for example, at the beginning of chapter 20, Undine is extremely happy because the life she is leading in Paris "seemed so perfect an answer to all her wants" (*CC*, 176). Life is defined in terms of her own particular needs. Paris is the perfect city: "Her senses luxuriated in all its material details" (*CC*, 176). Novelty, the quality scorned by Toryism, is what delights her, whether it be the "novelty and daring of the women's dresses" (*CC*, 176), the novelty of a "perfunctory dash through a picture show" (*CC*, 177), or the "the lingering visit to the last new milliner" (*CC*, 177), the novelty of the Nouveau Luxe, or the exhilarating novelty of "a tumultuous progress through the midnight haunts where 'ladies' were not supposed to show themselves, and might consequently taste the thrill of being occasionally taken for their opposites" (*CC*, 177).

The corollary of this selfishness is an utter inability to experience tender feelings or empathize with the feelings of others. Other people are just a nuisance. When Ralph writes to say that he is having difficulty paying the bills, Undine thinks "Always the same monotonous refrain! Was it her fault that she and the boy had been ill?" (*CC*, 178). Her son Paul is an obstacle to her freedom and spending and she is soon happy to pass him on to his father. Her sole aim at this point is to exchange her husband Ralph for Van Degen, and in using de Chelles's attention to her to excite Van Degen's jealousy.

This is a disguised eighteenth-century novel of sensibility, designed to show what happens when those without empathy or the semblance of virtue inherit the earth. It is a dystopian sentimental novel disguised as naturalism, a polemic on the subject of the assault on the good society that was taking place at the beginning of the twentieth century. Eighteenth-century novels of sensibility offered a reply to Hobbes's seventeenth-century claim that humans are innately selfish. In rejecting that philosophy Wharton was simultaneously rejecting the embrace of an art that is fashionable because it is novel. When Undine realizes that "literature was becoming fashionable" (*CC*, 178) she toys with the idea of a fashionably bohemian lifestyle, wearing "artistic dresses" (*CC*, 178) of the kind that Wharton would have noticed from her observation of the new arts in Paris. Such an art is represented as a superficial art, and *The Custom of the Country* is a devastating sociological critique of superficiality and of the "rising forces" that Ralph sees are destined to triumph. To rephrase Orwell's account of his own dystopian novel, *The Custom of the Country* is both a prophecy and a warning

7

Money, Politics, and Art: Questions of Commerce, Imperialism, and Gender

With *The Custom of the Country* Edith Wharton produced the kind of Balzacian *comédie humaine* novel that was also intended to appeal to the American readers who had bought the hundreds of thousands of copies of *The House of Mirth*. *The Custom of the Country* received good reviews and Wharton's royalties for the book suggest that it was a return to the financial success of her earlier novels.[1]

In wishing to produce art that was also commercially successful, Wharton was engaging with a problem that was to exercise the expatriate American novelists in the modernist period. As writers from the next generation, such as Fitzgerald and Hemingway discovered, the desire and need for success in the America marketplace clashed with the European aristocratic disdain for commercial success. Fitzgerald in particular sought the approval of the "highbrow" audience, while depending on an income from the "slicks" such as the *Saturday Evening Post*.[2] It is one of the great paradoxes of Wharton, confirming Pierre Bourdieu's point that all art is in commerce, that in *The Custom of the Country*, Wharton could conduct a devastating critique of the marketplace while eagerly monitoring its sales. She had indicated her attitude to the writing that the public at large found difficult in an early comment on Henry James: "[H]e talks, thank heaven, more lucidly than he writes."[3] She was well aware of the commercial implications of James's demanding style. His novels did not sell. The early modernist stall in the marketplace attracted few customers, and with the collapse of her marriage, she relied on healthy sales from fiction if she was to avoid a slide into either poverty or dependence. These were possibilities Wharton was determined to avoid, and free from a later, though by no means universal, modernist "contamination anxiety" she was untroubled by the notion that, as Walter Benjamin was to observe, in the age of mechanical reproduction, art's power was diminished.[4] She was also unworried by any thought that getting a good price for a story was prostituting one's art, the fear that obsessed Hemingway and Fitzgerald. As she had observed in *A Backward Glance*, Trollope had "killed off" Mrs. Proudie because he overheard somebody at his club saying "she had lived long enough, but that had not prevented the description of her death rivalling anything written by Balzac and Tolstoy."[5]

Money and Art: Mass Circulation versus Modernism

Wharton's interest in the sales of her fiction becomes particularly noticeable with the breakthrough commercial success of *The House of Mirth*. Even though Edith Wharton's verdict on 1905 had been that it had been a "good year," she was nonetheless alert to the thin ice on which her success stood. Fiction writing was a strategic release from the trap of the marriage in which she found herself, but it did not guarantee a complete escape, only periods of relief with a reason for being alone. It did, however, provide an independent income.

For Edith Wharton, the period between 1905 and 1913 proved personally traumatic but creatively productive. These were years of great contrasts: her precarious marriage finally collapsed, and she had an intense affair with Morton Fullerton. The success of *The House of Mirth* (1905) was followed by the relatively poor sales of the novels that followed, and she spent much time and energy making arrangements for the nursing of the declining Teddy Wharton and Henry James. By 1911 the burden of sickness that provides the crushing end to the narrative in *Ethan Frome* paralleled the wretched state of the two men to whom Wharton was linked by either legal or literary ties, while the lover who by 1910 had indicated that their relationship was over, had to be nursed gently toward publication himself.

Through all this turbulence Edith Wharton continued her work as a professional writer, as a woman who knew that her living and income depended on writing. Teddy Wharton had drawn on her money without her knowledge, and if she was to continue to travel, to own a car, and live in the style to which she had become accustomed, she knew that she would have to continue producing successful novels and short stories. For this very practical reason alone Wharton would have had problems with the strategy of the early modernists, or Georgians, for whom "better meant more difficult . . . a higher art for a more discerning and more dedicated, if smaller, readership."[6] Wharton could not afford a smaller readership.

Candace Waid has argued persuasively that the woman writer is a central trope in Wharton's early fiction and that the writing of letters is a coded narrative reference to the writing of fiction.[7] Waid points to the important role of letters in short stories such as "The Muse's Tragedy," *The Touchstone*, and "Copy," which all feature letters written by women. It is Waid's argument that Lily Bart is to be seen as Bertha Dorset's alter ego, and although Bertha is the actual writer of the letters that are central to the plot, Lily is mistaken for the author of the letters by the cleaning woman, and assumes the role of symbolic woman writer in the *tableau vivant*. Lily dies rather than publish the letters, and remains virginal and silent. Throughout the novel, however, she is associated with the materials and products of authorship: writing desks, book collecting, libraries, note-writing for Judy Trenor, the café in which women engaged in the publishing business gather. Wharton's subject, Waid argues, is the woman writer, and her profession the profession of letters. There was nothing dilettante about this.

The relationship between Edith Wharton's profession of authorship and the marketplace is described by Amy Kaplan: "Wharton's apprenticeship (*as a writer reveals*) her strategies for producing both a literary work, a professional self for the market at the turn of the century, (*and her*) effort to write herself out of the private domestic sphere and to inscribe a public identity in the marketplace."[8] As H. G. Wells shows in *Tono Bungay* (1909), the turn of the century saw a particular kind of market emerge, as product was sold through advertising. People on the move demanded magazines, books, and newspapers for journeys and holidays and with the aid of advertising, reputations could be made overnight, as the success of Tono Bungay, the quack medicine, shows. Wells's novel is a satire on the wastefulness of commercial excess, where worthless products could be marketed successfully. For the novelist, however, dependent on the income from writing, the arrival of the new commerce was a welcome development.

Wharton's keen eye for the market is registered by the way that she records in her diary for 1905 the outstanding sales of *The House of Mirth*. The book appeared on October 14, with an initial run of 40,000. On October 30, 20,000 more were pressed, and on November 11 she records that another 20,000 were required. Thereafter sales really shot up: on December 20, 100,000 copies were printed, while on Friday, December 8, she records with obvious pride that 120,000 more were being produced. Writing was not simply art, it was necessary sales and stark economics, and on the blank end page of the diary, there is a calculation for the royalties on 140,000 copies— 31,300 dollars. Her success continued: in November the novel had been the best seller in the whole United States for that month and was the most rapid sale of any book published by Scribner's. The success continued into the new year: on January 1, 1906 *The House of Mirth* was still New York's best seller, and in February and March it was once again the best-selling book in the United States.

Wharton was not to repeat that triumph, and her expenses as she traveled relentlessly ate into this money. The continuing pressure of the need for commercial success is suggested by a cutting she had taken from the August 25, 1911 issue of *Scribner's Magazine*, now part of the Beinecke Collection. A one-page advertisement announced a new novel, *The Winning of Barbara Worth*, by Harold Bell Wright, and Wharton had marked with her familiar red crayon the paragraph that says that in the biggest edition ever printed of any novel (250,000 copies), A. L. Burt Company would publish *The Calling of Dan Matthews* in a Popular Edition on September 15. Readers are reminded of the popularity of this writer in another part of the advertisement, which announced that "Over 700,000 copies (thirty-five car loads) of *The Shepherd of the Hills* have been sold" (Beinecke Collection). Wharton had underlined the "thirty-five car loads," duly impressed. In the years following her death, this commercial success led to her categorization as an interesting, popular novelist who had ignored modernism and now looked dated.

Her reputation has risen, however, as critics have resisted and questioned the usual categorizations. This is Amy Kaplan: "By studying Wharton as a realist, I situate her writing at the intersection of class and gender, without reducing her career to a simple expression of either category."[9] Kaplan acknowledges the work of feminist critics who have identified Wharton's relentless exposure of the commodification of women as one of the key agendas of modernity, but she wishes to resituate her afresh before she becomes shunted into a fresh siding marked "women's literature: precursors in the history of the representation of women's struggle for power." To Kaplan, Wharton is an author "who wrote at the intersection of the main market of popular fiction, the tradition of women's writing and a realistic movement that developed in an uneasy dialogue with twentieth-century modernism."[10] Her sharp analysis of the power of culture, gender, society, and class in subject formation makes her more amenable to critical theory than does the late romantic celebration of the individual that was modernism's central concern. As Wharton's reputation has risen, that of modernism has faltered, and Virginia Woolf's line of demarcation of 1910 is seen to be only the horizontal axis of a cultural map of the early twentieth century. There is also a vertical political axis, a line that separates those writers for whom the political model of the ideal state was aristocratic from those whose model was democratic. Wharton may have rejected what she saw as the cultural solipsism of modernism, but it not easy to decide whether this was for either progressive or conservative reasons. On the one hand her concern in fiction with the full spectrum of society sounds enlightened, benevolent, and inclusive, perhaps even democratic. On the other, the politics of her writing are consistent with that of the conservative majority from her period and class. These need not necessarily debar a writer from sympathy with modernism, but in Wharton's case it is symptomatic of a worldview that saw the implications of modernism as a threat to the ordered society, and not an opportunity to improve it. It is instuctive to see traces of the assumptions that underpinned Wharton's idea of the good society and the organization of the state.

The Politics of Empire: Race and Othering

Modernism grew out of a late nineteenth-century aesthetic that privileged art before politics. To a writer like Henry James, "fiction is an impression"[11] that can destroy the separation between thinking and experiencing, which the modern world has created. But Wharton was always the lucid thinker who was reticent about stepping into the modernist pool of ambiguity and uncertainty for its own sake. She was amused by, but not sympathetic to, those artists who made a great deal of the suffering and agonies of art. Her artistic characters, such as Ralph Marvell, are often weak and ineffectual. Her concern is not with the internal struggle of the self, but with the outer interactions of individuals. Of Fulvia and Odo in *The Valley of Decision* she had written that they were "just little bits of looking-glass in which fragments of the great panorama are reflected."[12] Like Undine in *The Custom of the Country* they serve to reflect the image of the wider society. That reflection, however, is not an obviously contrived and rose-tinted one, designed to flatter conservative values. Balzac provided an influential precedent, and David Bellos's appraisal of Balzac could apply equally to Wharton: "Balzac the novelist is actually more subtle, and more cynical, than Balzac the propagandist of conservative values."[13] It is worth examining Wharton's conservative values during this prewar period of writing success to see if (and possibly, where) this contrast between novelist and propagandist proves to be the case.

The political rhetoric of Edith Wharton's fiction between 1900 and 1914 is informed by perceptions and opinions developed during the conflict between old and new ideologies in the latter part of the nineteenth century, combined with a readiness to locate with anthropological detachment inherited Old New York attitudes in the context of a broader dialectic. The novels themselves are true dialectics, but ultimately have a point or argument that is more pronounced than Balzac's in his *Comédie Humaine*. For Wharton, the point, whether ethical, social, or moral, always has political implications.

Wharton had grown to maturity during a period in which her inherited values were under challenge. These challenges were not immediately threatening but were reflected in the questioning of assumptions about religion and in the argument for reform and the bettering of the conditions of the working class. Other subjects, such as sexual behavior, were not discussed openly in the mainstream of the new mass circulation newspapers, but found expression instead in the specialist discussion of anthropology, medicine, and the new field of psychiatry. Although homosexuality and the open expression of female desire were still pathologized,[14] writers such as Edward Carpenter, Marie Stopes, and Havelock Ellis, cloaking their arguments in scientific or abstract language, began to quietly question some of the sexual prejudices of society. Other social changes were taking place almost too quickly for debate, as the era of mass production advertising and mass consumption began.

The first fourteen years of the twentieth century witnessed evidence of a growing anxiety about the turn events were taking. In English, French, and American newspapers and magazines confident assumptions about empire, social inequality, and gender were gradually undermined as the beliefs inherited from Victorian conservatism were challenged and unsettled by events such as the Boer War, German imperial ambitions, and by the reported rhetoric of socialists and suffragists. In the discourse of anxiety, allusions to the challenge to empire, to anarchism, to the "woman question," and to the "New Woman" become common. Was this unrest indicative of cultures' decline? Wharton may have come to believe in aesthetic decadence and Anglo-Saxon extinction, but did she also believe, as Kassanoff argues, with the contemporary view of George Edward Woodberry, a Columbian University professor, that a race must die at the point of perfection?[15] Or is it more plausible that she continued to agree with the Anglo-Saxon Social Darwinists, such as Herbert Spencer and Teddy Roosevelt, who argued from a natural selection and eugenicists' position that the Anglo-Saxon race was superior and deserving of "racial" dominance? It is time to review the extent to which Wharton's pre–World War I writing endorses the prevalent views of the ruling class in Europe and America on the three subjects of empire, poverty, and gender. An assessment of Wharton's politics in these matters will not be the defining factor in her relationship with modernism, however, because modernism included artists who were imperialists and those who were skeptical of imperialism, socialists and conservatives, suffragettes, and antisuffragettes. But evidence of the aristocratic Toryism that characterizes her politics helps explain why she could not subscribe to the aesthetic preoccupations of modernism. Her inclination was to turn her insights on the world, not on herself.

Wharton, like other writers of the early twentieth century such as Conrad and Woolf, is at her most politically difficult when it comes to a subject European and American men were expansive about, but on which women were more reticent: empire and its effects. At first glance the rhetoric of Wharton's fiction seems to endorse standard early twentieth-century white imperialist views of race and religion. People of color are largely invisible in these texts, even though their work and produce provides the basis for much of the wealth enjoyed by the principal characters. It is a white Anglo-Saxon world that we observe in her fiction, with the searchlight sometimes thrown on the occasional Jewish presence.

The late nineteenth century, when the frontier in the United States was declared officially closed, saw American expansionism translated into the "manifest destiny" of U.S. imperialism. It was a vision of Pacific dominance applauded by Kipling in his 1899 poem "The White Man's Burden," subtitled "The United States and the Philippine Islands." Rudyard Kipling approved of the British Empire and its achievements, and viewed empire as a responsibility to be shared by the superior races in the world. It was the mission of Americans to take on the burden of the former Spanish empire, and it was their thankless duty to manage the lesser races that fell under their control:

> To wait in heavy harness
> On fluttered fold and wild—
> Your new-caught, sullen peoples,
> Half devil and half child.[16]

Such depictions appeared without comment in the cartoons of *Punch*, where "natives" are made to look either savage or ridiculous, and where anyone who was not white, be they Turkish, Japanese, Arab, or African, was shown in a stereotypical way that suggested inborn flaws of character and general loathsomeness.

In the resurrection and recovery of Wharton's work that took place in the 1970s and 1980s, criticism tended to be evasive about Wharton's cultural politics, seeing her more unattractive rhetorical positionings as subordinate to her acute analysis of the position of women within marriage. More recently, however, there has been a willingness to confront this awkward issue. In a withering attack on the politics of her writing, Stuart Hutchinson charges Wharton with "recurrent and creatively unexplored prejudices about sex, race, and class."[17] In this essay[18] Hutchinson discusses Wharton's failure to go beyond what he sees as a superficiality and complacency in her imaginative rhetoric. In *The House of Mirth*, argues Hutchinson, Wharton is guilty of a general failure "to reach beyond her central character's sentimentality" (he cites Lily's sentimentalizing of the working girl Nettie Struther). Questions about the racial (and racist) implications of Lily's Anglo-Saxon whiteness contribute to the uncertainty in the presentation of transgressive women. Both Undine in *The Custom of the Country* and Sophy in *The Reef* are presented rather ambiguously. There is something rather appealing about Undine's zest for life, but this interest is ultimately subordinated to a rhetorical censure, a shift that also applies to the representation of Sophy, the "misguided" new woman. Most disturbing is Wharton's unappealing representation of Jews in her novels, and the ease with which Ralph can liken his mother and grandmother to the "vanishing denizens of the American continent doomed to rapid extinction with the advance of the invading race."[19]

In Edith Wharton's travel writing there is not a great deal to suggest that she saw unfamiliar people as anything but "Other." Lacan's "Autre" represents symbolically the principle of difference that emerges during the Oedipal triangle that structures desire and creates the unconscious and the decentered subject. The Other is not the object of desire. Instead, it is the cause of desire, and without desire there cannot be self-definition. We define ourselves when we conceptualize that there is something we are not.[20] Some women reacted to the experience of being subjugated and "othered" by developing an identification with the oppressed races of the white hegemony, while others transferred their oppression onto these people. Wharton's writing places her somewhere in the middle of this spectrum.

Wharton's cruise in the *Vanadis* in 1888, her visits to Tunisia and Algeria in 1914, and her visit to Morocco in 1917 yielded writing that show her responding to "the mystery of the 'East,'" and to the exoticism of Africa.[21] There is a consistency in her racial and imperial attitudes during this thirty-year period. Her sketches of Morocco in particular, with their many references to the beneficence of her host General Hubert Lyautey and his administration's "modernizing" influence on Morocco, seem to offer an endorsement of French colonialism and her acceptance of the theory of imperialism.[22] In this view European colonial powers served the useful function of ridding the colonized power of its more unpleasant aspects. Spencer D. Segalia thinks that the position is more complicated than this,[23] arguing that although Wharton praises Lyautey, she does not support his "associanist" philosophy, which encouraged close contact between colonizers and colonized. A believer, as many of her contemporaries were, in "racial purity," she feared miscegenation and was against the mixing of races. Segalia also makes the point that in one respect Wharton resists Western stereotypes of gender, in that the Arab women of the harem are not sexualized, even though "negro" women are.

Morton Fullerton, who had been Wharton's lover in 1908, had given a glimpse of the standard male freedom to evaluate Arab women in his 1891 book *In Cairo*. Fullerton describes some Egyptian women going down to the river, and gives full play to the voyeuristic male gaze:

> The average among the women are of a far coarser order, fat to use an ugly word, and sometimes patched with collops of flesh. Even the merest girls, who were often attractive, had frequently the full physical development of mothers of more northern races . . . There was a certain appropriateness, however, . . . in the swelling lines of the bust of these dark-skinned maidens, in the rich fullness of animal development it betokened, here in a land where nature seemed bursting with the plenitude of life.[24]

In the late-Victorian period such descriptions of the "exotic" passed as artistry. By 1917, however, the war was having an impact on Wharton's reading of colonialism. Benstock considers that it is not until World War I that Wharton is able to consider poverty and destitution as something that is caused by politicians and therefore preventable, and that even then it is because of the vivid political action that is war. Benstock contrasts Wharton's 1888 perspective with that evident in 1917: "In 1888, starving babies and legless beggars were 'local atrocities,' but in 1917, they called to mind the ravages of World War I."[25]

It was in 1888 that the recently married, twenty-six-year-old Edith Wharton had kept the journal that described her experience on the cruise of the *Vanadis*. The *Vanadis* was a boat hired by Teddy Wharton's friend James Van Alen, and supported by a crew of sixteen, which included two stewards and two cooks. The three Americans took an expensive and adventurous long cruise in the Mediterranean, visiting North Africa and cruising through the Aegean. The journal, only rediscovered in 1991, was apparently lost and forgotten by Edith Wharton, who in *A Backward Glance* claimed that before 1918 she never kept a diary, but as this remark conveniently ignores the revealing journal covering the brief affair with Fullerton, which she would not have forgotten, perhaps she is being economic with the truth.[26] Her comments and observations are perceptive as always, but while she can admire beauty in landscape and people, she can sometimes blur the two together when the scene is not so attractive. In describing the Greek town of Euripo, for example, she observes: "The inhabitants of Euripo are a sullen, ill-favoured lot, and as for the town, a short walk sufficed to convince us that it has nothing to recommend it but its fine double girdle of walls and the fortress in the middle of the channel."[27] The tendency to identify the unfamiliar as "other," and to include people as the objects of otherness was common among even the most perceptive European travelers, as we see in the novels of Joseph Conrad, for example. Conrad had the advantage of having traveled widely throughout the world as a sailor, and was able to bring an understanding of imperialism that saw the effect the practice had on the perceptions of its agents. In 1888 Wharton was only just beginning to extend her travels beyond Western Europe. In the section of her journal called "Cattaro and Cettinje" she describes a visit to Montenegro: "The people we met on the road were mostly of the poorer class, and their dresses, although picturesque, were shabby and ragged, especially those of the women who, being the drudges of the community, are seldom as gaily dressed as the men."[28] Throughout her journey in the eastern Mediterranean, Wharton writes as the privileged traveler, observing with an interested and educated eye, but inclined to offer a patronizing de haut en bas cultural perspective. In "Amorgos and Astypalia" she describes a visit to the town of Khora, in Amorgos:

> Then we went to the village school, which the priest in charge invited us to see. As we stepped in the room, a hundred and twenty five little Greek boys rose with one accord from their seats and made a kind of military salute, which they repeated as each member of our party crossed the threshold. They were a nice, clean-looking set, but I should not think that their education would advance very quickly, as we found the priest gossiping with some friends outside the door, while the boys were apparently left to their own devices. We left some money with the priest to give the boys a treat, and continued on our way through the village.[29]

In "Rhodes" "A donkey was engaged for me . . . but the saddling of the donkey on the quay drew about us such a crowd of Turks, Jews and infidels, that I retreated to the Street of the Kings and mounted in the august shadow of the Auberges France and Castille."[30] During the decade after the *Vanadis* journey, a cluster of past and present military issues encouraged Edith Wharton to confront and reassess the nature of political action, the reality of the community, and the effective "othering" of people. She had long carried with her the knowledge that her father had avoided action in the American Civil War by not registering on the army list. As a wealthy New Yorker there was no great danger, and he could easily have sold his call-up papers if need be. But the failure of her father to do his civic duty clearly preyed on her mind and found its way into the plot of the 1895 short story "The Lamp of Psyche." In 1898 Wharton was in Washington during the time of the great Spanish-American War fever, heated to a boiling point by the loss of the *Maine*. The jingoism was palpable, and for many historians the explosion on the *Maine* marks the moment at which American imperialism began. But it was a much more singular military event in Europe, the Dreyfus case, that provides us with a glimpse of Wharton's otherwise unarticulated political judgments.

Alfred Dreyfus was a French army captain who in 1894 was charged and found guilty of betraying his country. The evidence was highly suspect, and the judgment was famously denounced by Zola in his article "J'accuse." There was an appeal and a second trial in 1899, on which Fullerton reported, and the guilty verdict was confirmed. The issue divided French society, and although Wharton's close companion Paul Bourget, the French writer and critic, considered Dreyfus guilty, she did not share this view and, influenced perhaps by Zola's "J'accuse," which had created a sensation in France, was prepared to disagree with him. The Dreyfus affair was as highly charged as it was mainly because Dreyfus was Jewish. Those who condemned him often gave free rein to their anti-Semitism. In their eyes, using the charge of treason as a justification, Dreyfus was French but not-French.

Novels such as *The House of Mirth* seem to reflect uncritically the dominant Western discourse of anti-Semitism with its own particularly pervasive form of "Othering."[31] In her essay "The Perfect Jew and *The House of Mirth*" Irene Goldman Price[32] emphasizes how Wharton's view of Jews would have been influenced by her reading of Hippolyte Taine and William Lecky, who Wharton claimed "were among the formative influences of my life."[33] Both assumed a distinct difference of race (as opposed to religion) and were inclined to generalization and stereotyping. Mr. Rosedale is described as "a plump rosy man of the blond Jewish type"[34] for whom Lily Bart feels an intuitive repugnance. Her view is apparently endorsed by Judy Trenor, who had "declared that he was the same little Jew who had been served up and rejected at the social board a dozen times within her memory" (*HM*, 16). The issue is whether such observations on religion and race are accepted by the rhetoric of the narrative or presented with the voice of critical irony. Goldman-Price calls for a greater clarity in the discussion of Rosedale, wondering why he should be discussed as a Jew when he is not religious, and arguing that to say simply that the treatment is anti-Semitic is to gloss over the issue. She cites Hildegarde Hoeller's study, which claims that the novel reveals Wharton's anxieties about race, with Lily's racial specialization being set up in opposition to Rosedale's Jewishness.[35]

Wealthier Jews are the more obvious subjects for pejorative comment in Wharton's fiction, but the Catholicism of Italians and the French is also invested with a dark side in Wharton's earlier writing, especially in *Madame de Treymes* and *The Custom of the Country*. Even in *The Valley of Decision,* Wharton's first published full-length novel, which she wished to be an even-handed representation of Catholicism, there are sinister, secretive, and powerful Jesuits, and the state is often shown as the puppet of the Church. "Foreign" intelligent women are a threat, and the Church recognizes that Fulvia has to be silenced.

The link that many American women saw between the oppression of people on the grounds of race, and their own oppression as women (the movement for women's suffrage growing out of the antislavery movement) does not seem to be made by the women in Wharton's novels. In *The Valley of Decision,* Fulvia wishes for political reform, but does not call for a reassessment of the role of women. Wharton may have wanted to avoid the charge of anachronism, because events take place in the years around 1774 and Mary Wollstonecraft's *Vindication of the Rights of Woman* was not published until 1792, but she could have made her main woman character a pioneer in this (as in other matters) if she had wanted to.

In attributing to Fulvia the downfall of Odo, the principal character, and in allowing Fulvia to deliver her doctoral address only then to be shot, Wharton seems to be expressing the same reservations about the education of women that surface in *A Backward Glance*. Similarly, Shari Benstock argues that there is evidence of Wharton's unchanging perspective on the world beyond Europe in that the Edith Wharton who made a visit to Algiers in March 1914 had substantially the same views of race as the Wharton who had sailed on the *Vanadis* twenty years earlier. Algiers was a city full of "effeminacy, obscenity or black savageness."[36] The journey into southern Tunisia is a journey into the mystery of the desert, into the exotic world of the Arabian Nights. She visited Carthage and stayed for ten days in Tunis, admitting on her return to Naples that in North Africa she had been gloating at people for the past month. Benstock comments that

Wharton's friend Lady Stanhope might have viewed Edith Wharton as a wealthy, self-interested tourist ogling natives.[37] Stuart Hutchinson argues that Wharton "never bothered to imagine things from Caliban's point of view."[37] She, like Joseph Conrad, may have been much traveled, but her travels reinforced, rather than challenged, a developed inclination toward the imperialist point of view.

Wharton's nascent imperialism was cultivated in an environment and in a society where such views were the orthodoxy. In a letter to Sara Norton written in 1901 Wharton describes herself, only half mockingly, as a "rabid Imperialist."[39] She objected to the Spanish-American War,[40] not because the United States was flexing its imperial muscles, but because the enemy was a European country that she knew well. In France and England she mixed with historians and political analysts who had published articles and books endorsing American expansionism. England and France were imperial powers and their right to colonize remained unquestioned in the circle in which she moved.

Wharton's position on the subject of imperialism has important consequences for her writing. Frederick Wegener, commenting on the letter to Sara Norton in which Wharton calls herself a "rabid Imperialist," considers the significance for her published work of the "imperial sensibility that fundamentally shaped her social and political views."[41] Wharton's understanding of progressivism, whether on the subject of women in marriage, social questions such as euthanasia and divorce, factory conditions or materialism, is traceable in her fiction, but should be read alongside her view of global politics and her acceptance of imperialism. Such a reading holds in check any tendency to embrace Wharton as a feminist, socialist, or subversive writer, even when evidence of feminist, socialist, and subversive rhetoric can be traced in her work. This is a point in its own right, and is not a defining issue that sets her apart from modernism. As the case of Ezra Pound was to show, it was possible to be anti-Semitic, misogynistic, and hold protofascist views and still be a modernist. Having said that, for all her wealth and privileges, Edith Wharton contemplated poverty and the poor in a way that Pound did not.

Moral, Psychological, and Physical Poverty

It would be easy to see the "good" year 1905, referred to in her diary entry, as the most successful and reassuring year in Edith Wharton's life. *The House of Mirth* had been a success, both financially and critically. The novel itself has a dark ending, but the sad decline and death of the lonely, outcast Lily Bart explores a predicament that is apparently in striking contrast to the prosperity enjoyed by its author. Wharton was married and lived in a fine house in the Berkshires, she had an impressive circle of friends that included Henry James, and she was not staring into anything remotely like the feared Edwardian abyss, conjured up by H. G. Wells, Jack London, E. M. Forster, and Theodore Dreiser. It is partly because she was so insulated from the poverty of the class that demanded a voice in the twentieth century, so restricted to a privileged society, and so clearly a writer mindful of the market that her work was for a long time denied critical approval. She may often have been able to chronicle the mores and eccentricities of her class with the satirical eye of a twentieth-century American Jane Austen, but the mid-twentieth-century critic favored different subjects and forms. The mannered world of Old New York appeared rather precious and old-fashioned compared with the glimpses into the urban abyss provided by Dreiser, Conrad, Lawrence, and Eliot. As Virginia Woolf was to say of the writing produced by her own popular contemporaries Bennett, Galsworthy, and Wells, "life is not . . . like this."[42] But it is reasonable to say of the work produced by the early modernists: life, for the majority, was not quite like this, either.

In 1905 Edith Wharton's fiction was addressing very modern issues,[43] and these books have endured despite the disappearance of Old New York, the worst excesses of factory exploitation, and the specific turn of the century examples of rural and urban poverty. Furthermore, it is not the case that Wharton's fiction ignored contemporary issues or failed to engage with contemporary politics or forms. They do engage, sometimes quite explicitly, but more often subtly and indirectly, reflecting Wharton's interest in an anthropological reading of history, culture, and politics. The fiction is mediated by a narrator who has done a great deal of thinking about political issues.

Wharton's first adult novel, *The Valley of Decision* (1902) may have emerged opportunely at a time when, as Frederick Wegener reminds us, there was popular interest in what Frank Luther Mott calls "a series of historical and cloak-and-sword novels" that were congenial companions to the American expansionist ideology at the turn of the century.[44] Blake Nevius, on the other hand, asks whether it is "simply by accident that during the heyday of progressivism in this country Mrs. Wharton chose to write a novel so contrary in spirit to that vast movement of philosophy and reform sponsored by scientists, social workers and even politicians . . ."[45]

Wharton's novel, however, does confront the issue of material poverty, albeit the poverty of eighteenth-century Italy. When the central character Odo, now the heir apparent to a dukedom, returns to the farm on which he grew up, he feels the inadequacy of the reformist philosophy into which he has come into contact in privileged Turin, reflecting a belief in the need for urgent, immediate philanthropic action rather than structural reform: "His mind had of late run much on economic abuses; but what was any philandering with reform to this close contact with misery? It was as though white hungry faces had suddenly stared in at the windows of his brightly-lit life. What did these people care for education, enlightenment, the religion of humanity? What they wanted was fodder for their cattle, a bit of meat on Sundays and a faggot on the hearth.[46] Although overlong and rather rambling, the novel ponders a number of explicitly political questions. Odo's education in the ways of the world is sharply influenced by a view expressed by the priest Crescenti:

> Even in this quiet retreat . . I hear much talk of abuses and of the need for reform; and I often think that if they who rail so loudly against existing institutions would take the trouble to trace them to their source, and would, for instance, compare this state as it is to-day with its condition five hundred or a thousand years ago, instead of measuring it by the standard of some imaginary Platonic republic, they would find, if not less subject for complaint, yet fuller means of understanding and remedying the abuses they discover.
>
> (*VD*, 259)

This ameliorative, or gradualist view of history is greeted by Odo as a revelation, and the narrator's voice seems to briefly merge with Wharton's:

> How was it that among the philosophers whose works he had studied none had thought of tracing in the social and political tendencies of the race the germ of wrongs so confidently ascribed to the cunning of priests and the rapacity of princes? Odo listened with growing interest while Crescenti, encouraged by his questions, pointed out how the abuses of feudalism had arisen from the small landowner's need of protection against the northern invader, as the concentration of royal prerogative had been the outcome of the King's intervention between his great vassals and the communes. The discouragement which had obscured Odo's outlook since his visit to Pontesordo was cleared away by the discovery that in a sympathetical study of the past might lie the secret of dealing with present evils. His imagination, taking the intervening obstacles at a bound, arrived at once at the general axiom to which such inductions

pointed; and if he afterward learned that human development follows no such direct line of advance, but must painfully stumble across the wastes of error, prejudice and ignorance, while the theorizer traverses the same distance with a stroke of his speculative pinions; yet the influence of these teachings tempered his judgment with charity and dignified his very failures by a tragic sense of their inevitableness.

(*VD*, 260)

Yet even here there is qualification and a measure of narrative distance. If Odo welcomes a view of the world that attributes present failure (including his own) to history, the narrator reminds us of the greater complexity of human development that Odo is himself to learn. The phrase "tempered his judgments with charity," however, is an expression of such narrative approval that it promises to be at one with Wharton's own politics.

This is not to suggest that Wharton was a confident apologist for existing inequalities. Neither she nor Odo is the eternal fatalist or cynic. At this stage in the novel he strongly believes that wrongs should be righted, and a later exchange with the Duchess is one that Wharton might well have had with a wealthy relative, where the only course would be to bite her tongue and avoid argument:

"Why do you concern yourself with politics?" she went on with a new note in her voice. "Can you find no diversion more suited to your rank and age? Our court is a dull one, I own—but surely even here a man might find a better use for his time."

Odo's self-possession returned in a flash. "I am not," cried he gaily, "in a position to dispute it at this moment"; and he leaned over to recapture her hand.

(*VD*, 314)

Politics to Wharton was something more than a mere "diversion" and later novels, such as *The House of Mirth*—and more manifestly, *The Fruit of the Tree* and *Ethan Frome*—emanate partly from her desire to write the novel of social realism or naturalism. Lily Bart, like Hurstwood in *Sister Carrie,* falls into a spiral of decline, driven ever lower by forces outside her control. How much Wharton knew about the experience of the urban and rural poor it is difficult to say, but *Bunner Sisters* and *Ethan Frome* are novellas that powerfully convey the effect of want. Her very first story, "Mrs. Manstey's View," published in 1891 when she was twenty-eight, had depicted the plight of a lonely, elderly woman whose sole pleasure is the view from her third-floor New York boardinghouse in a poor district. The poverty depicted in these works, and in *The House of Mirth,* is as much the poverty of emotion as it is the lack of money, though the two are inextricably linked, so that the "elision of class boundaries" in the novel forces the imagery of (psychological) poverty to the center of the novel, thus acting as a surrogate for the central problem of gender inequality.[47]

All four of these texts by Wharton convey a barrenness and a bleakness that comes from a set of social conventions that deny women (and men) happiness if they do not have the freedom that money can provide. If the charge of romanticizing working-class poverty can be leveled at the final section of *The House of Mirth*, it cannot be leveled at the depiction of poverty in *Bunner Sisters* and *Ethan Frome*. In both *Bunner Sisters* and *Ethan Frome*, the absence of children emphasizes the poverty of feeling, but the situation is very different in *The House of Mirth*, where there is less poverty and Lily's childlessness is the corollary of her decisions about being wed. Lily's avoidance of marriage except on her own terms makes her vulnerable to gossip, the cruel social disease that makes her the outcast. She must live by her own work, and as an unmarried woman her fate may eventually be that of the Bunner sisters, a prospect so depressing that she resorts to the sedative chloral, an accidental overdose of which kills her.

The prospect of a life of empty relationships, drugs, and drudgery, all made more awful with the onset of age, is a prospect confronted by many women writers later in the twentieth century. At the turn of the century, however, the possibility of the fall into the abyss of urban poverty was very real, and is a male anxiety confronted by writers as diverse as Wells, Jack London, E. M. Forster, and Knut Hamsun. The horrors of a mutant species of the kind we meet in *The Time Machine*, the depressing spectacle of the London poor that we meet in *The People of the Abyss*, the basement-dwelling Leonard Bast and the deranged hero of *Hunger* forced to eat his own manuscript, all signal the deep anxiety about the effects of poverty on human beings, and fears of degeneration and Darwinian decline.

In Forster's case this is linked in *Howards End* to anxieties about deracination, as the pervasiveness of machinery, hotels, and new-money transience means that all are in danger of serious psychological dislocation and rootlessness, be they rich or poor. Such an anxiety is also reflected in Wharton's novel, illustrating the transatlantic nature of these fears. In the moments before taking the final sedative, Lily reflects on what it is that is threatening her ruin, and she diagnoses a social sickness that she fears more than poverty:

> It was no longer, however, from the vision of material poverty that she turned with the greatest shrinking. She had a sense of deeper impoverishment—of an inner destitution compared to which outward conditions dwindled into insignificance. It was indeed miserable to be poor—to look

forward to a shabby, anxious middle-age, leading by dreary degrees of economy and self-denial to gradual absorption in the dingy communal existence of the boarding-house. But there was something more miserable still—it was the clutch of solitude at her heart, the sense of being swept like a stray uprooted growth down the heedless current of the years. That was the feeling, which possessed her now—the feeling of being something rootless and ephemeral, mere spindrift of the whirling surface of existence, without anything to which the poor little tentacles of self could cling before the awful flood submerged them. And as she looked back she saw that there had never been a time when she had had any real relation to life. Her parents too had been rootless, blown hither and thither on every wind of fashion, without any personal existence to shelter them from its shifting gusts. She herself had grown up without any one spot of earth being dearer to her than another: there was no centre of early pieties, of grave endearing traditions, to which her heart could revert and from which it could draw strength for itself and tenderness for others.

(*HM*, Penguin edition, 319)

Anxieties about rootlessness, degeneration, and heredity were reflected in the turn of the century debates about intelligence, instinct, sexual behavior, eugenics, race, and evolution. Wharton was interested in many of these issues, which during her lifetime were undergoing a reevaluation. In the mid-nineteenth century a biological, Darwinian reading of human behavior had dominated progressive scientific thinking, but Russel Wallace, Huxley, and Spencer, Franz Boas, James Fraser, and Freud contributed to a striking shift toward an emphasis on social and cultural factors. The richness and complexity of these debates is traceable in Wharton's fiction,[48] while such issues as incest, mother instinct, and the tribal nature of human behavior are found both in the scientific discourse and the discourse of Wharton's early twentieth-century fiction.[49] Her novels provide a social Darwinist analysis of human social evolution in which the movement is sometimes upward, as in *The Custom of the Country,* occasionally downward, as in *The House of Mirth,* and sometimes with a glance down toward the very bottom of the social well, as in *Bunner Sisters.*

Poverty and the Abyss

Bunner Sisters has as its subject those people who live close to the urban abyss. The two sisters who run a very modest dress repair shop in a poor district of New York are kept from the abyss only by their industry and economy, the elder sister Ann Eliza's belief in the virtues of self-sacrifice, and both sisters' dream of marriage. But it is the younger sister Evelina's marriage to an opium addict that destroys them both. Evelina is abandoned and dies of consumption. Ann Eliza is forced to sublet the shop and look for sales work, for which she is now too old.

The novella announces many of the themes that Wharton was to explore in her studies of the rich that are her novels of Old New York. The dream of romance offered by engagement and marriage, even to such an unattractive figure as the unhealthy clock-mender Herman Ramy, is shown to be the illusion that the narrative voice always hints that it will be, when Ramy is revealed to have married only for the money he manages to extract from both sisters primarily to feed his addiction. Marriage is a commercial arrangement among the poor as well as among the rich. Ramy blackmails Evelina into getting her sister to part with the money that he knows she possesses. The wedding is to be postponed because Ramy has supposedly calculated they do not have enough money to move to St. Louis where he has a job lined up. Evelina gives Ann Eliza an insight into his cool calculations: "He says he's got to lay by another hundred dollars before he'll be willing to take me out there."[50] The narrative voice, which filters its comments through Ann Eliza's perception of events, alerts us to what is going on, even though the full details are not revealed until much later: for a while Ann Eliza pondered this surprising statement; then she ventured: "Seems to me he might have thought of it before" (*BS*, 275–76). The later discovery of the betrayal and deception has a profound effect on Ann Eliza not because it brings to her awareness the sordid details of "the drug fiend" (though it certainly does that), but because it destroys her belief in the virtue of renunciation.

This is a story of the surrogate pleasure yielded by self-sacrifice. Ramy initially proposes to Ann Eliza, but though she had earlier dreamed of such a proposal, she has come to believe that it is her younger sister that he finds attractive, and having made this adjustment and convinced herself of its rightness, she would rather sacrifice her own happiness than her sister's (Evelina is clearly besotted with the clock-mender by this stage). Yet such renunciation has yielded only the ruin of the sister she loves like a daughter. Worse than being unrewarded, it has seemingly been punished. Ann Eliza is so startled she questions the Puritanical ethic on which her life has been based: "For the first time in her life she dimly faced the awful problem of the inutility of self-sacrifice. Hitherto she had never thought of questioning the inherited priniciples which had guided her life. Self-effacement for the good of others had always seemed to her both natural and necessary; but then she had taken it for granted that it implied the securing of that good." (*BS*, 303). And the loss of belief means that the abyss, that symbol of the horrific brutalization brought about by the degenerative effects of poverty, an image that appears in so much English and American fiction at the turn of the century, comes that much closer: "She felt that she could no longer trust in the goodness of God, and that if she was not good he was not God, and there was only a black abyss above the roof of Bunner Sisters." (*BS*, 303).

Like Leonard Bast in *Howards End* (1911) the Bunner sisters live in a basement. A world underground can be reassuring, as it is in an Edwardian children's story such as *The Wind in the Willows* (1908), but the futuristic horrors of the subterranean world of cities had been imaginatively explored by H. G. Wells in *The Time Machine* (1895). Forster, in *Howards End*, explored the sociological implication of the abyss in Edwardian London, as had Jack London eight years before in his documentary account *The People of the Abyss* (1903). A metaphor for the repressed fears of the subconscious, it is a place of psychological and material discomfort.

Wharton's account of New York deprivation reveals a similar anxiety about the grinding effects of poverty, and the bleakness of tone was supposedly responsible for the reluctance of publishers to take up this tale. The sisters' shop is in a "shabby basement" in a side-street "already doomed to decline." The "Bunner Sisters" sign is in "blotchy gold," and the shop is in a building whose shutters have "weak hinges," while the adjacent premises consist of a "cheap lunch-room" and a shabby hotel where it "was obvious from the chronic cluster of refuse-barrels at its area-gate and the blurred surface of its curtainless windows, that the families frequenting the Mendoza Hotel were not exacting in their tastes." (*BS*, 225). As the street advances eastward, it rapidly falls "from shabbiness to squalor" and the refuse covering the street by the end of the day is listed in all its unpleasant detail. Ramy's accommodation is no better. When Ann Eliza visits his shop she has "a glimpse of a dingy room with a tumbled bed" (*BS*, 233), and her romantic odyssey to the market in the hope of meeting him is contrasted with the description of the "damp and cold" morning whose early light makes the street look "its meanest and most neglected," and the meeting with the butcher, whom she approaches "across the tessellation of fish-scales, blood and saw-dust" (*BS*, 235). The willingness to disregard the awfulness of this poverty and squalor, and the unattractive appearance of Ramy with his "threadbare overcoat" and "shabby hat," his "row of yellowish teeth with one or two gaps," his "sunken cheeks and prominent eyes" and so on, is only comprehensible when we read how the possibility of marriage offers Ann Eliza an escape so that "for the first time in her long years of drudgery she rebelled at the dullness of her life" (*BS*, 236). It is a life of grinding tedium: "Intolerably monotonous seemed now to the Bunner sisters the treadmill routine of the shop, colourless and long their evenings about the lamp, aimless their habitual interchange of words to the weary accompaniment of the sewing and pinking machines." (*BS*, 245). But for the unmarried woman without family, there is an even more awful prospect. When Eveline begins her period of engagement to Ramy, Ann Eliza can only recall "that she got up each morning with the sense of having to push the leaden hours up the same long steep of pain." Only stoicism and her "idolatrous acceptance of the cruelties of fate" allow her to survive the prospect of an old age of lonely spinsterhood.

There are moments when this grimness is relieved by a lightness and irony of tone at which Wharton was to prove herself so adept. Occasionally this is at the expense of the sisters, as when Ramy ends his first visit "with an abruptness which would have startled anyone used to the subtler gradations of intercourse" (*BS*, 244). More obviously it is realized through the lively Miss Mellins, whose life is never without vivid incident involving, apparently, encounters with burglars, would-be poisoners, customers who have seen ghosts, and others who are being shadowed by detectives: "A sceptical observer might have explained Miss Mellins's proneness to adventure by the effect that she derived her chief mental nourishment from the *Police Gazette* and the *Fireside Weekly*" (*BS*, 246). These are brief Dickensian touches of humor in a narrative whose style is more characteristically that of an implacable naturalism that was to be more fully realized in Dreiser's *Sister Carrie*. But the excitement of the "tumult of the streets" and "the engulfing roar of Broadway or Third Avenue" (*BS*, 232) is glimpsed only rarely. Yet we know that Wharton admired the French naturalists, and *Bunner Sisters* explores the theme of entrapment and deceit in marriage at a time when she had been married for seven years and was beginning to discover the penalties in the contract into which she had entered. It is a political statement about an institution central to Victorian society.

If there are significant changes in the subject matter of Wharton's major novels from *The House of Mirth* (1905) to *The Fruit of the Tree* (1907) to *Ethan Frome* (1911), and then to *The Reef* (1912) and *The Custom of the Country* (1913) there are also continuities. These are manifest in the concern with the way that local culture shapes behavior, and in the special position of women, so that in some ways *The Custom of the Country* may seem to be a straightforward return to the territory that had proved so successful in 1905. The public liked her treatment of these subjects, and her books that dealt with wider, uncomfortable social issues did not seem to satisfy the market of readers she had created.

There is some evidence that Wharton's need to make money from her novels prevented her from writing about the poor in the way that she would have wished. *The Fruit of the Tree*, with its depiction of the industrial community, had not been well received. Although she returned to the subject of the poor in *Ethan Frome*, it did not sell well. *Summer*, the 1917 novella that Wharton characterized as a response to *Ethan Frome*'s winter, returned to the subject of rural isolation, but depicted a community containing both rich and poor. But if, for either commercial or aesthetic reasons, the poor were not to be her subject, then there was another group that was made "poor" culturally, and that she had discovered she could write about with a forensic, surgical accuracy: women. The irony was that it was not a group with which she herself publicly identified in any way whatsoever.

Gender: Closely Observed Women

At the heart of the argument I have been advancing is the issue of Wharton's attitude to the society of which she felt herself to be a part. I have suggested that her criticisms of that society always come from the position of an insider, and that she never identifies imaginatively with someone who sees it from the outside, or who wishes to destroy it. In this sense her criticisms are like those from within the family. You may find fault with your grandfather, brother, or mother, but you do not wish to see them dead. Wharton may find fault with the institution of marriage, but she does not wish to see it abolished. That is why she rejects bohemianism, and that is why she is uneasy about modernism. They both wished to knock down fences that she would rather rearrange.

Her argument with modernism is linked inextricably to her relationship with the social group that enjoyed high status and the social responsibilities that accompanied privilege. Wharton was not a solitary person. She was not friendless. She cultivated friendships, with both men and women. Her busy social life and constant traveling meant that she did not have, or did not allow herself time to reflect on existential questions about a world without meaning, principally because she considered such questions self-indulgent and self-centered. I am not suggesting that she was stuck in a Victorianism that she was unable to escape for it is clear that during the period 1900 to 1914 she entertained political ideas and chose a sexual adventure that showed she could defy her upbringing. Her decision not to abandon values with which she had been brought up was a deliberate choice made after reflection and contemplation. At its heart, however, as a political decision it does reflect a peculiarly Victorian suspicion of self-indulgence, manifested a hundred years earlier as a horror, not of solitary art, but of solitary sex. In the nineteenth century, masturbation became pathologized partly because it seemed to symbolize a world without God, and therefore a world in which there was no authority. If God went, then so did the ordered hierarchic universe. Such fears were evident in the tensions during the Enlightenment period, where ideas of self-fulfillment and "self governing, go-getting individuals collided with fears of moral anarchy."[51] Solitude became the source of vice political licentiousness and was regarded with suspicion.

Nowhere is the elevation of the social above the solitary more evident in Wharton's fiction than in her discussion of women. Women are central to her work, but they are always women who are perceived in relationship to others. They are not solitary women by inclination. Sometimes this social relationship is of a very unwelcome kind, and determined by social mores that observed, judged, and confined women, whether through the institution of marriage or superficial assumptions about female beauty. In Wharton's novels female characters are the sites on which questions about politics, culture, and desire all converge. Although Wharton's own position was aggressively antisuffrage, and in her final years she wrote with as much bitterness as irony of the influence of the "monstrous regiment" of the emancipated (*ABG*, 41), the issues raised by the treatment and experience of the women who formed her principal subjects (Lily Bart, Undine Spragg, and the Countess Olenska are the most lengthily examined characters in her fiction) inevitably raised questions about the kind of society that shapes and restricts these women.

It may not have been an inner circle, but the list of Wharton's women friends is a long one. In the period between her childhood and 1915 she was at various times close to Sara Norton, Margaret Terry Chanler, Minnie Jones, Beatrix Jones Farrand, Elsina Tyler, Mary Berenson, and Minnie Bourget. Some of these married into her family, some of these were relatives, and some were the wives of her male friends. As with so much else in her life and work, her contact with women was sometimes paradoxical. Her mother Lucretia seems to have been a cold, distant figure, while Wharton's relationship with Catherine Gross, the German employee who spoke French to Wharton, was close and enduring. The friendship with women such as

"Daisy" Terry went right back to childhood, while friendship with women such as Sara Norton and Minnie Bourget began when Wharton was in her thirties.

On the whole these were conservative women who accepted their place in the social hierarchy and conformed to nineteenth-century expectations of women, whether they were daughters, mothers, wives, or servants. In their correspondence with Wharton, they were not critical of the roles assigned to them. These were by no means New Women, or radical women. Female suffrage was not their cause.

In contrast, all of Edith Wharton's fictional women (and in the poorer communities the men, too) are subject to damaging restraints. Wharton believed that there should indeed be brakes on human behavior imposed by society, but the paradox is that while the fiction argues that these brakes are applied unequally to men and women, Wharton's public and private communications rarely advance this as an argument. They do not do so because, as a writing woman, Wharton did not wish to be excluded from that class in which her father, mother, and husband moved. There was a price to pay, however. That class was her sanctuary, but it was also her prison. Wharton explores this paradox in her early fiction, where it is possible to identify a number of key themes[52] that relate to the interrelated politics of class and gender. These themes include politics and the female body, commerce, women and conspicuous consumption, and the puritanical need for suffering. Only the last takes us in the direction of modernism, for the need for suffering, a need whose importance should not be underestimated in Wharton's belief system, may lead to a political conservatism (one accepts one's fate because it is God's will) but it can also lead to introspection, which in the early modernist period led many artists to contemplate consciousness rather than the religious soul. It is evident that this was not the case for Wharton, for all of the other themes demonstrate Wharton's fascination with the social, rather than the solitary, the cultural rather than the existential. Though this made her work look familiar compared to the unfamiliarity of writing by Virginia Woolf, Gertrude Stein, and Dorothy Richardson, her concern with the social is her great strength, however inveterately Tory the reasons for it may have been. That is not to say that early modernist writers showed no awareness of the social, nor that a desire to illustrate the inner workings of consciousness is a symptom of an unhealthy preoccupation with the self. It is simply an argument that Wharton's representation of women is an excellent illustration of her awareness of the power of the community in shaping the individual. Her fiction is a ventriloquism for a political voice that otherwise was silent.

Politics and the Female Body

In *The House of Mirth* Edith Wharton explored the issue of the female body, the dressing and arrangement of the body, and the significance of woman as adornment and art. Women are taught from an early age to see themselves as others see them, to be the objects of the male gaze, and to satisfy and please that gaze. Lily Bart is taught by her mother that her beauty is the family's only asset:

> Only one thought consoled her, and that was the contemplation of Lily's beauty. She studied it with a kind of passion, as though it were some kind of weapon she had slowly fashioned for her vengeance. It was the last asset in their fortunes, the nucleus around which their life was to be rebuilt.
> (*HM*, 34)

Lily's very name is suggestive of beauty and decoration, associated as it was with aestheticism, art nouveau, and flower symbolism. She perceives her own beauty to be the potential agent of something fine, and in so perceiving she avoids vanity and translates bodily beauty into art, aesthetics, and sensibility. The narrator describes this aspiration with gentle irony:

> There was in Lily a vein of sentiment . . . which gave an idealizing touch to her most prosaic purposes. She liked to think of her beauty as a power for good, as giving her the opportunity to attain a position where she should make her influence felt in the vague diffusion of refinement and good taste. She was fond of pictures and flowers, and of sentimental fiction, and she could not help thinking that the possession of such taste ennobled her desire for worldly advantages;
> (*HM*, 35)

Early in the novel Lily is examined by Selden as an object of art, something that is fashioned, made, and glazed, as base clay can be made into something beautifully shaped and glazed. Although his keen eye notices that her hair is perhaps slightly "brightened by art" there are natural qualities to admire in her little ear and black lashes. It is evolution that has made her in this form, and sacrificed others in the making. He is dissatisfied with his initial idea that she has been "produced":

> He was aware that the qualities distinguishing her from the herd of her sex were chiefly external: as though a fine glaze of beauty and fastidiousness had been applied to vulgar clay. Yet the analogy left him unsatisfied, for a coarse texture will not take a high finish; . . .
> (*HM*, 5)

Later in the novel Lily quite literally appears as a work of art, when she chooses Reynolds's *Mrs. Lloyd* as the subject she wishes to represent in the *tableaux vivants*. Yet she has chosen a painting that completely allows herself to be the object of attention: it is the loveliness of Lily Bart that is gazed upon, not the illusion of Mrs. Lloyd. Selden feels that for the first time he is seeing the "real Lily Bart": in impersonating beauty without the distraction of costume or surroundings, she has presented what she actually is, free from the shadows of position and circumstances that threaten to make a tragedy of her life. The narrator clearly plays with the ambiguities and ironies of this "revelation" and Wharton was undoubtedly aware that Reynolds was a portrait painter who would often paint the head of his subject and leave the body and dress to an employee.

Although Lily is aestheticized in this scene, she is also the subject of a cruder, more voyeuristic male gaze. Gus Trenor's comments end the scene on a baser note, in which the studied female body is the preoccupation:

> Gad, what a show of good-looking women; but not one of 'em could touch that little cousin of mine. Talk of jewels—what's a woman want with jewels when she's got herself to show? The trouble is that all these falbals they wear cover up their figures when they've got 'em. I never knew till tonight what an outline Lily has.
>
> (*HM*, 138)

As Trenor knows full well, society based on the integration of money and marriage demanded jewels. We have already noted that six years before the publication of *The House of Mirth* Thorstein Veblen had argued in *The Theory of the Leisure Class* that the display of women among the privileged class served the function of "conspicuous consumption," and that their dress, possessions, and daily public appearance provided confirmation of the man's success in ways in which his own dedication to work made impossible.[53]

But Lily is not married, and so her body is what counts. She is only twenty-nine, but that is not regarded as young for an unmarried woman. Her age, and the imminent process of aging, is signaled from our very first sight of Lily:

> Selden had never seen her more radiant. Her vivid head, relieved against the dull tints of the crowd, made her more conspicuous than in a ballroom, and under her dark hat and veil she regained the girlish smoothness, the purity of tint, that she was beginning to lose after eleven years of late hours and indefatigable dancing. Was it really eleven years, Selden

found himself wondering, and had she indeed reached the nine-and-twentieth birthday with which her rivals credited her?

(*HM*, 4)

In so much of Wharton's fiction, including *The House of Mirth*, "The Muse's Tragedy," and *The Custom of the Country*, the central woman is constantly regarded as a beautiful object, when she wishes to be regarded as a complex person. It is not surprising that the woman interiorizes the dominant male (and thus normative) perception, and becomes anxious if she is not living up to it. It is not until well into the novel that we see Lily worrying about the passing of youth and beauty, and then it is because she realizes that it may mean she is losing her hold on society. Selden has sailed to the West Indies, she reads in the evening paper, and then gazes at herself in the brightly lit mirror: "The lines in her face came out terribly—she looked old; and when a girl looks old to herself, how does she look to other people?" (*HM*, 179). It is not the loss of desire, but the loss of desirability that haunts many of Wharton's fictional women. It is a truism but an important part of the narrative rhetoric for all that: men can age and lose little of their charm, power, energy, and attractiveness. For women wishing to succeed in society, or to have relationships, or both, youthful beauty is everything. At the beginning of "The Pretext," a short story included in the 1908 collection *The Hermit and the Wild Woman*, the central character Mrs. Ransom notices that her "hair had grown too thin" and that "her lips were too pale; and there were lines in the corners of her eyes."[54] She later learns that the young man who has made her ardent again was simply using her as a pretext to cover his interest in someone else. Margaret Ransom looks in the mirror, and in recalling Dawnish's first visit she sees the significance of her situation: "It was just a year since then—the elms were budding again, the willows hanging their green veil above the bench by the river. But there was no trace of youth left in her face—she saw it now as others had doubtless always seen it."[55]

She stoically and resolutely turns to the paper she must complete for the imminent meeting of the Higher Thought Club. Any hopes she may have had are crushed, but she accepts life's punishment with fortitude.

Commerce, Women, and Conspicuous Consumption

What is most clearly understood is the link between the prescribed roles for women and the operation of both commercial and aristocratic society. In both cases women are required by the men who dominated privileged society to be decorative; they are encouraged not to be independent and are prohibited from having careers because women supply the means by which men display their prosperity and wealth. Marriage is thus a commercial transaction and part of the marketplace, as described in Veblen's *Theory of the Leisure Class*. One of the messages of *The House of Mirth* is that the price to be paid by middle-class women for independence is poverty. The political message is clear. Moneyed society monitors and enforces class divisions not only through the social exclusion of those who do not conform to the conventions, but through the greater threat of financial ruin or severance. In her postwar years Wharton may have thought that the order of the old society was worth preserving, but before World War I she exposed in her fiction the ruthless and damaging means by which that society held on to its power and influence and her argument in her 1917 study of the difference between American women and French women[56] is that it is precisely because in France women are given the opportunity to be businesswomen, mothers, and artists all at the same time that they are allowed to be become adult. The American system produces an environment for women that has the properties of a Montessori infant school, producing what Wharton identifies as a childish individualism that contrasts with the mature roles played by women in France. All of this is traceable to the paradox that whereas in America boys and girls are together in childhood, but separated as adults, in France the opposite is the case.

In writing about women Wharton is commenting on the society that produces a particular model of womanhood, and the institutions of marriage and the family that sustain this model. Bauer notes that Wharton's prewar novels, *The House of Mirth* and *The Custom of the Country*, trace women's entry into society, while her later fiction traces women retreating from mass culture. The new society is no better than the old. Bauer argues that by 1917 Wharton's fiction had reached the rhetorical position that argues that not only are marriage and female sexuality matters of economic exchange, the patriarchal family is intrinsically incestuous, a conclusion pointed toward in both *Ethan Frome* and *The Reef*. In *Summer*, Wharton's 1917 novella, argues Bauer, Charity, the central character "must reject the notion of sexuality as economic exchange": she forgoes her "value" and her "power" and gives herself freely to Harney. Ultimately Charity's relationship with Harney allows her to separate herself from North Dormer and the pressure of incest, whether it is coming from her relatives on the mountain or her adopted "father," the lawyer Royall. Bauer concludes: "In rejecting the oedipal configuration, Charity sounds Wharton's death knell for the family as a functioning unit."[59]

Such a conclusion makes it sound as if by 1917 Wharton was ready to write fiction that in a deliberately encoded way celebrates women who had challenged and escaped the patriarchal world of the traditional American and European family. I do not think that is the case, but the fact her fiction clearly permits such a subversive reading is a measure of the extent to which the polyphonic rhetoric of the novels contrasts with the narrow certainties of the political rhetoric with which Wharton identified in her own circle.

Gender: Gentle Ladies and New Women

In *A Backward Glance* Wharton claims that in all of her experience she had only met three highly intelligent, cultured women who could hold a conversation in male company. In her fiction there are few "modern" women who are presented with any empathy, and even these few are presented somewhat ambiguously. Both Fulvia in *The Valley of Decision*, and Justine in *The Fruit of the Tree* have question marks put next to them by the narrator. In *The House of Mirth* Lily Bart may sit on the cusp of the category known as the modern woman, but her streak of acquiescence presents as many challenges to the model as does the convention-breaking Mrs. Norma Hatch. None of the women in *Ethan Frome* is in a position to be modern, while the ambition and power of Undine Spragg is presented as an object lesson in the awfulness of a certain kind of woman that new money and old assumptions about marriage has created. Even the potentially independently spirited Sophy Viner is a prisoner of conventional marriage arrangements, and in the role of private tutor takes us right back to the position in which young women find themselves in the novels of Charlotte Brontë.

Does Wharton's fiction contain a rhetoric that argues the case for the equality of women? When asked in 1924 to write an essay on the question "Women: Have They Got What They Want?" Wharton replied that she had been "entirely out of sympathy with woman-suffrage."[58] Most of the women with whom she mixed endorsed that view. She did have social contact with women such as Nancy Astor, who was a feminist and was elected as the first woman MP in 1919, but Astor herself was a Conservative, and her "vulgarity and superficiality" offended the more dedicated activist Sylvia Pankhurst when she encountered her in 1914.[59] In any case, Wharton's personal contact was reserved for outright antisuffragist lobbyists such as the novelist Mrs. Humphry Ward. Moreover, after 1907 she was based in France, a country that had complicated attitudes to women. The influence of the Church was just one of these complicating factors. On the one hand it reinforced traditional, family roles for women. But on the other hand, the priest served as a rival to the husband's authority, often knowing through confession his sexual secrets, thus providing women with a secret power.[60] For this, and other reasons, feminism in France did not lead to the widespread campaign of suffragist militancy that was evident in England and condemned by Mrs. Humphry Ward, whose house at Tring she was renting when war broke out. The vote was not, therefore, part of Wharton's campaign for women's rights. In public she subscribed to no such campaign, but do the novels tell a different story about her views of the relationship between women and men?

Edith Wharton's attitude to gender was complex. She had been brought up to assume the nineteenth-century role prescribed for women, and in "Life and I"[61] she says that one of her preoccupations as a little girl was to look pretty and to wear pretty frocks. She attached importance to her dress and appearance throughout her life, and in public conducted herself in a way that was consistent with the expectations of a strong American woman of the privileged class.

The other childhood preoccupation identified in "Life and I" is the appetite for learning and the thirst for knowledge. That was not considered feminine, as she soon discovered. Her mother sought to distract her by introducing small girls as playmates. Edith invariably tired of them, and asked permission to go to her room where she could make up her own stories. There were other ways in which Edith Jones did not conform to the roles required of conventional women. As an adult she married but then divorced. She did not have children. She was interested in the sciences as well as the arts. Despite such signs of resistance, she seems to have accepted that there is an innate difference determined by sex, and that the important thing was to understand the essential character of that difference rather than to question the categories themselves.

Her complex attitude to gender was reflected in her attitude to writing, as Nancy and R. W. B. Lewis describe in the introduction to her *Letters:*

> Edith Wharton, as one might say, was nothing if not a dialectical personality. In the fall of 1907, she received from Robert Grant, the Boston judge and a novelist whose work she esteemed, a long and balanced analysis of her novel *The Fruit of the Tree*. She was happy, she replied, that he had liked the construction of the book, but agreed with him that in the interest of firm construction, she had allowed her characters to remain little more than "mere *building-material.*" She drew a distinction—a trifle muddled in formulation, but clear and compelling in essence—between *conceiving* a novelistic subject, like a man, "that is, rather more architectonically &

dramatically than most women," and *executing* the subject like a woman, via a marshaling of "small incidental effects" and a technique of "episodical characterization."[62]

The Lewises then go on to consider the implications of the two narrative modes, "the masculine and the feminine, the dramatic and the accumulative," as applied to her letters, where, they argue, the two alternate and mingle. They reject the argument, put forward by Janet Malcolm in a *New York Times* review of the Library of America edition of Wharton's fiction,[63] that Edith Wharton "hated, feared and distrusted women,"[64] though they concede that she shied away from literary women such as May Sinclair, and that after the war the comments in her letters are increasingly out of sympathy with women who are fighting for equality. They agree with Elizabeth Ammons, who in *Edith Wharton's Argument with America* attributes this to the impact of the war itself and the way that it caused her to feel much greater affection for the conventions of a society that the war had virtually destroyed.[65]

In *French Ways and their Meaning*, written and published serially during World War I and later as a book in 1919, Wharton argues that American women suffer from being cut off from the intellectual stimulation provided by men. They are not treated as adults, but as children. They therefore learn to behave as children. Shari Benstock comments on the paradox contained in Wharton's argument, which seems to be leading to a condemnation of patriarchy, but stops short:

> Wharton always articulated her notions of the "feminine" in the context of the "masculine," seeing women in relation to men, emphasizing the cultural (and for her, possibly innate) superiority of the male mind to the female consciousness. She did not hold men responsible for "narrow(ing) down" women's interest, but rather focused her attention on the effect on such narrowing in women's lives. Thus her praise of a French society that allowed women an equal part in social interaction and offered a co-operative partnership in marriage was founded on resentment of the restrictions imposed upon American women by marriage, an institution she did not immediately identify as patriarchal.[66]

As a novelist Edith Wharton was practicing an art in which work by English women writers formed part of the literary canon, but with the exception of George Eliot, Wharton does not dwell on the achievements of these women in her letters. Jane Austen and the Brontës[67] are mentioned only in passing, while a contemporary writer such as Virginia Woolf was resented for the critical enthusiasm for her postwar novels that had led to the disparagement of Wharton's own work, as we have seen. Stream of consciousness writing appeared too undisciplined to appeal to the Wharton whose contact with James reinforced her belief in the importance of writing as carefully arranged art. As Frederick Wegener points out, Edith Wharton did not value her abilities as a critic, seeing criticism as the province of men. Women critics in her novels and short stories are satirized, as are women who give lectures and speeches. The role of women is to listen and to comment, even in the Parisian salon. Wharton seems to have identified the critical faculty as masculine, tending to produce gushing admiration for the criticism produced by her male circle of friends, while disparaging her own.

If this aspect of her view of gender did not change, and if in general her later, post–World War I view of "new" women became increasingly entrenched and reactionary, it is all the more surprising that her attitude to women's suffrage did undergo some modification some time before 1915. In a tribute to Jean du Breuil de Saint-Germain, who was killed in 1915, Edith Wharton acknowledges his contribution to the feminist cause and the way that he influenced her own understanding in the years before the war:

> It is Jean du Breuil who opened my eyes to a question of which—I admit it to my shame—I had not until then understood the immense social implications. In a few words, he made me see that the only thing that matters, to the feminist movement, is the fate of those women "whom the brutal economic law of big-city life waits to devour," of those poor hardworking women who accept their long misery with an animal fatalism because they do not know that they have a right to a more humane existence. In short, one would be tempted to say that women who argue for the right to vote could very well do without it, but it is necessary for those women, so much more numerous, who do not even know what it is, or why others are demanding it in their name![68]

It is this category of woman that we have glimpses of in the final section of *The House of Mirth,* and who may have been the original conception behind the novel that was originally to be *Justine Brent;* Wharton's paradoxical attitude to her own sex is brought out in "The Long Run" (1912). Paulina Trant is in some senses a "new woman." She smokes, she talks subversively, and she does as she likes. She marries a dull man, because she is poor but fond of enjoyment. The price she pays is one that society made all women of that class and period pay. She becomes her husband's possession, as the would-be lover Merrick feels resigned to accept: "She was Trant's and not mine: part of his luggage when he travelled as she was part of his household furniture when he stayed at home . . ."[69] As a rhetorical comment this is as revealing and politically charged as the opening of *The Awakening*, where the narrator foregrounds Mr. Pontellier's perception of his wife as she comes up from the beach: "'You are burnt beyond recognition," he added, looking at his wife as one looks at a valuable piece of personal property which has suffered some damage."[70] Wharton allows her male characters to observe the weaknesses of their own sex. The remarks are sometimes presented casually, and the very lightness of their presentation makes them all the more effective. In "The Long Run" Merrick observes: "Many a man—I'm talking of the kind with imagination—has thought he was seeking a soul when all he wanted was a closer view of its tenement."[71]

The tone is that of the gentleman's club, rather than that of the sharp satire reserved for Undine or Bertha Dorset. But even though men in Wharton's fiction are often treated more indulgently than women, their very shortcomings are made apparent by the regular appearance of the weak male in her narratives.

Gender Questions: Wharton, Fullerton, and Indadequate Men

The persistence of flawed, inadequate men represented as the central male "types" in Wharton's novels[72] has been linked, quite understandably, to the flawed character of the men who featured prominently in her life.[73] If the fictional Otto, Lawrence Selden, Amherst, George Darrow, Ralph Marvell, and Newland Archer all had their personal shortcomings, then so did Edward Wharton, Walter Berry, Henry James, and Morton Fullerton. There is a particular kind of dilettante who crops up time and time again. Knowledgeable, sophisticated, often a collector, he is, like the first Mr. Leath, an utter bore and more often than not unreliable and hypocritical.

There is another recurrent type, the failed artist, that critics find puzzling. Why should a writer who was so successful return again and again to the theme of the artist who fails? Ralph Marvell fails to write the novel that he has been working on for so long, and commits suicide. Dick Peyton in *Sanctuary* is a failure as an architect. There are failed painters and poets. It is an odd preoccupation for someone who knew setbacks, but whose work in the wake of the enormous success of *The House of Mirth* was guaranteed a publisher.

A simple biographical answer might be that Morton Fullerton provides the source for a ready model of the unsuccessful writer. Both James and Wharton tried to and did indeed help him in his writing, but concluded that he would never become the artist that they wanted him to be, one that accorded to their model of the good writer, possibly because journalism had irrevocably damaged him. It is easy to see Fullerton as a minor writer and principally a scoundrel, the man who carried on relationships with other women at the same time as his affair with Edith Wharton, the man who was untrustworthy. Because James and Wharton are fine writers, it is tempting to accept their judgments of Fullerton's talents as final, and thus relegate Fullerton to the role of peripheral figure intellectually and aesthetically, whose main role in Wharton's life is sexual and erotic. In this study I have tried to show that Fullerton's knowledge of international politics enriched the debates into which Wharton was drawn, and that he offered a less precious, aesthetically detached, and patrician view of the world than the other men in her inner circle. Fullerton's *Patriotism and Science* begins with a fine dedication to his father and the influence of his tolerant liberalism:

> To my father
>
> On whose library shelves the sight of Plato touching shoulders with John Howe the Puritan preacher, and of the poet Shelley enduring with unwonted tranquility his two old companions on either hand, Balzac and the author of the "Divine Legation of Moses," while just beyond stood Lucretius, the "Thousand and One Nights," and Adam Smith, suggested to me, the boy, the value of the social virtue of tolerance, and although it impressed at first the special charm of literature, suggested without much ado the larger interest of life.[74]

Fullerton brought an important intelligent and perceptive reading of international politics into Wharton's life. In the "Democracy" section of *Patriotism and Science*, he says that books such as *Le gouvernement démocratic* by Emile de Caveleye, Bagehot's work in England, Bryce's in America, and Boutmy's in France all made "us" think about democracy and the structure of government. It was a subject that exercised him in the years before he met Edith Wharton. In his essay "English and Americans," which appeared in a slightly revised form in *Patriotism and Science*, Fullerton writes of the unedifying deadlock of business in the House of Representatives: "[I]t illustrated on a large scale an important point that Mr. Bagehot was always making, the greater working efficiency of the parliamentary form of government over the presidential in its union of the legislative and executive functions."[75] Both of his political books were prophetic. *Problems of Power* accurately predicted the conflict of World War I, while *Patriotism and Science* contains some quite provocative comments about patriotism in its opening section "On a Certain Danger in Patriotism." Against a background of jingoism in England and the United States, Fullerton warns that patriotism is not always a good thing, and that there will come a day when we will feel pity for the inscription "He died for his country."

Fullerton recommends the phrase "passion for the planet" (which he did not coin) and warns of the dangers of arrogance in colonialism. He offered a perspective that Wharton was not to receive from any other member of her circle of close male friends and provided an influence that is not limited to their sexual affair.

Defining a Soul: The Conservative Influence of Religion and the Acceptance of Suffering

There is some evidence[76] that Edith Wharton, the woman born into New York Protestantism, ended up seriously contemplating entry to the Roman Church. Each tradition offered something attractive and something repellent. Catholicism offered ritual, but it also required submission. Protestantism offered textual authority and charity, but it also made sexual desire the most wicked of sins. Kenneth Clark saw an echo of Calvinist belief in her practice of having a circle of friends, the "elect." Yet the interest in the lives of those beyond that circle, her servants, the local villagers, and the victims of war, reflected a compassion that was more spiritually Catholic in character.

What Wharton seems to have moved away from is the mysticism of religious belief, which is explored in her writing of the early 1900s. She was too much of a rationalist for that. Thus she was resistant to the popular late nineteenth-century esoteric revival, whether expressed in the form of Theosophy, the New Science, or New Thought. Theosophy, with its cult of Isis and interest in world religions was antiscientific (in her New York apartment Madame Blavatsky kept a stuffed baboon representing Darwin), although it claimed to be the New Science. New Thought, like the Christian Science movement founded by Mary Baker Eddy, grew out of the metaphysical religious healing movement started by Phineas Parkhurst Quinby in the 1860s, which argued that illness was the product of wrong belief. New Thought emphasized the primacy of the mind in the universe, the immanence of God, and the essential goodness of human nature. It was an optimistic set of beliefs, in that it offered the hope that ultimately all humankind could enjoy prosperity, but its claim that the mind could be used for healing was an affront to the world of observable fact to which Wharton adhered. In *The House of Mirth* the narrator gently mocks the enthusiasm for such beliefs, including a sideswipe at butterfly enthusiasms for political reform: "Mrs. Fisher's latest hobby was municipal reform. It had been preceded by an equal zeal for socialism, which had in turn replaced an energetic advocacy of Christian Science."[77]

Edith Wharton's interest in science and rationalism, combined with her endless curiosity about human behavior, conveniently came together in the new field of anthropology. She believed that novels could be anthropological studies of various societies, ranging in her case from the Old New York world of *The House of Mirth* to the impoverished west Massachusetts world of *Ethan Frome*. *The Custom of the Country* is the novel in which the anthropological approach is most explicit, with Ralph using the language of anthropology to discuss the contact of the new-money people with Old New York society:

> Ralph had never taken his mother's social faiths very seriously. Surveying the march of civilization from a loftier angle, he had early mingled with the Invaders, and curiously observed their rites and customs. But most of those he had met had already been modified by contact with the indigenous: they spoke the same language as his, though on their lips it had so often a different meaning. Ralph had never seen them actually in the making, before they had acquired the speech of the conquered race.
> (*CC*, 51)

The Custom of the Country has been criticized for its failure to judge Undine.[78] The reader assumes she is a monster, but the narrative does not say so. This may be because Wharton did not mean us to see her as a monster but as the product of cultural forces over which she has no control. The coolness of the presentation, therefore, is the coolness of the social scientist. In Wharton's case this is allied to a natural predisposition to accept hurt philosophically, and this acquiescence partly explains her silence on political matters.

The willing acceptance of suffering and pain is the corollary of a suspicion of pleasure and enjoyment, and in New England writing that acceptance is rooted in Puritanism. Suffering is a means of expiating guilt, and whereas in many sects the mortification of the flesh and the punishment of the body is the means by which that suffering is ensured, Puritanism finds virtue in the more psychological and long-term strategy of self-denial. Self-denial on this earth leads to treasures in the next. The better life is the harder life.

The rhetorical endorsement of suffering in Wharton's writing is evident in her approving underlining of the Keats quotation about the schooling of an intelligence in her copy of his letters and in her choice of title for *The House of Mirth*.[79] The Old Testament judgment in Ecclesiastes that fools occupy the house of mirth is preceded by two stark and rousing calls to mortification: "It is better to go to the house of mourning than to go to the house of feasting: for that is the end of all men; and the living will lay it to his heart. Sorrow is better than laughter: for by the sadness of the countenance the heart is made better."[80]

Wharton found an endorsement for a belief in the educative value of suffering in George Eliot, whose work she had considered in her 1902 review of Leslie Stephens's biography.[81] Eliot's *Adam Bede* contains the famous narrative reflection: "Deep, unspeakable suffering may well be called a baptism, a regeneration, the initiation into a new state."[82] Wharton's 1892 poem "Experience" had celebrated the way that over a period of time an alchemical change occurs whereby grief can be turned into gold. Pain and loss have long been identified as the important ingredients of love. In Christianity the penitent suffers to be closer to Christ and God. In twelfth-century Provence the troubadours produced ballads of courtly love in which the very fact that the desired mistress was unattainable inflamed the desire, so that there was implicit joy in pain. In the twentieth century, Lacan has argued that sexual desire springs from the experience of loss. Suffering is a necessary part of the individual's education, Wharton's narratives at times wish us to believe. She had suffered from the coldness of a distant mother, a cruel breakdown of an engagement in which her "intellectuality" and "ambition" were given by the society gossip sheet *Town Topics* as the reasons for the couple's parting of ways.[83] She suffered constant ill health until she moved away from the sea. She suffered from a marriage to a man who not only did not share her interests in literature and art, but felt threatened by her developing career as an author. Teddy's father, William Craig Wharton, had committed suicide, and she feared that Teddy too could descend into madness. Suffering seemed an inevitable and necessary part of life, even if love eventually appears. In *The Valley of Decision* Fulvia tells Odo: "To be near you I must go from you. To love you I must give you up" (*VD*, 484). But in *Ethan Frome,* the narrative protests at the awfulness of pointless and endless suffering, which far from educating the spirit causes embitterment and the hardening of the soul. Too much pain does not school an intelligence. Wharton, moreover, did not believe that her own personal pain should ever be transcribed directly into narrative. Autobiography was a bad source of fiction, she believed.

Wharton was not an ascetic. She loved travel, art, and beautiful clothes. She longed for emotional and sensual fulfillment. Yet if the rhetoric of her novels finally questions the need for suffering, it never questions the need for work. In this respect she was the true Massachusetts Protestant, driven to succeed by the need to employ every ounce of her energy productively. It is in this sense that I have identified Wharton as a Massachusetts writer, even though she was born in

New York and spent much of her life in Europe. In the ten years from 1900 to 1910, she produced a prodigious volume of work, and this was the product of disciplined and energetic commitment to the writer's craft. Much of this work was produced at The Mount, a retreat where she could be relatively free from distractions. This work is informed by a political awareness that is initially quite explicit in the fiction, both in terms of subject matter and argument. This explicitness always makes concessions to her more conservative readers by offering such qualifications as the following:

> [Alfieri's] political theories were but the enlargement of his private grievances, but the mere play of criticism on accepted institutions was an exercise more novel and exhilarating than the wildest ride on one of his half-tamed thoroughbreds.
>
> (*VD*, 127)

Such a comment, however, reveals that by 1902, when *The Valley of Decision* (from which this comes) was first published, Wharton was not intellectually hostile to the challenging of established institutions, even if the tone is condescending and the specific reference is to the questioning that took place in Europe during the revolutionary period of the late eighteenth century. The collision of two worlds, that of the established order and that of the new ideas, was the subject of Wharton's first published novel, and it is a political subject repeatedly examined, albeit in a variety of forms and settings, in the extensive range of fiction that she produced in the productive prewar years. In August, 1914, however, the notion of what was meant by "the world" was to change, and Wharton's world was to change with it.

8

Politics and Paradoxes: Toryism, Modernism, and War

> Mrs. Wharton's intellectuality positively freezes the fingers with which one turns her page.
> —Van Wyck Brooks, *America's Coming of Age* (1915)

> I must protest, and emphatically, against the suggestion that I have "stripped" New York society. New York society is still amply clad, & the little corner of its garment that I lifted was meant to show only that little atrophied organ—the group of idle and dull people—that exists in any big & wealthy social body.
> —Edith Wharton, letter to William Roscoe Thayer, 11 November 1905, *HL*

A Radical American Tory

STRICTLY SPEAKING, THE TERM "TORY" SHOULD BE RESERVED FOR the English landed class from the seventeenth century onward. Their heyday was the period of the Restoration and they were united by a belief in monarchy, stability, the value of land and the country house, the idea of noblesse oblige, and the preservation of manners and polite behavior. They were a group that was gregarious within its own class, believing in the importance of social gatherings of a not very intellectual kind, such as balls, dinners, shoots, and riding to hounds. The arts were supported through the purchase of books for libraries and paintings and music for private concerts, but such patronage was intended largely for the purpose of decorating their houses. The house, the countryside, and its land was what really mattered, which was why architecture on the grand scale was valued.

In many important respects Wharton identified with an Anglo-American version of this ideology, though its English representatives would have denied that it was an ideology. She loved her French houses and their gardens, as she had valued the Mount, and in 1914 was planning to buy a country house somewhere in southern England. Wharton believed in political stability, the need to be hospitable, well dressed, and polite, and many of these practices could be anchored in the foundation of a country house. Yet there were too many shortcomings in the Tory lifestyle for her to be completely comfortable with it. Wharton had grown up in New York City, and seemed to enjoy the rush of the cosmopolitan world. She was an adventurer, a traveler. She was an intelligent and inquisitive woman, deeply interested in the arts. These were not Tory virtues.

She rebelled, therefore, against the more unthinking parts of Toryism. Its unquestioning adherence to the Catholic Church (in its French version) or in England, its endorsement of field sports and the unspoken belief that women were not capable of intelligent conversation or the management of affairs meant that the Tory lady's life was not for her. Yet there were, at the beginning of the eighteenth century radical Tories, such as Jonathan Swift, and it was to this tradition of criticism that she was most close politically. Wharton's satire, like Swift's, is not to cause social revolution, but to preserve tradition from its own foolishness or irrationality. Swift may have been devoted to church and state, but he could not accept his forebears' belief in the divine right of kings. Wharton, similarly, was far too much a product of America to accept uncritically the paraphernalia of monarchy and aristocracy, even though she mingled socially with people from that world. Her fiction became the space in which she could explore political questions about such a Toryism from the inside.

It might be thought that such a sympathy with many of the tenets of Toryism was what prevented her from embracing modernism. This is not the case. As Kaplan and Simpson point out, in rejecting Edwardianism modernist writers in England were rejecting not the conservatism, but the liberalism with which it was associated. Ironically, they argue, it was the outsider status of Lawrence, Joyce, T. S. Eliot, Forster, and Woolf that fueled their modernism, an "underlying anxiety that they stood outside the culture and audience for which they wrote"[1] (sexuality and gender being the outsider factors in the case of the last two). As an American woman, Wharton, in theory, might have had two reasons to share this sense of cultural exclusion. But her Old New York pedigree cushioned her from this outsider experience, and she "did not need to move from outsider to insider status . . . by producing the new art."[2]

Between the completion of *The Custom of the Country* in 1913 and her death in 1937 Edith Wharton stayed loyal to Europe. She spent much of the early years of World War I involved in war work with refugees and orphans, raising money and organizing workshops. She visited the front and in the final year of the war bought Pavillon Colombe, north of Paris, living there until her death. During these postwar years she continued to produce short stories, novels, and novellas, and wrote the much-praised novel, *The Age of Innocence* (1920), which was not only a best seller but was awarded the Pulitzer Prize. Her decision to return to France from Tring in England as soon as war broke out is indicative of her Tory sense of noblesse oblige.

As an American Wharton could have retreated to the United States and thus avoided the war itself, but she chose not to do so. Instead she responded to the new situation by taking on a new role as an organizer of war relief and the dissemination of new kinds of writing. Her visits to the front in 1915 led to the publication of the essays included in *Fighting France: From Dunkerque to Belfort*. To help finance her war support work she collected original war texts, which included prose, poetry, artwork, and music, and published these as *The Book of the Homeless* in 1916. Later in the war, in 1918, she published the patriotic novel *The Marne*, and began work on another novel, *A Son at the Front*, which she preferred to describe as a study in psychology.[3] The war temporarily resolved the paradoxes about class, marriage, and art that informed her politics and writing before 1914. The plight of the refugees became her primary concern and the focus for all activity. In 1914 Joyce began work on *Ulysses*. In that same year the outbreak of war caused Wharton to abandon her plan of living and writing in England. Instead she made straight for France and made a profession of the charity work that in peacetime her society normally regarded as an appropriate diversion or hobby.

So it is that Wharton, who had traveled ceaselessly, now decided to commit herself to France at just the time when thousands of French and Belgian refugees were becoming homeless, and when the easy option would be to stay in England or retreat to America. This was just the latest of the many contradictions, like that of being an American Tory, that characterize the years 1900–1914. Several of these unresolved paradoxes are traceable in two short stories that were first published on the eve of the war, "The Long Run" (1912) and "The Triumph of the Night" (1914). Though these paradoxes remain largely unresolved in her fiction, there is usually a clear privileging in the rhetoric of one side of the political argument, even when the other is advanced clearly and forcefully.

Exile and Rootlessness

By 1912 Edith Wharton had embarked on a self-imposed exile from America that was to continue until her death in 1937. Although France was her base throughout all these years, with homes in Paris, just outside the capital, and on the Mediterranean coast, she moved between the city and the coast on a regular basis and did not abandon the restless movement that characterized her entire life. In his letter of December 1912 praising *The Reef* Henry James identified, not without an acknowledged irony, what he saw as her only shortcoming as a novelist: "[Y]our only drawback is not to have the homeliness and the inevitability and happy limitation and the affluent poverty of a country of your own (comme moi, par example!)."[4] Whether it was to compensate for the lack of roots or an atavistic return to our ancestral nomadic lifestyle, Wharton was frequently on the move, seeking new sights and experiences. The excitement of travel is conveyed in "The Long Run"[5] when Merrick is trying to convey the thrill of embarking on a relationship with Paulina Trant: "Haven't you, sometimes, at the moment of starting on a journey, some glorious plunge into the unknown, been tripped up by the thought: 'If only one hadn't to come back'? Well, with her one had the sense that one would have to come back; that the magic ship would always carry one farther. And what an air one breathed on it! And, oh, the wind, and the islands, and the sunsets!"[6] It is true that this image is primarily a metaphor for the beginning of passion, but this enthusiastic parallel could only have been produced by someone who delighted in travel as Wharton did. At the same time, there was a psychological and constitutional price to pay for this experience of never being tied to one place. In "The Triumph of the Night"[7] the narrator reflects on his emotional fragility, having fled his host's house in the belief that he has seen a ghost: "That was what his rootless life had brought him to: for lack of a personal stake in things his sensibility was at the mercy of such trifles. . . . Why else, in the name of any imaginable logic, human or devilish, should he, a stranger, be singled out for this experience? . . . Unless, indeed, it was just because he was a stranger—a stranger everywhere—because he had no personal life, no warm screen of private egotisms to shield him from exposure, that he had developed this abnormal sensitiveness to the vicissitudes of others."[8]

Wharton was well aware of the paradox of embracing a moral position that valued tradition, custom, and history while living the life of the deracinated. Disturbing questions would have haunted her: Can the value of custom only be seen by those who have lost it? And by contributing to the restlessness of the planet, and by seeking to experience the traditions of others vicariously through travel, is one contributing to its erosion and decline? In 1920, when the war had reinforced her sense of cultural loss, she recalled affectionately Henry James's observation, made in *The American Scene* in 1907, that it "takes a great deal of history to make a little tradition, a great deal of tradition to make a little taste, and a great deal of taste to make a little art."⁹ Wharton wished to create, but also to preserve, and the two somtimes contraditory impulses, were of equal strength in her life. Each had its own outlet, so that fire, before World War I, was kept apart from powder.

Writing Critically

After the war the paradoxes that her life and writing contained re-emerged, but the balance had shifted. Edith Wharton did not join with modernism in either its subject of individual consciousness nor in using the experimental, fragmentary technique that became one of its characteristic features, and she was scornful of much of the new writing that was being lauded. The nineteenth-century New York society world whose hypocrisies she had highlighted no longer seemed quite so bad to her now that it had been swept away in its entirety. As Michael Millgate points out, her successful 1920 novel, *The Age of Innocence*, "rarely sounds those notes of bitterness and satire so strongly audible in *The House of Mirth* and *The Custom of the Country*."[10] She became more strident in her derision of American materialism and popular culture. In her biography of Wharton, Shari Benstock describes an increasingly entrenched, illiberal woman, whose anti-Semitism seems to be fueled by her new fondness for Catholicism and her resentment of the "new" Europe and America in which immigration had created ethnic diversity. She disliked the education of women, believing, in Benstock's words, that "erasing differences between sexes and social classes, the intermingling of customs and the overthrow of traditions could bear no rich cultural fruit."[11] Yet the fact that her publicly stated views became more reactionary should not lead us to assume that her writing ceased to develop. The subject matter may appear to be stubbornly nostalgic, but the treatment is not. As Preston points out: "[S]ometimes, as Wharton recognised, it is easier to analyse one's own country and background from afar, and her most profoundly backward-looking novels, the ones set in Old New York, or among the descendants of that world, were all products of the 1920s, written after the war (which she experienced wholly and vividly in France) after she was thoroughly expatriated."[12] With the exception of *The Age of Innocence* and one or two short stories, Wharton's postwar work was for a long time considered inferior to her prewar writing. There have been attempts to revisit and reevaluate this work, particularly in Dale M. Bauer's *Brave New Politics*, which concentrates on work published from 1917 onward. Bauer argues, as I have been doing here, that Wharton's fiction often includes a reading of politics that is more complex than her publicly stated one. It also reveals an interest in issues that are more contemporary than a preoccupation with the novels of Old New York, which she continued to produce after the war, would lead us to believe. Bauer discusses Wharton's 1917 novella *Summer* as a narrative that reflects the contemporary debates about eugenics, abortion, degeneracy, and patriarchy.[13] Wharton rejects here, Bauer argues, the doctrine of maternal culpability, which blamed mothers for eugenic decline. Mountain degeneracy is matched by Royall's degeneracy. For the lawyer, who wishes to possess his adopted daughter sexually, there is the safe retreat of the Masonic society, which reinforces patriarchal rights and values. But even Royall "cannot play all the middle class masculine roles at the same time" (father, lawyer, husband to the same woman), and in showing this Wharton offers a keen indictment of marriage. The book is, arguably, "Wharton's blunted criticism of the patriarchal sexual economy . . . and the incestuous nature of patriarchal marriage."[14]

The success of her novels eventually convinced Edith Wharton that writing novels and short stories was something that she could do well. Even so, she was critical of all her works—*The House of Mirth, The Reef,* and *The Custom of the Country* were all the subject of anxious reflections and a consciousness that things could have been done differently. But Wharton was prepared to accept that there had been sufficient critical approval to support the case that they had some merit.

When it came to writing criticism herself, however, she was completely lacking in confidence.[15] She wrote to her friend William Crary Brownell that writing the essays that appeared in the first half of *The Writing of Fiction* was terrifying, that the writing of the Proust essay eventually included in the same volume dogged her "like Banquo," and that she would "tremble like an aspen" when Brownell read the first of these essays.[16] She produced more critical work than this might suggest, but it was clearly an ordeal for her. She reviewed specific books often as a favor to the friend or acquaintance who had written them. And she did not value her critical work enough to ensure that it was collected together and published as a single volume, *The Writing of Fiction* being the one rare exception.

This lack of confidence is puzzling, as Wharton was an astute and intelligent critic, and the body of fiction that she had written gave her the authority to write about the work of others. Wegener speculates that it might be explained by her feeling that she had received no training in journalism or criticism, and had not received a formal education at school or university. Her lack of belief may also explain why she did not discuss politics except in response to the specific needs and interests of friends, most notably William Morton Fullerton. Politics and criticism were seen as male discourses, and even though she must have known she could write as intelligently on these subjects as any of her male peers, in her social group it was perhaps not seen as the correct thing that a woman ought to be doing.

Modernism and the Politics of Art and Home

There is a revealing sentence in the first chapter of *The Writing of Fiction* where Wharton is discussing developments in French fiction, which she much admired:

> What was new in both Balzac and Stendhal was the fact of their viewing each character first of all as a product of particular material and social conditions, as being thus or thus because of the calling he pursued or the house he lived in (Balzac) or the society he wanted to get into (Stendhal), or the acre of ground he coveted, or the powerful or fashionable personage he aped or envied (both Balzac and Stendhal).[17]

Such a view is consistent with her understanding of her goal in writing *The House of Mirth*, her first successful novel. In the letter to Professor Thayer, expressing admiration for his *Atlantic* essay on history, Wharton was delighted that he had recognized her intention in writing this novel: "I am particularly & quite extraordinarily pleased with what you say of my having—to your mind—been able to maintain my reader's interest in a group of persons so intrinsically uninteresting except as a social manifestation."[18] What is revealing about both these statements is the endorsement that they provide of the novelists' need to acknowledge the role of society and material conditions in shaping human behavior. Extended politically that becomes a socialist point of view, but in Wharton's case it is a political view that had its roots in science and observation, practices which interested Balzac and Stendhal respectively, and was developed by her reading of Darwin. To leap from the shaping discourses of her class into socialism would not have been impossible, but her class belief that in this direction lay immorality prevented her. For the other great quality she admired in the novel was its didactic value, what it can teach us about moral behavior. There was no relativism in Wharton, nor any sense of the meaninglessness of existence that produces nihilism and despair: "A good subject, then, must contain in itself something that sheds a light on our moral experience. If it is incapable of this expansion, this vital radiation, it remains, however showy a surface it presents, a mere irrelevant happening, a meaningless scrap of fact torn out of its context."[19] Linked to this was Wharton's belief that art should not separate itself from society and withdraw from the mainstream. It was a belief that extended to culture as a whole, and partly explains her decision to live and work in France, for there culture "is an eminently social quality, while in Anglo-Saxon countries it might be called anti-social."[20] It is a belief that separates her from the modernism of Virginia Woolf with her emphasis on the need to move away from the public to the private sphere. But the attention given to Woolf's essays on modern fiction has been queried recently, most notably by Douglas Hewitt, who argues that not only is Woolf's criticism always cited because it is so convenient but also because there is little else that can be used. Hewitt queries Woolf's logic in suggesting that a characteristic of the new writing is that it favors the small over the big, rejects material detail, and ignores the political for the psychological. Joyce can incorporate more material detail than Bennett, Conrad's politics are crucial to his novels, and Lawrence, Proust and Faulkner show more than a glimpse of the public world. Perhaps, muses Hewitt, "fiction is too much of a social art to reject society for very long."[21]

From the very beginning of her writing career, Wharton had a very clear idea about the kind of fiction that she valued and the kind that she intended to write. In a letter to Robert Grant, written in response to her reading of his novel *The Undercurrent*, she writes with the confidence of a successful author:

> Every piece of fiction is an anecdote that exemplifies something, an instance. The lives of your characters are bound to touch at all points other lives irrelevant to the special anecdote you are telling about them, & part of the process of art is to discard these irrelevancies, however interesting they are in themselves.[22]

Ironically this was written while she was in the middle of writing her "first novel," *The Valley of Decision*, which in many ways breaches that rule, but thereafter she sticks closely to this artistic principle, whose emphasis on special anecdote and incident, as opposed to individual epiphany, takes it closer to Mr. Bennett than to Mrs. Brown.

There are many ways of responding to Wharton's fiction, and the sustained critical analysis applied over the past thirty years has led to some very divergent readings of her work. The apparent political conservatism of the world she writes about, and the views of the characters who inhabit that world, have been examined closely, and Wharton has emerged favorably from this examination. The writing is seen by many to be progressive, liberating, prescient, and consistent with a view of the world that many critics would see as desirable in the world of today. If *A Backward Glance* is cautious and elitist, that is because Wharton "jams her messages to herself" as Judith Fryer says.[23] For Annette Zilversmit, "Wharton's literary narratives have always been the encoded inscriptions of female desire waiting to be released and recovered."[24] And recognition is now afforded the postwar novels, which for a long time were ignored or considered inferior. Recent studies have not only recovered these novels from obscurity, but have made claims for them that suggest they surpass the prewar fiction. Judith L. Sensibar comments on the increased sophistication of Wharton's political analysis as the years pass, so that she moves from her studies of upper-class urban American women— like Lily Bart, who is colonized by the patriarchal gaze in *The House of Mirth*—to more politically and psychologically complex and inclusive rendering of colonizing processes. This change is registered most clearly in her later fiction and prose.[25]

Do Wharton's politics undergo any significant changes between 1900 and 1914? Does she question the need for the ordered society she so admired in *A Motor-Flight Through France?* Her 1919 study of the French, *French Ways and their Meaning*, might not suggest so, for in Blake Nevius's words, it is an endorsement of qualities observed in her 1908 study:

> Throughout the ranks of French society the diffusion of certain traits is apparent: a reverence for tradition, a sense of continuity with the past, taste, intellectual honesty, absolute probity in business, a love of privacy and a respect for the practical and intellectual abilities of women. And all of these traits are embodied equally in the manners which are apparent in the various levels of this rich culture.[26]

This does not suggest much of a change, but we need to remember that this was originally written during a war in which her American audience had not initially supported the French, and was published after a war that had destroyed so many of the features that Nevius's summary identifies as being attractive to her. Was she less in love with them five years earlier, in the summer before the war began?

There is a key question to be asked about Wharton's writing, now that she is properly recognized as a significant American writer of the early twentieth century, and that is the extent to which she moves beyond the cultural and political assumptions of her class and period. In an attempt to redress the wrong of a neglected literary reputation, there is always the danger of idealizing the literary subject who has been ignored, condemned or slighted in some way. As a public woman Wharton dressed in conformity with the fashions and styles of the period, and took pains to look as smart and attractive as possible. Critics have noted the many innovative garments in her textual wardrobe, and in the more enthusiastic cases of celebratory criticism there is sometimes a tendency to treat Wharton as the empress of writing and to invent for her clothes that on closer scrutiny she appears not to be wearing. Wharton does not espouse the political cause of feminism, socialism, or any kind of radicalism, whether bohemian, antiimperialist, or stream of consciousness modernist. As long ago as 1963 Diana Trilling raised questions about Wharton's belief in democracy: "[Wharton's] commitment to the democratic principle, if it can be said to have existed at all, existed only in a much transmogrified form."[27] That said, I think that during the pre-war period there is movement in her reading of the politics of government, but that it shifts from an inherited conservatism to a form of social determinism (though Wharton rejected the philosophical determinism and argued that the individual is always responsible for his or her fate) but no further. *The Valley of Decision* is informed by a politics that is sympathetic to idealism, but sees attempts to introduce utopian change suddenly as naive. There should be reform, but not revolution, as that leads to chaos and the release of dangerous forces destructive to the necessary ordering of society. *The House of Mirth* points to the consequences for values of the triumph of wealth over manners, and acts as a warning. Readers are presented with a group of people who do no good, and if we are not alert to Wharton's politics, we may wonder why they should not be swept away. But the novel is predicated on the belief that though they do harm, destroying Lily in their selfishness, they should be reformed, not taken to the guillotine. The moral is the same of that of *The Wind in the Willows*. Nettie Struther, the poor mother with the baby, looks up to the privileged class, and, in the rhetoric of the novel, their duty is to be more like Gerty Farish, who does have a sense of noblesse oblige, charity, and philanthropy. *Ethan Frome, The Reef,* and *The Custom of the Country* all point to the inevitability of the triumph of economics over love, over taste, and over tradition. That is a considerable political shift, and though it offers no recipe for change, it does provide an analysis of society that considers the relationship between art, life, and money in a less simplistic way than the new fiction of modernism, whose individualism she rejected.

To say that an increasingly deterministic position informs Wharton's novels is not to suggest that the fiction embodies the nihilism of modernity in which meaning and hope have been lost.[28] Many of her novels from 1900–1914 provide case histories in which well-meaning individuals are trapped or destroyed by circumstance, or in which only the selfish survive. But if art or sensibility does not have the potential to transform as it has in Henry James, Wharton shares James's rarely expressed, but fundamental belief that the world would be a better place in the future. It is the outbreak of war and the devastation that it will cause that undermined that belief, as James observes: "The plunge of civilization in this abyss of blood & darkness by the wanton feats of those 2 infamous autocrats is a thing that so gives away the whole long age during which we had supposed the world to be, with whatever abatements, gradually bettering, that I have to take it all now for what the treacherous years were all the while really making for a <u>meaning</u> is too tragic for words."[29]

It is difficult not to see Wharton as holding political views that many would now regard as reactionary. But in America, England, and France, the period 1900 to 1914 was a reactionary time, and many modernists too held reactionary views. Two recent studies of modernism emphasize that what was unbearable about modern life was the disappearance of the assured place of the artist, leading to what David Trotter calls "paranoid modernism."[30] This is not Wharton's theme. On the other hand, there is a claim made about modernist writers that seems wholly applicable to Wharton and the dissonance between her public politics and the politics of her fiction. Sara Blair draws attention to recent critical readings of the distasteful right-wing politics of Wyndham Lewis and the French writer Céline: "Literary theorists Fredric Jameson and Julia Kristeva . . . have powerfully argued that specific literary performances undercut, exceed, or problematize the explicit commitments of their authors."[31] It is not that writers are above politics, it is that their imaginative writings accommodate a polyphonic breadth of political readings. There is also a strand of modernism that Wharton does have much in common with politically and intellectually. This is the strand represented and influenced by T. E. Hulme,[32] who argued that original sin, even in its secular form, had to be acknowledged as a fact of life, as human nature was never going to change fundamentally. Accept that, and appropriate art and action would follow. It is a belief that shaped Wharton's writing, and when the war came, it determined her actions.

The Book of the Homeless

It is one of the paradoxes of Wharton's life that for this woman who spent so much time traveling in Europe and North Africa, and spent more than half her life exiled from the land of her birth, homes were so important. The Mount, the Rue de Varenne, Pavillon Colombe, and Hyères were places to which she knew she could return as to friends or a family. There is nothing remarkable in this. In the theory of prospect refuge,[33] it is claimed that the most secure position for the human psychology is the one that provides refuge but allows a prospect. To see widely without a refuge to which the individual can return is unsettling. To have a refuge, but no vantage point, is confining. At the end of *The Custom of the Country*, a wistful tribute is given to the value of the French home: "It was natural that Americans, who had no homes, who were born and died in hotels, should have contracted nomadic habits; but the new Marquise de Chelles was no longer an American, and she had Saint Désert and the Hôtel de Chelles to live in, as generations of ladies of her name had done before her."[34]

Wharton's first two books had been about homes, and as we saw, both *The Decoration of Houses* and *Italian Villas and Their Gardens* emphasize the importance of the decoration, architecture, and garden layout in creating an environment that is conducive to human conversation, contact, and sensibility. The home may sometimes be the private place of retreat, but it is also the place of reception and social intercourse. The home is neither fortress nor castle, but the place in which one lives as a secure member of a community. The home provides areas that are private and areas that are designed for more public activities. It is a very practical realization of the political organization of human society. The absence of a home, "unhomeliness" is one translation of the German word for the uncanny, and although James felt that this sense of dislocation was to her disadvantage, it may actually have allowed her social and political insights that her otherwise privileged existence denied her.

There is a certain consistency, therefore, that in a time of crisis, when the outbreak of war forced so many refugees from Belgium to become homeless, that the writer and traveler who had discussed the problem of being adrift, who valued so much the stability and heritage that a fixed society could provide and pitied those who became divorced from it, should turn her attention to the needs of the homeless.

In 1915 Edith Wharton gathered together contributions from writers and artists from America, England, France, and other countries, and after editing the collection, they were published as *The Book of the Homeless* and sold to raise money for the charity that would support the refugees. It is frequently mentioned in passing in Wharton discussions, but these sometimes casual references do not do justice to this remarkable book. For here is a document that is striking testimony to the practical, political action of Edith Wharton. Both she and Theodore Roosevelt, in their respective introductions, describe the scale of the refugee support that is needed and give a glimpse of the scale of the work that is being done. Wharton refused to be overwhelmed.

The published book is the size of a children's annual from the middle of the twentieth century, and at first glance might be mistaken for one. It is, however, a book containing work by a remarkable collection of artists from a period in which late Victorian, Edwardian, Georgian, and modernist writing was circulating in an environment not yet aware of the separating categories that were to be retrospectively applied to this art. The book brings together work from artists as diverse as Charles Dana Gibson (of the Gibson Girl) and Max Beerbohm, and Claude Monet and Lèon Bakst. Popular, satirical, impressionist, and modernist work is all represented, but with a strong bias toward high art and high culture.

There are contributions from Thomas Hardy, Joseph Conrad, and Henry James; there are poems from Yeats, Santayana, and Alice Meynell. Wharton may have had reservations about some of the work of the new generation of artists, but here is work by Cocteau, Rodin, and Stravinsky. Bakst's *Mènade* gestures toward Picasso and cubism just as Edward Howland Blashfield's *A Woman's Head* looks back to the Pre-Raphaelites. This is a broad, unifying, catholic collection of material. Some of the contributors, like John Singer Sargent and Mrs. Humphry Ward, were extremely well known and sit comfortably by the hearth of the establishment. There are Edwardian writers such as Gosse, Maeterlinck, and Galsworthy, and Georgian writers such as Rupert Brooke, who was to be dead before the book was published. Henry James was responsible for securing Brooke's piece, through Brooke's literary agent, and also had the job of persuading W. D. Howells not to withdraw the piece he had submitted.[35] As well as American writers such as Howells there were French writers such as Paul Bourget, and the alphabetical order creates some odd bedfellows, with Bourget being preceded by Laurence Binyon and Binyon by a contribution from Sarah Bernhardt. The onset of war was the agency that allowed a diversity, which dissolved many of the usual cultural frames.

The quality of the work itself may not always be rare, except in the sense that there cannot be many documents from the period like this, but what is so impressive is the coming together of men and women who by nature and temperament are usually so solidly individualistic. The book is a collective act, a political act, and textual evidence of a great achievement by Wharton that survives and has a resonance that the bare recording of facts and the official French honor of a decoration does not.

The book does not transcend politics, however, for even in its production there was a hierarchy of editions, with the very best in large format and limited to 175 copies, with these 175 de luxe copies subdivided into numbers 1–50, which were even more exclusive and lavish. Even Theodore Roosevelt possessed only a numbered copy between 51 and 175.[36] Nor was Wharton's war work to lead to any lasting political conversion. After the war Wharton did not ask questions about the organization of the state and its impact on the poor that made her think society should be radically reorganized. If this provided an opportunity to see a connection between the way that an extreme example of state activity, namely war, was destructive and ruthless in its impact on the mass of people and the way that governments generally operated, it was an opportunity not taken. But it was an opportunity not taken by the working class either, who ignored the call from socialist organizations not to fight a capitalist war, appealing to workers from all counties to unite against it. The war was widely seen by the western alliance as a unique event, with Germany cast in the role of the evil power rather than as a country reacting belligerently in the more general struggle for economic supremacy.

The Book of the Homeless remains a different achievement from Wharton's other works. Wharton's novels are fine novels, beautifully written, and full of brilliant satire, sharp observation, and serious questions. Wharton's political views do not eclipse or overshadow the fiction, which is a place in which a whole polyphony of political and ethical voices compete to be heard. There is a consistent argument in this fiction, but these are not polemics. The politics is implicit, and often unpredictable. Such is the achievement of Wharton in her pre–World War I fiction, which one hundred years later is now read by more people than ever before.

The Book of the Homeless is not now read, but it is an important historical and material object designed to bring food and clothing to the men, women, and children who were in desperate need of help. It is the product of direct action and direct politics, not intended to change behavior and more concerned with raising money than raising awareness. It offers a confirmation of the political outlook that underpins Wharton's fiction. It is an act of noblesse oblige and provides evidence that in a crisis, duty came before self, the vindication of the principle that the fictional Lily Bart's honorable repayment of debt at the end of *The House of Mirth* had demonstrated ten years earlier.

Apart from Modernism: Reprise

The ambiguities implicit in the phrase "apart from modernism" are intended to suggest three senses in which Wharton's work can and should be regarded in relation to modernism. There is a sense in which those who have sought to include Wharton under the umbrella "modernism" are correct. Aspects of her work in 1911 and 1912 are like parts from the gathering wave of modernism, and had she given up writing with *The Reef* it might well have been reasonable to speculate that this and *Ethan Frome* represented an experiment with form that the discovery of Proust would have encouraged her to take further. But Wharton did not stop with *The Reef*, though nearly all of her later work is outside the scope of this particular study, which stops when the full impact of the war became apparent in 1915. Even taking into account this later writing, however, beyond the specialist field of Wharton studies there has been no great evidence of a move to include her in discussions of *modernist* writing by women. In the anthology *The Gender of Modernism,* published in 1990 and dedicated by the editor Bonnie Kime Scott "to the forgotten and silenced makers of modernism," Edith Wharton's work is not included. She appears in the index only once, being mentioned in the same breath (once again) as John Galsworthy in a letter by Nella Larsen.[37]

This is both apt and unfortunate. She is *apart from modernism* in that her work resists the call to take art out of history, economics, and politics. She rejected modernism on these grounds, and leveled against modernism a similar charge to the one that modernism itself had leveled against realist fiction, namely that the new writing was indiscriminate in its cataloguing of detail. Modernism turned the camera from the outer world to the inner, but still lacked the ability to discriminate between what was important and what was unimportant.[38] Wharton held firm to a belief in this distinction, and was convinced that there should be order in art as there should be order in society. Her aesthetic and social politics are thus consistent.

At the same time, it is important to be clear about what did *not* distinguish Wharton from modernism. As we saw in the previous chapter, it was not the marketing of her work that sets her apart, because it is now acknowledged that many modernist writers were actively involved in the marketplace. James Joyce, for example, set up the first cinema in Dublin with the aid of a Continental backer in 1909, won a franchise to sell Irish Aran sweaters on the Continent, and planned to set up a Dublin broadsheet newspaper called *The Goblin,* all of which perhaps help explain the otherwise bizarre friendship between the bourgeois Bloom and the bohemian Stephen near the end of *Ulysses*.[39] It was not Wharton's technique that set her apart from modernism, as she was clearly interested in the techniques used by Henry James, Joseph Conrad, and Proust, and experimented with some of them in *Ethan Frome* and *The Reef*. It was not her class origins per se, because modernist writers came from all classes. It was certainly not her nationality, since American writers were at the vanguard of modernism. Finally, despite the dominance of men in the modernist canon, it cannot have been a matter of gender, because Virginia Woolf, Gertrude Stein, and Dorothy Richardson advanced experimental writing to such an extent that for some modernist writing with its fluidity, cyclical character, and refusal to focus on action and plot is an emergent *women's writing*. It was none of these things. Instead it was a political separation, determined by Wharton's conception of art as something that has an important role to play in the good society. Life was not the chaotic, random, fluid phenomenon that modernism alleged.

An objection to this setting of Wharton apart from modernism can obviously be raised on the grounds of the arbitrariness of categories. Why not interpret "modernism" less rigidly so as to include some of Wharton's work? The case for the elasticity of the term "modernism" is well illustrated by critical discussion of whether naturalism itself, a category of writing characterized by its domestic interiors, "the conflict of individual aspiration and social obligation, the pull of personal inclination against the duties of kinship, the clash of tradition and self fulfilment,"[40] features that bring to mind Wharton's work, should be considered one of the truly modernist movements. The call for inclusiveness is well made, but on the grounds that the politics that informed Wharton's idea of the purpose of art differed so fundamentally from that of key practitioners from Conrad to Joyce, I still think it useful to think of Wharton alighting from the modernist train when she realized what its destination might be.

Although Nella Larsen and Virginia Woolf dismissed Wharton as an Edwardian writer, she has long since avoided the fate of being bracketed unthinkingly with Galsworthy. Yes, she may have been unable to escape her class, and her ideal of the home may be a "quintessentially aristocratic ideal."[41] Her American Tory politics may mean that she believed that life is possible only "in the very society she is attacking."[42] Yet here is a great paradox. The bustling city with its vulgar materialism is rejected in favor of the country house and its traditions of the family. In the years before World War 1, however, Wharton traveled ceaselessly and never established her own Tory country house family, except in surrogate form through her inner circle of friends.

8: POLITICS AND PARADOXES

Similar conundrums inform her writing. There is at times a narrowness of rhetoric, implicit in the fiction and explicit in her other writing, concerning race, class, and empire. Such a rhetoric is highly problematic for the twenty-first-century reader, and the restoration of her reputation should not seek to gloss over or avoid this. But Edith Wharton is the writer of important, powerful, early twentieth-century novels that celebrate connection and community rather than human severance and isolation. It is this commitment to humankind as a social species, sometimes constrained by society but never liberated by being alone, that puts her at odds with what she perceived to be the aims of some of the early modernist writers. The achievement of Edith Wharton involves a recognition of the ground that radical Tories and anticapitalists paradoxically share, namely their opposition to selfish individualism, whether justified by bourgeois or artistic values. Both bourgeois individual and self-conscious artist are vulgar and vain. Unlike socialists, however, Wharton favored a community that is caring but hierarchical. In her writing, however, this instinctive loyalty is subjugated beneath a sharp critical analysis, which, after *The Valley of Decision*, never sacrifices the fiction for propaganda.

Apart from modernism, therefore, this complex, polished satirical writing was emerging from Wharton's pen between 1900 and 1915. In its refusal to lock itself inside the artist's studio, it was exploring a world in which the power of economics and the drive toward rootlessness was examined by Wharton's critical intelligence in ways that utterly connect with the questions being asked about the culture of the West in our twenty-first-century world. Her fiction is, paradoxically, more modern now than it was in 1915.

Appendixes

Appendix 1: Desire and the Regulation of Sexuality in Edith Wharton's Writing, 1907–17

EDITH WHARTON'S MARRIAGE TO TEDDY WAS AN UNHAPPY ONE, AND Shari Benstock alludes to the contemporary gossip that the absence of children revealed the absence of sexual intercourse.[1] Whether that is or is not the case, there is evidence that in the years immediately before 1910, part of Edith Wharton was longing for the sexual fulfillment that she believed was the experience of other women, and that her brief affair with Morton Fullerton was as much a controlled decision not to deny herself that possibility as it was a desperate need for Fullerton himself. In this sense her desire approximates more closely to the more positive model of Deleuze and Guattari (1972), that it was not a sign of absence or lack, but a desiring-machine that produces the object of desire. The lover is made from the wanting, and the fact that Edith Wharton was simultaneously preoccupied with caring for Teddy, who was increasingly ill, caring for Henry James who was suffering a bout of depression over the fortunes of an American edition of his works, and editing her own writing, suggests that she was not the slave but the controller of desire. The object of desire was one who seemed to offer not only sexual but also intellectual companionship, something missing in her own marriage. The fusion of the erotic and the transgressive, the intellectual and the political (Fullerton was a political journalist) meant that the relationship was particularly intense and charged for Edith Wharton.

Wharton wished for the fulfillment of a sexual relationship, and her private writings show that she imagined that she might experience this in the quietness of the forest or in some remote country inn. In fact, she was only able to spend a limited number of nights with Fullerton. One of these was at Charing Cross Station where she wrote the poem "Terminus," whose disturbing images of snatched joy leading to death, oblivion, and a return to duty contrast with the rapture of the language in the note sent to Fullerton in which the poem was enclosed: "I beg you dear, send back the poem soon. *Je suis si heureuse*—it breaks over me like a great tide."[2] There were other nights together, during a motor car tour of Essex with Henry James, and in Boulogne as they cross the Channel on their way back to Paris. In her biography of Edith Wharton, Benstock concludes that Wharton and Fullerton first became lovers during this June 1909 liaison at the Charing Cross railway terminus, but Dwight says that the sexual relationship began in February or March 1908, a perception confirmed by the tone of the letters written to Fullerton at the time and by R. W. B. Lewis and Nancy Lewis's interpretation of them (Lewis and Lewis, eds., *Letters*, 1988). Marion Mainwaring, in her recent biography of Fullerton (2001) casts great doubt on some of the Lewises' interpretations, and suggests that the sexual relationship began in May 1908. It is important to establish when the change from friendship to intimacy occurred because of the complex relationship between the physical world of the body and the world of the mind and writing.

Mainwaring and Dwight are undoubtedly correct in the importance they attach to the commencement of the private diary that Wharton begins following Fullerton's visit to The Mount in October 1907, and in the entries in Italian for February, March, and April 1908 with their allusions to the passion of Paolo and Francesco in Dante's *Inferno*. Things were advanced enough that spring for Wharton to be able to confide to her diary on May 19: "I have drunk of the wine of life at last, I have known the thing best worth knowing, I have been warmed through and through, never to grow quite cold again until the end."[3]

In the immediate afterglow of this experience she wrote a series of sonnets: "The Mortal Lease" and the poem "Life." "The Mortal Lease" was published in *Artemis to Actaeon and Other Verses* in 1909, a collection that reflects Wharton's interest in Diana the hunter, love and adultery, and may be read as the reply of the hunter of words to the hunter of bodies. Although the eight-poem sonnet sequence includes poems written as early as 1902 and harks back to a former era in terms of tone and rhetoric, to Paula Bernat Bennett it is of interest "as an example of a genre that has recently evoked considerable interest from women poets, possibly because the structure of the sonnet sequence creates a meditative framework through which poets can examine the significance of desire in their lives."[4] The sonnets also reveal evidence of the way in which anxieties about passing time and missed opportunities act as the spur to submit to desire, to take the proffered kisses, to seize the day and the Moment:

> The Moment came with sacramental cup
> Lifted—and all the vault of life grew bright
> With tides of incommensurable light—
> But tremblingly I turned and covered up
> My face before the wonder.
>
> "Mortal Lease" Sonnet 6

In her diaries and letters she had noted her belief that Nietzsche was right to identify the denial of the body and the suppression of pleasure as a product of a corrupting instinct toward death, an argument made more explicit by Freud in 1911, the same year in which *Ethan Frome* was published.

The new note of rapture and eroticization found itself into much of the writing of this period. In the poem "Life" images of the dormant reed awakened by the lips of the Life with the invitation to

> once more
> Pour the wild music through me

describe the awakening of the male reed by a female Pan, enacting the kind of gender reversal explored in *Ethan Frome*. (Pan made his reed pipe—or syrinx—to console himself after his pursuit of the nymph Syrinx had been thwarted when she cried to her river-god father to turn her into a reed, her wish being immediately granted.) Put alongside the outline of "Beatrice Palmato," a story that was never completed,[5] the poems suggest an even more eroticized subtext of sexual release through transgressions, which in the surviving fragment are exoticized as oral sex, orgasm, and incest with a Levantine father figure. In "Life" the fellatio imagery—for such it appears to be—is first phallocentric (the reed) and then gynocentric (*pierced, lipped,* and the throat reference in the striking final lines of the following section):

> Life
>
> Nay lift me to thy lips, Life, and once more
> Pour the wild music through me—
>
> I quivered in the reed-bed with my kind
> Rooted in Lethe-bank, when at the dawn
> There came a groping shape of mystery
> Moving among us, that with random stroke
> Severed, and rapt me from my silent tribe
> Pierced, fashioned, lipped me, sounding for a voice,
> Laughing on Lethe-bank and in my throat

> I felt the wing-beat of the fledgling notes
> The bubble of girl-like laughter in my throat.
>
> ("Artemis to Actaeon," 7)

The poem continues by exploring the adventures of the reed as it is "played" by the female Pan who

> warming me with her,
> And as he[6] neared I felt beneath her hands
> The stab of a new wound that sucked my soul
> Forth on a new song from my throbbing throat

And as confirmation that gender roles become blurred and dissolve in erotic activity the poem continues:

> "His name,—his name?" I whispered, but she shed
> The music faster, and I grew with it,
> Became a part of it, while Life and I
> Clung lip to lip, and I from her wrung song
> As she from me, one song, one ecstasy,
> In indistinguishable union blent,
> Till she became the flute and I the player.

There is further pain to be mingled with the pleasure. Following the challenge from the lyre-god Life makes more demands of the willing reed:

> "Wait" she laughed
> And in my live flank dug a finger-hole
> And wrung new music from it. Ah, the pain!

Once experienced, the mingling of pleasure and pain created by desire becomes a much yearned for experience:

> But evermore it woke
> And stabbed my flank with yearning for new music and new pain.

This association of ecstasy and pain, stabbing and wounding, provides us in the poetry with a direct revelation of Wharton's reflection on "life" (meaning both the specific erotic sense in which the word is used by Wharton and the more general idea of a personal philosophy) than is apparent in the more detached voice that is apparent in third person narrative fiction. To Candace Waid this poem, and the others in this collection, signals Wharton's desire to know and see, and to escape silence.[7] The reed in "Life" cannot produce music, but wishes to be played. There is a dread of muteness, of not knowing, and as in a poem "Vasilius in Zante," about a sixteenth-century anatomist found guilty of dissecting a woman before she was dead, the thirst for knowledge sometimes exacts a terrible price. Yet Vasilius's pioneering study "The Structure of the Body" is presented as the vindication for his mistakes. The alternative, silence and the lack of investigation, would be worse and transgression is sometimes necessary.

"Life" is discussed by Gloria Erlich,[8] who is particularly interested in exploring desire as part of an incest theme, particularly one in which the older man comes between lovers—as in *Summer*, where Lawyer Royall is ostensibly Charity's adopted father but may be her actual father.[9] None of this is to suggest that we should assume—or that it is in any way helpful to assume—a direct correlation between fiction and life, for to Erlich the nucleus of Wharton's fantasy life is "the displacement of her sexuality onto words and books."[10] Yet when Edith Wharton began a first draft of her autobiography she called it "Life and I," and it begins with a moment of dawning sensuality intermingled with childhood simplicity:

> My first conscious recollection is of being kissed in Fifth Avenue by my cousin Dan Fearing. It was a winter day, I was walking with my father, and I was less than four years old, when this momentous event took place . . . and I remember distinctly his running up to me, and kissing me, and the extremely pleasant sensation which his salute produced. . . . Thus I may truly say that my first conscious sensations were produced by the two deepest-seated instincts of my nature—the desire to love and to look pretty.
>
> (Wharton [n.p.])

The enduring sensation, still remembered, would support the argument that however inadequate and unsatisfactory Fullerton may have been as a man, as a lover he allowed Edith Wharton to experience physical and sensual pleasure of the kind that remained long in her memory, and against which all subsequent writing was written.

The relationship with William Morton Fullerton, which many find somewhat puzzling,[11] is more explicable if it is seen as a previously imagined affair with a moral libertine, one whose own sexual history had incestuous overtones: he had nearly married his cousin, a woman who he had been brought up to believe was his sister. Embodied in the writing of daily letters, the incipient love affair conflates with childhood desires for dominant, older men such as her father, whom Wharton greatly admired. But, as I argued earlier, the relationship is also an important intellectual and political one, because Fullerton was a serious and able student of international politics, which his profession as a journalist and his authorship of books gave substance to.

The novel written immediately after the affair with Fullerton, and after the publication of *Artemis to Actaeon, Ethan Frome*, is not such a long way from this theme of transgressive sex, desire, and politics. In the French draft of the novel Mattie is Hart's niece, and in the published story she is the daughter of his wife's cousin. Ethan is not that much of an older man—twenty-seven to Mattie's twenty—but he is jealous of the young bachelors, such as Denis Eady, who dance with Mattie. When the young Eady asks her to go for a ride on his cutter, Frome, overhearing and spying like a character in a Thomas Hardy novel (the description of the dance seen through the windows is reminiscent of the description of the dancing in *The Return of the Native*), dreads that she may accept, and the later attempted suicide can be read as Ethan's way of preventing her from having any other admirers than him: at the beginning of the novel, when he hears that others have nearly crashed into the big elm that night he boasts that he could steer clear of the tree if he wanted to. But as in *Summer*, where Charity, now married to her father/lover has a momentary impulse to escape and take flight "but it was only the lift of a broken wing," and as in the outline of "Beatrice Palmato" where Beatrice commits suicide when she reveals (by overreacting to her husband's innocent kissing of their six-year-old daughter) what her own incestuous past has been—a severe price is paid for any transgression.

The sense of transgression—the sense of consciously taking part in an act that is taboo and forbidden—is the essential ingredient in these texts, Erlich argues, and the explanation for the choice of Fullerton, whose reputation as a libertine, as a man who had a close relationship with his sister/cousin and other women (some of whom were blackmailing him), and as the man with whom she chose to have an affair is precisely that he was so obviously ephemeral. It is generally agreed that she did not know that he had been married, that he was bisexual, and that Henry James found him so excitingly "tactile"—but his manner and the reputation that she did know about was enough. She submitted to his authority precisely because in the context of a sexual relationship it was an improper authority. As in the legend of Tristan and Iseult, a translation of which she was reading during this period, it was a relationship both pure and impure. Desire created the object, chose the object, enacted and enjoyed the object, and ultimately wrote the object into being in novels and poems: "In terms of incest desires, Edith Wharton has yearned in imagination for much that Morton Fullerton flirted with and acted out."[12] Ultimately there has to be renunciation, however. Once the thing has been achieved, it must end. In the title poem "Artemis and Actaeon" there is the line "Because I love thee thou shalt die," for by dying, immortality—the preservation of the moment—is possible. In her later writing, the sense of self-sacrifice becomes even more acute and paradoxical. In *The Age of Innocence* Madame Olenska says to Newland Archer "I can't love you unless I give you up."

That novel chronicles the price paid in self-sacrifice and the weakness of men. The men around Wharton were weak, but the Lewises are a little dismissive of Fullerton. Wharton found him not only physically attractive; there was contact of mind as well as body. They could talk freely, and she could enjoy the kind of free conversation with Fullerton that she could enjoy with Henry James, but James was no potential lover; he was not sexually interested in women, and was even older than Teddy. Fullerton may have been far from ideal, but he satisfied a cerebral as well as a sensual need. The intellectual gap in her marriage is suggested by Teddy's disarmingly frank comment in a letter to Sally Norton, one of Edith Wharton's friends: "You know I am no good on Puss's high plain of thought—but you will agree that no lady of talent is as well turned out as she is." (February 26, 1907).

In *Ethan Frome* the feeling that Ethan has found a soul mate is what initially draws him to Mattie: he is more "sensitive than the people about him to natural beauty" and "hitherto the emotion had remained in him as a silent ache" until he appears to find a kindred spirit in Mattie. But the text, which is full of qualifications, and in which the word "seemed" constantly recurs, is hesitant here too: "When she said to him once 'It looks just as if it was painted!' it seemed to Ethan that the art of definition could go no further, and that words had at last been found to utter his secret soul."[13]

Ethan Frome was written after the affair with Fullerton was over, but when it was not yet completely cold. In tone the text conveys a sense of loss and hopelessness—the drive toward death—that is absent from Edith Wharton's own mood at the time, as captured by the letter written to Fullerton on New Year's Eve 1909 when she seemed to acknowledge that their fleeting relationship was already history, but could be revived through language and memory:

My Dearest and Ever Dearest,

Are you happy when you sit and talk to me like that? If you are, nothing else matters—at least not this last day of December, just a little more than a year after the day on which you wrote me: "The letters survive, and everything survives."

During that year you have given me some divine hours, and I want to remember them alone tonight.

It's true that I am not "strong" when you are near me, but when I leave here next week the change will come of itself, naturally, and I shall gradually get used to seeing you less—I suppose!

(Benstock, 229)

Did this profound and intense relationship with Fullerton affect the form and argument of her writing? It would be wrong to underestimate its importance in her personal life, but equally it would be wrong to exaggerate its importance for her writing. Before the relationship with Fullerton she had just completed a novel with a more explicit social and political message. After the relationship she was to write novels in which the triangle of two women and one man mirrors the triangle of two men and one woman that she was part of. But it would do well to separate the sexual relationship from the professional and intellectual one, which preceded and outlived the brief affair. Both were writers, and Candace Waid argues that in *Ethan Frome* Wharton is confronting the problem of the silent woman, who is in this sense the barren woman. The vision at the end of *Ethan Frome* is of a pair of women and a man who have neither health, love, art or children. It is a world from which there is no escape.

Appendix 2: Recent Readings of *The House of Mirth*

Although Gavin Jones's emphasis on the idea of poverty in his reading of *The House of Mirth* is meant as a corrective to the earlier critical emphasis race, in some respects his analysis complements Jennie Kassanoff's argument that the novel should be read alongside contemporary debates in museum journals and elsewhere about the need to preserve vanishing species of American wildlife.[14] Kassanoff argues that Lily is represented as an example of a threatened, vanishing species. Kassanoff's reading of Lily as a specimen of an endangered species draws on contemporary discourses about zoos, taxidermy, museums, and vanishing wildlife. She also sees the novel's politics as consistent with the ones noted in the earlier discussion of *The Valley of Decision*. Here also, Kassanoff observes, "[D]emocracy threatens the nation with civic unrest, cultural decline, and even the wholesale redistribution of wealth."[15]

Although Kassanoff's "extinction" argument is persuasive, the situation is complex. It is certainly the case that Roosevelt, among others, made the case for preservation in museums and national parks. Roosevelt, with whom Wharton had a family link, was both hunter and conservationist. But he believed utterly in the superiority of what he called the Anglo-Teuton race, and was convinced that Anglo-Saxons were destined to conquer because of their capacity to rule, organize, and administer better than any other race.[16] Such a doctrine might wish to see Lily displayed in a museum (this is the gloss Kassanoff put on the the *tableau vivant* scene), but in evolutionary theory, the stronger individuals who surround her deserve to triumph by virtue of their strength.

If there is a Jamesian influence, it is in the subject, rather than in the style of the novel. It has been seen, by Elizabeth Ammons among others, as paralleling Henry James's *Daisy Miller*, with Winterbourne and Selden as detached, coldhearted dilettantes whose judgments are sophisticated but found wanting. Its difference, which is its achievement, is in giving us in Lily Bart the point of view of the woman as decorative object that in *Daisy Miller* is denied to the reader. We do not hear Daisy. We do hear Lily. Both are flowers, both Americans judged and ruined by the society that excludes them. But whereas Daisy has a surname that signifies ordinariness, Lily's surname may be a shortened form of the word for exchange, "barter," but it is also the common abbreviated form of baronet, the bottom rung on the ladder of aristocratic titles. It is a conclusion to which Kassanoff seems to be moving in her description of Lily's "reawakened desire for aristocratic rootedness."[17]

The success of the novel is not surprising. It drew on a tradition of social commentary that was the hallmark of the nineteenth-century novel. Its marvelously satiric tone, which Q. D. Leavis[18] likens to the best of Jane Austen and George Eliot (though lacking the moral purpose of the novels by these writers)[19] has been compared by Paul Pickrel[20] (as Carol Singley has noted)[21] to *Vanity Fair*, itself a parody of *Pilgrim's Progress*. Wharton's dry, sardonic descriptions delay the recognition of the way that acid is doing its work, quietly and remorselessly, though this is to suggest a cruel commentator. The reader's reaction is likely to be a quiet smile, rather than a wince, though the smile is as much the smile of relief that the target is another, and not the reader: "Mrs. Gryce had a kind of impersonal benevolence: cases of individual need she regarded with suspicion, but she subscribed to Institutions when their annual reports showed an impressive surplus."[22] This is relatively gentle irony, of the kind we also see applied to Mr. Gryce, who had made a fortune out of "a patent device for excluding fresh air from hotels."[23] But the satire can be excoriating in its contempt for its subjects: "[Lily] looked down the long table, studying its occupants one by one, from Gus

Trenor, with his heavy carnivorous head sunk between his shoulders, as he preyed on a jellied plover, to his wife, at the opposite end of the long bank of orchids, suggestive, with her glaring good-looks, of a jeweller's window lit by electricity. And between the two, what a long stretch of vacuity! How dreary and trivial these people were!"[24]

APPENDIX 3: SCIENCE, EVOLUTION, AND EMERSONIAN TRANSCENDENTALISM IN *THE CUSTOM OF THE COUNTRY*

In the earlier discussion of Wharton's work I touched on two issues, gender and science, whose politics can be brought together historically by considering the kind of dualism and binary opposition (science versus art, men versus women) that fin de siècle debates about these issues constructed. Though these debates clearly have a bearing on all of Wharton's pre-1914 novels, the particular idea of dualism and evolution, the concept which links both gender and science, has a special significance for *The Custom of the Country*.

In an important discussion of the intellectual landscape of the turn of the century, Judith Fryer mapped in her essay "Women and Space: The Flowering of Desire"[25] the established territories marked out for men and women, and how these were reflected in architecture and design. At a broad political level this involves a clear separation of the public and the private spheres. As Virginia Woolf made clear, there were certain spaces from which women were excluded, and these included the collections of the British Museum and much of the world of Oxford and Cambridge Universities. Women had assigned to them the sphere of the social and public arena, of dinner parties, tea, and public events, but were denied rooms of their own. Without such spaces, how can they create works of art? The answer is that they cannot, and so this cultural separation creates gender. Social and economic conditions determine the role and achievement of women. Fryer sees an anticipation of this in Wharton's early short story "The Valley of Childish Things" (a title that invites contrast with that of her serious novel *The Valley of Decision*) in which a little girl one day leaves her playroom and her lesson books to see something of the world beyond. She undertakes an arduous journey to a plateau on a mountain where there are men and cities and "useful arts." But finding it bleak and cold she returns, expecting to find the companions she has left behind as developed as herself, and the one fellow adventurer she has chanced to meet. But they have remained as children, and when she expresses surprise and disappointment to her fellow traveler, he seems unconcerned, and reminds her to look after her complexion. The emphasis is clearly on the assumptions made about women and the spaces (and priorities) that have been allocated to them, but men too remain in the playroom.

Science, too, provided a dualistic metaphor, as Fryer reminds us. In 1900 Henry Adams stood in the Gallery of Machines at the Paris Exposition, and the sight of the great dynamo engine, which in his autobiography becomes a symbol of entropy, becomes a metaphor for that process of disintegration that will lead to the loss of unity that art and architecture of the Middle Ages possessed. Santayana, a poet and thinker much admired by Wharton, used the modern architecture of the skyscraper, which engineering science was able to create as a symbol of the American male's achievement and will, while the colonial mansion is the symbol of the sphere occupied by the American intellect couched in a "genteel" tradition, which is predominantly female. Fryer points out that Wharton's first full-length publication, *The Decoration of Houses,* inscribes the division between the public and the private, with doors that can be locked to allow retreat into such spaces as the (with)drawing room. The industrial revolution confirmed the division between the world and the house when it brought to an end cottage industries and rural life, in which the house was the center of work. Thorstein Veblen saw the division of activity and place confirmed by the division in the construction of gender, but attributed this not to industrial developments but to an evolutionary development, which saw the emergence of a leisure class. Women, with their display of manners, dress, and the observance of ceremony, were a stage in the Darwinian project.

Wharton's novel has also been discussed in relation to Darwin and Emerson. The Darwinian theme, to be more accurate the theme from Herbert Spencer of "survival of the fittest," is clear in *The Custom of the Country* from the way that Undine survives by adaptation, and Ralph dies from his failure to adapt. Ceccelia Tichi argues that the argument of *The House of Mirth* is that death is preferable to degeneration, and that in it Wharton expresses her preference "for extinction over eugenic degradation."[26] Tichi then goes on to discuss *The Custom of the Country,* drawing attention to the "saurian" features of Peter Van Degen as a way into a discussion of the flexibility of lizards and amphibians, but also their cold-bloodedness. She passes over the opportunity to discuss the dinosaur association, which is more problematic but surely worthy of comment, suggesting as it does great lumbering beasts who dominate the landscape but have a narrow intelligence. The problem is that this suggests that they face extinction, whereas it is the Marvells of this world for whom this is the more immediate fate. Yet commercialism and the destruction of manners is the monster, and dinosaurs had featured as monsters from the outdoor exhibit at the Great Exhibition to Conan Doyle's *The Lost World*.

Evolution, originally reassuring (the story of human progress from fish to homo sapiens), was ultimately anxiety making, as H. G. Wells had shown in *The Time Machine*. If the dinosaurs could become extinct, then so could human beings, as the time traveler discovers when he goes far into the future at the end of Wells's novel. Even in the short term, the evolution of society and ideas can destroy. In "Undine Spragg and the Transcendental I," Julie Olin-Ammentorp and Ann Ryan argue that by the 1890s the Emersonian ideal had been appropriated and distorted.[27] "Self-Reliance" became the model for a "can-do society," justifying self-advancement and material achievement. Olin-Ammentorp and Ryan suggest that *The Custom of the Country* contains its own binary commentary on Emerson, a writer who was very important to Wharton, and reflects the kind of ambiguity about his status that we find in "The Angel at the Grave," in which the daughter of a now forgotten transcendentalist is rewarded for her faithful keeping alive of his memory by the news brought by a visiting scholar that his philosophy may now seem quaint but his scientific ideas were pioneering. In *The Custom of the Country*, Olin-Ammentorp and Ryan argue, Ralph, who shares Emerson's first name, represents the transcendentalist ideal, but his moment of transcendental epiphany is presented ironically, alongside Undine's boredom with the Italian countryside. Elmer Moffatt, they argue, not entirely convincingly is the embodiment of the corruption of Emersonianism. He is self-reliant, he does not conform, and he loves beauty. The last two claims are questionable, but at least their case here is more convincing than that made about Undine, whose dynamism and adaptability they also see as Emersonian, challenging nineteenth-century conventions of sentimental female behavior. More persuasive is Tichi's argument in her essay[28] that the Emersonian influence is traceable to Emerson's division of the constituents of nature into two parts, and that Undine and Marvell represent these two parts. The advancement of Undine and the decline of Marvell clearly poses a problem for the narrator, who casts Undine as the underwater sprite who has not only evolved rapidly into the successful woman of the early twentieth century, but has done so in a way that American culture almost makes inevitable, because it provides no other outlet for women of drive and ambition. As in the majority of Wharton's fiction, there seems to be no political alternative, no preferred option. The organic unity (assuming it ever existed) of the transcendental model is no longer sustainable in the Gilded Age.

The leisured class, in which both she and Henry James so fundamentally believed, had nowhere to go. We have seen that the bohemian model was not acceptable for either men or women, because it sacrificed the tradition of customs and manners, and for women in particular it entailed a sexual freedom that was ultimately pernicious. The new world of Moffatt and Van Degen offered energy and activity, as even Mr. Spragg comes alive when he enters the office building, but that was a world from which women were excluded, and it was a world in which money replaced aesthetics as the intellectual capital. As there could be no salon in twentieth-century America, it is not surprising that France seemed to provide some glimmer of hope, though France, too, was not without its drawback, as *The Custom of the Country* shows. And France, too, is vulnerable to the invasion of both Moffatt and Undine, whose final alliance is a marriage of similar sensibilities.

It is this sense of an unstoppable force, a wave in historical development that cannot be turned back, that provides the case for a particularly political reading of this novel. Robert L. Caserio[29] has argued that we should not overlook the centrality of Elmer Moffatt as the representative of that great political and financial confidence type that we find elsewhere in Snopes and Frank Cowperwood, for example. Critics such as Cynthia Griffin Wolff have been misled into thinking that it is Charles Bowen who is a reliable guide to the events that unfold in *The Custom of the Country*, perhaps because Wharton herself may have thought so, if pressed. The text, an untrustworthy ideological construct (as Caserio reminds us, Fredric Jameson recommends that we see novels in this light), has Bowen in the wise, but ultimately Olympian mode of Henry James. James, like the ancient Greeks, condemned the Elmer Moffatts of this world who negotiate a way through the city for purely personal rather than for public reasons. But the novel shows us that Moffatt is no more untrustworthy than language itself, eloping with the very young Undine and marrying her in Opake, Nebraska. Caserio makes much of this opacity, and the fact that his initial defeat cannot prevent his ultimate triumph. It is for this reason that the narrator withholds explicit information about Undine's first marriage, so that it can be made clear that Undine's progress is predicated on a lie. The discovery that the "invader" can totally outwit the "aboriginal," and succeed in constructing an appearance that is underpinned by a lie, is what demolishes Ralph's belief in the adequacy of his own values and brings him to suicide. He must pass away so that she can succeed. That is the way of evolution. But more than that, it is the marketplace that rules here, as Wai-Chee Dimock[30] argued that it ruled *The House of Mirth*. The instability of a world without absolutes, in which a lie will serve as well as a truth, means that everything is reduced to its exchange value. Language, like marriage, is valuable only because of what you can do with it. It has no intrinsic worth in itself.

Appendix 4: Living in the Bentham's Panopticon: Surveillance and the Remorseless Gaze

An image that makes a frequent appearance in Wharton's fiction is that of the scrutinizing eye. It is the central image in her most famous "ghost" story, "The Eyes," and it is an image that haunts Merrick in "The Long Run," when he begins his relationship with Paulina Trant: "There she stood; and as this queer sensation came over me I felt that she was looking steadily at me, that her eyes were voluntarily, consciously resting on me with the weight of the very question I was asking."[31] It is an image used in "The Triumph of the Night," where the gaze of the ghostly figure behind Mr. Lavington, seen only by Faxon, the central character, when he looks from Lavington's nephew Frank Rainer to their host:

> . . . Faxon raised his eyes to look at Mr. Lavington. The great man's gaze rested on Frank Rainer with an expression of untroubled benevolence, and at the same instant Faxon's attention was attracted by the presence in the room of another person, who must have joined the group while he was upstairs searching for the seal. The new-comer was a man of about Mr. Lavington's age and figure, who stood just behind his chair, and who, at the moment when Faxon first saw him, was gazing at young Rainer with an equal intensity of attention. The likeness between the two men—perhaps increased by the fact that the hooded lamps on the table left the figure behind the chair in shadow—struck Faxon the more because of the contrast in their expression. John Lavington, during his nephew's clumsy attempt to drop the wax and apply the seal, continued to fasten on him a look of half-amused affection; while the man behind the chair, so oddly reduplicating the lines of his features and figure, turned on the boy a face of pale hostility[32]

The observing, judging eye is rarely absent from her fiction, as characters assess women, paintings, and opera house audiences with critical eyes, sometimes with the aid of glasses. It is frequently a cold, remorseless look. But sometimes it is simply the look of the keen, inquiring observer. Both senses can be seen in relation to Emerson, whose famous "transparent eyeball" image conveyed the sense of calm, selfless observation to which all transcendentalists should aspire. His New England philosophy was different from that Puritanism of two centuries earlier, which had subjected women to the critical gaze as their bodies were examined for marks of the devil. Yet both traditions see the eye as a moral agent, as an instrument of God. Wharton draws on both traditions. To Lacan it was not the gaze of the observer that was important, but the gaze of the Other. Elizabeth Grosz comments on the distinction between "another" and "the Other," and the more serious effect of the latter: "The gaze must be located outside the subject's conscious control. If it is outside, for Lacan, unlike Sartre, this means that the gaze comes always from the field of the Other. It is only the gaze which can, as Sartre astutely observed, reduce me to shame at my very existence. But it is not the gaze of an other; it is the Other's gaze. It is the result of being located in the field of the Other."[33]

Although earlier I expressed reservations about the usefulness of a general theory of shame that applied affect theory to Wharton's novels and found (most noticeably) evidence of shame nearly everywhere, there is an important point that Lev Raphael makes in his conclusion that offers a clue to the possible significance of this recurrent description of shaming experiences. The significance comes from observing more closely the representation and agency of this shame: "Wharton's universe is pervaded by shame and the imagery of exposure: glaring lights and glaring eyes. Exposure is a terrible possibility that haunts the fictional domain, sometimes through the seemingly inhuman nature of newspapers and magazines."[34] Whereas Raphael sees this largely as a matter of character formation through personal humiliation, the broader application of this insight brings us to the issue of surveillance and power, as discussed by Foucault in *Discipline and Punish*.[35] Inspection and examination is the means by which sophisticated society disciplines, regulates, and orders the subject, and by means of the all-pervasive gaze, for which Foucault uses the image of the panopticon, subjects engage in self-regulation. Raphael points us in this direction by drawing attention to the agency of newspapers and magazines in this process. The humiliating reporting of divorce or infidelity in the popular press is a powerful incentive for men and women to regulate their own behavior, and if married, to seek to regulate the behavior of their partners.

Equally powerful deterrents are the two public humiliations of Lily that occur in rapid succession in the narrative. Preceding the moment when Lily learns that she has been largely passed over in her aunt's will is the public insult that occurs when Bertha Dorset announces in front of a large gathering that Lily will not be returning to the Dorsets' yacht. It is the public nature of this insult that makes it so devastatingly an act of punishment. It is observed by so many, and Lily has no option but to bow to her disgrace in the eyes of others and leave quietly, even though she has done nothing wrong. Both are mortifying moments of personal humiliation that Lily manages bravely, but they are also significant political moments, showing how the wealthy can exercise power over their dependants by determining how others see them. Lily has no option but to remain silent in the face of injustice because she wishes to be rewarded by the society that plays to these rules. It is her identification with this society, as it is Undine's similar identification, that Wharton shows us, not because she wishes us to feel sorry for the individual Lily or feel contempt for the individual Undine, though these may be important rhetorical necessities, but because she wants to demonstrate that there is no other choice for the individual. The price to be paid for resistance is exclusion.

The indictment of the society and class that has this power is not that it excludes, however, but that it sometimes excludes the innocent and embraces the mercenary. There is no doubt that Wharton is making a point about gender as well, because women in particular in this society are subject to inspection and physical examination much more than men. Beauty is the main currency of women such as Undine and Lily, and Anna's lack of beauty is cushioned, but not compensated for, by her inherited wealth. Women are under the surveillance of both men and women, and their appearance becomes the main means by which they are judged. Undine craves for attention and hates being ignored. In the mirror she imagines herself being admired.[36] Lily is not so vain, but she knows full well the effects that she can create, and her moment of "triumph" is in the pose as the Mrs. Lloyd, whose beauty won her the marriage that Lily is never to have. Cynthia Griffin Wolff discusses the narrative implications of the representation of the gaze in this novel:

Early on Lily is observed by Percy Gryce and she knows that she herself is the object of his gaze, and she knows that action of any kind will diminish the potency of her "femininity" at this moment. In these "visual" transactions throughout the novel, the narrator often plays a crucial role—explicating Lily's thought process and revealing it to the reader in ways that make it inescapably clear the extent to which Lily can "see" all the implications of her situation. In this regard, it is important to realize that *this* narrator must necessarily be "gendered" female: that is, one of the narrator's central functions in *The House of Mirth* is to direct the reader's attention to two things that women MUST know—and that *they must keep secret*—hidden from the tyranny of the male gaze.

1. The studied, careful effort that is required to appear "naturally feminine" and . . .

    2. The regular habit women have of scrutinizing men and analyzing men's behavior—all the while appearing to be merely dependent, observant, and passive.[37]

The importance of the gaze explains the significance of the theater in these novels, where not only is display institutionalized and formalized, but it operates at a number of levels. Women like Sophy are keen to see the performance of a famous actress in a Parisian theater, while women like Undine go to the theater to be seen. As John Berger observed, though perhaps without fully acknowledging Cynthia Griffin Wolff's second point, men look at women and women look at themselves being looked at. Thus women are objectified and regulated.

In her study *Displaying Women*[38] Maureen E. Douglas discusses late nineteenth-century anxieties in New York about the public display of the contours of the female body in theater tableaux and how this was seen as more threatening to public morals than the sanctioned display of prostitutes.

Men, too, can be controlled by surveillance. The piercing eyes that scrutinize men, such as Faxon and Merrick, indicate the fear of exposure of transgressive behavior. The ghosts that visit warn of judgment from beyond the grave. Wharton's ghost stories, perhaps, provide a verdict on class and behavior that goes well beyond a view that she could ever have any desire to make publicly. If the eyes that look at women can be turned on men, then men will learn some important truth about themselves. But this theme in her fiction and letters also confirms a belief in an external, inescapable, terrifying judgment ever present in life, represented by the scene from the *Eumenides*, which haunts Lily Bart.[39] Orestes shares a cave of the oracle with the sleeping Furies. His "implacable huntresses" may be asleep, but they were always there in the dark corners, and would inevitably awake and righteously restore the established order.

Wharton's sense of the ever-present Furies, and her frequent reminders in her fiction of the feeling of being observed, suggest that her view of the world corresponds to a deep Freudian sense of the need for observation and control, of the kind proposed by Jeremy Bentham in the closing years of the eighteenth century. Bentham had in mind a monitoring tower, which he called a panopticon, which could be used in prisons. The prisoners occupy cells, which in Foucault's extrapolation, become "small theatres in which each actor is alone, perfectly individualised and perfectly visible."[40] It is quite a suitable metaphor for the modernist version of the estranged artistic consciousness that Wharton thought something to be avoided, not examined in forensic detail.

Notes

Chapter 1. "Schooling an Intelligence"

1. Edith Wharton, *A Backward Glance* (1934; repr., New York: Charles Scribner's Sons, 1993), 114. Hereafter referred to as *ABG*.

2. The passage occurs in a letter from John Keats to George and Georgiana Keats, 21 April 1819. Keats rejects the Christian concept of a "vale of tears" in favor of Keats's concept of a "vale of Soul-making." In order to convert an Intelligence into a Soul, the individual must welcome the education of experience, in which the heart must "feel and suffer in a thousand diverse ways." See Keats *Selected Poems and Letters*, selected by Robert Gittings and ed. Sandra Anstey (Oxford: Heinemann, 1995), 175.

3. Whitman's opening paragraphs whimsically review the perils and strains of his life: "Perhaps the best of songs heard, or of any and all true love, or life's fairest episodes, sailors', soldiers' trying scenes on land or sea, is the résumé of them, or any of them, long afterwards, looking at the actualities away back past, with all their practical excitations gone. How the soul loves to float mid such reminiscences! . . . So here I sit gossiping in the early candlelight of old age—I and my book—casting backward glances over our travel'd road. After completing, as it were, the journey—(a varied jaunt of years, with many halts and gaps of intervals—or some lengthen'd ship-voyage, herein more than once the last hour had apparently arrived, and we seem'd certainly going down—yet reaching port in a sufficient way through all discomfitures at last)" Whitman, "A Backward Glance O'er Travel'd Road," in G. Schmidgal, ed., *Walt Whitman*, 377.

4. *ABG*, 63.

5. R. W. B. Lewis, *Edith Wharton: A Biography* (1975); Cynthia Griffin Wolff, *A Feast of Words: The Triumph of Edith Wharton* (1977); Shari Benstock, *No Gifts from Chance* (1994). Percy Lubbock's earlier work, *Portrait of Edith Wharton* (1946), is more of a memoir than a biography.

6. In his review of "The Hermit and the Wild Woman" (1908), H. L. Mencken wrote: "I have read Conrad and Kipling on the deck of a smelly tramp steamer, with my attire confined to a simple suit of pajamas, and somehow, the time, the place and the garb seem in no wise indecent: but after I had passed the first story in Mrs. Wharton's book, I began to long for a velvet smoking jacket and a genuine Havana substitute for my corncob pipe." H. L. Mencken, "A Road Map of the New Books," *Smart Set* 27, no. 1 (January 1909): 157–58. Included in S. T. Joshin, ed., *H. L. Mencken on American Literature* (Athens: Ohio University Press, 2002), 147.

7. Nicky Mariono, *Forty Years with Berenson* (London: Hamish Hamilton, 1966), 165.

8. For an account of Frances Hodgson Burnett's work and life see Gretchen Gerzina, *Frances Hodgson Burnett* (2004).

9. Malcolm Bradbury and James McFarlane, eds., *Modernism: A Guide to European Literature, 1890–1930* (London: Penguin, 1976), 26.

10. José Ortega y Gasset, "The Dehumanizaton of Art" in *The Dehumanization of Art and Other Writings on Art and Culture* (Garden City, N.Y.: Doubleday, 1956).

11. David Lodge, "The Language of Modernist Fiction: Metaphor and Metonymy," in Bradbury and McFarlane (1976), 484.

12. Conrad was eight years older than Wharton.

13. H. L. Mencken, "The Anatomy of Ochlocracy," *Smart Set* 64, no. 2 (February 1921): 143. A review of *The Age of Innocence* included in S. T. Joshin, ed., *H.L. Mencken on American Literature* (Athens: Ohio University Press, 2002, 149–50.

14. Webster's Collegiate Dictionary (1916; repr., Springfield, Mass.: Merriam Company, 1923), 627.

15. Martin Halliwell, *Modernism and Morality* (Basingstoke, U.K.: Palgrave), 2001, 11.

16. In a recent view of Eric Auerbach's *Mimesis: The Representation of Reality in Western Literature* (Princeton, 2003), Terry Eagleton compares Auerbach's response to modernism with Lukács's: "The upbeat humanism of both men affronted by the downbeat outlook of the Modernists. Both are doctrinal life-affirmers, high-European humanists dismayed by the flaccid melancholia of the late bourgeois world." Terry Eagleton, "Pork Chops and Pineapples," *London Review of Books*, 23 October 2003, 18.

17. For Mansfield on Richardson, see Katherine Mansfield, *Notes on Novelists* (Constable, 1930), 42, and the discussion in Trodd, *Women's Writing in English* (1998), 63–64. For Woolf on Joyce, see chapter 3 of this study.

18. Susan Goodman, *Edith Wharton's Inner Circle* (Oxford: Oxford University Press, 1994), 66.

19. Dale M. Bauer, *Edith Wharton's Brave New Politics* (Madison: University of Wisconsin Press, 1994).

20. Blake Nevius, *Edith Wharton: A Study of her Fiction* (Berkeley: University of California Press, 1961).

21. Carol J. Singley, ed., *A Historical Guide to Edith Wharton* (Oxford: Oxford University Press, 2003), 9.

22. Lev Raphael, *Edith Wharton's Prisoners of Shame* (London, Macmillan, 1991).

23. Kathy Fedorko, *Gender and the Gothic in the Fiction of Edith Wharton* (Tuscaloosa: University of Alabama Press, 1995).

24. See, for example, her essay, "Extinction, Taxidermy, Tableaux Vivants: Staging Race and Class in *The House of Mirth*," *PMLA* 115, no. 1 (January 2000): 60–74. I will be referring to this, and her recent book, *Edith Wharton and the Politics of Race* (2004), later in this study.

25. Janet Beer writes of Kate Orme, in *Sanctuary:* "Kate is, in topographical terms, constructed in the colonial relationship to her father . . . Governed, as she is, her welfare is irredeemably adjunct to the well-being of the centre, in this instance the centre of self-satisfaction and selfishness that is her father. She is, like territory, to be disposed and maintained in the most economically expedient and profitable manner." Janet Beer, *Kate Chopin, Edith Wharton and Charlotte Perkins Gilman: Studies in Short Fiction* (London: Macmillan, 1997), 104.

26. Judith L. Sensibar writes of the change from Wharton's studies of upper-class American women: "like Lily Bart, who is colonized by the patriarchal gaze in *The House of Mirth*—to more politically and psychologically complex and inclusive ren-

derings of colonizing processes." Judith L. Sensibar, "Edith Wharton as Propagandist and Novelist," in Colquitt et al., *A Forward Glance: New Essays on Edith Wharton* (London: Associated University Presses, 1999), 150.

27. Stephanie Lewis Thompson, *Influencing America's Tastes* (Gainsville: University Press of Florida), 2002: 92.

28. Sylvia Plath is one such example. Plath and Wharton also share a number of other qualities, interests, and experiences. They both depended on writing for their incomes, they wrote both poetry and prose, they admired Nietzsche and translated Ronsard, they had failed marriages, and they are often discussed in relation to a single, influential male writer (James or Hughes).

29. John Keats letter to George and Georgiana Keats, letter 123 (dated here Sunday, 14 February 1819), in M. B. Forman ed., *The Letters of John Keats* (London: Oxford University Press, 1947), 336.

30. Letter to Sara Norton, 7 July 1908, in R. W. B. Lewis and Nancy Lewis eds., *The Letters of Edith Wharton* (New York: Collier Books, 1988), 159. Hereafter referred to as *Letters*.

31. *ABG*, vi.

32. Edith Wharton, preface to *Ghosts* (1937), Reprinted in Frederick Wegener, ed., *Edith Wharton: The Uncollected Critical Writings* (Princeton: Princeton University Press, 1999), 273.

33. Edmund Burke, *A Philosophical Enquiry into the Origins of our Ideas of the Sublime and Beautiful* (1757).

34. Harold Bloom, for example, in his "Freud and the Sublime: A Catastrophe Theory of Creativity," in Maud Ellman, ed., *Psychoanalytic Literary Criticism* (London: Longman, 1994), 182. See Nicholas Royle, *Uncanny*, 14.

35. Bauer, *Edith Wharton's Brave New Politics*, 11.

36. "The New Frenchwoman," in *Edith Wharton Abroad: Selected Travel Writings, 1888–1920*, ed. Sarah Bird Wright Chivers Press, 1992), 287. Originally appeared under the title "Is there a New Frenchwoman?" in the *Ladies Home Journal*, April 1917, 34:12.

37. Jennie A. Kassanoff, *Edith Wharton and the Politics of Race* (Cambridge: Cambridge University Press, 2004).

38. Although the evidence comes from the post–World War I period, the following comment shows that such reading took place with enthusiasm: "Edith whirled through *Punch*, the *Times Literary Supplement*, and the illustrated papers." Extract of letter from Bernard Berenson to Nicky Mariano, Christmas Day 1931, quoted in Mariano, *Forty Years*, 169.

39. Louis Althusser "Ideology and Ideological Statue Apparatuses," in Julie Rivkin and Michael Ryan, eds., *Literary Theory: An Anthology* (Oxford: Blackwell, 1998) 294–304.

40. Terry Eagleton, *Literary Theory* (Oxford: Blackwell, 1983), 173.

41. Edith Wharton, letter to Sara Norton, 10 May 19—— (probably 1910 as the letter refers to Henry James's "The Velvet Glove" in the March *English Review*). Letters from Edith Wharton to the Norton family 1906–1922; bms AM 1193; 336–54 Houghton Library, Harvard University (hereafter referred to as *HL*).

42. Henry James, letter to Edith Wharton, 24 February 1912. Typed copy in Percy Lubbock collection, of Henry James manuscripts; bms AM 1237.16, *HL*.

43. Women's prison in London in which suffragists were incarcerated.

44. Henry James, letter to Edith Wharton, 13 March 1912. Typed copy in Percy Lubbock collection, of Henry James manuscripts, bms AM 1237.16, *HL*.

45. Henry James, letter to Edith Wharton, 29 May 1912. Typed copy in Percy Lubbock collection, of Henry James manuscript, bms AM 1237.16, *HL*.

46. "The Victim," *Punch*, 6 March 1912 175.

47. Susan Goodman, *Edith Wharton's Inner Circle*, 95. She quotes from a comment made by Bernard Berenson made in an 1890 letter to Mary Costello. See H. Kiel, ed., *The Bernard Berenson Treasury* (New York: Simon and Schuster, 1963), 38.

48. Henry James, letter to Edmund Gosse, 11 October 1912. Typed copy in Percy Lubbock collection, of Henry James manuscript, bms AM 1237.16, *HL*.

49. Henry James, letter to H. G. Wells, 10 July 1915. Typed copy in Percy Lubbock collection, of Henry James manuscripts, bms AM 1237.16, *HL*.

50. *Atlantic Monthly*, July–December 1909, 840–44, Lamont Library, Harvard University.

51. *Atlantic Monthly*, July–December 1910, 785–87, Lamont Library, Harvard University. This is an unusual poem addressed to a "Dear Sister," who has stayed with the speaker through thick and thin.

52. *Atlantic Monthly*, January–June, 1910, 145, Lamont Library, Harvard University.

53. Letter from Edith Wharton to Bliss Perry, 8 August 1905. Letters to Bliss Perry, 1905–7, bms AM 1343, *HL*.

54. William Roscoe Thayer, "The Outlook in History," *Atlantic Monthly*, July 1905, 65–78.

55. Edith Wharton, letter to William Roscoe Thayer, 11 November 1905. Letters to William Roscoe Thayer, bms AM 1081 (1893), *HL*.

56. Henry Dwight Sedgwick, "The Mob Spirit in Literature," *Atlantic Monthly*, July 1905, 9–15.

57. Ibid.

58. See Goodman, *Inner Circle*, 95.

59. Edmund Wilson, *The Wound and the Bow* (London: W. H. Allen, 1952) 181.

60. Nevius, *Edith Wharton*, 52.

61. Carol J. Singley, ed., *A Historical Guide to Edith Wharton*, introduction.

62. Malcolm Bradbury, *The Expatriate Tradition in American Literature*, British Association for American Studies, pamphlet no. 9 (Durham: BAAS, 1982), 23.

63. *Punch* carried a full-page cartoon in 1912 showing a Pandora's box marked "Present from the USA" releasing a cacophony of ragtime singers and players, while in the foreground the female spirit of "Music," has dropped her lyre and clutches her fingers to her ears. See *Punch*, 9 April 1913, 275. (See jacket cover).

64. Bradbury, *The Expatriate Tradition*.

65. Ibid., 24.

66. Ibid.

67. Nancy Bentley, "Edith Wharton and the Science of Manners," in *The Cambridge Companion to Edith Wharton*, ed. Millicent Bell (Cambridge: Cambridge University Press, 1995), 47–67.

68. Candace Waid, *Edith Wharton's Letters from the Underworld* (London: University of North Carolina Press, 1991).

69. Eagleton, "Pork Chops and Pineapples." Eagleton is describing Erich Auerbach.

70. In *The Political Unconscious*, for example, Fredric Jameson has argued for the "priority of the political interpretation of texts." Fredric Jameson, *The Political Unconscious: Narrative as a Socially Symbolic Act* (New York: Cornell University Press; London: Routledge, 1981), 17.

71. Unlike classic psychoanalytic theory, which examines how mental processes such as fantasy operate at the individual level, articulations of political-unconscious theory, building on Jameson, "pave the way for understanding how fantasies operate at the individual and cultural level and are shaped by material forces." Wendy S. Hesford, "Reading Rape Stories: Material Rhetoric and the Trauma of Representation," in *College English* 62, no. 2 (November 1999): 192–229. Cited quotation is from 205.

72. Axford et al., *Politics: An Introduction* (London and New York: Routledge, 1997); R. Hague, M. Harrop, and W. Breslin, *Comparative Government and Politics* (Basingstoke: Macmillan, 1994).

73. Edith Wharton, *A Motor-Flight Through France* (New York: Charles Scribner's Sons, 1908), 9.

74. Edith Wharton, letter to Bliss Perry, 8 August 1905, bms AM 1343 (540.544), *HL*. Perry was editor of *Atlantic Monthly* from 1899–1909.

75. William Roscoe Thayer, "The Outlook in History," in *Atlantic Monthly* 96 (July 1905), 65–78.

76. Ibid., 71.

77. The full quotation from Shari Benstock, *No gifts from Chance*, 25, reads:

From a contemporary perspective, Lucretia's attitudes seem to verge on pedantry, if not undue exercise of parental authority. But they were based on European practices intended to maintain the cultural system by molding children to the expectations of society. Monitoring children's reading both for the appropriateness of subject matter and reading level was a responsibility French parents, for example, took very seriously. French children were not given free run of the family library (as in America) and young ladies especially were to be shielded from harsh realities and crude forms of expression. Preparing her daughter to become a matron in old guard New York, Lucretia Jones unwittingly directed Edith's steps towards Europe and French ways. Appreciating long-held traditions and regularized habits, Edith was drawn (even in childhood) to cultural conservatism that valued preservation over innovation.

78. Hugh Broghan, in chapter 17 of *The Penguin History of the United States of America* (London: Penguin Books, 1985), 386–87, notes:

The America which fought the Civil War was still in many crucial respects the America which fought the Revolution. The great majority of the population was Protestant, and of English, Welsh, Scottish or Irish descent. It had an outlook that may be summed up crudely as republican, middle-class and respectable. Above all it was rural, in origins, residence, outlook and occupation: the 1860 census classified five out of every six Americans as rural dwellers. All this was to change dramatically between Appomattox and the First World War. The Jeffersonian republic of farmers, from being an aspiration, became a memory. In its place, instead of a plain dignified, provincial society, clinging to the edge of a continent yet gazing eagerly westward, there entered the twentieth century, a continental nation, hugely rich and productive, populous, harshly urbanized, heavily industrialized, infinitely various in its ethnic origins, its religions, languages and cultures, transformed into the first fully modern society by its rapidly evolving technology.

79. *ABG*, 9.
80. Ibid.
81. Ibid., 16.
82. Ibid.
83. Ibid.
84. Ibid., 59.

85. The fuller quotation in *ABG*, 6, reads:

> The readers (and I should doubtless have been among them) who twenty years ago would have smiled at the idea that time could transform a group of *bourgeois* colonials and their republican descendants into a sort of social aristocracy, are now better able to measure the formative value of nearly three hundred years of social observance: the concerted living up to long-established standards of honour and conduct, of education and manners. The value of duration is slowly asserting itself against the welter of change, and sociologists without a drop of American blood in them have been the first to recognize what the traditions of three centuries have contributed to the moral wealth of our country. Even negatively, those traditions have acquired, with the passing of time, an unsuspected value. When I was young it used to seem to me that the group in which I grew up was like an empty vessel into which no new wine would ever again be poured.

86. Ibid., p 6.
87. Edith Wharton, letter to Sarah Norton, 20 October (1909?), bms AM 1088.1, *HL*.
88. Benstock, *No Gifts from Chance*, 419–20.
89. Carol J. Singley, *Edith Wharton: Matters of Mind and Spirit* (1998), 45.
90. Edith Wharton, *The Touchstone*, in *Madame de Treymes: Four Short Novels* (London: Virago, 1984), 12.
91. Kate Tunstall, in her review of many Louise Roberts's *Disruptive Acts* in the *London Times Literary Supplement*, 21 March 2003, 32, observes:

> The Anglo-American New Woman—a term coined in 1894 by the British journalist Sarah Grand for the *North American Review*—would never do in France, for she was insufficiently concerned with her personal appearance. Quickly reified in the French cultural imagination as cigarette-smoking, bicycle-riding, bookish and plain, not to say ugly, and worse still, foreign, she was easily dismissed as ridiculous. French feminists would need to adopt more covert tactics. . . . The New Woman was transformed into the *éclaireuse*, a feminine version of the *éclaireur*, a military term for a soldier who goes in advance of the troops for intelligence purposes.

92. Mary Louise Roberts, *Disruptive Acts: The New Woman in Fin-de-Siècle France* (Chicago: University of Chicago Press, 2003).
93. This led to a fear of dark, mysterious indefinable presences, and ironically (or perhaps, significantly) for a person who was later to write so many ghost stories, a terrible fear of these tales, so severe that she could not bear to think of these books downstairs in the library and had to destroy them. See Benstock, *No Gifts from Chance*, 27, see also Edith Wharton "Life and I" in *Edith Wharton's Novellas and Other Writings* (New York: New York Library of America, 1990), 1079–80.
94. Ibid., 78–97. Benstock acknowledges that Wharton's inactivity during the year 1895 has led to the conclusion that she had some kind of breakdown at this time, but challenges the belief that she underwent a rest cure in the late 1890s. Benstock considers that the illnesses to which Wharton was subject during this period were connected with her continuing sinus problems. "Psychological interpretations of her physical 'breakdowns' and 'rest cures' often overlook or discount the physiological sources of her ailments. Stress and overwork increased her vulnerability to sinus irritation, throat infections, flu, bronchitis, asthma, and lung infection" (95).
95. *AGB*.
96. Ibid., 208–9.
97. *Punch*, 29 January 1908, 74.

98. "Cold storage, deplorable as it is, has done far less harm to the home than Higher Education" (*ABG*, [1993], 41).

CHAPTER 2. SKIRTING MODERNISM

1. Edith Wharton, letter to Sara Norton, 5 June 1903, in Lewis and Lewis, eds., *Letters*, 84.
2. Edith Wharton, *A Motor-Flight Through France* (New York: Scribner's, 1908).
3. Blake Nevius, *Edith Wharton*, 69.
4. See the letter to William Crary Brownell, 14 February 1902, in Lewis and Lewis, eds., *Letters*, 58.
5. Edith Wharton, *The Valley of Decision* (New York: Charles Scribner's Sons, (1902). All subsequent quotations are from the 1914 reprint edition, referred to hereafter as *VD*.
6. Gian Franca Balestra, "Edith Wharton's Italian Tale: Language Exercise and Social Discourse," in Colquitt et al., eds., *A Forward Glance: New Essays on Edith Wharton* (Newark: University of Delaware Press, 1999) 207–20. See page 210 for the proposed dating of this exercise.
7. Outline in the privately printed 1907 edition of *The Education of Henry Adams*, in which Henry Adams discusses the theory of acceleration and the dynamic theory of history.
8. An idea explored much later by Freud in *Civilisation and its Discontents*.
9. William Godwin, *Enquiry Concerning Political Justice*, abridged and ed. K. Codell Carter (1798; Oxford: Clarendon Press, 1971) 58.
10. Benstock, *No Gifts from Chance*, 166.
11. Edith Wharton, letter to William Crary Brownell, in Lewis and Lewis, eds., *Letters*, 48.
12. Edith Wharton, *A Motor-Flight Through France*, 140.
13. For Hewlett's introduction, see Stendhal, *Chartreuse de Parma* (London: William Heinemann, 1923), v—xxii.
14. Edith Wharton, review of *The Fool Errant*, by Maurice Hewlett (New York: Macmillan, 1905). Reprinted in Frederick Wegener, eds., *Edith Wharton: The Uncollected Critical Writings* (Princeton: Princeton University Press, 1999) 110–15.
15. See William L. Vance, "Edith Wharton's Italian Mask: *The Valley of Decision*," in *The Cambridge Companion to Edith Wharton*, ed. Millicent Bell (Cambridge: Cambridge University Press, 1995) 169–98.
16. *VD*, 79. There is irony in the presentation, of course, but the target of the irony is both Cantapresto and the philosophy he attacks.
17. This is no coincidence. In a letter providing information about the novel for her publisher, Wharton wrote "The close of the story pictures the falling to pieces of the whole business at the approach of Napoleon," in Lewis and Lewis, eds., *Letters*, 58.
18. In their June 1902 review of *The Valley of Decision*, the *Catholic World* took offense at this and other representations of Catholicism in the novel. See Vance, "Edith Wharton's Italian Mask," 188.
19. This is quite a playful device, with its own pseudofootnote provided "by a female friend of the author" (*VD*, 556). Yet Arthur Young (*sic*) is one of the actual

sources of background knowledge that Wharton acknowledges in her autobiography (see *ABG*, 84).

20. "Vernon Lee was the first highly cultivated and brilliant woman I had ever known" (*ABG* 87).

21. Vernon Lee, "The Valley of Decision." Published in Italian in *La Cultura* (1903). Translated and republished in Millicent Bell, ed., *The Cambridge Companion to Edith Wharton*, 199–202.

22. Here, for example, is a comment made in a study published relatively recently (Roger Magraw, *France, 1815–1914: The Bourgeois Century* [1992], 17) some ninety years after *The Valley of Decision:*

> Despite recent attempts by French, British and American writers to reinterpret the French Revolution, the only plausible, coherent analysis remains that of scholars who, in the tradition of the great French historian George Lefèbre, see it as a "bourgeois revolution." If one looks beneath the surface of the conflicts and chaos which shook French society between the 1780s and 1815 it becomes evident that the "bourgeoisie" has been the major beneficiary of those changes which occurred. It was they who were ideally positioned to monopolize posts in the bureaucracy and army vacated by the aristocracy, as careers became "open" if not to talent, then at least to men of wealth, education and initiative rather than to birth alone.

23. Vance, "Edith Wharton's Italian Mask," 193.

24. Nevius, *Edith Wharton*, 50.

25. Elizabeth Ammons, "Edith Wharton's Hard-working Lily: *The House of Mirth* and the Marriage Market," in *Edith Wharton's Argument with America* (Athens: University of Georgia Press, 1980).

26. Lev Raphael, *Edith Wharton's Prisoners of Shame* (London: Macmillan, 1991).

27. Wharton, *Madame de Treymes* (London: Virago Press, 1984) 172; hereafter referred to as *MdT*.

28. See letter to William Crary Brownell, 14 February 1902, in Lewis and Lewis, eds., *Letters*, p 58.

29. Gavin Jones, "Poverty and the Limits of Literary Criticism," *American Literary History* 15, no. 4 (Winter 2003): 765–82. The quotation is from 779.

30. A situation found in *Hard Times* and *Great Expectations*.

31. Edith Wharton, *The House of Mirth* (1905; New York and London: Norton, 1990), 248–49. Hereafter referred to as *HM* with page number following in text.

32. Stephen Blackpool's final wish is that workers and masters should "come together more": "I ha' seen more clear, and ha' made it my dyin' prayer that aw' the world may on'y coom toogether more, an' get a better understan'in' o' one another." Charles Dickens, *Hard Times*, book 3, chapter 6, "The Starlight."

33. Babies and children are largely, but not entirely, absent from *The House of Mirth*. Lily is not, therefore, singled out for her barrenness, the beautiful but sterile woman that Sylvia Plath excoriated. Good women like Gerty Farish remain single and childless.

34. See John Higham, *Send These to Me: Immigrants in Urban America* (Baltimore: Johns Hopkins University Press, 1984).

35. Edith Wharton, *The House of Mirth* (Penguin, edition, 1985), 273–74. For Queenie Leavis discussion, see Q D Leavis (1938) "Henry James's Heiress: The Importance of Edith Wharton" in F. R. Leavis, *A Selection from Scrutiny*, vol. 2 (Cambridge: Cambridge University Press, 1968), 124–36. See 128.

36. Edith Wharton, *The Writing of Fiction* (1925), 29.

37. Singley, *Edith Wharton: Matters of Mind and Spirit*, 84.

38. Ibid., 83.

39. See Maureen Honey, "Erotic Visual Tropes." Honey discusses the work of the art historian Bram Dijkstra in *Idols of Perversity: Fantasies of Feminine Evil in Fin-de-Siecle Culture* (New York: Oxford University Press, 1986).

40. Jennie A. Kassanoff, "Extinction, TAxidermy, Tableaux Vivants. Staging Race and Class in *The House of Mirth*, *PMLA* 115 (January 2000): 60–74. See 70. Hereafter "Staging Race."

41. Durkheim was also active in supporting the case for Dreyfus. His influence on sociology is profound, and he outlined its approach in *The Rules of Sociological Method* (*Les Règles de la méthode sociologique* (1895).

42. Wai-Chee Dimock, "Debasing Exchange: Edith Wharton's *The House of Mirth*," *PMLA* 100, no. 5 (1985): 783–92. The quotation is on 784.

43. Ibid., 785.

44. Ibid., 788.

45. Ibid., 789.

46. Ibid., 787.

47. Mary Cadwalader Jones, "Woman's Opportunities in Town and Country," in *The Woman's Book 2* (New York: Charles Scribner's Sons, 1894), 201–10. This extract was reprinted in the 1990 Norton edition of *The House of Mirth*, 282.

48. See Judith Fryer, "Reading Mrs. Lloyd," 27. The arguments cited by Fryer are to be found in Elaine Showalter, "The Death of the Lady (Novelist): Wharton's *The House of Mirth*," *Representations* 9 (Winter 1985): 136, and Elizabeth Ammons, *Edith Wharton's Argument with America* (Athens: University of Georgia Press, 1980) 43.

49. Dimock, "Debasing Exchange," 790.

50. In a footnote Dimock pays tribute to the potential radicalism of the novel's political position: "Wharton seems to pit the bourgeoisie against both the aristocracy and the working class. While her assumption is never articulated, it nevertheless makes her something of an involuntary Marxist in this respect" (792 n. 18).

51. Benstock, *No Gifts from Chance*, 159.

52. Magraw, *France*, 251.

53. Jennie A. Kassanoff, "Corporate Thinking: Edith Wharton's *The Fruit of the Tree*," *Arizona Quarterly* 53 (Spring 1997): 25–29. James W. Tuttleton, "*The Fruit of the Tree:* Justine and the Perils of Abstract Idealism," in *The Cambridge Companion to Edith Wharton*, ed. Bell.

54. Tuttleton, 157—68.

55. See Edith Wharton, letter to Upton Sinclair, 19 August 1927 "It seems an excellent story until the moment, all too soon, when it becomes a political pamphlet. I make this criticism without regard to the views you teach, and which are are detestable to me." See Lewis and Lewis, eds., *Letters*, 500.

56. Kassanoff, "Corporate Thinking," 49.

57. Edith Wharton, *The Fruit of the Tree* (London: Virago Press, 1984), 633.

58. A point noted by Deborah Carlin. See "To Form a More Imperfect Union: Gender, Tradition, and the Text in Wharton's *The Fruit of the Tree*," in Bendixen and Zilversmit *Edith Wharton: New Critical Essays*, 57–77. For her comments on the positions taken by critics, see 59.

59. Margaret McDowell and Elizabeth Ammons, for example.

60. See Deborah Carlin, "To Form a More Imperfect Union," for example.

61. Ibid.

62. Donna Campbell, introduction to *The Fruit of the Tree*, by Edith Wharton, vii–viii. (Boston, Mass.: Northeastern University Press, 2000), vii–vii.

63. *ABG*, 153.

64. Jack Lindsay, *George Meredith* (1956), 185.

65. Inthe introduction to *The Fruit of the Tree*, xix–xx, Cambell notes:

[B]oth seek to transcend social class as a category through an insistence on professionalism. Further, each profession rejects the model of the Veblenian body at leisure—the useless body, the body that does not work—as a mechanism for defining class, instead providing a model in which intellect must express itself continually through the useful body in a kind of unending service to the helpless at both ends of the social spectrum, the powerless or disabled mill hands and the idle rich. Often seen as a novel about physical bodies— mechanized bodies, workers' bodies, women's bodies, bodies broken into fragments ("hands"), bodies existing as symbolic sites of power struggle or spectacles of display—*The Fruit of the Tree* thus also addresses the question of the mind in service of the body.

66. Wharton's next novel, *Ethan Frome*, returns to the subject of the working poor, as seen through the eyes of a working professional engineer for whom circumstance has created a temporary enforced idleness.

67. Katherine Joslin draws attention to Wharton's extensive scientific reading in the context of perceived differences between "male" and "female" writing. In her essay, "Gender and *The Fruit of the Tree*," she discusses the oft-described flaws in the construction of the novel in terms of Wharton's doubts about her abilities as a novelist, expressed as the tension between her desire to put a female discourse into a male architectonic structure. See Katherine Joslin, "Architectonic or Episodic? Gender and *The Fruit of the Tree*," in Colquitt et al., *A Forward Glance*, 62–75.

68. Campbell notes that Dickinson's "Euthanasia: From the Note-Book of an Alpinist" had appeared in the February 1906 issue of *Littell's Living Age* (see Campbell, introduction, in *The Fruit of the Tree*, xv).

69. Ibid., xxvi–xxvii.

70. See Shari Benstock, "Landscapes of Desire."

71. *The Hermit and the Wild Woman and Other Stories* and *A Motor-Flight Through France* were published in 1908. *Artemis to Actaeon and Other Verses* was published in 1909.

Chapter 3. Apart from Modernism?

1. Roslyn Dixon, "Reflecting Vision in *The House of Mirth*," in *Twentieth Century Literature* (1987): 211–22; see 221.

2. Carol J. Singley, ed., *A Historical Guide to Edith Wharton* (Oxford: Oxford University Press, 2003) 8.

3. Terry Eagleton, *Exiles and Émigrés* (London: Chatto and Windus, 1970).

4. Shari Benstock, "Landscape of Desire: Edith Wharton and Europe," in *Wretched Exotic: Essays on Edith Wharton in Europe*, ed. Katherine Joslin and Alan Price (New York: Peter Lang, 1993).

5. Millicent Bell, "Edith Wharton in France," in *Wretched Exotic*, ed. Joslin and Price, 61.

6. Ibid. Bell's argument here is much more convincing than her later invitation to the reader to compare Wharton to a "frontiersman who detached himself from his origins" because she improvised her life, "like a frontiersman." (65). Wharton as Calamity Jane does seem to be stretching it a little.

7. In this respect they are quite unlike Wharton's "Inner Circle" and I am not persuaded by Susan Goodman's argument that there are parallels between the two, even if there is a direct link in the person of Bernard Berenson, who knew Roger Fry.

There are so many differences, many conceded by Goodman, that it is difficult to see this as a subject warranting a whole chapter.

8. Singley, ed., *A Historical Guide to Edith Wharton*, 13.

9. Dale M. Bauer, "Wharton's 'Others': Addiction and Intimacy," in *A Historical Guide to Edith Wharton*, ed. Singley, 115–146.

10. Bauer does not mention this, but in an undated letter that probably dates from 1915, as it seems to hint at *French Ways and their Meaning* (Wharton writes that she is using the French as "a stick to beat our own egregiousness with"), Wharton comments, "Sex obsession is ruining France, but it is better than drink, and better too than the American contempt for women. So who is going to solve this problem?" Letters from Edith Wharton to William Morton Fullerton, 31 August 19 (1915?) HL.

11. Fredric Jameson, *Postmodernism and Consumer Society*, in Hal Foster, ed., *Postmodernism* (1982; repr., 1985). In this essay Jameson argues that modernism prepares the way for an art that replicates and is absorbed by consumer capitalism, and that art is postmodernism.

12. Ibid., 114.

13. See Fredric Jameson, *Signatures of the Visible* (1992: 201–3) and *Postmodernism, Or, The Cultural Logic of Late Capitalism* (1992).

14. Stan Smith *The Origins of Modernism: Eliot, Pound, Yeats and the Rhetoric of Renewal* (London: Harvester Wheatsheaf, 1994) 234.

15. Ibid., 239.

16. Carola M. Kaplan and Anne B. Simpson, eds., *Seeing Double: Revisioning Edwardian and Modernist Literature* (Basingstoke: Macmillan, 1996).

17. Ibid., xi.

18. Edmund Wilson, *Axel's Castle* (1931; repr., London: Flamingo, 1984).

19. Raymond Williams discusses the emergence of modernism in "When Was Modernism" in *The Politics of Modernism* (1989), 31–35. Williams emphasizes the metropolitan conditions that were necessary for the emergence of modernism, and the influence on technology and art, in "Metropolitan Perceptions and the Emergence of Modernism" in the same text, 37–48.

20. In a review of *The Cambridge History of Political Thought* (ed. Ball and Bellamy), Vernon Bogdanor writes that "in terms of political thought there was considerable continuity between the period before and after 1914. Indeed, the years between 1880 and 1914 were . . . exceptionally creative in political thought, being the years in which many of the preconceptions of the nineteenth century came to be challenged by thinkers such as Nietzsche, Freud and Pareto. . . . Terence Ball and Richard Bellamy are right to locate the beginning of the century "roughly in 1880, when the major European states had been largely established and the era of liberal regimes began." *Times Literary Supplement*, (London), 19/26 December 2003, 14.

21. Smith, *Origins of Modernism*, 234.

22. Charles Sowerwine, *France since 1870: Culture, Politics and Society* (Basingstoke, U.K.: Palgrave, 2001), 99.

23. Virginia Woolf, "Modern Fiction," in *The Common Reader* (London: Harmondsworth, U.K.: Penguin Books, 1925), 89.

24. E. M. Forster diary, 13 January 1908. Quoted in P. N. Furbank, *E. M. Forster: A Life, Vol. 1, The Growth of the Novelist, 1879–1914* (London: Secker and Warburg, 1977), 161–62. The E. M. Forster papers are at King's College, Cambridge.

25. See Bury, J. P. T., *France 1814–1910*, (London: Routledge 1991), 217–227 for a discussion of France on the eve of World War I.

26. With one exception: "Some of them still maintained a closed circle in the Faubourg St. Germain in Paris" (Bury, 222). This was the part of Paris in which the Whartons made their home in 1906.

27. Ibid.

28. Martin Green, *The English Novel in the Twentieth Century* (London: Routledge and Kegan Paul, 1984) 153–54.

29. Review of *Pointed Roofs*, by Dorothy Richardson. Anonymous review,er, *The Saturday Review* 16 October 1915.

30. The review of *Pointed Roofs* appeared under the heading "An Original Book."

31. Edith Wharton, *The Writing of Fiction* (London: Charles Scribner's Sons, 1925), 12–13.

32. Ibid., 14.

33. Ibid., 17.

34. Frederick Wegener, *Edith Wharton: The Uncollected Critical Writings* (Princeton: Princeton University Press, 1996), 44.

35. Frederick Wegener, "Form, 'Selection' and Ideology in Edith Wharton's Anti-Modernist Aesthetic," in *A Forward Glance*, 116–38.

36. Ibid., 131.

37. Edith Wharton, "The Great American Novel," *Yale Review*, July 1927. Reprinted Frederick Wegener, ed., *Uncollected Critical Writings*, 151–58.

38. See introduction to the 1922 edition of *Ethan Frome* and *A Forward Glance*, 126.

39. Edith Wharton, "Permanent Values in Fiction," *Saturday Review of Literature*, 7 April 1934. Reprinted in Wegener, ed., *The Uncollected Critical Writings*, 175–79. See 179.

40. Edith Wharton, "Tendencies in Modern Fiction," *Saturday Review of Literature*, 27 January 1934. Reprinted in Wegener, ed., *The Uncollected Critical Writings*, 170–74; "Permanent Values in Fiction," *Saturday Review of Literature*, 7 April 1934. Reprinted in Wegener, *Uncollected Critical Writings*, 175–79.

41. Benstock, *No Gifts from Chance*, 419.

42. Carol J. Singley, ed., *A Historical Guide to Edith Wharton* (Oxford: Oxford University Press, 2003).

43. Judith L. Sensibar "'Behind the Lines' in Edith Wharton's *A Son at the Front*: Re-Writing a Masculinist Tradition," in *Wretched Exotic*, ed. Joslin and Price, 241–58. The quotation is from 253.

44. *Wretched Exotic*, ed. Joslin and Price, 14.

45. Susan Goodman, "Edith Wharton's Inner Circle," in *Wretched Exotic*, ed. Joslin and Price, 43–60.

46. Ibid., 48.

47. This claim about Bourget's influence is made in *The Wound and the Bow*, 177.

48. Shari Benstock, "Landscape of Desire," in *Wretched Exotic*, ed. Joslin and Price, 19–42. The quotation is from 32.

49. Letter from Edith Wharton to Sara Norton, 7 July 1909, *HL*.

50. Ibid. Richard Parkes Bonington (1802–38) exhibited with Constable and Reynolds. The Wallace collection in London contains thirty-five of his works.

51. See carbon copy listing those approached, included in "Sixteen Letters to Barrett Wendell," *HL*.

52. See Hermione Lee, "Edith Wharton's library," in The *Observer Review*, 2 August 1998, 15. The London *Observer* is a Sunday newspaper.

53. Proust for reasons of health, and Wharton for reasons of privacy.

54. *ABG*, 214–15.

55. As is her comment on the possible necessity for the writer to admire the society s/he satirizes, which could be a view of her own position as well as that of Proust.

56. *ABG* 213–14.

57. Bradbury, *The Modern British Novel*, (London: Penguin, 1994), 5.

58. Benstock, "Landscape of Desire," in *Wretched Exotic*, ed. Joslin and Price, 385.

59. Virginia Woolf, "American Fiction," *Saturday Review of Literature*, New York, 1925. (See Benstock, "Landscape of Desire," 385 n. 67 in *Wretched Exotic*, ed. Joslin and Price).

60. The Woolfs could not agree to publish the book because of its size and because of fears that they would be charged with obscenity. Virginia Woolf explained her other objections in a letter to Lytton Strachey: "[M]oreover, I don't believe that his method, which is highly developed, means much more than cuttung out the explanations and putting in the thoughts between dashes. So I don't think we shall do it." *The Letters of Virginia Woolf,* ed. Nigel Nicolson and Joanne Trautmann, 6 vols., letter 924, 23 April 1918 (London: Hogarth Press, 1975–80), 2:234. Later in her diary (26 September 1922) Woolf was to confirm her feeling that she felt the novel a failure, pretentious and unfocused, the kind of book a bored schoolboy might have produced.

61. See, for example, Jonathan Crary, *Techniques of the Observer* (London: MIT Press, 1999).

62. Ibid., 11.

63. Sowerwine, *France since 1870,* 98.

64. Singley, *Edith Wharton: Matters of Mind and Spirit,* 24.

65. Singley argues that this is because Wharton favored a more rigid, secure religion because of a felt need for absolutes, something that both Calvinism and Catholicism provided. Hence the occasional attraction of those two belief systems. She thus believed in what Singley calls a "Limited Naturalism" where life is largely deterministic and governed by laws and forces, but individuals nevertheless have some degree of moral choice. See Singley, ibid., 64.

66. George Santayana (1863–1952), born in Spain and raised in Boston where he became a professor of philosophy at Harvard, argued that humans possess the reasoning faculty not to engage in dreams (he was opposed to German idealism), but to engage in logical deductions based on facts and evidence. Like Wharton he moved to Europe, living in France, England, and Italy.

67. He was also interested in history and is responsible for the famous quotation that says that those who forget history are "condemned to repeat it."

68. Hermione Lee cites the following evidence of Wharton's response: "In Santayana's *The Life of Reason*, next to 'In some nations everybody is by nature so astute, versatile, and sympathetic that education hardly makes any difference in manners or mind' she writes 'France.'" Hermione Lee, "Edith Wharton's Library," in *The Observer Review,* 2 August 1998, 15 .

69. Singley, *Edith Wharton: Matters of Mind and Spirit,* 9.

70. Wharton's copy was the 1898 edition, and it has a bookplate from her Saint-Brice sous Forêt library in her house outside Paris. Despite this, the age of the edition may suggest that she owned the book before World War I.

71. "[I]n or about December 1910 human character changed." Virginia Woolf, "Mr. Bennett and Mrs. Brown," in *Collected Essays*, vol. 1 (London: Hogarth Press, 1966), 321.

72. Jameson, "Post Modernism and Consumer Society", 114.

73. P. A. Lee-Browne, *The Modernist Period: 1900–45* (London: Evans Brothers, 2003), 50.

74. Edith Wharton to Bernard Berenson, 14 June 1913, Bernard Berenson collection, Villa I Tatti (Harvard Library). See also Benstock, "The Landscape of Desire," in *Wretched Exotic,* ed. Joslin and Price, 281.

75. Raymond Williams, *The Politics of Modernism* (London: Verso, 1990), 34.

76. Williams in *The Politics of Modernism,* 50, describes the situation thus:

[I]n 1888 . . . Nietzsche [was] to write of Strindberg's play *The Father:* "It has astounded me beyond measure to find a work in which my own conception of love—with law as its means and the deathly hatred of the sexes as its fundamental laws—is so magnificently expressed." Strindberg confirmed the mutual recognition: "Nietzsche is to me the modern spirit who dares to preach the right of the strong and the wise against the foolish, the small (the democrats)."

77. Williams comments on Strindberg's celebration of Nietzsche:

This is still a radicalism, and indeed still daring and violent. But it is not only that the enemies have changed, being identified now as those tendencies which hitherto had been recognized as liberating: political progress, sexual emancipation, the choice of peace against war. It is also that the old enemies have disappeared behind these; indeed it is the strong and the powerful who now carry the seeds of the future: "Our *evolution* . . . wants to protect the strong against the weak species, and the current aggressiveness of women seems to me a symptom of the regress of the race." The language is that of Social Darwinism, but we can distinguish its use among these radical artists from the relatively banal justifications of a new hard (lean) social order by the direct apologists of capitalism. What emerges in the arts is a "cultural Darwinism," in which the strong and daring radical spirits are the true *creativity* of the race. Thus there is not only an assault on the weak—democrats, pacifists, women— but on the whole social and moral and religious order. The "regress of the race" is attributed to Christianity, and Strindberg could hail Nietzsche as "the prophet of the overthrow of Europe and Christendom." (Ibid.)

78. Benstock, "The Landscape of Desire," in *Wretched Exotic,* ed. Joslin and Price, 282.

79. Gerald Sykes, review of *Virginia Woolf: The Critical Heritage,* in *Nation* (New York), 16 December 1931, 284–86.

80. She was not alone among careful readers of the period in reaching this judgment. In 1948, in *The Great Tradition,* F. R. Leavis wrote of Joyce "[I]t seems plain to me that there is no organic principle determining, informing, and controlling into a vital whole, the elaborate analogical structure, the rendering of consciousness, for which *Ulysses* is remarkable, and which got it accepted by a cosmpolitan literary world as a new start. It is rather, I think, a dead end, or at least a pointer to disintegration. . . ." (F. R. Leavis, *The Great Tradition* [London: Chatto and Windus, 1948], 15).

81. Sigmund Freud, "Repression" (1915), in Angela Richards, ed., *Sigmund Freud,* vol. 11, *On Metapsychology: The Theory of Psychoanalysis* (London: Penguin Books, 1984).

82. Lewis and Lewis, eds., introduction in *Letters.*

83. Most notably by Edmund Wilson in "The Ambiguity of Henry James" (1934).

84. Kenneth B. Murdock, introduction to *Henry James: The Turn of the Screw and the Aspern Papers* (London: Dent/Everyman, 1969).

85. Sigmund Freud, "The 'Uncanny,'" (1919), in Albert Dickson, ed., *Sigmund Freud:* vol. 14, *Art and Literature* (London: Penguin Books, 1988), 339–76.

86. Freud, "The 'Uncanny,'" 367.

87. Nicholas Royle, *The Uncanny*, (Manchester: U.K.: Manchester University Press, 2003).
88. Martin Heidegger, "The Origin of the Work of Art," in *Poetry, Language, Thought*, trans. Albert Hofstadter (New York: HarperColophon Books, 1975).
89. Julia Kristeva, *Strangers to Ourselves*, trans. Leon S. Roudiez (New York: Columbia University Press, 1991).
90. Hélène Cixous, "Fiction and its Phantoms: A Reading of Freud's *Das unheimliche* ('The Uncanny')," trans. Rober Densomè, *New Literary History* 7, no. 3 (1976): 525–48.
91. Freud, "The 'Uncanny,'" 362.
92. Edith Wharton, *Collected Stories, 1891–1910*, 814. Hereafter referred to as *CS*.
93. Freud, "The 'Uncanny,'" 362.
94. Wharton, "The Eyes," in *CS 1891—1910*, 810–13.
95. Ibid., 816.
96. "For if they were a projection of my inner consciousness, what the deuce was the matter with that organ?" *CS, 1891–1910*, 817.
97. Terry Castle, *The Female Thermometer*, (Oxford: Oxford University Press, 1995), 175.
98. Edith Wharton, letter to Bernard Berenson, 21 February 1922, in Lewis and Lewis, eds., *Letters*, 450–51.
99. Lewis and Lewis, eds., *Letters*, introduction, 10.
100. Joy Dixon, *Divine Feminine: Theosophy and Feminism in England*, (Baltimore: Johns Hopkins University Press, 2000).
101. Elaine Showalter, review of Joy Dixon's *Divine Feminine: Theosophy and Feminism in England*, in the *Times Literary Supplement*, 24 May 2002, 8.
102. Edith Wharton, preface to *Ghosts* (New York: Appleton Century, 1937), vii–xii. Reprinted in *Edith Wharton: The Uncollected Critical Writings*, ed., Wegener, 270–73.
103. Dyman also discusses their reading gender. The ghost stories are discussed primarily in relation to Wharton's life, however: "Wharton's ghost stories provide an illuminating look at her personal conflicts and concerns projected on a cultural screen." See Jenni Dyman, *Lurking Feminism: The Ghost Stories of Edith Wharton* (New York: Peter Lang, 1996).
104. Kathy Fedorko, *Gender and the Gothic in the Fiction of Edith Wharton* (London: University of Alabama Press, 1995).
105. Janet Beer and Avril Horner, "'This isn't exactly a ghost story': Edith Wharton and Parodic Gothic," in *Journal of American Studies* 37, no. 2 (August 2003): 269–87.
106. See, for example, "A Haunted House," by Virginia Woolf, "The Rocking-Horse Winner," by D. H. Lawrence, and "The Dead" by James Joyce.
107. Fredric Jameson, in "The Existence of Italy," in *Signatures of the Visible*, 159–60, for example, describes the attitudes of the "Screen Group" to mid-twentieth-century film:

> for whom, as Dudley Andrews has observed, the great modernist auteurs (Hitchcock, Fellini, Bergman, Kurosawa et al.) are as aesthetically dishonest and ideological as the traditional Hollywood ones. Indeed, for Screen, these "moderns" are if anything more suspicious than the conventional forms of Hollywood "realism," where the unconscious—Freudian, deconstructive, or even political—can still slip through the cracks in the form, and undo and subvert an iconic surface which the "modernists" are then in their turn concerned to seal and to stamp with the signature of their unique style of "genius."

108. Jameson himself, however, in "The Existence of Italy," 162–63, offers an alternative to the postmodern critique of its predecessors and encourages us to turn the hourglass of realism/modernism upside down:

> Returning now to the historical issue of realism itself, the most obvious initial way of estranging and renewing this concept would seem to consist in reversing our conventional stereotype of its relationship to modernism. The latter, indeed, we celebrate as an active aesthetic praxis and invention, whose excitement is demiurgic, along with its liberation from content; while realism is conventionally evoked in terms of passive reflection and copying, subordinate to some external reality, and fully as much a grim duty as a pleasure of any kind. Pleasure is, however, generally in aesthetic experience an exercise of praxis, and even the various aesthetics of play are easily adjusted to forms of production by way of a notion of freedom as control over one's own destiny.
>
> Something will be gained, therefore, if we can manage to think of realism as a form of demiurgic praxis; if we can restore some active and even playful/experimental impulses to the inertia of its appearance as a copy or representation of things. Meanwhile modernism may itself be momentarily rethought by experimenting with the provisional hypothesis that, grim duty or not, it is now to be seen as the passive-receptive activity, a discovery procedure like Science . . .

109. Carol J. Singley, *Edith Wharton: Matters of Mind and Spirit* (Cambridge: Cambridge University Press, 1998).

110. Edith Wharton, letter to Morton Fullerton, 8 June 1908, in Lewis and Lewis, eds., *Letters*, 151.

111. Ibid., 152.

112. Edith Wharton, letter to Margaret Terry Chanler, 9 June 1925, in Lewis and Lewis, eds., *Letters*, 483.

113. Thomas à Kempis, *The Imitation of Christ* (London: Dent, 1968), 227.

114. Edith Wharton, "The Angel at the Grave," in *CS*, vol. 1, 276.

115. See Singley, *Edith Wharton*.

116. Edith Wharton, letter to Bernard Berenson, 7 June 1921, in Lewis and Lewis, eds., *Letters*, 441.

117. Edith Wharton, "A Reconsideration of Proust," *Saturday Review of Literature*, 27 October 1934. Reprinted in Weener's *Edith Wharton: The Uncollected Critical Writings*, 179–84.

118. Edith Wharton, "A Reconsideration of Proust," *Saturday Review of Literature*, 27 October 1934. Reprinted in Wegener's *Edith Wharton: The Uncollected Critical Writings*, 182.

119. Edith Wharton, "Marcel Proust," in *The Writing of Fiction* (London: Charles Scribner's Sons, 1925), 153.

120. Ibid., 154.

121. Edith Wharton, "A Reconsideration of Proust," *Saturday Review of Literature*, 27 October 1934. Reprinted in Wegener's *Edith Wharton:The Uncollected Critical Writings*, 182.

122. Ibid.

123. "Style in this definition is discipline; and the self-consecration it demands, and the bearing it has on the whole of the artist's effort, have been admirably summed up by Marcel Proust in that searching chapter of "A l'Ombre des Jeunes Filles en Fleurs' where he analyzed the art of fiction in the person of the great novelist Bergotte." See Edith Wharton, *The Writing of Fiction*, 24.

124. Edith Wharton, "Marcel Proust," in *The Writing of Fiction*, 155–56. The book is a collection of three essays that appeared the year before in *Scribner's Magazine* (what

Wharton called Fiction I, II, and III) and the essay on Proust written for the *Yale Review*.

125. Malcolm Bowie, *Proust among the Stars* (London: HarperCollins, 1998). See chapter 4, "Politics," 126–74.

126. Ibid., 148.

127. Ibid.

128. Ibid., 149.

129. For a discussion of Proust's comic vision, see Roger Shattock, *Proust's Way*, (London: AllenLane The Penguin Press, 2000), chapter 3.

130. Edith Wharton, *ABG*, 49.

131. Edith Wharton, "The Great American Novel," in Wegener, *Edith Wharton: Uncollected Critical Writings*, 156.

132. See Helen Killoran, *Edith Wharton: Art and Allusion* (Tuscaloosa: University of Alabama Press, 1996), 200 (endnote 10 here also refers to James R. Mellow's *Charmed Circle: Gertrude Stein and Company* [New York: Frederick A. Praeger], 1974).

133. See Virginia Woolf, "Mr. Bennett and Mrs. Brown," in *Hogarth Essays* (London: Hogarth Press, 1924) and in *Collected Essays*, vol. 1 (London: Chatto and Windus, 1966), 319–37. For the accusation of materialism, see "Modern Fiction," in *The Common Reader* (1925). Republished by Penguin (Harmondsworth, U.K.: Pelican Books, 1938), 145–53. At least parts of this essay were written in 1919.

134. Edmund Wilson emphasized the significance of the description of interior detail in *The Custom of the Country*. See *The Wound and the Bow* (1952), 179.

135. Benstock, *No Gifts from Chance*, 390.

136. Woolf, "Mr. Bennett and Mrs. Brown," 324.

137. Ibid., 320.

138. Marcel Proust, *À la recherche de temps perdu* (*Remembrance of Things Past*), vol. 1, *Du côté de chez Swann* (1913). Translated into English by CK Scot Moncrieff as *Swann's Way*, part 1 (London: Chatto and Windus, 1971), 252.

139. Benstock, *No Gifts from Chance*, 292.

140. Proust, *À la recherche*, 250.

141. Lewis and Lewis, eds., *Letters*, introduction, 11.

142. See, for example, W. Lawrence Hogue *Race, Modernity and Postmodernity* (New York: State University of New York Press, 1996) and Marianne Dekoven "Modernism and Gender" in *The Cambridge Comparison to Modernism*, ed., Michael Levenson, (Cambridge: Cambridge University Press, 1999, 174–93.

143. Bradbury and McFarlane, eds., *Modernism: A Guide to European Literature*, Penguin edition, (1991) 393.

Chapter 4. *Ethan Frome,* Modernism, and a Political Argument

1. Jennie Kassanoff, "Corporate Thinking," in Arizona Quarterly, (1997): 49–50.

2. "Eveline" probably dates from 1903. Many of the stories included in *Dubliners* were published in newspapers before being published in book form. See Stan Gebler Davies, *James Joyce: Portrait of the Artist* (London: Sphere Books, 1977) 85–86.

3. "Eveline," in *Dubliners,* by James Joyce (1914; London: Granada Publishing, 1977), 35. All subsequent quotations are from this edition.

4. Ibid.

5. Ibid., 33.

6. Ibid.
7. Ibid., 35.
8. Ibid., 37.
9. This parallel is explored by Linda Costanzo Cahir in "Edith Wharton's *Ethan Frome* and Joseph Conrad's *Heart of Darkness*," in *Edith Wharton Review* 19.1 (Spring 2003): 20–23.
10. Ibid., 21.
11. See Carol J. Singley, *Edith Wharton: Matters of Mind and Spirit,* chapter 3.
12. David Lodge, *The Modes of Modern Writing* (London: Edward Arnold, 1991), 152.
13. Gertrude Stein, *Tender Buttons* (1911; New York: Dover Publications, 1997), 3.
14. David Lodge, *Modes,* 151.
15. See Susan Goodman, *Edith Wharton's Inner Circle,* especially chapter 3.
16. William Morton Fullerton, "English and Americans," in *Fortnightly Review,* vol. 47 (January–June 1890) (London: Chapman and Hall), part 1, 242–55; part 2, 731–40.
17. Letter from Henry James to William Morton Fullerton, February 1890, Henry James collection, bms AM 1014.4, *HL.*
18. Dated 1 January 1909, by which time Wharton and Fullerton had met and commenced their close relationship.
19. In 1905 the journal serialized "A Modern Utopia," Wells's account of a world state.
20. William Morton Fullerton, *Patriotism and Science: Some Studies in Historic Psychology* (Boston: Roberts Bros., 1893).
21. Letter from Henry James to Morton Fullerton, 19 December. James could be referring to the Diamond Jubilee, the funeral of Queen Victoria, or the coronation of Edward VII, bms AM 1014.4, (*HL.*)
22. William Morton Fullerton, *In Cairo* (London: Macmillan, 1891), dedication, vi.
23. This is comparable with the circumstances of Sylvia Plath's novel, where it is at first difficult to see any connection between the world of *The Bell Jar* and the London in which it was written.
24. Eric Cahm, "Revolt, Conservatism and Reaction in Paris, 1905–1935," in Bradbury and McFarlane, *Modernism: A Guide to European Literature* (1991), 162–71. For Cahm's discussion of classical French values see 168–69.
25. See, for example, the section "Philosophy in the Conversation of Mankind," with its allusion to Michael Oakeshott's "The Voice of Poetry in the Conversation of Mankind," in Richard Rorty, *Philosophy and the Mirror of Nature* (Oxford: Blackwell, 1994), 389–94.
26. M. M. Bakhtin, *The Dialogic Imagination: Four Essays,* trans. Michael Holquist (Austin: University of Texas Press, 1981).
27. Wharton had observed the world of rural Massachusetts from her car seat during excursions from The Mount in her recently acquired automobile. Thus in writing *Ethan Frome,* she was imagining this world with the feeling of displacement experienced by the narrator. Morton Fullerton had grown up in Waltham, Massachusetts, so the setting had a variety of personal associations.
28. Roger Magraw in *France, 1815–1914: The Bourgeois Country* (1992), 227–28, describes the situation as follows:.

> French secondary and higher education has been attacked for its failure to adapt to the requirements of an industrial society. Critics point to the failure of Fortoul's efforts to create a scientific baccalauréat syllabus, and to the continued higher prestige of the classical and

philosophy streams in the lycées. Observers like Renan cited the poor quality of university science and the absence of both financing and research as a major factor in the war defeat of 1870. The continued expansion of Catholic secondary schooling, which came to control 50 er cent of pupils, was, obviously, not the fault of republican anticlerical politicians. Yet the anti-positivist, anti-rationalist ethos of these colleges, and their tendency to "cram" pupils for baccalauréat exams as an entry to military and bureaucratic careeers, could be viewed as diverting sections of the elites away from industry and science. Although Durey's technical schools had 900 pupils by 1871, and had been designed to supply industry with its qualified "NCOs," their success was limited. They lacked prestige, and failed to expand. One 1913 survey claimed that only 7 per cent of entrants to commerce and industry had adequate technical training. As Terry Shin concludes, the dominance of the *École Polytechnique* was healthy neither for France higher education nor for industry . . . Their training was largely abstract, with little experimental work. They tended to despise "practical" engineers . . . The net outcome has sometimes been portrayed in pessimistic terms. Camille Cavillier, head of the Pont-à-Mousson engineering works, claimed to be driven "mad with rage to see that in our country, where education is pursued to a high level, it so impractical . . . the young are all studying to be scholars, none to do anything practically useful." Yet the professed gloom of such technocratic philistines was a little exaggerated by 1900. . . . Chemistry faculties flourished in Nancy and Paris, hydroelectricity courses emerged at Grenoble, regional industry began to rely on the applied science of its local university. . . . C. Day has emphasized the significant role played by the *École Centrale des Arts et Métiers* in attracting pupils from the middle bourgeoisie and training graduates in applied science for the engineering, chemical and electrical sectors. Between 1897 and 1909 five major provincial universities established engineering degrees. The society of professional engineers quadrupled its membership to 6,000 between 1882 and 1914.

29. See, for example, chapter 2, note 64.
30. Kassanoff, "Corporate Thinking," *Arizona Quarterly* (1997): 25–59.
31. William Morton Fullerton, *Patriotism and Science*, 133.
32. Emile de Laveleye, *Le Gouvernement dans la Démocratie*, 2 vols. (Paris: Félix Alcan, 1891).
33. Fullerton, *Patriotism and Science*, 130.
34. Ibid., 169.
35. Kate Gschwend, "The Significance of the Sawmill: Technological Determinism in *Ethan Frome*," in *Edith Wharton Review* 16, no. 1 (Spring 2000): 9–13.
36. Wegener writes:

> While the nuances of the interrelationship between commercial exigencies abroad and their imaginative assimilation in Wharton's writing need to be scrutinized more fully, one cannot avoid noticing the degree to which her fiction—alertly registering so many aspects of colonial business enterprise—tacitly assents to the emergence of an imperial economy in the West. Nowhere is this alertness sharper than in her attention to the dominance of Western investment in the sort of projects she has in mind in praising the "the interior development of Morocco" under the French Protectorate (IM.218)—the construction of roads, bridges, railways, ports, and so on. This attention underlies the remarkable frequency with which Wharton's imagination gravitates toward the figure of the engineer, a commanding new professional "type" in the United States and elsewhere by the time her literary career began.

Frederick Wegener, "'Rabid Imperialist': Edith Wharton and the Obligations of Empire in Modern American Fiction," in *American Literature* 72, 4 (December 2000), 783–812. The cited quotation is from 796–97. "IM" is Wegener's citing of Wharton's *Inside Morocco* (New York: Scribner's, 1920).

37. Elizabeth Ammons, "The Engineer as Cultural Hero and Willa Cather's First Novel, *Alexander's Bridge*," *American Quarterly* 38 (Winter 1986). See 750–53.

38. Wegener cites the following edition: Edith Wharton, *Ethan Frome* (New York: Signet, 1987), 6, 3.

39. Wegener, "'Rabid Imperialist,'" 801.

40. Archibald Cary Coolidge, *The United States as a World Power* (New York: Macmillan, 1908).

41. Wegener "'Rabid Imperialist,'" 784.

42. The context of the quotation is as follows:

> As one explores the lives and writing of those whom Wharton came to know in "that compact and amiable little world" of prewar Paris the unanimity of their beliefs regarding colonialism in France becomes more and more conspicuous. Even among the friends and acquaintances only briefly mentioned in her letters and memoirs, it is hard to find an exception to this consensus on the worthiness of the new Gallic empire. Scholars have long been aware of the socially and intellectually conservative disposition of Wharton's circle in the Faubourg Saint-Germain; only some slight additional probing is required to demonstrate just how close its members all came to represent the entire pro-imperialist elite of the *belle époque*.

Wegener, "'Rabid Imperialist,'" 791. The quotation describing "that compact ... world" is from Edith Wharton's *A Backward Glance* (New York: Appleton, 1934), 259.

43. For example, "Americans are the western pilgrims, who are carrying along with them that great mass of arts, sciences, vigor, and industry which began long since in the east; they will finish the great circle." *Letters from an American Farmer* (1782), letter 3. Reprinted in Christopher Ricks and William L. Vance, eds., *The Faber Book of America* (London: Faber and Faber, 1994), 242.

44. Here Shotter is discussing C. B. Macpherson's "The Politician's Theory of Possessive Individuals": "Macpherson's account could very well figure as one of the major texts of identity explored in this book, for he shows how the notion of 'possession,' although clearly not the source of other important concepts—such as freedom, rights, obligations and justice—has none the less powerfully shaped their interpretations, and hence our notions of how we are (or should be) related to one another and hence, what and who we are" (136). J. Shotter, "Social Accountability and the Social Construction of 'You,'" in *Texts of Identity*, ed. John Shotter and Kenneth J. Gergen, 136. (London: Sage Publications, 1989).

45. See Sandra M. Gilbert and Susan Gubar, *No Man's Land,* vol. 2, *Sexchanges* (London: Yale University Press, 1989), 131.

46. New York *Call* (1912). Copy of review in the Beinecke Rare Book Room, Yale University, New Haven, Connecticut.

47. Catherine Belsey, *Desire: Love Stories in Western Culture* (Oxford: Blackwell, 1994).

48. Neither is it a very easy term to use, signifying different practices in different contexts. Its use usually indicates that the writer is interested in the construction of the discursive subject, but discussions of such constructions may be informed by a Lacanian notion of lack and unrealizable desire for the other, or they may be informed by a more "positive" concept of desire as motivating force, which cuts across structural oppositions (mind/body, nature/culture) and functions as an imperative that motivates.

49. Simone de Beauvoir, *The Second Sex* (London: Picador 1988). 1988.

50. Edith Wharton, *Ethan Frome,* ed. Robin Peel (Cambridge: Cambridge University Press, 1999), 29.

51. Benstock, *No Gifts from Chance,* 229.

52. Letter dated 5 June 1908, in Lewis and Lewis, eds., *Letters.*

53. Rosemary Brooke (1997).
54. Gloria Erlich, *The Sexual Education of Edith Wharton* (Berkeley: University of California Press, 1992), xii.
55. Carol Wershoven, *The Female Intruder in the Novels of Edith Wharton* (Madison, N.J.: Fairleigh Dickinson Press 1982), 22.
56. Ibid., 40.
57. Candace Waid, introduction to *A Backward Glance*, by Edith Wharton (London: Everyman/Dent, 1993).
58. *A Backward Glance*, 195–96, reads:

"Ethan Frome" . . . was frequently criticised as "painful" and at first had much less success than my previous books. I have a clearer recollection of its beginnings than of those of my other tales, through the singular accident that its first ages were written—in French! I had determined, when we came to live in Paris, to polish and enlarge my French vocabulary; for though I had spoken the language since the age of four I had never had much occasion to talk it, for any length of time, with cultivated people, having usually, since my marriage, wandered through France as a tourist . . . To bring my idioms up to date I asked Charles Du Bos, to find, among his friends, a young professor who would come and talk with me two or three times a week. An amiable young man was found; but being too amiable ever to correct my spoken mistakes, he finally hit on the expedient of asking me to prepare an "exercise" before each visit. The easiest thing for me to write was a story; and thus the French version of "Ethan Frome" was begun, and carried on for a few weeks. Then the lessons were given up, and the copy-book containing my "exercise" vanished for ever. But a few years later, during one of our summer sojourns at The Mount, a distant glimpse of Bear Mountain brought Ethan back to my memory, and the following winter in Paris I wrote the tale as it now stands, reading my morning's work aloud to Walter Berry [a relative and close friend], who was as familiar as I was with the lives led in those half-deserted villages before the coming of motor and telephone. We talked the tale over page by page, so that its accuracy and "atmosphere" is doubly assured—and I mention this because not long since, in an article by an American literary critic, I saw "Ethan Frome" cited as an interesting example of a successful New England story written by some one who knew nothing of New England! "Ethan Frome" was written after I had spent ten years in the hill region where the scene is laid, during which years I had come to know well the aspect, dialect and mental and moral attitude of the hill-people.

59. Elizabeth Ammons, *Edith Wharton's Argument with America* (Athens: University of Georgia Press, 1980), 270.
60. Charlotte Perkins Gilman, "Men and Art," in *The Man Made World* (1911).
61. Ammons, *Argument*, 277.
62. This point is argued by Gilbert and Gubar in *Sexchanges* (1989).
63. The poem is quoted in Janet Gray, *She Wields a Pen: American Women Poets of the Nineteenth Century* (London: Dent, 1997).
64. Cynthia Griffin Wolff, "Edith Wharton," in *A Dictionary of Literary Biography*, vol. 9, part 3 (Detroit, Mich.: Broccoli Chlark), 1981, 133.
65. *Ethan Frome*, ed. Robin Peel, (Cambridge: Cambridge University Press, 1999), 49.
66. Wolff (1981), 133.
67. Max Nordau, *Degeneration* (1895).
68. See Gilbert and Gubar, *Sexchanges*, 153.
69. Nordau, *Degeneration*, cited in Redmond O'Hanlon *Joseph Conrad and Charles Darwin* (Edinburgh: Salamander Press, 1989), 48–49.
70. Millgate, "Edith Wharton," in *The New Pelican Guide to English Literature*, ed. Boris Ford, vol. 9, *American Literature* (London: Penguin Books, 1991) 263–277. See 274.

318   APART FROM MODERNISM

71. Harold Bloom, introduction to *Modern Critical Views: Edith Wharton* (New York: Chelsea House Publishers). Reprinted in Edith Wharton, *Ethan Frome and Other Stories* (Philadelphia and London: Running Press/Courage Books, 1996), 169–75.

72. Edith Wharton seems to have discovered Nietzsche during her affair with Fullerton, when she was most sympathetic to the idea of transgression.

73. Harold Bloom, introduction to *Modern Critical Views*, 171–72.

74. Edith Wharton, "Life and I," in *Edith Wharton: Novellas and Other Writings* (New York: Library of America, 1990), 1073.

75. Ibid., 1074.

76. Carol J. Singley, *Edith Wharton: Matters of Mind and Spirit* (Cambridge: Cambridge University Press, 1998), 107.

77. Daniel J. Schneider, *Symbolism: The Manichean Vision: A Study in the Art of James, Conrad Woolf and Stevens* (Lincoln: University of Nebraska Press, 1975).

78. William Morton Fullerton, "English and Americans (Part II)," *Fortnightly Review*, no 281 (May 1890), 739. Fullerton is quoting from Cousin.

79. David Lodge in Bradbury and McFarlane, *Modernism*, 481.

80. Martin Halliwell, *Modernism and Morality: Ethical Device in European and American Fiction* (Basingstoke, U.K.: Palgrave, 2001) 48.

Chapter 5. Vulgarity, Bohemia, and *The Reef*

The second epigraph at the beginning of the chapter is from Lewis and Lewis, *Letters*, 483.

1. Edith Wharton, "Life and I," in *Edith Wharton: Novellas and Other Writings*, with notes by Cynthia Griffin Wolff (New York: Library of America, 1996) 1071–96.

2. Ibid., 1081.

3. Acquiring and developing the right house (and garden) was enormously important to Edith Wharton. When she discovered Sainte Claire, the house in Hyères, which she was determined to occupy, she wrote to Royall Tyler that she felt as if she were going to get married "to the right man at last." Lewis and Lewis, eds., *Letters*, 417.

4. Ibid., 93.

5. Jennie Kassanoff, "Staging Race and Class in *The House of Mirth*," PMLA 115 (2000), 62.

6. Wharton's impatience with America continued when it failed to enter the war on the side of France and England, and her dissatisfaction is evident in the pages of her 1919 study comparing France and America, *French Ways and their Meaning*. After the war Wharton became even more irritated, regretting the spread of American popular culture. See Benstock, *No Gifts from Chance*, 396.

7. See R. W. B. Lewis *Edith Wharton: A Biography*, 331.

8. Grant Allen, *The Woman Who Did* (1895; London: Richards Press, 1927).

9. Gloria C. Erlich, "The Female Conscience in Edith Wharton's Shorter Fiction: Domestic Angel or Inner Demon," in Millicent Bell, ed., *The Cambridge Companion to Edith Wharton* (Cambridge: Cambridge University Press, 1999) 98–116. The quotation is from 107.

10. Arthur Conan Doyle, "A Scandal in Bohemia" (first published in the *Strand Magazine*, July 1891). Republished in *Great Works of Arthur Conan Doyle* (New York: Chatham River Press, 1987), 1. This was an early Sherlock Holmes adventure,

though "A Study in Scarlet" (1887) and "The Sign of Four" (1890) had already established Holmes's reputation.

11. *ABG*, 46.

12. Virginia Nicholson, *Among the Bohemians* (London: Viking, 2002). This quotation is taken from an edited extract published in *The Guardian* (London), 19 October 2002, G2 section, 34–35. See also R. W. Seton-Watson, *A History of the Czechs and Slovaks* (London: Hutchison and Company, 1943).

13. Rosemary Hill, review of *Bohemians: The Glamorous Outcasts*, by Elizabeth Wilson, *London Review of Books*, 6 March 2003, 21.

14. Kenneth Grahame, "A Bohemian in Exile," in *Pagan Papers* (London: John Lane, the Bodley Head, 1898), 131–46. *Pagan Papers* is a book that shows the turn of the century fascination for wandering, Pan and pantheism, and the countryside, all of which feature in *The Wind in the Willows*.

15. Edith Wharton, *A Motor-Flight Through France*, 46.

16. Ibid., 47.

17. Edith Wharton, *The Reef* (1912; London: Virago, 1983), 26. Hereafter referred to as *TR* with page number following.

18. Ibid.

19. John Steane, "Not Stimulating Enough to be Heard Often," in *Puccini: La Bohème* (Cardiff: Welsh National Opera, 1984), 5.

20. For Edith Wharton's father's interest in the opera see R. H. B. Lewis, *Edith Wharton*, 23. For Edith Wharton and the opera, see Benstock, *No Gifts from Chance*, 281.

21. Paul Gavarni was a French painter (1804–66) whose scenes of everyday life were praised by Balzac. In 1847 he came to London and produced a series of studies of the poor.

22. Edith Wharton, *Sanctuary* in *Madame de Treymes: Four Short Novels*, 123.

23. Although Virginia Woolf's essay on Carlyle's house was published as part of "the London Scene" series on "Great Men's Houses" in *Good Housekeeping* in 1924, a newly discovered notebook from 1909 seems to record the visit to the house that provided the source of the article. See Doris Lessing, "Sketches from Bohemia," in *The Guardian Review*, 14 June 2003, 4–6.

24. Grant Allen, *The Woman Who Did* (1895; London: Richard Press, 1927), 72.

25. Arthur Ransome, *Bohemia in London* (London: Chapman and Hall, 1907), 276.

26. Ibid., 280.

27. Henry James to Lilla Cabot Perry, 3 January 1912. See Fred Kaplan, *Henry James: The Imagination of Genius* (London: Hodder and Stoughton/Sceptre 1992), 542.

28. Henry James, letter to Edith Wharton, 19 November 1911. Typed copy in Percy Lubbock collection of Henry James Manuscripts; bms AM 1237.16, *HL*.

29. Henry James, letter to Mary Cadwalader Jones, 4 January 1912. Typed copy in Percy Lubbock collection of Henry James Manuscripts; bms AM 1237.16, *HL*.

30. The setting for this party may not appear to be specified, but based, presumably, on the reference to the hired "gallery" and the Chelsea environment in which Kate's widowed sister lives, Philip Hensher refers to the "shattering moment in *The Wings of the Dove* when Kate and Merton first meet at a Bohemian party in Chelsea." Philip Hensher, Introduction to Henry James, *The Ambassadors* (London: Penguin Books, 2001) vii.

31. See Benstock, *No Gifts from Chance*, 266–268.

32. Henry James to Howard Sturgis, 5 August 1912. See Kaplan, *Henry James*. (1993), 543.

33. Edith Wharton to Charles Scribner, 27 November 1911, in Lewis and Lewis, eds., *Letters*, 262–63.
34. Grant Allen, *The Woman Who Did*, 26.
35. Ibid., 94.
36. Ibid., 64.
37. See, for example, Carol Singley, *Edith Wharton: Matters of Mind and Spirit*. Singley argues that wisdom (sophia) of Old Testament Jewish culture is suppressed and replaced by the "logos" of the New Testament. In effect, Singley explains, this is the suppression of the feminine, a suppression that is acted out in the novel.
38. Edith Wharton, *The Custom of the Country* (Oxford: Oxford University Press, 1995), 241–43. Hereafter referred to as *CC*.
39. Linked to the earlier novella, *The Pomegranate Seed*, one of the novels written by Margaret Aubyn, the dead woman writer in *The Touchstone*.
40. Hermione Lee, keynote address at "Edith Wharton in London" conference, University of Surrey, London, July 2003. See also "In our Time," Bohemianism, BBC Radio 4, 9 October 2003.
41. In Wharton's next novel, *The Custom of the Country*, all that is vulgar in Undine Spragg is traceable to her Midwest roots.
42. Perhaps there is also a satirical echo of the name of Anna's mother-in-law, Madame de Chantelle.
43. To use Genette's narratological term.
44. *TR*, 191.
45. *CC*, 178.
46. Ibid., 303.
47. Janet Beer, *Kate Chopin, Edith Wharton and Charlotte Perkins Gilman: Studies in Short Fiction* (London: Macmillan, 1997), 101.
48. H. G. Wells's short story "In the Abyss" first appeared in *The Idler* in October 1896.
49. Nevius, *Edith Wharton* (1961), 90.
50. "In [Virginia Woolf's] 1909 notebook is a little sketch, called 'A Modern Salon,' about Lady Ottoline Morrell, who played such a role in the lives and works of many of the artists of her time, from DH Lawrence to Bertrand Russell." Doris Lessing, "Sketches from Bohemia," 5.
51. "I am deeply dissatisfied with [*The Reef*], as it missed the final revision which I like to give at leisure, owing to the fact that the proofs were lost for nearly a month on their way to me." Edith Wharton, letter to Theodora Bosanquet (Henry James's secretary), 15 December 1912, Theodora Bosanquet collection, *HL*.
52. Henry James to Howard Sturgis, 10 December 1912, Henry James collection, bms AM 1094, *HL*.
53. Henry James, letter to Edith Wharton, 4 December 1912. Typed copy from Percy Lubbock collection of Henry James Manuscripts; AM 1237.16 *HL*.
54. Margaret Forster, ed., "Racine," in *The Oxford Companion to English Literature* 1991, (Oxford: Oxford University Press, 1991).
55. Benstock, *No Gifts from Chance*.
56. Marilyn French, introduction, *TR*, vii.
57. Dale M. Bauer, *Edith Wharton's Brave New Politics*, 25.
58. In *Writing Back: Sylvia Plath and Cold War Politics* (London: Associated University Presses, 2002).
59. See Bauer, *Edith Wharton's Brave New Politics*, for example.
60. Joseph Conrad, "Karain: A Memory," in Joseph Conrad, *Tales of Unrest* (London: Unwin, 1898).

61. Bauer, *Edith Wharton's Brave New Politics*, 23.
62. The letters cited are letters 23.7 and 67.1 from the Edith Wharton collection at the University of Texas at Austin. See Mainwaring, *Mysteries of Paris*, 208 and 308.
63. William Morton Fullerton, *Problems of Power* (London: Constable and Company, 1913), 117.
64. Ibid., 178–79.
65. Gloria Erlich, "The Female Conscience in Edith Wharton's Shorter Fiction: Domestic Angel or Inner Demon?" in *The Cambridge Companion to Edith Wharton*, ed. Millicent Bell, 98–116. See 107.
66. Michael Millgate, "Edith Wharton," in Boris Ford, ed., *American Literature* (London: Penguin Books, 1991), 269. The essay (263–77) is an abridged version of the introduction to *The Constable Edith Wharton*, 4 vols. (London: Constable, 1966).
67. See Dale M. Bauer, "Wharton's 'Others': Addiction and Intimacy," in Carol J. Singley, ed., *A Historical Guide to Edith Wharton* (Oxford: Oxford University Press, 2003) 115–46.
68. Oscar Wilde, *Salome, The Duchess of Padua, Vera*, in *The Works of Oscar Wilde*, (New York: Lamb Publishing, 1909), 19.
69. Bram Dijkstra, *Idols of Perversity: Fantasies of Feminine Evil in Fin De Siecle Culture* (New York and Oxford: Oxford University Press, 1986).
70. Bauer, *Edith Wharton's Brave New Politics*, 23.

Chapter 6. John Jay Chapman, "Social Order and Restraints"

Epigraph at the beginning of this chapter is from Edith Wharton, *The Custom of the Country* (Oxford: Oxford University Press, 1995), 59. Subsequent references are to this edition and will be given as *CC* followed by page number in the text.

1. For a discussion of Ford's politics, see Jesse Matz, *Literary Impressionism and Modernist Aesthetics*, (Cambridge: Cambridge University Press, 2002).
2. Letter to William Crary Brownell, June 1904, in Lewis and Lewis, eds., *Letters*, 91.
3. Edith Wharton, *A Motor-Flight Through France* (New York: Charles Scribner's Sons, 1908) 5. Subsequent references to this edition will be abbreviated as *MFTF* follwed by the page number and given in the the text.
4. J. J. Chapman "The Harvard Classics," in *Science* 30, no. 270 (1 October 1909): 440–43; new series (New York: Science Press). It had appeared in *Science* because it concludes that Harvard needs the "high priest of science" on its governing body in order to protect it from the businessmen.
5. In his later years, after World War I, in which he had lost a son, Chapman supported some very unpleasant causes. He became obsessively anti-Catholic and anti-Semitic and was happy to be published in Ku Klux Klan propaganda.
6. Letter from Edith Wharton to Sarah Norton, 20 October (1909?), Sara Norton, Letter from Edith Wharton, bms 1088.1, *HL*. Although Chapman's article appeared in the November 1909 issue of *Science*, it was likely that this was available in the weeks before that month.
7. See M. A. De Wolfe, *John Jay Chapman and His Letters* (Boston: Houghton Mifflin, 1937).
8. J. J. Chapman, letter to his son, December 1915. See Richard B. Hovey, *John Jay Chapman: An American Mind* (New York: Columbia University Press, 1959), 364fn65.

9. J. J. Chapman, "La Vie Parisienne," in *Greek Genius and Other Essays* (New York: Moffat Yard, 1915) 292–317.

10. Hovey, *John Jay Chapman* (1959).

11. Chapman, "La Vie Parisienne," 304.

12. Kenneth Clark, *Another Part of the Wood: A Self Portrait* (London: John Murray, 1974) 204.

13. In an undated letter written sometime between 1911 and 1919, Edith Wharton wrote: "I don't mind being called 'cynical and depressing' by the sentimentalists as long as those who see the 'influences' recognize my ability to see them too." Letter to Barrett Wendell, 8 May. Sixteen letters from Edith Wharton to Barrett Wendell; Barrett Vandell, Letters from Edith Wharton, bms AM 1907.1, *HL*.

14. Kenneth Clark, *Another Part of the Wood*, 204.

15. Nancy Bentley, *The Ethnography of Manners,* (Cambridge: Cambridge University Press, 1995).

16. Ibid., 164.

17. Ibid., 161.

18. Ibid., 177.

19. William Morton Fullerton *Problems of Power* (New York: Scribner's; London: Constable and Co., 1913), introduction, ix.

20. Ibid., vii.

21. Ibid., book 3, chapter 3, 225.

22. Ibid.

23. Ibid.

24. Bauer, *Edith Wharton's Brave New Politics*, 23.

25. Ibid., 20.

26. Iibd.

27. Fullerton, *Problems of Power,* 2.

28. Ibid., book 1, chapter 1.

29. Ibid., book 2, chapter 3, especially 9.

30. See Millicent Bell, "Edith Wharton in France," in *Wretched Exotic: Essays on Edith Wharton in Europe,* ed. Joslin and Price, 71.

31. Fullerton, *Problems of Power,* 177–78.

32. Q. D. Leavis, "Henry James's Heiress" in *Scrutiny*, volume 7 (1938). Republished in F. R. Leavis, ed., *A Selection from Scrutiny*, vol. 2, (Cambridge: Cambridge University Press, 1968), 124–36. The quotation is from 129.

33. Harold Bloom, introduction to *Modern Critical Views: Edith Wharton* (n.p.: Chelsea House, 1986). Reprinted in *Edith Wharton: Ethan Frome and Other Stories* (Philadelphia: Courage Books, 1996) 170–75. The quotation is from 170.

34. "[Undine] is a perfect and monstrous emblem of the time." Cynthia Griffin Wolff, *A Feast of Words* (1977), 233. "Yet Undine is not a monster. She is felt to be less of one than Rosamund Vincy, George Eliot's masterpiece on the same pattern, and there is a stimulus to be derived from a display of her tactics." Q. D. Leavis, "Henry James's Heiress," 130.

35. See Michael Millgate, "Edith Wharton," in Boris Ford, ed., *American Literature* (London: Penguin Books, 1991), 271. Millgate argues that the element of disgust and caricature is evident "from the moment when we learn her first name and how she came by it" (ibid). Such a reading hardly does justice to the way in which the social construction of an Undine is treated in this novel. Personal animus is an insufficient explanation for the subtle presentation of Undine's progress.

36. Gilman, *Women and Economics* (1898), 121.

37. Ibid., 79.

38. Betsy Klimasmith, "The 'Hotel Spirit': Modernity and the Urban Home in Edith Wharton's *The Custom of the Country* and Charlotte Perkins Gilman's Short Fiction," *Edith Wharton Review* 18, no. 2 (Fall 2002): 25–34.

39. Edith Wharton and Ogden Codman, *The Decoration of Houses* (New York: Charles Scribner's Sons, 1897), 5.

40. Edith Wharton, *Italian Villas and Their Gardens,* with pictures by Maxfield Parrish (London: John Lane, the Bodley Head, 1904). The book is dedicated to Vernon Lee.

41. Thorstein Veblen, *The Theory of the Leisure Class: An Economic Study of Institutions* (New York: Macmillan, 1899; repr. New York: Dover Publications, 1994).

42. Peggy Anne McNamara, "The Language of Money in the Fiction of Henry James," (Ph.D. dissertation, Rice University, 1976), 5. Cited in Hanno Kabel, "Money, Alienation and the Leisure Class: Henry James, Edith Wharton, Thorstein Veblen," in ZAA 44, no. 4 (1996) 346–57. Kabel's book is a study of the relationship between Veblen's book and two novels—Wharton's *The Age of Innocence* and Henry James's *The Ambassadors..*

43. It is ironic, therefore, that the *Penguin Guide to English Literature* (1991) not only has the whole of American Literature as volume 9, but has the Michael Millgate essay on Wharton as the last one *before* the section called "The Modern Age."

44. These reviews were sent to Edith Wharton by Macmillan and are part of the Edith Wharton Collection at the Beinecke Library at Yale.

45. Unknown to Wharton, the title had recently been used for a collection of short stories by Mary Crawford Fraser (Mrs. Hugh Fraser) published in 1899 under the title *The Custom of the Country: Tales of New Japan.*

46. Helen Killoran, *Edith Wharton: Art and Allusion* (1996), 44. Killoran attributes the play to Beaumont and Massinger, but this must be a mistake.

47. Nancy Bentley drew attention to this quotation in 1995. See Nancy Bentley, *The Ethnography of Manners,* (Cambridge: Cambridge University Press, 1995), 160.

48. Charlotte Perkins Gilman, *Women and Economics* (1898; repr. London: G. P. Putnam's Sons, 1908; New York: Harper and Row, 1966).

49. Ibid., 213.

50. Ibid.

51. See Elaine Showalter, "Spragg: The Art of the Deal," in M Bell, (1995), 92.

52. Ibid.

53. R. W. B. Lewis, *Edith Wharton: A Biography.*

54. Edith Wharton, letter to Robert Grant, 25 July 1900, *HL.*

55. Honoré de Balzac, *Cousin Bette,* trans. Sylvia Raphael (1846; Oxford: Oxford University Press, 1998), 116.

56. Waid, *Edith Wharton's Letters from the Underworld,* 225n20.

57. "The literary tradition out of which Wharton writes is that of the late Trollope of *The Way We Live Now* and *The Prime Minister.*" Stephen Orgel, introduction, *The Custom of the Country,* by Edith Wharton (Oxford: Oxford University Press, World's Classics, 1995), xv.

58. Orgel, xviii.

59. Frusk is a word that sounds like the unpleasant infection frush, a disease that afflicts horses. The word derives from the Old English word for frog.

60. "If Raymond de Chelles had been English he would have been a mere fox-hunting animal, with appetites but without tastes; but in his lighter Gallic clay the wholesome territorial savour, the inherited passion for sport and agriculture, were blent with an openness for finer sensations, a sense of the come-and-go of

324   APART FROM MODERNISM

ideas, under which one felt the tight hold of two or three inherited notions, religious, political, and domestic, in total contradiction to his surface attitude." (*CC*, 172).

Chapter 7. Money, Politics, and Art

1. See R. W. B Lewis, *Edith Wharton* (1993), 351. Lewis says that the Scribner's sales figures have not survived.
2. For a discussion of this, see Sarah Churchwell, "Four Thousand Dollars a Screw: The Prostituted Art of F. Scott Fitzgerald and Ernest Hemingway," forthcoming.
3. Lewis, *Edith Wharton*, 124.
4. For a discussion of the role of marketing see Kevin J. H. Dettmar and Stephen Watt, eds., *Marketing Modernisms: Self-Promotion, Canonization and Rereading* (Ann Arbor: University of Michigan Press, 1996). The phrase "contamination anxiety" is discussed in Michael Murphy "'One Hundred Per Cent Bohemia': Pop Decadence and Aestheticization of Commodity in the Rise of the Slicks," in Dettmar and Watt, *Marketing Modernisms*, 61–89 See especially 65–66.
5. Edith Wharton, *A Backward Glance*, 134.
6. Carola M. Kaplan and Anne B. Simpson, eds., *Seeing Double: Revisioning Edwardian and Modernist Literature* (London: Macmillan, 1996), introduction, xii.
7. Candace Waid, *Edith Wharton's Letters from the Underworld* (London: University of North Carolina Press). See especially chapter 1, "Women and Letters," 15–49.
8. Kaplan, *Social Construction* (1988: 67).
9. Ibid., 66.
10. Ibid.
11. For a discussion of early modernism, as impressionism see Jesse Matz, *Literary Impressionism and Modernist Aesthetics* (Cambridge: Cambridge University Press, 2001).
12. Edith Wharton to Sara Norton, 13 February 1902, Lewis and Lewis, eds., *Letters*, 57.
13. David Bellos, introduction to Honoré de Balzac, *Cousin Bette*, (Oxford: Oxford University Press, 1992) xiv.
14. A recent study has suggested that the machinery of justice was less threatening than has been assumed and that it was the social isolation and shame that was the real punishment for those convicted of homosexual offenses in the nineteenth century. See Graham Robb, *Strangers: Homosexual Love in the Nineteenth Century* (London: Picador, 2003).
15. Jennie Kassanoff, "Staging Race" (2000), 70.
16. Rudyard Kipling, "The White Man's Burden," in *The Portable Kipling*, ed. Irving Howe (London: Penguin Books, 1982), 602.
17. Stuart Hutchinson, "Sex, Race, and Class in Edith Wharton," in *Texas Studies in Literature and Language* (Winter 2000): 431.
18. Ibid., 431–44.
19. Ibid., 440. The quotation is from *CC*, 47.
20. See Jacques Lacan, *Écrits* (1977a) and the *Four Fundamentalist Concepts* (1977b).
21. See Shari Benstock, *No Gifts from Chance*.
22. Ibid., 336–37.
23. Spencer D. Segalia, "Reinventing Colonialism: Racism and Gender in Edith Wharton's *In Morocco*," in *Edith Wharton Review* 17, no. 2 (Fall 2001): 22–31.

24. W. M. Fullerton, *In Cairo* (London: Macmillan, 1891), 49.

25. The fuller argument in Benstock, *No Gifts from Chance,* 65–66, reads:

> The desire to explore and plunder, trading silver for trinkets, belong to her "archaelogical ardours." Carried away by the experience of unearthing the ancient past, she averted her eyes from squalor, except in Ithaca, where she claimed never to have seen "greater appearances of misery and poverty." A few days later in Montenegro, however, the desolation was so complete that even the colorful and handsome national dress, which was expensive and required by the prince for holiday celebrations, could not distract her from the human suffering. . . . She made no comment, however, on living conditions in societies where women had no legal or civil rights. Thirty years later, visiting Morocco as a guest of the French government, her perspective was still Western, Christian, and colonialistic, but her attitude had changed toward the circumstances in which Arab women and children lived. In 1888, starving babies and legless beggars were "local atrocities," but in 1917, they called to mind the ravages of World War I.

26. Edith Wharton, *The Cruise of the Vanadis,* ed. Claudine Lesage (Amiens: Sterne, 1992).

27. "Mount Athos," in Wharton, *The Cruise of the Vanadis,* 106.

28. "Cattaro and Cettinje," in Wharton, *The Cruise of the Vanadis,* 124.

29. "Amorgos and Astypalia," in Wharton, *The Cruise of the Vanadis,* 62.

30. "Rhodes," in Wharton, *The Cruise of the Vanadis,* 72–73.

31. See Jacques Lacan, *Écrits: A Selection,* trans. Alan Sheridan (London: Tavistock, 1977), 172.

32. Irene Goldman-Price, "The Perfect Jew and *The House of Mirth:* A Study of Point of View," in *Edith Wharton Review* 16, no. 1, 1–9. Originally appeared in *MLA Studies* 23.2 (Spring 1993): 25–36.

33. Edith Wharton, letter to Sara Norton, 16 March 1908, in Lewis and Lewis, *Letters,* 136.

34. Edith Wharton, *The House of Mirth* (Middlesex, Engalnd: Penguin, 1985), 14. Subsequent references in the text are to this edition and are given as *HM* followed by the page number.

35. Hildegarde Hoeller, "The Impossible Rosedale: Race and the Reading of Edith Wharton's *The House of Mirth,*" *Studies in American Jewish Literature* 13 (1994): 14–20.

35. Benstock *No Gifts from Chance,* 293; citing Wharton's letters, Lewis and Lewis, eds., *Letters,* 305–319.

37. Ibid., 294.

38. Stuart Hutchinson, "Sex, Race, and Class in Edith Wharton," in *Texas Studies in Literature and Language* (Winter 2000): 440.

39. Edith Wharton to Sara Norton, 12 March 1901, in Lewis and Lewis, eds., *Letters,* 45.

40. Frederick Wegener, "'Rabid Imperialist': Edith Wharton and the Obligations of Empire in Modern American Fiction," *American Literature* 72, no. 4 (December 2000): 783–812.

41. Ibid., 784.

42. Virginia Woolf, "Modern Fiction" (appeared originally as "Modern Novels" in Times Literary Supplement 10, no. 3 [1919]) in *The Common Reader* (Harmondsworth, U.K.: Penguin Books), 148.

43. The London *Guardian*'s review of *The Greater Inclination* noted that the stories "are extremely modern." *Guardian,* 11 July 1899.

44. Frederick Wegener, "'Rabid Imperialist,' 794.

45. Nevius, *Edith Wharton* 49–50.
46. Edith Wharton, *The Valley of Decision* (New York: Charles Scribner's Sons, 1914), 223–24. Subsequent references in text are given as *VD* followed by the page number.
47. Gavin Jones, "Poverty, Gender and Literary Criticism: Reassessing Wharton's *The House of Mirth,*" *Comparative American Studies* 1, no. 2 (2003): 153–77. See 155.
48. See Carl N. Degler, *In Search of Human Nature: The Decline and Revival of Darwinism in American Social Thought* (New York/Oxford: Oxford University Press, 1991).
49. See Dale M. Bauer , p35 and passim.
50. Edith Wharton *Bunner Sisters* in Edith Wharton, *Madame de Treymes* (London: Virago, 1984), 275.
51. See Barbara Taylor, "Too Much," review of *Solitary Sex: A Cultural History of Masturbation*, by Thomas Laquer, in the *London Review of Books*, 6 May 2004, 22.
52. Some of these themes are suggested by Cynthia Griffin Wolff in her introductory essay to the Penguin edition of *The House of Mirth* (Middlesex, U.K.: Penguin Books, 1985), vii–xxvi.
53. Thorstein Veblen, *The Theory of the Leisure Class* (New York: Macmillan 1899), chapters 3 and 4.
54. Edith Wharton, "The Pretext," in *Collected Stories: 1891–1910* (New York: Library of America, 2001), 633.
55. Ibid., 660.
56. Edith Wharton, "French Ways and Their Meaning," in *Edith Wharton Abroad: Selected Travel Writings 1880–1920*, ed. Sarah Bird Wright (London: Chivers Press, 1992), 278–95.
57. Bauer, 48.
58. Benstock, *No Gifts from Chance*, 265. See also 387 for Wharton's vitriolic and anti-Semitic comments about the education of professional women.
59. See Martin Pugh, *The Pankhursts* (London: Allen Lane, Penguin Press, 2001), 308.
60. See Sowerwine, *France*, 79.
61. "Life and I," in Edith Wharton, *Novellas and Other Writings* (New York: Library of America, 1990) 1069–96. "Life and I" is an early draft of Wharton's autobiography and consists of three chapters only. It was probably written in 1923 and then abandoned, according to Cynthia Griffin Wolff.
62. Lewis and Lewis, eds., *Letters*, 7.
63. Janet Malcolm, review of Library of America volume of Edith Wharton's fiction. R. W. B. Lewis and Nancy Lewis give no further details, but the reference is to Janet Malcolm, "The Woman Who Hated Women," *New York Times Book Review*, 16 November 1986, 11–12. See Lewis and Lewis, eds., 8.
64. Ibid.
65. Elizabeth Ammons, *Edith Wharton's Argument with America* (Athens: University of Georgia Press, 1980).
66. Shari Benstock, *Women of the Left Bank: Paris, 1900–1940* (London: Virago Press, 1987) 67.
67. Wegener notes that Wharton felt that *Wuthering Heights* would have been a better novel if Emily Brontë had not peopled it with madmen. Wegener, *Edith Wharton: The Uncollected Critical Writings*, 45.
68. Edith Wharton, "Jean du Breuil de Saint-Germain," in Wegener, *Edith Wharton: The Uncollected Critical Writings*, 200–201.
69. Edith Wharton, "The Long Run," in *Collected Stories, 1911–1937*, 124.

70. Kate Chopin, *The Awakening* (New York: Norton Critical Edition, 1994) 4.
71. Edith Wharton, "The Long Run," in *Collected Stories, 1911–1937,* 121.
72. Something observed by Edmund Wilson in his chapter "Justice to Edith Wharton," in *The Wound and the Bow.* (London: Alcuin Press, 1941) 184.
73. See, for example, Michael Millgate, "Edith Wharton," in Boris Ford, ed., *American Literature* (London: Penguin Books, 1991) 270.
74. Fullerton, *Patriotism and Science,* dedication.
75. Fullerton, "English and Americans" Part 2, in *Fortnightly Review,* no. 281 (May 1890): 740.
76. See Benstock, *No Gifts from Chance,* 427–28.
77. Edith Wharton, *The House of Mirth* (1905; London: W. W. Norton and Company, 1990), 39.
78. See, for example, Stuart Hutchinson, "Sex, Race, and Class in Edith Wharton," *Texas Studies in Literature and Language* 42, no. 4 (Winter 2000): 439: "[I]f there is monstrousness in [Undine] Wharton does not recognize it and offers no appropriate response to it."
79. "The heart of the wise is in the house of mourning; but the house of fools is in the house of mirth" (Ecclesiastes 7: 4).
80. Ibid., verses 2 and 3.
81. Wharton was unhappy with George Eliot's intricate and contrived plots, but defended her demonstration of scientific reasoning and her concern with important moral questions. See review of *George Eliot,* by Leslie Stephens, in *The Bookman* (May 1902), reprinted as "George Eliot," in Wegener, ed., *Edith Wharton* 71–77.
82. George Eliot, *Adam Bede,* chapter 42 (1859; London: William Blackwood and Sons, 1901) 647.
83. See Benstock *No Gifts from Chance,* 1994, 46.

Chapter 8. Politics and Paradoxes

1. Kaplan and Simpson, *Seeing Double,* xv.
2. Ibid.
3. For a discussion of this novel, see the introductory essay by Shari Benstock in Edith Wharton, *A Son at the Front* (1923; DeKalb Northern Illinois University Press, 1995), vii–xvi.
4. Henry James to Edith Wharton, 4 December 1912. Typed copy in the Percy Lubbock collection of Henry James manuscripts, bms AM 1237 16, *HL.*
5. Edith Wharton, "The Long Run," *Atlantic Monthly* (1912); *Xingu and Other Stories* (1916). Included in *Collected Stories, 1911–1937* (2001), 112–40.
   Ibid., 123.
7. Edith Wharton, "The Triumph of the Night," *Scribner's Magazine* (1914); *Xingu and Other Stories* (1916). Included in *Collected Stories, 1911–1937,* 141–65.
8. Ibid., 159.
9. Edith Wharton, "Henry James in His Letters," *Quarterly Review* 234 (1920): 199.
10. See Michael Millgate, "Edith Wharton," in Boris Ford, ed., *American Literature* (London: Penguin Books, 1991) 273.
11. Benstock, *No Gifts from Chance,* 388.
12. Preston *Edith Wharton's Social Register,* (2000), 32.
13. See Bauer, *Edith Wharton's Brave New Politics,* chapter 1, "*Summer* and the Rhetoric of Reproduction."

14. See Elizabeth Ammons, *Edith Wharton's Argument with America* (Athens: University of Georgia, 1980), 133. See also Bauer, 35.
15. Frederick Wegener, *Edith Wharton: The Uncollected Critical Writings* (1999), 3.
16. Ibid., 3–5.
17. Edith Wharton, *The Writing of Fiction* (1925) 6–7.
18. Edith Wharton, letter to William Roscoe Thayer, 11 November 1905, *HL*.
19. Edith Wharton, *The Writing of Fiction* (1925), 29.
20. *ABG*, 173.
21. Douglas Hewitt, *English Fiction of the Early Modern Period, 1890–1940* (London and New York: Longman, 1988), 133.
22. Edith Wharton, letter to Robert Grant, 5 December, The Mount, Lenox. Robert Grant, seven letters from Edith Wharton bms AM 1115, *HL*. *HL* has questioned the date (1904?) but the following suggests that it was written before the publication of *The Valley of Decision:* "Please excuse this slipshod letter, with half the words left out. It means that I am still hard at work on that great and faultless opus, in which all my theories with regard to the art of fiction are being applied with that exquisite facility & proud confidence of success which as you are so truly characteristic of the author in the middle of his—& still more her—first novel."
23. Judith Fryer, *Felicitous Space: The Imaginative Structure of Edith Wharton and Willa Cather* (Chapel Hill: University of North Carolina Press, 1986) 161.
24. Annette Zilversmit, "All Souls": Wharton's Last Haunted House and Future Directions for Criticism," in Bendixen and Zilversmit *Edith Wharton: New Critical Essays*, 315–29. See 326.
25. Judith L. Sensibar, "Edith Wharton as Propagandist and Novelist," Colquitt et al., eds., *A Forward Glance, Edith Wharton*, 149–71, See 150.
26. Nevius, *Edith Wharton*, 74.
27. Diana Trilling, "*The House of Mirth* Revisited," *American Scholar* 32 (1962–63): 113–26. The quotation is on 114.
28. So I am not persuaded that Lily Bart falls into a decline in *The House of Mirth*, because she not only discovers that there is no moral center to society; she discovers that there is no moral center in herself. This is Roslyn Dixon's argument. But Lily does retain a moral center, in refusing to use the letters that will permit her escape at the expense of someone else. Roslyn Dixon, "Reflecting Vision in *The House of Mirth*," in *Twentieth Century Literature* (1987): 211–22.
29. Henry James, letter to Howard Sturgis, 4/5 August 1914, Henry James Collection, Letters, Henry James to Howard Sturgis, bms AM 1094 *HL*, *HL*.
30. David Trotter, *Paranoid Modernism* (Oxford: Oxford University Press, 2001).
31. Sara Blair, "Modernism and the Politics of Culture," in Michael Levenson, ed., *The Cambridge Companion to Modernism* (Cambridge: Cambridge University Press, 1999), 157–74. The quotation is on 162.
32. Robert Ferguson, *The Short Sharp Life of T. E. Hulme* (London: Allen Lane, 2002).
33. Jay Appleton, *The Experience of Landscape* (London: John Wiley, 1975).
34. *CC*, 321.
35. Letter from Henry James to Edith Wharton, 21 August 1915 See copies of letters from James to Edith Wharton, Percy Lubbock Collection, *HL*.
36. The Houghton Library has Theodore's Roosevelt's deluxe copy, no. 147, and a smaller, standard copy of the book presented to the Roosevelt House Library in 1927 and personally signed by Edith Wharton.
37. Bonnie Kime Scott, *The Gender of Modernism: A Critical Anthology* (Bloomington: Indiana University Press, 1990), 216.

NOTES

38. This is discussed by Laura Saltz in "Image to Text: Modernist Transformations in Edith Wharton's 'The Muse's Tragedy,'" in *Edith Wharton Review* 19, no. 2 (Fall 2003): 15–21.

39. This subject is discussed in Declan Kiberd, "Bloom in Bourgeois Bohemia," in the *Times Literary Supplement*, 4 June 2004, 14–15.

40. Bradbury and McFarlane, *Modernism: A Guide to European Literature* (Penguin, 1991), 192.

41. Stuart Hutchinson, ed., *Edith Wharton: The House of Mirth, The Custom of the Country, The Age of Innocence* (Basingstoke, England: Palgrave Macmillan, 1998).

42. Ibid., 33. Hutchinson is paraphrasing Alfred Kazin.

Appendixes

1. Benstock, *No Gifts from Chance*, 60.
2. Ibid., 215.
3. Edith Wharton papers. Lily Library, Indiana University.
4. Paula Bernat Bennt, ed., *Ninettenth Century Americna Women Poets: An Anthology* (Oxford: Blackwel, 1998), 341.
5. The unpublishable erotic fragment was discovered among the Wharton papers and was published in R. W. B. Lewis, *Edith Wharton* (New York: Harper and Row, 1975), appendix C, 545–48. It describes an incestuous sexual consummation with an explicitness unique in Wharton's writing.
6. The "he" refers to a god.
7. See Candace Waid, *Edith Wharton's Letters from the Underworld* (1991), 53–60.
8. See Erlich (1992) *Sexual Education*. Erlich discusses "Life" as an example of the "hand motif," which, she argues, can either suggest autoeroticism, or as in the "Beatrice Palmato" fragment (the name itself possibly signifying the hand) mutual masturbation directed by a controlling, dominant figure.
9. The issue of fatherhood, both symbolic and real, is discussed by Rhonda Skillern in "Becoming a 'Good Girl': Law Language and Ritual in Edith Wharton's *Summer*," in *The Cambridge Companion to Edith Wharton*, ed. Millicent Bell, 117–36.
10. Erlich, preface, xii.
11. Much light is thrown on Fullerton's character by Marion Mainwaring in *Mysteries of Paris: The Quest for Morton Fullerton* (Hanover, N.H.: University of New England Press, 2001), though the book's revelations make Wharton's infatuation even more baffling to those who expect passion to be guided by reason.
12. Erlich, 100.
13. *Ethan Frome*, (Cambridge University Press), 38.
14. Gavin Jones, "Poverty and the Limits of Literary Criticism," *American Literary History* 15, no. 4 (Winter 2003): 765–82. For Kassanoff, see Jennie Kassanoff. "Extinction, Taxidermy, Tableaux vivants: Staging Race and Class in *The House of Mirth*," *PMLA* 115, no. 1 (January 2000): 60–74.
15. Kassanoff, "Staging Race," 66.
16. See, for example, Roosevelt's *New Nationalism* (1910).
17. Kassanoff, "Extinction," 68.
18. Q. D. Leavis, "The Importance of Edith Wharton," in *Scrutiny*, vol. 7, 1938. Reprinted in *A Selection from Scrutiny*, vol. 2 (Cambridge: Cambridge University Press, 1968), 124–36.

19. Ironical, in the light of Wharton's contention that a narrative must have a moral purpose, as we shall see later.

20. Paul Pickrel, "*Vanity Fair* in America: *The House of Mirth* and *Gone with the Wind*," *American Literature* 58 (1987): 37–57.

21. Singley, *Edith Wharton*, (1998), 73.

22. Edith Wharton, *The House of Mirth* (1905; New York and London: Norton, 1990), 20.

23. Ibid., 21.

24. Ibid., 45.

25. Judith Fryer, "Women and Space: The Flowering of Desire," in *Prospects* 9 (1984), 187–230.

26. Ceccelia Tichi, "Emerson, Darwin and *The Custom of the Country*," in Carol J. Singley, *A Historical Guide to Edith Wharton*, 89–114. See 93.

27. Julie Olin-Ammentorp and Ann Ryan, "Undine Spragg and the Transcendental I," in *Edith Wharton Review* 17, no. 1 (Spring 2001): 1–9.

28. Tichi, "Emerson, Darwin and *The Custom of the Country*," 99.

29. Robert L. Caserio, "Edith Wharton and the Fiction of Public Commentary," *Western Humanities Review* 30, no. 3 (Autumn 1986): 189–208.

30. Dimock, "Debasing Exchange," 783–92.

31. Edith Wharton, "The Long Run," *Collected Stories, 1911–1937*, 121.

32. Edith Wharton, "The Triumph of the Night," *Collected Stories, 1911–1937*, 149–50.

33. Elizabeth Grosz, *Jacques Lacan: A Feminist Introduction* (London: Routledge, 1995), 81.

34. Lev Raphael, *Edith Wharton's Prisoner of Shame*, (London: Macmillan, 1991), 319.

35. Michel Foucault, *Surveiller et Punier*, trans. Alan Sheridan as *Discipline and Punish* (1975; London: Penguin, 1991). See especially chapter 3, "Panopticism."

36. *Custom of the Country*, 15.

37. Cynthia Griffin Wolff, "Lily Bart and Masquerade," in *A Feast of Words*, 427.

38. Maureen E. Douglas, *Displaying Women: Spectacles of Leisure in Edith Wharton's New York* (New York: Routledge, 1998).

39. *Eumenides* is the third play in the *Oresteia* trilogy by Aeschylus. Orestes is pursued by the Eumenides for killing his mother Clytemnestra. The cave scene is recalled by Lily in *The House of Mirth* (1985), 148.

40. M. Foucault, *Language, Counter-memory, Practice: Selected Essays and Interviews*, ed. D. F. Bouchard (Oxford: Blackwell, 1977), 200.

Works Cited

WORKS BY EDITH WHARTON

1897. *The Decoration of Houses.* With Ogden Codman. New York: Charles Scribner's Sons.

1905. *The House of Mirth.* Repr., New York: Norton, 1990.

1902. *The Valley of Decision.* Repr., New York: Charles Scribner's Sons, 1914.

1904. *Italian Villas and their Gardens.* London: John Lane/The Bodley Head.

1905. *The House of Mirth.* Repr., Harmondsworth, U.K.: Penguin, 1985.

1906. *Madame de Treymes* in *Madame de Treymes: Four Short Novels.* Repr., London: Virago, 1994.

1907. *The Fruit of the Tree.* With an introduction by Donna Campbell. Repr., Boston: Northeastern University Press, 2000.

1908. *A Motor-Flight Through France.* New York: Charles Scribner's Sons.

1909. *Artemis to Actaeon and Other Verses.* London: Macmillan.

1910. *Tales of Men and Ghosts.* London: Macmillan and Co.

1911. *Ethan Frome.* Edited by Robin Peel. Cambridge: Cambridge University Press, 1999.

1912. *The Reef.* London: Virago, 1983.

1913. *The Custom of the Country.* Oxford: World Classics/Oxford University Press, 1995.

1916. *Bunner Sisters* in *Madame de Treymes and Other Stories.* Repr., New York: Scribner's, 1970.

1917. *Summer.* New York: Appleton.

1920. *Inside Morocco.* New York: Scribner's.

1923. *A Son at the Front.* Repr., Dekalb: Northern Illinois University Press, 1995.

1925. *The Writing of Fiction.* London: Charles Scribner's Sons.

1929. *Hudson River Bracketed.* New York: D Appleton.

1932. *The Gods Arrive.* Repr., London: Virago Press, 1987.

1934. *A Backward Glance* London: Constable, 1972; London: Dent/Everyman, 1993.

1965. *Ethan Frome and Summer.* Repr., With an introduction by Michael Millgate. London: Constable.

'Life and I.' N.p. Previously unpublished autobiographical fragment probably written in early 1920s. Included in *Edith Wharton: Novellas and Other Writings* (1990). New York: Edited by Cynthia Griffin Wolff. Charles Scribner and Sons.

1992. *The Cruise of the Vanadis.* Edited by Claudine Lesage. Amiens, France: Sterne.

1996. *Ethan Frome and Other Stories.* Philadelphia: Running Press/Courage Books.

Other Works

Alexander, Neville. 1997. 'Toward a National Language Plan for South Africa from the Language Plan Task Group'. Paper delivered at *English Teachers Connect*, University of Witwatersrand, Johannesburg.

Allen, Grant. 1895 *The Woman Who Did*. Repr., London: Richard Press, 1927; Oxford: Oxford University Press, 1995.

Ammons, Elizabeth. 1980. *Edith Wharton's Argument with America*. University of Georgia Press.

———. 1986. "The Engineer as Cultural Hero and Willa Cather's First Novel, *Alexander's Bridge*. " *American Quarterly* 38 (winter): 750–53.

———. 1991. "Gender and Fiction." In the *Columbus History of the American Novel*, edited by Emory Elliott. New York: Columbia University Press.

Anstey, Sarah. 1995. *Keats: Selected Poems and Letters*. Oxford: Heinemann.

Appleton, Jay. 1975. *The Experience of Landscape*. London: John Wiley.

Axford, B., G. H. Browning, R. Huggins, B. Rosamond, and J. Turner. 1997. *Politics: an Introduction:* London: Routledge.

Bakhtin, M. M. 1981. *The Dialogic Imagination: Four Essays*. Translated by Michael Holquist. Austin: University of Texas Press.

Balzac, Honoré de. 1846/1998. *Cousin Bette*. Translated by Sylvia Raphael. Oxford: Oxford University Press.

Bauer, Dale M. 1994. *Edith Wharton's Brave New Politics*. Madison: University of Wisconsin Press.

Beauvoir, Simone de. 1988. *The Second Sex*. London: Picador.

Beer, Janet. 1997. *Kate Chopin, Edith Wharton and Charlotte Perkins Gilman: Studies in Short Fiction*. London: Macmillan.

Bell, Millicent, ed. 1995. *The Cambridge Companion to Edith Wharton*. Cambridge: Cambridge University Press.

Belsey, Catherine. 1994. *Desire: Love Stories in Western Culture*. Oxford: Blackwell.

Bendixen, Alfred, and Annette Silversmit, eds. 1992. *Edith Wharton: New Critical Essays*. New York: Garland Publishing.

Bennett, Paula Bernat, ed. 1998. *Nineteenth Century American Women Poets: An Anthology*. Oxford: Blackwell.

Benstock, Shari. 1987. *Women of the Left Bank 1900–1940*. London: Virago Press.

———. 1994. *No Gifts from Chance: a Biography of Edith Wharton*. London: Hamish Hamilton.

Bentley, Nancy. 1995. *The Ethnography of Manners: Hawthorne, James, Wharton*. Cambridge: Cambridge University Press.

Bhabha, Homi K. 1994. *The Location of Culture*. London: Routledge.

Bloom, Harold. 1986. Introduction to *Modern Critical Views: Edith Wharton*. London: Chelsea House Publishers. Reprinted in *Edith Wharton: Ethan Frome and Other Stories*. Philadelphia: Courage Books. 1996, 170–75.

Bogue, Ronald. 1989. *Deleuze and Guattari*. London: Routledge.

Booth, Howard J., and Nigel Rigby, eds. 2000. *Modernism and Empire*. Manchester, U.K.: Manchester University Press.

Bowie, Malcolm. 1998. *Proust Among the Stars*. London: HarperCollins.

Bradbury, Malcolm. 1982. *The Expatriate Tradition in American Literature*. British Association for American Studies, Pamphlet No. 9. Durham, U.K.: BAAS.

———. 1994. *The Modern British Novel*. London: Penguin.

Bradbury, Malcolm, and James McFarlane. 1976. *Modernism—A Guide to European Literature 1890–1930*. Repr., London: Penguin Books, 1991.

Bridges, Margaret. 1997. 'Whose Desire?' *European English Messenger* (Spring) Logruno, Spain: E.S.S.E.

Brogan, Hugh. 1985. *The Penguin History of the United States of America*. London: Penguin Books.

Brooke, Rosemary. (n.p.) Translation of French exercise ("Hiver").

Brookner, Anita, ed. 1988. *The Stories of Edith Wharton*. Vol. 1. London: Simon and Schuster.

———. 1989. *The Stories of Edith Wharton*. Vol. 2. London: Simon and Schuster.

Brooks, Van Wyck. 1916. *America's Coming of Age*. New York: R. W. Huebsch.

Bury, J. P. T. 1991. *France 1814–1910*. London: Routledge.

Bush, Julia. 2000. *Edwardian Ladies and Imperial Power*. London:Cassell/Leicester University Press.

Butler, Christopher. 1994. *Early Modernism: Literature, Music and Painting in Europe 1900–1916*. Oxford:Oxford University Press.

Butler, Judith. 1990. *Gender Trouble: Feminism and the Subversion of Identity*. London: Routledge.

Carner, Mosco. 1958. *Puccini*. Repr., London: Duckworth, 1974.

Carter, William C. 2000. *Proust: A Life*. New Haven: Yale University Press.

Castle, Terry. 1995. *The Female Thermometer*. New York: Oxford University Press.

Chapman, J. J. 1915. *Greek Genius and Other Essays*. New York: Moffat Yard.

Chodorow, Nancy J. 1994. *Femininities, Masculinities, Sexualities*. Lexington: University Press of Kentucky.

Chopin, Kate. 1899. *The Awakening*. Repr., New York: Norton Critical Edition, 1994.

Clark, Kenneth. *Another Part of the Wood: A Self Portrait*. London: John Murray, 1974.

Colquitt, Clare, Susan Goodman, and Candace Waid, eds. 1999. *A Forward Glance: New Essays on Edith Wharton*. Newark: University of Delaware Press.

Conan Doyle, Arthur. 1987. *Great Works of Arthur Conan Doyle*. New York: Chatham Rive Press.

Conrad, Joseph. 1898. *Tales of Unrest*. London: Unwin.

Coolidge, Archibald Cary. 1908. *The United States as a World Power*. New York: Macmillan.

Copjec, Joan. 1995. *Read my Desire: Lacan against the Historicists*. London: MIT Press.

Crary, Jonathan. 1999. *Techniques of the Observer*. London: MIT Press.

Dattmar, Kevin, and Stephen Watt, eds. 1996 *Marketing Modernism: Self-Promotion, Canonizaton and Rereading*. Ann Arbor: University of Michigan Press.

Davies, Stan Gebler. 1977. *James Joyce: Portrait of an Artist*. London: Sphere Books.

De Laveleye, Emile. 1891. *Le gouvernment dans la démocratie*. Paris: Félix Alcan.

De Wolfe, M. A. 1937. *John Jay Chapman and His Letters*. Boston: Houghton Mifflin.

Degler, Carl N. 1991. *In Search of Human Nature: The Decline and Revival of Darwinism in American Social Thought*. New York: Oxford University Press.

Deleuze, Gilles, and Felix Guattari. 1972/translated by Robert Hurley, Mark Seem, Helen Lane 1977. *Anti-Oedipus.* New York: Viking.

———. 1975/translated by Dana Polan 1986. *Kafka: Toward a Minor Literature.* Minneapolis: University of Minnesota Press.

Dickson, Albert, ed. 1988. *Art and Literature.* Vol. 14 of *Sigmund Freud.* London: Penguin Books.

Dijkstra, Bram. 1986. *Idols of Perversity: Fantasies of Feminine Evil in Fin-de-Siecle Culture.* New York: Oxford University Press.

Dimock, Wai-Chee. 1985. "Debasing Exchange: Edith Wharton is *The House of Mirth.* PMLA 100(5): 783–92.

Dixon, Joy. 2001. *Divine Feminine: Theosophy and Feminism in England.* London: John Hopkins University Press.

Douglas, Maureen E. 1981. *Displaying Women: Spectacles of Leisure in Edith Wharton's New York.* New York: Routledge.

Drabble, Margaret, ed. 1991. *The Oxford Companion to English Literature.* Oxford: Oxford University Press.

Dupree, Ellen. 1999. "The New Woman, Progressivism, and the Woman Writer in Edith Wharton's *The Fruit of the Tree.*" *American Literary Realism,* (Winter) 31: 44–62.

Dwight, Eleanor. 1994. *Edith Wharton: An Extraordinary Life.* New York: Harry N. Abrams.

Dyman, Jenni. 1996. *Lurking Feminism: The Ghost Stories of Edith Wharton.* New York: Peter Lang.

Eagleton, Terry. 1970 *Exiles and Émigrés.* London: Chatto and Windus.

———. 1983. *Literary Theory.* Oxford: Blackwell.

Eliot, George. 1859. *Adam Bede.* Repr., London: William Blackwood and Sons, 1901.

Ellis, Havelock. 1908. "Studies in the Psychology of Sex: Sexual Inversion; 'The Nature of Sexual Inversion.'" In *Desire and Imagination,* 1995, edited by Regina Barreca. London: Meridian/Penguin.

Erlich, Gloria. 1992. *The Sexual Education of Edith Wharton.* Berkeley: University of California Press.

Fedorko, Kathy. 1995. *Gender and the Gothic in the Fiction of Edith Wharton.* Tuscaloosa: University of Alabama Press.

Ferguson, Robert. 2002. *The Short Life of T. E. Hulme.* London: Allen Lane.

Fletcher, John, and Philip Massinger. 1619. *The Custom of the Country.* In *The Works of Francis Beaumont and John Fletcher* Vol. One. Repr., London: George Bell and Sons and A. H. Bullen, 1904, 482–589.

Ford, Boris, ed. 1991. *American Literature.* London: Penguin Books.

Forman, M. B., ed. 1947. *The Letters of John Keats.* London: Oxford University Press.

Forster, Margaret. 1985. *The Oxford Companion to English Literature.* Oxford: Oxford University Press.

Foucault, Michel. 1975. *Surveiller at Punier.* Translated by Alan Sheridan as *Discipline and Punish.* London: Penguin, 1991.

———. 1977. *Language, Counter Memory, Practice: Selected Essays and Interviews.* Edited by D. F. Bouchard. Oxford: Blackwell.

———. 1986. *The History of Sexuality.* New York: Random House.

Franck, Dan. 2001. *The Bohemians.* London: Weidenfeld and Nicolson.

Freud, Sigmund. 1915. "Repression." In Angela Richards, ed., 1984, *On Metapsychology: The Theory of Psycholanalysis.* Vol. 11 of *Sigmund Freud.* London: Penguin Books.

Fullerton, William Morton. 1891. *In Cairo*. London: Macmillan.

———. 1893. *Patriotism and Science: Some Studies in Historic Psychology*. Boston: Roberts Brothers.

———. 1913. *Problems of Power.* New York: Scribner's.

Furbank, P. N. 1977. *The Growth of the Novelist 1879–1914*. Vol. 1 of *E. M. Forster: A Life*. London: Secker and Warburg.

Fryer, Judith. 1986. *Felicitous Space: The Imaginative Structure of Edith Wharton and Willa Cather.* Chapel Hill: University of North Carolina Press.

———. 1992. "Reading Antloyd." In *Edith Wharton: New Critical Essays,* edited by Alfred Bendixen and Annette Silversmit. New York: Garland Publishers, 27–53.

Gale, Robert L. *A Henry James Encyclopedia*. Westport, Conn.: Greenwood Press.

Gallagher, Catherine, and Stephen Greenblatt. 2000. *Practicing New Historicism.* London: University of Chicago Press.

Gerzina, Gretchen. 2004. *Frances Hodgson Burnett*. New Brunswick, N.J.: Rutgers University Press; London: Chatto and Windus.

Gilbert, S., and S. Gubar. 1989. *Sexchanges*. London: Yale University Press.

Gilman, Charlotte Perkins. 1908. *Women and Economics*. London: G. P. Putnam's Son.

———. 1911. "Men and Art." In *The Man Made World*. New York: Charlton.

Girard, René. 1965. "Triangular Desire." In *Deceit, Desire and the Novel*. Baltimore: Johns Hopkins University Press.

Godwin, William. 1798. *Enquiry Concerning Political Justice*. Abridged and edited by K Codell Carter. Oxford: Clarendon Press, 1971.

Goodman, Susan. 1994. *Edith Wharton's Inner Circle*. Oxford: Oxford University Press.

Grahame, Kenneth. 1898. *Pagan Papers*. London: John Lane/The Bodley Head.

Gray, Janet. 1997. *She Wields a Pen: American Women Poets of the Nineteenth Century.* London: Dent.

Green, Martin. *The English Novel in the Twentieth Century*. London: Routledge and Kegan Paul.

Hague, R., M. Harrop, and W. Breslin. 1994. *Comparative Government and Politics*. Basingstoke, U.K.: Macmillan.

Halliwell, Martin. 2001. *Modernism and Morality: Ethical Device in European and American Fiction*. Basingstoke, U.K.: Palgrave.

Heidegger, Martin. 1975. *Poetry, Language, Thought*. Translated by Albert Hofstadter. New York: Colophon Books.

Hewitt, Douglas. 1988. *English Fiction of the Early Modern Period 1890–1940*. London: Longman.

Higham, John. 1984. *Send Them to Me: Immigrants in Urban America*. Baltimore: Johns Hopkins University Press.

Hovey, Richard B. 1959. *John Jay Chapman: An American Mind*. New York: Columbia University Press.

Hunter, Ian. 1988. *Culture and Government*. London: Macmillan.

———. 1994. *Rethinking the School*. London: Allen and Unwin.

Hutchinson, Stuart. 2000. "Sex, Race, and Class in Edith Wharton." *Texas Studies in Literature and Language*. 42, no. 2 (Winter): 431–44.

James, Fredric. 1992. *Signatures of the Visible*. London: Routledge.

James, Henry 2001. *The Ambassadors*. London: Penguin Books.

Jameson, Fredric. 1981. *The Political Unconscious: Narrative as a Socially Symbolic Act.* New York: Cornell University Press.

———. 1982. "Postmodernism and Consumer Society." In Hal Foster, ed. *Postmodern Culture,* 111–25. London: Pluto Press, 1985.

———. 1991. *Postmodernism, Or, The Cultural Logic of Late Capitalism.* Durham, N.C.: Duke University Press.

———. 1992. *Signatures of the Visible.* London: Routledge.

———. 1998. *The Cultural Turn.* London: Verso.

Joshi, S. T., ed. 2002. *H. L. Mencken on American Literature.* Athens: Ohio University Press.

Joslin, Katherine, and Alan Price, eds. 1993. *Wretched Exotic: Essays on Edith Wharton in Europe.* New York: Peter Lang.

Joyce, James. 1914. *Dubliners.* Repr., London: Granada Publishing, 1977.

Kabel, Hanno. 1996. "Money, Alienation and the Leisure Class: Henry James, Edith Wharton, Thorstein Veblen." ZAA 44 4: 346–57.

Kane, Michael. 1999. *Modern Men: Mapping Masculinity in English and German Literature 1880–1930.* London: Cassell.

Kaplan, Amy. 1988. *The Social Construction of American Realism.* London: University of Chicago Press.

Kaplan, Carola M., and Anne B. Simpson. 1996. *Seeing Double: Revisioning Edwardian and Modernist Literature.* Basingstoke, U.K.: Macmillan.

Kaplan, Fred. 1993. *Henry James: The Imagination of Genius.* London: Sceptre/Hodder and Stoughton.

Kaplan, Louise J. 1991. *Female Perversions.* London: Penguin Books.

Kassanoff, Jennie. 2000. "Extinction, Taxidermy, Tableaux Vivants: Staging Race and Class in *The House of Mirth.*" PMLA 115 (January): 60–74.

———. 2004. *Edith Wharton and the Politics of Race.* Cambridge: Cambridge University Press.

Kempis, Thomas à. 1968. *The Imitation of Christ.* London: Dent.

Kiel, H, ed. 1963. *The Bernard Berenson Treasury.* New York: Simon & Schuster.

Killoran, Helen. 1996. *Edith Wharton Art and Allusion.* Tuscaloosa: University of Alabama Press.

Kristeva, Julia. 1991. *Strangers to Ourselves.* Translated by Leon S. Roudiez. New York: Columbia University Press.

Lacan, Jacques. 1977a. *Écrits: A Selection.* London: Tavistock.

———. 1977b. *The Four Fundamentalist Concepts of Psycho-analysis.* London: Hogarth Press.

Leavis, F. R. 1948. *The Great Tradition.* London: Chatto and Windus.

Leavis, Q. D. 1938. "Henry James's Heiress." *Scrutiny.* Repr. in F. R. Leavis, ed., *A Selection from Scrutiny,* Vol. 2. Cambridge: Cambridge University Press, 1968. 124–36.

Lee-Browne, P. A. 2003. *The Modernist Period: 1900–45.* London: Evans Brothers.

Levenson, Michael, ed. 1999. *The Cambridge Companion to Modernism.* Cambridge: Cambridge University Press.

Lewis R. W. B. 1975a. *Edith Wharton.* London: Constable.

———. 1975b. *Edith Wharton: A Biography.* New York: Harper and Row.

Lewis, R. W. B. and N. 1988. *The Letters of Edith Wharton.* London: Simon & Schuster.

Lindsay, Jack. 1956 *George Meredith*. London: The Bodley Head.
Lodge, David. 1977. *The Modes of Modern Writing*. Repr., London: Edward Arnold, 1991.
Magraw, Roger. 1992. *France 1815–1914: The Bourgeois Century*. London: HarperCollins/Fontana Press.
Mainwaring, Marion. 2001. *Mysteries of Paris: The Quest for Morton Fullerton*. Hanover, N.H.: University Press of New England.
Majumdar, Roger, and Allen McLaurin, eds. 1975. *Virginia Woolf: The Critical Heritage*. London Routledge.
Mansfield, Katherine. 1930. *Notes on Novelists*. London: Constable.
Marcus, Laura, and Peter Nicholls, eds. 2004. *The Cambridge History of Twentieth-Century English Literature*. Cambridge: Cambridge University Press.
Mariano, Nick. 1966. *Forty Years with Berenson*. London: Hamish Hamilton.
Matz, Jesse. 2001. *Literary Impressionism and Modernist Aesthetics*. Cambridge: Cambridge University Press.
Mellow, James R. 1974. *Charmed Circle: Gertrude Stein and Company*. London: Phaidon Press.
Millgate, Michael. 1966. "Edith Wharton." In *American Literature*, ed. Boris Ford, 263–77.
Nevius, Blake. 1961. *Edith Wharton: A Study of her Fiction*. Berkeley and Los Angeles: University of California Press.
New York *Call*. 1912. Unsigned review of Ethan Frome. February 4. Beinecke Rare Book and Manuscript Library, Yale University.
Nicholsan, Virginia. 2002. *Among the Bohemians*. London: Viking.
Nicolson, Nigel, and Joanne Trautmann. 1975–80. *The Letters of Virginia Woolf*. London: Hogarth Press.
Nordau, Max. 1895. *Degeneration*. New York: D. Appleton.
O'Hanlon, Redmond. 1984. *Joseph Conrad and Charles Darwin*. Edinburgh: Salamander Press.
Ortega y Gassett, José. 1956. *The Dehumanization of Art, and Other Writings on Art and Culture*. New York: Doubleday.
Peel, Robin. 2002. *Writing Back: Sylvia Plath and Cold War Politics*. Newark: University of Delaware Press.
Preston, Claire. 2000. *Edith Wharton's Social Register*. New York: St. Martin's Press.
Ransome, Arthur. 1907. *Bohemia in London*. With illustrations by Fred Taylor. London: Chapman and Hall.
Raphael, Lev. 1991. *Edith Wharton's Prisoner of Shame: A New Perspective on Her Neglected Fiction*. London: Macmillan.
Richards, Angela, ed. 1984. *On Metapsychology: The Theory of Psychoanalysis*. Vol. 11 of *Sigmund Freud*. London: Penguin Books.
Ricks, Christopher, and William L. Vance, eds. 1994. *The Faber Book of America*. London: Faber and Faber.
Rivkin, Julie, and Michael Ryan, eds. 1998. *Literary Theory: An Anthology*. Oxford: Blackwell.
Roberts, André Michael. 2000. *Conrad and Masculinity*. Basingstoke, U.K.: Palgrave.
Roberts, Andrew, ed. 1998. *Joseph Conrad*. Harlow, U.K.: Longman.
Royle, Nicholas. 2003. *The Uncanny*. Manchester, U.K.: Manchester University Press.

Schneider, Daniel J. 1975 *Symbolism: The Manichean Vision: A Study in the Art of James, Conrad Woolf and Stevens.* Lincoln: University of Nebraska Press.

Schreiner, Olive. 1899. "The Woman Question." In *An Olive Schreiner Reader: Writings on Women and South Africa.*

Scott, Bonnie Kime. 1990. *The Gender of Modernism.* Bloomington: Indiana University Press.

Sedgwick, Eve Kosofsky. 1985. *Between Men.* New York: Columbia University Press.

Seton-Watson, R. W. 1943. *A History of the Czechs and Slovaks.* London: Hutchisn.

Shattock, Roger. 2000. *Proust's Way.* London: Allen Lane/The Penguin Press.

Shotter, J. 1989. "Social Accountability and the Social Construction of 'You'" In *Texts of Identity,* edited by John Shotter and Kenneth J. Gergen. London: Sage Publications.

Singley, Carol J. 1998. *Edith Wharton Matters of Mind and Spirit.* Cambridge: Cambridge University Press.

———. 2003. *Edith Wharton's The House of Mirth: A Casebook.* Oxford: Oxford University Press.

———, ed. 2003. *A Historical Guide to Edith Wharton:* Oxford: Oxford University Press.

Smith, Stan. 1994. *The Origins of Modernism.* London: Harvester Wheatsheaf.

Snitow, Ann, Christine Stansell, and Sharon Thompson, eds. 1984. *Desire: The Politics of Sexuality.* London: Virago.

Sowerwine, Charles. 2001. *France since 1870: Culture Politics and Society.* Basingstoke, U.K.: Palgrave.

Stean, John. 1984. "Not Stimulating Enough to be Heard Often." In *Puccini: La Bohème.* Cardiff, U.K.: Welsh National Opera.

Stein, Gertrude. Paris 1911, New York 1914. *Tender Buttons.* Repr., Dover Publications, 1997.

Thacker, Andrew. 2003. *Moving Through Modernity.* Manchester, U.K.: Manchester University Press.

Thompson, Stephanie. 2002. *Influencing America's Tastes.* Gainesville: University Press of Florida.

Trodd, Anthea. 1998. *Women's Writing in English.* London: Longman.

Trotter, David. 2001. *Paranoid Modernism.* Oxford: Oxford University Press.

Veblen, Thorsten. 1899. *The Theory of the Leisure Class.* New York: Macmillan.

Vita-Finzi, P. 1990. *Edith Wharton and The Art of Fiction.* London Pinter Publishers.

Waid, Candace. 1991. *Edith Wharton's Letters from the Underworld.* Chapel Hill: University of North Carolina Press.

———. 1993. "Introduction." In *Edith Wharton: A Backward Glance.* London: Everyman/Dent.

Wegener, Frederick. 1999. *Edith Wharton: The Uncollected Critical Writings.* Princeton: Princeton University Press.

———. 2000. "'Rabid Imperialist': Edith Wharton and the Obligations of Empire in Modern American Fiction." *American Literature* 72, no. 4 (December): 783–812.

Wershovan, Carol. 1982. *The Female Intruder in the Novels of Edith Wharton.* Madison, N.J.: Fairleigh Dickinson University Press.

Whitman, Walt. 1888. "A Backward Glance O'er Travel'd Roads." In *Walt Whitman Selected Poems*. Edited by Gary Schmidgall, 1855–1892, New York: St. Martin's Press, 1999, 377–85.

Wilde, Oscar, 1909. *The Works of Oscar Wilde: Salome, The Duchess of Padua, Vera*. With illustrations by Aubrey Beardsley and others. New York: Lamb Publishing.

Williams, Linda. 1995 *Critical Desire: Psychic Analysis and the Literary Subject*. London: Edward Arnold.

Williams, Raymond. 1990. *The Politics of Modernism*. London: Verso.

Wilson, Conrad. 1992. *Giacomo Puccini*. London: Phaedron Press.

Wilson, Edmund. 1952. *The Wound and the Bow*. London: W. H. Allen.

Wolff, Cynthia Griffin. 1977. *A Feast of Words: The Triumph of Edith Wharton*. New York: Oxford University Press.

———. 1981. "Edith Wharton." In *A Dictionary of Literary Biography* Vol. 9, pt 3. Detroit: Broccoli Clark.

———, ed. 1990. *Edith Wharton: Novellas and Other Writings*. New York: Charles Scribner and Sons.

Woolf, Virginia. 1925. *The Common Reader*. Harmondsworth, U.K.: Penguin Books.

———. 1966. *Collected Essays* Vol. 1. London: Hogarth Press.

Wright, Sarah Bird, ed. 1995. *Edith Wharton Abroad: Selected Travel Writings 1888–1920*. London: Hale.

Index

À Kempis, Thomas, 98, 110, 111
Adams, Samuel Hopkins, 73
Age of Innocence, The, 143, 147, 150, 265, 267
Allen, Grant, 157, 165, 167, 222
Althusser, 25
"Angel at the Grave, The," 112
Aristotle, 139
Artemis to Actaeon and other Verses, 98, 281–85
Austen, Jane, 124, 147, 238, 255, 288
Awakening, The, 257

Backward Glance, A, 12, 13, 20, 36, 37, 40, 54, 88, 93, 147, 148, 233, 236, 253, 271
Baden-Powell, Robert, 87
Bakhtin, 145
Balzac, 89, 216, 225, 229–30, 269
Barnes, Natalie, 82, 139
Bataille, Georges, 69
Baudelaire, 157
Beardsley, Aubrey, 195–96
"Beatrice Palmato," 108, 170
Beerhbohm, Max, 275
Benjamin, Walter, 84
Bennett, Arnold, 96, 119, 120, 238, 270
Berenson, Bernard, 26, 28, 30, 35, 111, 118, 119
Bergson, Henri, 85, 114, 177
Bernhardt, 275
Berry, Walter, 111, 127, 352
Binyon, Laurence, 275
Blavatsky, Madame, 106, 259
Bleak House, 179–89
Bloom, Harold, 211
bohemianism, 158–74
Book of the Homeless, The, 23, 93, 265, 274–76

Bourdieu, Pierre, 225
Bourget, Paul, 45, 60, 88, 111, 157, 275
Bradbury, Malcolm, 16, 29–30
Brontë, Charlotte, 193, 253
Bronë, Ann, 160
Brontës, 136, 255
Brooke, Rupert, 275
Bunner Sisters, 76, 138, 240, 241, 242–46
Burnett, Frances Hodgson, 15
Burroughs, William, 127

Carlyle, 33
Carpenter, Edward, 230
Castle, Terry, 105
Cather, Willa, 82
Chapman, John Jay, 25, 30, 200–202
Chopin, Kate, 82
Churchill, Winston, 73
circle, Edith Wharton's, 35
Cixous, Hélène, 103
Clark, Kenneth, 203
Cocteau, 275
Conrad, Joseph, 17, 81, 126, 157, 188, 231, 234, 237, 238, 270, 275, 278
Custom of the Country, The, 22, 31, 42, 79, 108, 147, 173, 196, 197–224, 229, 232, 236, 242, 245, 251, 252, 260, 272, 274, 289–93

Daisy Miller, 178–79, 288
Darwin, 242, 259, 269
De Beauvoir, Simone, 140
De Crèvecouer, J. Hect. St. Jean, 136
Debussy, 97
Decoraton of Houses, The, 213, 274, 290
Deleuze and Guattari, 141
"Descent of Man, The," 117
Diaghilev, 129

341

Dreiser, Theodore, 17, 73, 91, 238
Dreyfus case, 235
"Duchess at Prayer, The," 111
Du Maurier, George, 157
Durkheim, 132, 133, 135

Eagleton, Terry, 81
Einstein, Albert, 85
Eliot, George, 47, 117, 175, 255, 261, 288
Eliot, T. S., 17, 81, 118, 238, 264
Ellis, Havelock, 141, 230
Emerson, R. W., 15, 112
engineering, 76, 216
Ethan Frome, 11, 22, 41, 74, 78, 122, 123–54, 240, 245, 246, 252, 253, 260, 261, 272, 277, 278, 285–87
"Eveline," 123–25, 154
"Eyes, The," 103–5, 293

Faulkner, William, 91
Fighting France, 265
Fitzgerald, F. Scott, 80
Ford, Ford Madox, 88, 95, 109, 144, 157, 198
Forster, E. M., 37, 86, 125, 238, 241, 264
Foucault, M., 105, 140, 294
Fournier, Alain, 203
French Ways and their Meaning, 54, 255, 271
Freud, 22, 102, 121, 144, 195, 242
Frome, Ethan, 77
Fruit of the Tree, The, 19, 41, 50, 54, 72–78, 133, 138, 245, 246, 253
Fuller, Margaret, 152
Fullerton, William Morton, 13, 20, 21, 25, 79, 82, 108, 110, 111, 127–29, 133, 135, 142, 145, 153, 169, 189, 211–12, 233, 234, 252, 257–59, 269, 284
"Fulness of Life, The," 97
Furies, the, 24, 196

Galsworthy John, 17, 89, 238, 275, 277, 278
Ghosts, 21, 107
Gibson, Charles Dana, 275
Gilman, Charlotte Perkins, 82, 146, 147–48, 152, 212
Gods Arrive, The, 103, 161–62
Godwin, William, 45

Gone with the Wind, 217
Gosse, Edmund, 275
Grahame, Kenneth, 160, 199
Graves, Robert, 84

H. D., 82
Hamsun, Knut, 103, 241
Hard Times, 219
Hardy, Thomas, 275
Hawthorne, Nathaniel, 136, 137
Heart of Darkness, 26
Hemingway, Ernest, 80
"Hermit and the Wild Woman," 111
Hermit and the Wild Woman and Other Stories, The, 79
Hobbes, 224
Hound of the Baskervilles, The, 205
House of Mirth, The, 19, 31, 41, 42, 54, 55, 60–72, 74, 132, 138, 147, 167, 175, 196, 215, 227, 232, 235, 237, 240, 242, 245, 249–52, 253–56, 257, 259, 260, 271, 272, 287–89, 294–96
Howards End, 241, 244
Howells, William Dean, 73, 275
Hudson River Bracketed, 103, 160–61
Hugo, Victor, 159
Hunger, 241
Hurston, Zora Neale, 82
Huxley, Thomas, 242

In Cairo, 233
incest theme, 186–87
Italian Backgrounds, 45
Italian Villas and their Gardens, 45, 213, 274

James, Henry, 13, 17, 22, 25–26, 27, 35, 43, 94, 95, 96, 111, 128, 136, 144, 164, 165–66, 175, 199, 225, 229, 252, 266, 275, 276, 278
James, William, 15, 85, 102, 112, 121,
Jameson, Fredric, 83, 99, 109
Jane Eyre, 139, 141, 193
John, Augustus, 165
Joyce, James, 16, 18, 81, 88, 91, 93, 99, 154, 264, 270, 277, 278

"Karain," 188
Kassanoff, Jennie A., 19, 20, 25, 123
Keats, 13, 20, 176, 260
Kingsley, Charles, 98

Kipling, Rudyard, 231
Kristeva, J., 103

Lacan J., 139, 176, 232, 261, 294
"Lamp of Psyche, The," 235
Larsen, Nella, 277, 278
Lawrence, D. H., 16, 91, 94, 95, 198, 203, 238, 264, 270
Leavis, F. R., 84, 118
Leavis, Q. D., 211, 288
Lee, Hermione, 14, 171
"Letters, The," 108
Lewis, Wyndham, 100
Lewis, R. W. B., 14
Lewis, Sinclair, 91
"Life," 282–84
Lodge, David, 16
London, Jack, 238, 241, 244
"Long Run, The," 257, 265, 266, 293

"Machine Stops, The," 125
Maeterlinck, 275
Mansfield, Katherine, 18, 91
Marne, The, 265
Maugham, Somerset, 162
Mencken, H. L., 17
Meredith, George, 17, 75–76, 97
Mew, Charlotte, 82
Meynell, Alice, 275
Middlemarch, 217
Modernism, 18, 22, 80–130
Monet, Claude, 275
Moore, George, 17
Morrell, Lady Ottoline, 175
"Mortal Lease, The," 282
Mother's Recompense, A, 90, 95
Motor Flight Through France, A, 27, 33, 37, 44, 47, 79, 199, 200, 271
Mrs. Dalloway, 90
"Mrs. Manstey's View," 240
Murger, Henry, 159, 162
"Muses's Tragedy, The," 227, 251

Nietzsche, 21, 97, 100, 111
Nordau, Max, 149, 150
Norris, Frank, 73

"Ogrin the Hermit," 97
Old New York, 11, 13, 23, 29, 35, 36, 37, 39, 117, 173, 191, 195, 212, 219, 238, 268

Ortega y Gassett, José, 16
Orwell, George, 224

Passage to India, A, 188
Patriotism and Science, 258
"Pelican, The," 110
"Permanent Values in Modern Fiction," 91
Persephone, 31
Plato, 139
Poe, 97
politics: definitions of, 11, 17, 32
"Pomegranate Seed," 170
Portrait of the Artist as the Young Man, A, 125
Pound, Ezra, 16, 31, 81, 88, 95, 100, 237
"Pretext, The," 251
Problems of Power, 189–91, 206–11, 258
Proust, Marcel, 82, 85, 93, 112–16, 121, 163, 203, 270, 278
Puccini, 162

Ransome, Arthur, 165, 175
Reef, The, 11, 16, 20, 22, 31, 33, 55, 59, 78, 108, 109, 155–96, 232, 245, 252, 272, 277, 278
Revolution: American, 49; French, 47
Rhys, Jean, 82
Richards, I. A., 84
Richardson, Dorothy, 17, 18, 82, 89, 106, 278
Riding, Laura, 84
Riis, Jacob, 61
Rimbaud, 159
Rise of Silas Lapham, The, 204
Rodin, 275
Roosevelt, 275
Rorty, Richard, 131

Saint Simon, 115
Salome, 195
Sanctuary, 55–57, 163, 173–74, 257
Sand, George, 160
Santayana, George, 98, 117, 275
Sargent, John Singer, 275
Schreiner, Olive, 149
Science, 132, 133, 134
Sinclair, May, 106, 255
Sinclair, Upton, 73
Sister Carrie, 240, 245
Son at the Front, A, 265

Sorel, Georges, 133
Spencer, Herbert, 174, 242
Stein, Gertrude, 16, 82, 99, 118–19, 126, 129, 278
Stendhal, 89, 269
Stopes, Marie, 230
Strauss, Richard, 195
Stravinsky, 100, 130, 275
Strindberg, August, 101
Summer, 137, 246, 252, 268
Swift, Jonathan, 264

Tales of Men and Ghosts, 102–9, 122
"Tendencies in Modern Fiction," 91
Tender Buttons, 126
Tono Bungay, 197, 204, 227
"Touchstone, The," 31, 38, 55–57, 170, 227
Traherne, Thomas, 90
Treymes, Madame de, 55, 57–60, 236
"Triumph of the Night, The," 265, 266, 293, 293
Trollope, Anthony, 97, 219, 226

"Valley of Childish Things, The," 97, 289
Valley of Decision, The, 20, 28, 42, 44–54, 59, 111, 229, 236, 238–40, 253, 261, 262, 270, 272, 289
Vanity Fair, 215, 216
Veblen, Thorstein, 76, 146, 214, 250, 252

Ward, Mrs. Humphry, 212, 253, 254, 275
Wells, H. G., 17, 27, 116, 174, 197, 227, 238, 241, 244, 291
Welty, Eudora, 214
West, Rebecca, 82
Wharton, Edith:
—poetry: *Artemis to Actaeon and other Verses,* 98, 281–85; "Life," 282–84
—prose: *The Age of Innocence,* 143, 147, 150, 265, 267; "The Angel at the Grave," 112; *A Backward Glance,* 12, 13, 20, 36, 37, 40, 54, 88, 93, 147, 148, 233, 236, 253, 271; "Beatrice Palmato," 108, 170; *The Book of the Homeless,* 23, 93, 265, 274–76; *Bunner Sisters,* 76, 138, 240, 241, 242–46; *The Custom of the Country,* 22, 31, 42, 79, 108, 147, 173, 196, 197–224, 229, 232, 236, 242, 245, 251, 252, 260, 272, 274, 289–93; *The Decoraton of Houses,* 213, 274, 290 "The Descent of Man," 117; "The Duchess at Prayer," 111; *Ethan Frome,* 11, 22, 41, 74, 78, 122, 123–54, 240, 245, 246, 252, 253, 260, 261, 272, 277, 278, 285–87; "The Eyes," 103–5, 293; *Fighting France,* 265; *French Ways and their Meaning,* 54, 255, 271; *The Fruit of the Tree,* 19, 41, 50, 54, 72–78, 133, 138, 245, 246, 253; "The Fulness of Life," 97; *Ghosts,* 21, 107; *The Gods Arrive,* 103, 161–62; "Hermit and the Wild Woman," 111; *The Hermit and the Wild Woman and Other Stories,* 79; *The House of Mirth,* 19, 31, 41, 42, 54, 55, 60–72, 74, 132, 138, 147, 167, 175, 196, 215, 227, 232, 235, 237, 240, 242, 245, 249–52, 253–56, 257, 259, 260, 271, 272, 287–89, 294–96; *Hudson River Bracketed,* 103, 160–61; *Italian Backgrounds,* 45; *Italian Villas and their Gardens,* 45, 213, 274; "The Lamp of Psyche," 235; "The Letters," 108; "The Long Run," 257, 265, 266, 293; *Madame de Treymes,* 55, 57–60, 236; *The Marne,* 265; "The Mortal Lease," 282; *A Mother's Recompense,* 90, 95; *A Motor Flight Through France,* 27, 33, 37, 44, 47, 79, 199, 200, 271; *Mrs. Dalloway,* 90; "Mrs. Manstey's View," 240; "The Muses's Tragedy," 227, 251; "Ogrin the Hermit," 97; "The Pelican," 110; "Permanent Values in Modern Fiction," 91; "Pomegranate Seed," 170; "The Pretext," 251; *The Reef,* 11, 16, 20, 22, 31, 33, 55, 59, 78, 108, 109, 155–96, 232, 245, 252, 272, 277, 278; *Sanctuary,* 55–57, 163, 173–74, 257; *A Son at the Front,* 265; *Summer,* 137, 246, 252, 268; *Tales of Men and Ghosts,* 102–9, 122; "Tendencies in Modern Fiction," 91; "The Touchstone," 31, 38, 55–57, 170, 227; "The Triumph of the Night," 265, 266, 293, 293; "The Valley of Childish Things," 97, 289; *The Valley of Decision,* 20, 28, 42, 44–54, 59, 111, 229, 236, 238–40, 253, 261, 262, 270, 272, 289
Wharton, Teddy, 30

Whitman, Walt, 13, 14, 111
Wilde, Oscar, 159, 195
Wilson, Edmund, 28, 84
Wind in the Willows, The, 199
Winter's Tale, The, 194
Wolff, Cynthia Griffin, 14
Wollstonecraft, Mary, 236
Woman who Did, The, 196, 222
Women and economics, 212, 216

Woolf, Virginia, 16, 18, 82, 85, 88, 90, 91, 95, 96, 99, 120–21, 231, 238, 255, 264, 270, 278
Writing of Fiction, The, 89, 113, 268, 269
Wuthering Heights, 139, 141

Yeats, W. B., 17, 31, 81, 275

Zola, Émile, 17, 88, 97, 235